The Coming Information Age

Annenberg/Longman Communication Books
George Gerbner and Marsha Siefert, Editors
The Annenberg School of Communications
University of Pennsylvania

Wilson P. Dizard

The Coming Information Age

An Overview of Technology, Economics, and Politics

Longman

New York & London

The Coming Information Age
An Overview of Technology, Economics, and Politics

Longman Inc., 19 West 44th Street, New York, N.Y. 10036
Associated companies, branches, and representatives
throughout the world.

Developmental Editor: Gordon T. R. Anderson
Editorial and Design Supervisor: Diane Perlmuth
Manufacturing and Production Supervisor: Anne Musso

P
92
.U5
D5
1982

Library of Congress Cataloging in Publication Data

Dizard, Wilson P.
  The coming information age.
  (Annenberg/Longman communication books)
  Bibliography: p.
  Includes index.
  1. Communication — United States. I. Title.
II. Series.
P92.U5D5   001.51'0973   81-17213
ISBN 0-582-28115-6   AACR2

Manufactured in the United States of America
9 8 7 6 5 4 3 2 1

For Lynn

Contents

Foreword by Ithiel de Sola Pool   ix

Preface   xiii

1. The Information Age   1
   The key element in the post-industrial equation

2. The American Stake   22
   How the U.S. future is affected by this change

3. The Technological Framework: Communications Networks   45
   The anatomy of high-capacity networks

4. The Technological Framework: Information Machines   68
   Computors: From filing cases to creative simulators

5. The Economics of the New Age   87
   The dollars-and-cents of the new changes

6. The Politics of Change   117
   The beginnings of a U.S. policy for the new age

7. Exporting the Information Society   148
   How U.S. information and communications changes are influencing other societies

8. The Open-Loop Future   181
   A look at future implications of current development in U.S. information and communications and some suggestions for a national strategy

Selected Bibliography   199

Index   201

Contents

Foreword

Wilson Dizard communicates. There are many of us, students of communications, who may know a lot about bits, baud, repeaters, cables, optical fibres, WARCs, and CCITT, but what we know is hard to communicate. Many of us wish we could communicate what we think we know as well as this book does.

What follows is, as the title tells us, an overview. It describes for non-technologists the new technologies of computers, semiconductors, satellites, and light guides. It introduces us to the burgeoning industry of electronic communications, the giants in it and the challengers. It summarizes the political debates about communications policy in the Congress and the FCC. And at the end we learn about the international controversies on free flow of information, direct satellite broadcasting and international data networks.

But the book is not just an overview. There is a consistent line of argument. The technical and economic review leads up to a political conclusion, one with which I am not sure that I agree. The conclusion seems to be that the United States needs to restructure its government to enable it to reach more coherent communications policies.

Dizard tells us about the erosion of the American lead in computers and electronics, and in particular about the Japanese challenge.
He explains the inadequacy of the Communications Act of 1934 and its
inappropriateness to the present era of communications abundance.
He describes the attempts to reach coherence of policy through the
White House Office of Telecommunications Policy and then the
National Telecommunications and Information Agency; he also reports their failure. He explains the essential diversity and pluralism of
this nation, and recognizes that as one of its strengths; he also takes
full note of the tradition of the First Amendment.

Given these facets of our national philosophy there are, I would
argue, severe limits to how much coherence of communications policy
there can or should be. Nor is it clear what kinds of persons have the
competence to create such policies. The technicians in the spectrum
allocation game, for example, rarely grasp the political and economic
issues with which they deal; the foreign service officers in the State Department rarely understand the technological implications of what they
are doing. (Dizard when he was in the foreign service was a rare exception.) Perhaps a certain amount of robust debate among the different parties is not a bad thing. In any case, the issue is raised in the
chapters to follow; it will be an active issue of national policy for decades to come.

The question of the U.S. lead in information technology is one
that needs to be looked at with detachment and sophistication. This
country has been the source of the computer and telecommunications
revolution. It leads the world in levels of penetration of such devices as
computers, telephones, word processors, satellites and CATV. Its
cultural products ranging from scientific books to TV shows are first in
the world market. Is that a good thing, a bad thing, or a morally neutral fact about which there may nonetheless be conflict of interest?

In the U.S.A. the erosion of our lead in information technology
has been a subject of alarm. It is in part a reflection of declining productivity. It is also a threat to one of our top sources of foreign exchange earnings. Politically, too, we tend to view the export of our
cultural products as a healthy influence towards world understanding
and democracy as well as a lever of influence for ourselves.

The same coin turned over is sometimes viewed by others as a
threat. Our major totalitarian adverseries, of course, view American
world communications with alarm. That need neither surprise nor disturb us. More serious is the fact that from countries we feel to be
friends we hear complaints about a threat to their culture or their
autonomy.

Dizard, I believe rightly, does not accept that line of argument. Nor is it just a matter of whose ox is gored. It is not a zero sum game. All countries are benefitted as any country improves its facilities for communicating or produces interesting cultural products. It is thus appropriate for Americans to be alarmed if we are doing less well than we have in the past in moving mankind's technologies of knowledge forward or in providing books, plays, and music that all enjoy. Nor are we hurt, but rather benefitted if other countries advance more rapidly than they have in their information activities. We gain by using their data bases, being able to phone or telex them cheaply and easily, or enjoying their works of art.

There is thus nothing parochial in Dizard's warnings as to problems in America's effectiveness in the world information market. One would hope that the warnings will be listened to, and at the same time one would hope that in every other country there are people giving similar warnings and urgings to their own people to move ahead in creating a freer and better flow of information.

In all that we have said above we have talked of both computing and communications. As this book and many other sources tell us, these technologies are converging to the point where they are hard to distinguish. Dizard quotes Anthony Oettinger's coinage, "compunications." The point about convergence is certainly true; these two technologies interpenetrate to such a degree that it is impossible to formulate policy for one and not for the other — as the F.C.C. has discovered. Yet historically they are two technologies which are quite distinct.

Starting in the middle of the 19th Century a revolution in communications began with the telegraph, later expanded by the telephone, then radio and TV. By using electronic signals instead of visible marks on a surface, it became possible to transmit messages instantaneously to a distance and to do that not only for written words, but also for representations of voice and graphics too. That was a revolution in information processing as significant as the two previous great revolutions in that field: the invention of writing, millenia ago, and the invention, 500 years ago, of a way to produce written messages in multiple copies.

The computer, in the middle of the 20th Century, was just as revolutionary to communications, but in a different way. For the first time an artificial intelligence was able to create or modify the messages that were transmitted. Every communications device before that took a message that had been composed by a human being and (with some occasional loss) delivered it unchanged to another human being. The computer for the first time provides a communication device by which a person may receive a message quite different from what any human sent. Indeed, machines may talk to each other.

Thus two revolutionary developments in communications within a century of each other have converged to create a kind of communications system quite unlike that which has ever existed before. This book introduces us to some of the implications of those technological developments.

Ithiel de Sola Pool

Preface

Arnold Toynbee once suggested that the twentieth century is the first time that mankind can seriously consider the welfare of the entire race. If this is true, it is largely because of events described in this book. These events involve the evolution, perhaps within the next half-century, of a universal electronic information network, capable of reaching everyone everywhere. It is the beginning of the information age.

This book is an interim report on these developments. Interim, because there are still formidable hurdles to realizing the network. Dramatic developments within the past two decades have assured that technology is no longer a serious obstacle. The problems are now almost wholly in the areas of economic and social affairs. We need to triangulate these two factors with technology in ways that will better identify the opportunities and the barriers to a new kind of information-rich civilization. There is an element of insistence in this task now, as the framework of the new communications and information structure begins to develop at a faster pace.

In providing an overview of these issues, I have tried to tread that thin line — supplying sufficient facts to clarify the issues while avoiding elaborate details that may obscure them. I have tried to keep in mind W. H. Auden's commandment, "Thou shalt not commit social science." Another pitfall to be avoided is the shimmering thin generality, a particular hazard in discussing such broad subjects as information and communications.

The emphasis throughout is on American ideas and actions. This is not chauvinistic conceit. It is rather a recognition of the fact that the fullest concept of the information age is being applied first in this country. I hope to correct any imbalance in a later book that will examine more fully the impact of the information age abroad among our industrial allies, in the developing nations, and in the communist states. The Europeans and Japanese may, in fact, move ahead of us in many applications of the new network during the coming decade. Their centralized governments' direction of communications affairs often permits faster decisions and actions. The American approach is, of course, different, with decision making shared by government and a complex private sector. This involves a considerable amount of confusion and overlapping. But the results are often more innovative, more exciting and, in the long run, probably more effective in providing a wider range of resources to more people.

We do need a stronger national consensus on our goals and actions in the communications and information area. However, in addition to better planning mechanisms, we also need, in Nigel Calder's phrase, "all the fallibility we can get . . . to preserve the absolute unpredictability and total improbability of our connected minds." This is a lovely paradox, and a saving one. In the final analysis, our ability to adapt the powerful new communications and information machines to these intensely human qualities will be the best measure of our success in the new age.

I owe a large debt of gratitude to many people who, in different ways, helped me with this work. They include the faculty and staff of the two institutions at which I taught while researching and writing — the National War College and the School of Foreign Service at Georgetown University. In particular, the staff at Georgetown's Lauinger Library, under the direction of Joseph E. Jeffs, was most helpful in meeting my research needs. I was able to complete the book while a Research Affiliate at MIT's Center for International Studies. Dr. Eugene Skolnikoff, director of the Center, and his staff provided invaluable assistance.

I must also acknowledge the helpful comments, both formal and informal, of Carroll Bowen, Philip Dizard, Herbert Dordick, Alex Edelstein, Glenn Fisher, Oswald Ganley, George Gerbner, Jonathan Gunther, Carol Lee Hilewick, Roland Homet, Neil Hurley, Kas Kalba, Donald LeDuc, Brenda Maddox, Leonard Marks, Anthony Oettinger, Edwin Parker, Joseph Pelton, Ithiel de Sola Pool, William Read, Jim Richstad, Glen Robinson, Wilbur Schramm, Anthony Smith, and Jon Vondracek, among others. Students in my Georgetown seminars on communications who assisted with specific research include Cynthia Cox, Hugh Dugan, Keelan Hadley, Bridget Kirwin, Susan Klinges, Peter Ling-Vannerus, Ann Llop, Ellen O'Connor, Eileen O'Hara, Jeff Perez, Laura Picchetti, Tamara Schiebel, and Jennifer Shupp. My four sons, John, Stephen, Wilson, and Mark, each provided useful comments. Finally, a special acknowledgement goes to my wife, Lynn, who brought to my efforts the invaluable chemistry of loving interest and informed criticism.

Wilson P. Dizard

Chapter One

The Information Age

The Wright brothers' flying machine was an unstable device, designed with just enough new information to permit it to move through a turbulent three-dimensional environment under its own power. The result was a successful fifty-nine–second flight on a windswept North Carolina sand dune. Previous experimenters had failed, many of them crashing because they could not match the available facts with the needs of powered flight.

The analogy is apt for the turbulence through which American society will be moving in the coming years. Our passage through difficult times involves infinitely more complex factors than the mechanics of wings, struts, and rudders in the Wright airplane. But the critical question will be the same: do we have sufficient information to carry us through the turbulence? As with the Wright brothers, the answer will tell whether we crash or soar, whether we are headed for a life-enriching culture in the twenty-first century or whether we collapse into political lassitude, economic stalemate, and social fragmentation.

These choices come at a time when technology offers a wider

range of information and communications resources than people have ever had. The resources are so pervasive and influential that it is now becoming clear that the United States is moving into a new era — the information age. Ours is the first nation to complete the three-stage shift from an agricultural society to an industrial one and to a society whose new patterns are only now emerging. One characteristic of the new age stands out among the welter of trends. This is the increasing emphasis on the production, storage, and distribution of information as its major activity. Our strategy for organizing the transition to this new environment will set the pattern and quality of American life well into the new century.

"Information age" is the kind of trendy label that satisfies our national penchant for slogans. It is, at best, an arbitrary name, useful primarily for identifying a set of ideas. The persistent structural problems of American society will not be dispersed by slogans. A cliché label is less important than a real perspective on where we are and where we want to be, as individuals and as a society, during the coming years.

The purpose of this book is to examine the transition to the new age, to test its implications, and to suggest strategies for managing it. The survey of developments presented here will show that what is happening is not simply a linear extension of what has gone on before. We are experiencing instead a qualitative shift in the thrust and purpose of American society in ways that call for a dynamic response.

The United States is the primary incubator of the changes pushing the world towards an information age. The energies of most societies are still largely absorbed in farming or early industrialization. Japan and the advanced nations of Europe are beginning the transition to a new communications and information environment, although they are not yet as deeply involved as we are. Like the rest of the world, they are watching this country, in Michel Crozier's phrase, as "the society which is inventing the future."

This is not a flag-waving conceit. The technologies of the information age were largely developed here, and they are being applied here first. This advantage is temporary, however. In the fast-moving new technocentric order, the lead time for innovation that can monopolize the market has been narrowed down to a few years at best. Technology transfer, legal or larcenous, is the order of the day. The research breakthrough made in a California laboratory shows up very quickly on production lines in Cologne or Osaka, often in an improved version. Technological isolationism — of the kind that led Chinese emperors to decapitate subjects who sold secrets — is no longer possible. America's lead in high technology gives us an edge in the transition to the new information environment. Our lasting influence, however, will depend upon our ability to design political and social strategies to match our technological potential in the coming years.

The rush to identify the new information age has resulted in a wide array of adjectival clichés. There are George Lichtheim's post-bourgeois, Rolf Dahrendorf's post-capitalist, Amitai Etzioni's post-modern, Kenneth Boulding's post-civilized, Herman Kahn's post-economic, Sidney Ahlstrom's post-Protestant, Lewis Feuer's post-ideological, and Roderick Seidenberg's post-historic societies. Richard Barnet adds a pragmatic note with his contribution: the post-petroleum society. Most of these epithets have been left at the post by a phrase popularized a decade ago by Harvard sociologist Daniel Bell: the post-industrial society. The common prefix of these labels suggests an autumnal quality to our age, a sense of ending. Neither Bell nor the other future-watchers have projected a grand design for what is to come, either out of intellectual prudence or simply out of awe at the many contentious prospects available.[1]

Nevertheless, each of them assigns great significance to the prospects examined here — the evolution of a more complex information and communications environment. They may approach the phenomenon from varying perspectives and draw different conclusions, but they share a sense of its importance. Professor Bell, in particular, puts the information factor at the center of his concept of the post-industrial society. He sees a seismic shift of the economy from goods production to information-based services, with professionals and technicians replacing business entrepreneurs as the preeminent social class. Knowledge becomes the pivot of innovation and policy making and technology the key to controlling the future. In Bell's view, a new intellectual technology will be created based on computers; problem-solving devices will replace intuitive judgments.

The future, Dr. Bell suggests, belongs to the eggheads. It is an intriguing notion, inevitably challenged by the eggheads he exalts. These challenges are in the tradition of Lewis Mumford, the most perceptive critic of twentieth-century industrial society. Early in his career, Mumford projected the growth of a humane, technology-based civilization. In his later years, he drew back, predicting instead a massive information-based military/industrial establishment run by an expanding, oppressive bureaucracy.[2] More recent critics, like Peter Stearns and Michael Harrington, continue to challenge euphoric projections for our collective future, sounding a warning against the assumption that powerful, resistant social structures can be readily modified to meet new demands.[3] All theory is gray, as Goethe reminds us, and most of what Dr. Bell and his academic defenders and detractors tell us is theory. However, out beyond the academic forums and lecture halls, massive changes in the information environment are changing the shape and thrust of American society in very concrete ways.

Until recently, there was little solid evidence of the dimensions of this change. Researchers relied primarily on the useful but incomplete studies of Princeton economist Fritz Machlup two decades ago. Machlup looked at what he called "the knowledge industries" — an umbrella phrase covering the educational system, the media, libraries, research institutes, and the like. He suggested that these industries and services were becoming a major force in the U.S. economy, and were expanding at a much faster rate than the industrial and agricultural sectors. In the early sixties, he estimated that the knowledge industries accounted for over forty percent of the work force and about a third of the annual gross national product.[4]

Machlup's study was an important first step in identifying the dimensions of information-based activities in the United States. Like most ground-breaking research, it raised more questions than it answered. A detailed survey of the changes identified by Machlup did not become available until 1977, when the U.S. Department of Commerce published a nine-volume report entitled *The Information Economy*.[5] Written mainly by Stanford economist Marc Uri Porat, the study confirmed and strengthened Machlup's thesis that the dominant trends in the U.S. economy involved information-related activities. The Commerce Department's study used different criteria than Machlup's in projecting a new view of the economy in which over forty-five percent of the gross national product is tied to information production and distribution, while nearly half the labor force is engaged in these activities. The study refined Machlup's analysis by dividing the information economy into two parts: a primary sector made up of the direct producers and distributors of information in the marketplace and a secondary sector consisting of the private and public bureaucracies that manage or regulate the economy. The distinction is significant, particularly because it identifies the heavy impact of bureaucratic activities, as distinct from marketplace factors, in the new information environment.

The Commerce Department study will be examined more closely in a later chapter. It is useful in providing a data base with which to identify the salient characteristics of a new kind of economy, increasingly concerned with the production, storage, and distribution of information. This development has all the characteristics of a permanent shift, and it is one whose implications are difficult to grasp. Some of the implications were defined in broad terms some years ago by the theologian/paleontologist Teilhard de Chardin when he described

> the increasing degree in which present-day thought and activity are influenced by the passion for discovery: the progressive replacement of the workshop by the laboratory; of production by research; of the desire for well-being by the desire for more being. . . . Research, which only yesterday was a luxury pursuit, is in the process of becoming a major, indeed the principal, function of humanity. As in the case of all organisms preceding it, but on an immense scale, humanity is in the process of "cerebralizing" itself.[6]

De Chardin's vision still seems utopian. Nevertheless, it is an early warning of the cultural changes implicit in the dry columns of statistics in the Department of Commerce report and other studies of the new information environment. Given the momentum with which we are moving into this environment, we need to get our bearings now and to develop a strategy for managing it.

What scenario can we project for an information-oriented society in the coming years? None of the theory or the research of the academics gives us clear indications. The closest historical precedent is the introduction of printing, an event to which the reaction was delayed and spread out over centuries.

Unlike printing, today's technologies have an almost instantaneous impact. The computer pioneer John von Neumann pointed out that modern technology increases the rate of change not so much by shortening the time involved as by expanding the areas — political, economic, and cultural — that are affected. In the communications and information fields, new technologies no longer develop in a linear fashion, separated by decades, with enough time in between for their implications to be sorted out and for them to be brought into active use. Now we are dealing with a wide range of converging technologies, which forces us to make immediate choices and leaves considerably less margin for error.

Forecasting change under these conditions is a risky business, particularly when it involves, as in this country, an already complex information and communications structure. Nevertheless, a general pattern is emerging. It can be seen roughly as a three-stage progression, beginning with changes in the basic information production and distribution industries, leading to a greater range of services available for other industries and for government, and resulting in a vastly expanded range of information facilities at the consumer level. It will be useful to take a summary look at this progression.

The first stage of transformation is already well underway. It is concentrated in what the Department of Commerce's 1977 study called the "primary information sector." This sector is dominated by a relatively small group of large corporations that are the builders and operators of the basic information and communications infrastructure. Their size and influence are awesome. The largest of them, the American Telephone and Telegraph Company, had in the late seventies a gross income greater than the individual gross national products of 118 foreign countries. The industry is dominated by acronymic giants. — IBM, ITT, RCA, GE, CBS, and so on. Clustered around them are groups of smaller firms with little-known names such as Digitech, Valtec, Transnet, and Micom. These minor players are no match for the giants in terms of economic power, but they represent an important trend. Many of them compete successfully against the established leaders by introducing innovative ideas and techniques with a flexibility and flair often lacking in the old-line companies. The result is a newly competitive tone in what has heretofore been a cautious, conservative sector of the economy. But, whether with established firms or feisty new challengers, the industry is building the high-technology infrastructure that will form the basic pattern for the information economy. A large part of the structure is already in place. Much of the rest of it is on the drawing boards, ready to be built and completed well before the end of the century.

Meanwhile, the next stage of the new information economy is emerging. It involves the industries and organizations, both private and public, that will be the primary users of the new high-technology network. Their dependence on the services of the new technology is already extensive, and it will increase exponentially during the eighties. The banking industry, for instance, is moving towards a universal electronic funds-transfer system that will gradually replace most of its paper transactions, including the more than forty billion checks written every year in the United States. The national health-delivery system will be supported increasingly by automated, computer-based data systems whose functions range from storage of medical records to long-distance monitoring of patients. The education industry, with its $100 billion annual budget, will move more rapidly into electronic learning systems. Hopefully, this industry will benefit from lessons learned in the sixties, when it attempted to automate instruction for

the wrong reason, that is, to save money rather than to improve the
learning process. Computer-assisted instruction, already used by millions of students, will become commonplace. Computer literacy will
be taught as a basic skill.

Some of the most extensive changes will take place in business
offices. The trend toward automated office operations is already running strong in large organizations. In the next decade, it will encompass even the smallest firms, making them essentially computer-based
communications centers. The automation of office procedures will
probably account for the largest dollar-volume share of the expanded
information sector in the next few years.

Meanwhile, the vast public sector bureaucracy is adapting to the
new technologies. The U.S. Government is now the largest single repository and dispenser of information, from cookbooks printed by the
Government Printing Office to maps of Mars produced by the Space
Administration. One small federal agency, the National Technical Information Service, is the largest publisher of books and reports in the
world, using a computer-based system that has almost nothing to do
with conventional printing presses.

The third and most far-reaching stage of the information age will
accelerate during the coming decade. This is the mass consumerization of high-technology information services. Communications and information resources in the United States are more complex than in
any other society in the world. They are relatively primitive, however, considering the prospects created by the application of available
technology to a new kind of mass information network. As inventor
Peter Goldmark put it, our communications are still in the tom-tom
stage. The changes are coming fast, however. Advanced information
and communications resources, now limited largely to use by big business and big government, can be extended to homes and small organizations, providing a wide range of computer-based information resources that is well beyond anything now available.

This possibility conjures up visions of whirring, blinking computers in the living room and other Sunday-supplement dreams. The
reality is somewhat different — and more reassuring. Most of the
new services will be made available through two devices already present in most American homes — the telephone and the television set.
These familiar instruments can be the links to a new kind of information richness.

In Britain, an information network with the unassuming name of
Prestel already supplies thousands of homes and offices with a full
range of computerized information services. The system is based on

the telephone, the TV set, and a "black box" attachment that costs less than two hundred dollars. The service is linked to hundreds of data bases, providing hundreds of thousands of "pages" of information which can be ordered up on the television screen by dialing the appropriate computer through the telephone system. The data ranges from the frivolous to the practical to the profound: *What is my horoscope for today? Who won the fifth race at Ascot this afternoon? Which library provides the best bibliographic information on the combinatorial mathematics of scheduling?* Prestel tells all, for a fee that is added to one's telephone bill at the end of the month. It is a working system that is being replicated in a half-dozen other European countries. There are ambitious plans for merchandizing similar services in this country by the mid-eighties.

Prestel and other projects that plug millions of people into a vastly expanded system of information services are Model T versions of what may be a taken-for-granted part of daily life by the end of the century. The present systems can only connect their subscribers to relatively large central computer banks. The next step, well within the capacity of present technology, will be to allow subscribers to develop their own data banks. This information can be sent to central data banks, passed on to other subscribers directly as a public service or for a fee, or stored for future reference. Here we will have a new kind of First Amendment democracy — every person his own data collector and publisher, unmediated by any authority, public or private, as long as he pays the telephone/computer service bill at the end of the month.

The full possibilities of this technology will be felt only in those democracies — a discouraging minority of the world's nations — that are committed to open inquiry and the ambiguity of conflicting challenges to authorized, conventional wisdom. The United States and like-minded societies have had only limited experience with such an environment until now because of technical and economic constraints on universal information access. But, we are beginning to grapple with the implications of the changeover. It will, for instance, affect the way in which we learn, not only in school but in the long years afterwards. For all our commitment to mass education, we are still living in a time of educational incapacity. Formal learning for adults is generally cut off in the late teens or the early twenties, leaving most of us diminished in an environment that requires lifelong retraining. With the new technology, continued learning will be more than a question of refresher courses and other "adult education." It will involve, rather, an environment that adds a stunning dimension to information seeking and creative thinking. Norman Macrae, an editor of the *Economist*, asks what will happen if the new technologies are applied in ways that remove the present limitations on lifetime access to information:

> The prospect is, after all, that we are going to enter an age when any duffer sitting at a computer terminal in his laboratory or office or public library or home can delve through unimaginable increased mountains of information in mass-assembly data banks with mechanical powers of concentration and calculation that will be greater by a factor of tens of thousands than was ever available to the human brain of even an Einstein. From the 99 percent perspiration and one percent inspiration that was Edison's definition of inventive genius before he died in 1931, we have in the four decades since his death already provided the machines that can reduce the main part of that perspiration much more than 99 times over. Because this will eventually make research a task that can be undertaken more effectively (even part-time) by many more people, this must surely increase the prospect by unearthing more people with Edison's or Einstein's divine afflatus. I do not believe that heretofore more than a small fraction of mankind's potential geniuses have ever had a chance to indulge in research work if they wanted to.[7]

The prospect of crowds of Einsteins and Edisons is enough to give us pause. More immediately, a full-scale information network will break the old constraining bonds of limited access to information resources. Computer scientists have a phrase that fits the new situation — "distributed intelligence." Until a few years ago, Norman Macrae's future geniuses were limited to large, centralized data bases. The new technologies — minicomputers and high-speed data networks — are changing this, making possible a new kind of flexibility and creative individualism. Geographically dispersed data terminals, each with its own information storage and computing capability, can operate independently, be linked to each other, or linked to large central data sources. The focus in computer development has moved from the relatively simple management of central data bases to new patterns of "distributed intelligence" — a phrase that defines much of the creative promise of the coming information age.

The image of the genius working at a computer terminal in a small room appeals to our pride of technological prowess as well as to our democratic faith in individualism. What is difficult to imagine is its replication tens of thousands or even millions of times. This calls for a quantum leap of both imagination and of faith in the promise of a new information environment. Our understanding of freedom, creativity, and democracy will take on different dimensions in the new era.

The promise is intangible and elusive. We are not going to vote on the information society one day any more than our eighteenth-century ancestors voted on the industrial age. There is no specific critical moment when we can decide how we want to handle the new environment. The issues are spread out in time and place, across a fragmented array of institutional decisions. As we shall see, this makes development of a broad strategy for the new age problematic. We have, in any event, moved beyond easy notions that we can fill our information needs simply by plugging in bigger and better machines. To be sure, the technology for such machines is available: the challenge is in applying them with a clear perception of social needs and in giving emotional texture to the new environment they will create. As Jacques Maritain once noted wryly, "The telephone and the radio do not prevent man from having two arms, two legs, two lungs, falling in love and searching for happiness."[8]

The technocratic visions of the thirties and forties, in which communications were a mechanistic linear process, collapsed under their shaky assumptions about human behavior. Many of the subtleties of the communications process still elude us and probably always will. However, its human dimensions are better understood now as a result of the increased attention given them by researchers in all disciplines from animal biology to mathematics. One of the most fruitful research areas has been the study of how animals, from dolphins to chimpanzees, communicate in elaborate patterns. Another has been the study of nonverbal human communications, the use of body gestures and other signals which, according to anthropologist Edward Hall, make up 70 percent of our communication patterns. The result, as Harold Lasswell noted, has been to reduce the parochialism of the larynx in our understanding of communications.

If it has not come up with final answers, the new research has emphasized the complexity of the communications process. Human beings are not information processors, but code crafters. They don't think straight, if "straight" is taken to mean adhering to standards of right-thinking predetermined by some higher authority. This ambiguity is the most subtle and useful quality we bring to the task of fashioning a truly creative information environment. In this work, we are heirs to the great tradition of men and women who, through the ages, have sought to organize knowledge for civilizing purposes.

Success in our generation will depend on the degree to which we shape the new information technologies in accordance with human values. For most of this century, futurists and planners have imagined human progress in terms of a technological society, a chromium wilderness in which emotional richness has been overtaken by programmed happiness. H. G. Wells, among others, described this solemnly in his works. Aldous Huxley added the saving grace of satire in *Brave New World*. We have moved away from these monstrous models towards more humanistic ones, in which machines are a subordinate rather than a controlling factor. The cold metaphor of the impersonal, technocratic machine is being replaced. The new metaphor is a blooming, buzzing garden in which each of us — including those new Einsteins and their computers — can cultivate a personal plot. This involves combinations of order and disorder, as well as the surprises that spring from the widened boundaries of creative imagination.

Programmed utopia or blooming, buzzing garden — these are, in simplified form, the alternative ways in which we can begin to understand our choices in the emerging information environment. It is a familiar problem for Americans. The tensions between democratic, humanistic ideals and technocratic imperatives thread through our history. However, the new information machines add an insistent, even urgent, dimension to this conflict. They do this by amplifying intelligence dramatically in much the same way that the machines of the Industrial Revolution amplified physical strength. Computers and other information machines are the new motor power, pulling us towards a transformed society faster than we can understand where we are going. The machines can help orient us in these ambiguous passages, but they are not panaceas. Their mechanical innards do not contain certain formulas for surviving and thriving.

Neither will we find the answers at the Delphic shrines of the technocrats and their systems-analysis dogmas. As Herbert Stein has pointed out:

> The dream of thinking everything out before we act, of making certain we have all the facts and know all the consequences, is a sick Hamlet's dream. It is the dream of someone with no appreciation of the seamless web of causation, the limits of human thinking, or the scarcity of human attention. The world outside is itself the greatest storehouse of knowledge. Human reason, drawing upon the pattern and redundancy of nature, can predict some of the consequences of human action. But the world will always remain the largest laboratory, the largest information store, from which we will learn the outcomes, good and bad, of what we have done. Of course, it is costly to learn from experience, but it is also costly, and frequently much

less reliable, to try through research and analysis to anticipate experience.[9]

Who sets the social directions and policies in this complex new environment? Government is only one of the major actors in the process. Industry, labor, the financial community, and universities each play critical roles. Given the sensitivity of the subject, the process demands a new kind of awareness of the relationship between technology, economics, and social needs. Decisions on the future pattern of communications and information resources differ from those dealing with, say, medical care or housing. Communications and information policies involve basic questions of personal identity and values. The overriding concern should not be specific programs or techniques but rather the pattern by which influence is exerted and information becomes effective in a pluralistic society. Strategic decisions will depend on how we see ourselves and project our own interests as we face an uncertain future. A large democracy thrives only when its citizens share enough information, beliefs, and assumptions to function together in a rough consensus. This consensus becomes more important as the pace of change accelerates, upsetting present assumptions and clouding future expectations. We need to collectivize our intelligence, not in centralized, authoritarian fashion, but by encouraging dialogue based on shared information and leading toward agreement on strategies for surviving and thriving as individuals and as a society.

This imperative for both personal and communal awareness is underscored by political scientist Karl Deutsch.[10] He suggests that we are coming closer to the boundaries within which our intellectual equipment is able to cope with present complexities. He calls for greater emphasis on "intelligence amplification," using information technologies to increase human understanding. Part of the problem with this is our ignorance about the capabilities of the new machines. We tend to see them primarily as improved means for storing and distributing information. Their greatest value, however, may be as satellites of consciousness, monitoring and identifying social needs in much the same way as the NASA Landsat satellite monitors earth's environmental conditions. This calls for a new kind of information and communications pattern well beyond our present limited system, one that is universal, interactive, and accessible to everyone.

One advantage we have is in not being bound by the easy assumptions of earlier generations about the value of technical progress; we see more clearly the contradictions involved in this process.

The French sociologist, Jacques Ellul, has developed a sobering catalogue of these paradoxes. He points out that:

- All technical progress exacts a price; that is, while it adds something on the one hand, it subtracts something on the other.
- All technical progress raises more problems than it solves, tempts
  us to see the consequent problems as technical in nature, and
  prods us to seek technical solutions to them.
- The negative effects of technological innovation are inseparable
  from the positive. It is naïve to say that technology is neutral, that
  it may be used for good or bad ends; the good and bad effects are,
  in fact, simultaneous and inseparable.
- All technological innovations have unforeseeable effects.[11]

These strictures apply with particular sensitivity to the spread of communications and information technologies. For all our willingness to
assume that the new networks are a good thing, there are warning
signals to the contrary. Consider, for example, Citizen's Band radio,
that new form of electronic populism which has given over thirty million Americans their own two-way broadcasting capabilities. Advertisers of CB sets stress safety and convenience as benefits of their products. There may be such advantages, but they mask the deeper
reasons for the CB craze. The less advertised factor is CB's appeal to
more personal needs. Communications researcher Bert Cowlan sees
the CB phenomenon as:

> a desire to overcome alienation and to have the opportunity to man-
> age one's own communication system, coordinate one's own re-
> sources to survive in what many perceive as an increasingly hostile,
> bureaucratic, and depersonalized, costly, inefficient and high-risk
> environment.[12]

The CB user may broadcast in an urgent megavoice, but he
or she often displays a penchant for anonymity with a glamorized
pseudonym. Tom, Dick, Harry, and Mary Jones turn into Crusader
Rabbit, Super Stud, the Ace of Spades, and Crazy Mama. As one of
the characters in the excellent 1977 film, *Citizen's Band*, says about
CB's influence in a small town: "Everyone in this town is somebody
they're not supposed to be."

The tendency to hide one's identity behind an electronic shield
can be found in another well-known phenomenon — the unlisted
phone number. Once the preserve of a self-conscious minority, the

unlisted number is now common. Almost a million phone numbers in New York City are not listed.[13] The private number is a symbol, albeit an absent one, of the dark side of our assumptions about the importance of being in touch, of being part of the network. It is a reminder that, for many people, the openness promised by new communications technologies is a threat, not a promise.

These examples are not aberrations, but merely some of the doubts, fears, and other human frailties we bring with us to the expanded information environment. The promising aspect of the new technologies is that they may expand democratic humanistic options, allowing more sharing of responsibilities and rewards. They can, obversely, have less rewarding effects, propping up outmoded institutions and narrow interests. Such rigid use of technology leads to political alienation and social unrest, resulting in the kind of bloody-minded Ludditism that characterizes so much of the popular attitude toward impersonal technologies and the managers who control them. In the short run — the next decade or two — the first attempts to apply the information machines effectively will compound this problem. This process will call not only for technical efficiency but also for a new kind of democratic equity, a person-centered perspective that assumes neither men nor machines need to be changed radically before human progress can take place.

We are moving into a new ecology of information, defined in large part by the computer's ability to amplify intelligence. This liberating potential of the information machines is still only partially understood. In these first decades of computer technology, the machines have been regarded primarily as useful, somewhat exotic storage bins and calculating devices. Their misuse and underuse is characteristic of our technological and social illiteracy. The problem is computer literacy, a subject just beginning to engage the attention of researchers and educators.

British critic George Steiner has observed that computer language may be a more logical common tongue than English or any other so-called world language. Probably, a new polyglot will develop from computer-oriented English and ideograms. A sort of universal Pidgin may emerge, similar to the special patois that airline pilots use as they take off and land in a multilingual range of cultures.

Developing a comprehensible, comprehensive language is only part of the problem of computer literacy. Equally important is developing a level of literacy that will stimulate creative use of the machines as intelligence amplifiers by nontechnical users. As computer scientist Alan Kay puts it: "Simple tasks must be simple and com-

plex ones must be possible."[14] Kay and his colleagues at the Xerox
research center in Palo Alto are among the groups studying ways in
which to expand creative application of personal computing systems.
Significantly, they have turned to the inventiveness of young children
for their insights. The project, known as SMALLTALK, involves
hundreds of children, ranging in age from six to fifteen, who are
given wide latitude to program computers. Along the way, the Xerox
researchers have learned a lot about learning, particularly about the
fragile balance between free exploration and structured curricula.
Similar research at MIT's Artificial Intelligence Laboratory confirms
the computer's simulating value in expanding the prospects for
imaginative learning.[15]

Children have taught the SMALLTALK researchers to program
more imaginative uses of the simulating property of computers. Most
adults use computer simulation as a crutch to confirm their versions
of reality. Children have far fewer inhibitions. They use the computer
to create what Kay and his colleagues call "splendid nonsense,"
simulations that stretch the limits of human imagination beyond conventional ideas. This may be the greatest force unleashed by the new
high-capacity information machines, with games played by children
pointing to a new kind of expanded human creativity. The computer
programs created by children in the Xerox lab are the modern equivalent of the "splendid nonsense" with which the movers and shakers of
civilization have always challenged conventional thinking.

The stumbling blocks to realizing this potential lie not in those
who exaggerate the computer's capability, but in those who fear it.
There is a disturbing tendency to retreat from the implications of
the new machines, to deny the possibility of a viable technology-
powered democratic society. These antitechnology forces, the new
Luddites, seek solace in astrology, artificial Waldens, and bad poetry.
Most of us still accept, if with some reservations, the traditionally
American secular faith in technology and its benefits. We recognize
that technology is not an all-purpose solution. In a divided world, it
exerts a powerful influence in keeping us divided. Nevertheless, as
Harold Lasswell has noted, an effective information and communications system, at home and abroad, is needed to sustain the powerful
trends pushing us toward a new form of world order — the shaping
and sharing of basic values and the introduction of specific procedures
for more stable social and economic development.[16]

Whether such a pattern can be realized will depend not only on
our own efforts but ultimately on decisions made in a hundred and
fifty highly diverse societies beyond our borders. Each of them must

deal, in its own cultural context, with the new information machines, and with the need for difficult institutional changes at the political, economic, and social level. American experience has a powerful attraction for other societies searching for their own versions of a new Eden. The difference now is the renewed strength and universality of the search. There is, as Janet Flanner says, a strong wind blowing for all men of different colors on different parts of the globe, with a steady, unending velocity, unlike the limited cyclonic gusts of the past. Americans have had practical experience with this liberating spirit for more than two centuries; for others, it is a traumatic new experiment.

In its transference overseas, the American example has taken on a wider identity. It is the gospel of modernization. Since modernization describes much of the psychic environment in which the global information age is developing, it is an important part of our story. Modernization is the doctrine of organized universal betterment. As a worldwide civil religion, it is more influential than nationalism or such limited movements as democracy, fascism, or communism. It shows itself as a psychic mass migration toward a better life. Once this idea makes contact with a society, it diffuses in ways that irrevocably affect traditional institutions and values. It becomes the universal social catalyst, changing everyone it touches.

The gospel of modernization has had to undergo adjustment to some persistent realities since it was first proclaimed in the 1950s. The tone then was one of unalloyed missionary zeal, involving the transformation of the world's underdeveloped areas into local versions of middle-class American suburbs. Reluctantly, its proponents have had to scale down this vision considerably in recent years. Modernization now tends to be described in such uninspiring terms as the New International Economic Order. The emphasis is on sober subjects such as technology transfer, export subsidies, protection prices for raw materials, and the like. Nevertheless, behind the facade of this new sobriety, faith in modernization remains strong. It is a gospel that speaks to the common desires of human beings, as the British critic. Malcolm Muggeridge, once stated:

> What they all want . . . is what the Americans have got — six lanes of large motor cars streaming powerfully into and out of gleaming cities; neon lights flashing, and juke boxes sounding and skyscrapers rising, story upon story into the sky. Driving at night into the town of Athens, Ohio (pop. 3,450), four bright colored signs stood out in the darkness — "Gas," "Drugs," "Beauty," "Food." Here, I

thought, is the ultimate, the *logos* of our time, presented in sublime simplicity. It was like a vision in which suddenly all the complexity of life is reduced to one single inescapable proposition. These could have shone forth as clearly in Athens, Greece as in Athens, Ohio. They belonged as aptly to Turkestan or Sind or Kamchatka.... There are, properly speaking, no Communists, no capitalists, no Catholics, no Protestants, no black men, no Asians, no Europeans, no Right, no Left and no Center.... There is only a vast and omnipresent longing for Gas, for Beauty, for Drugs and for Food.[17]

Western democratic capitalism has undoubtedly fostered and diffused the modernization idea faster than any other system. However, it would be wrong to equate modernization exclusively with America's own political and economic experience. Many of our mistakes in dealing with the Third World are based on this kind of misperception. Nevertheless, the American example stands as a major force, despite the apparent erosion of our political and economic influence abroad in recent years. "America is a gigantic theater," wrote Ceasare Pavese, "where, with greater candor than elsewhere, is being played out the drama of us all." The drama others are observing now is an America moving beyond the conventional modernization process into an advanced evolutionary phase in which information rather than material production is the focus.

This is usually demonstrated in economic terms, but the American contribution goes further in defining its social dynamics. We add the hitherto startling notion that we expect to live through two or more sets of futures in one lifetime. This is reflected in an educational system that, at its best, prepares for a future that is unpredictable, different, and — still the American hope — qualitatively better. This is a long psychic jump, not without peril, from the assumptions of most other societies with their still-powerful legacies of hierarchal immobility. Such traditions are being eroded everywhere as the gospel of modernization spreads.

Americans proselytize most effectively when they do so least consciously. In his masterful work on propaganda systems, Jacques Ellul emphasizes that unstructured "social propaganda" as expressed in Hollywood films or the *Reader's Digest* has far more impact than the highly organized propaganda attempts of the nazis, communists, or even our own government's programs of official political persuasion aimed at overseas audiences through the Voice of America. The impact of unintended American social influence — from Levis jeans to IBM computers — is a potent part of the dynamics of modernization.

The coming of the information age complicates the modernization process. Even the limited communications channels available over the past three decades served as powerful diffusers of the new gospel. The new communications and information machines will speed this diffusion dramatically. The developing high-technology networks around the world are predominantly American in style, as is the tone of most of the modernization messages flowing through them.

A new map of the globe is being drawn. It is an information map, comparable to a weather map in that it indicates environmental conditions rather than linear directions. The map shows a dense mass of organized information over North America, with smaller masses over Europe, Japan, and the Soviet Union. Elsewhere the density of information shades off into thinness. The new technologies can change this map radically by helping create a global knowledge grid. How much of the grid can be in place by the end of the century? By the year 2010? To what extent will political, economic, and ideological factors cause delays?

The answers will depend on the strategies and actions we choose during the coming decade, both within our domestic framework and in our relations with other societies. Americans have tended to see the modernization process in terms of the political and economic power it may confer on us. This view is shortsighted. The end benefit, to us and to every other society, will be a stunning global dimension to learning and knowledge. This new dimension can convert our fixation on modernization into a powerful civilizing force.

We are heirs to a great tradition of men and women who saw the organization of available information as a basic condition of human progress. It is the tradition of Ptolemy I Soter (305–283 B.C.) who founded the great library of Alexandria, the first attempt to gather all the world's books in one place and catalogue them scientifically. Its collection of perhaps 700,000 volumes was not matched again until the past century. The destruction of the library in 391 A.D. was a major disaster for Western civilization, reducing the stock of organized knowledge to a few hundred manuscripts. Fortunately, the tradition was kept alive by small groups of Benedictines and other monks, who copied and preserved the few works that survived. The next great step, following the invention of printing and cheap paper, was the work of the French Encyclopedists and their equally enlightened Scottish counterparts, the creators of the *Encyclopaedia Britannica*. Both attempted to summarize the world's knowledge in one set of books. Theirs was an astonishing effort, with (in the case of the

French) direct revolutionary implications. The concept spread to the development of the modern Alexandrine counterparts — the Library of Congress, the British Museum library, and other great library centers.

In the early part of this century, H. G. Wells proposed the development of a World Brain, a project for gathering and storing all information in one place, using the latest technologies. His World Brain was dismissed as fantasy at the time, but the concept is realizable today in the computer, whose capabilities go well beyond those he proposed. The contents of the Library of Congress, over thirty million volumes, could now be stored microelectronically in a relatively small room. Reduced to digital computerized form, the Library's total holdings could eventually be transmitted in a few minutes over high-capacity networks. These may not be practical possibilities, but the growth of massive data banks, linked to users throughout the world by high-speed circuits, already constitute a new civilizing force in the great tradition of Alexandria, Monte Cassino, the Encyclopedists, and the great modern library centers.

Here is a challenge to match the promise of our democratic society as we move towards a new century. In little more than a generation, the technology to match this challenge has moved from the laboratories into everyday use. Our applications have been primitive compared to the potential of the new machines. The United States has expanded its information production to the point that it is now the repository of the largest share of the world's organized knowledge. Greater benefits may come, however, not from the knowledge we give or sell to other societies, but from what we receive over the new electronic circuits from them. We need these outside resources not simply as accretions to our own knowledge inventory but for the health of our society. They are needed, as the veteran diplomat George Kennan once said:

> Just as rain is by the desert and needed . . . for our sakes alone, for our development as individuals and as a nation, lest we fall into complacency, sterility and emotional decay; lest we lose our sense of the capabilities of the human spirit, and with it much of our sensitivity to the possible meaning and wonder of life itself.[18]

The American influence on a global knowledge network will depend primarily on what we do as a nation. The issue is the development and application of technologies vital to the future of our democratic society and its place in the world. A strategy will emerge either by design or default; for the present, we have not decided which it will be. Given our reluctance to turn over the decision and control functions in this area to government, we have relied largely on haphazard, unstructured decision making, driven primarily by economic forces that have given us the most advanced communications and information structures in the world. The question is whether we can continue on the same course in the same manner or whether we have arrived at a moment when a different national strategy is needed.

How does a society shape strategies for its survival? There is no formula to guide us into an uncertain future with its combination of enhanced intelligence capabilities and greater social ambiguities. Our greatest resource in meeting the challenge is a three-pound electrochemical device, slightly alkaline, which runs on the power of glucose at twenty-five watts. It is the human brain. It has one striking advantage which even the most sophisticated computer will eternally lack — the power of divine afflatus, imagination, or even just common sense.

Notes

1. Daniel Bell first outlined his post-industrial thesis in *The Coming of Post-Industrial Society* (New York: Basic Books, 1973), p. 212 *et passim*. For a more recent version of Bell's ideas, see his "The Social Framework of the Information Society," in *The Microelectronics Revolution*, ed. Tom Forester (Cambridge, Mass.: M.I.T. Press, 1981), pp. 500–49.

2. Lewis Mumford, *The Pentagon of Power* (New York: Harcourt Brace, 1970), pp. 293–99.

3. Peter Stearns, "Is There a Post-Industrial Society?" and Michael Harrington, "Post-Industrial Society and the Welfare State," in *Libraries in Post-Industrial Society*, ed. Leigh Estabrook (Phoenix: Oryx Press, 1977), pp. 8–18, 19–29.

4. Fritz Machlup, *The Production and Distribution of Knowledge in the United States* (Princeton, N.J.: Princeton University Press, 1962).

5. U.S. Department of Commerce, *The Information Economy*, 9 vols. Office of Telecommunications special publication 77–12 (Washington, D.C.: Government Printing Office, 1977).

6. Teilhard de Chardin, *The Future of Man* (New York: Harper & Row, 1969), pp. 166 and 173.

7. Norman Macrae, "Multinational Business," *The Economist* (London) (January 22, 1972), p. 10.

8. Julie Kernan, *Our Friend, Jacques Maritain* (New York: Doubleday, 1975), p. 177.

9. Herbert Stein, "Designing Organizations for an Information-Rich World," in *Computers, Communications and the Public Interest*, ed. Martin Greenberger (Baltimore: Johns Hopkins University Press, 1971), p. 47.

10. Karl W. Deutsch, *The Nerves of Government* (New York: The Free Press of Glencoe, 1963).

11. Jacques Ellul, "The Technological Order," *Technology and Culture*, 3 (Fall 1962): 394.

12. Bert Cowlan, "Communications for the Individual and Extension of Choice" (Paper presented before the annual conference of the International Institute of Communications, Washington, D.C., September 1977), p. 4. See also Jon T. Powell and Donald Ary, "Communications Without Commitment," *Journal of Communication*, 27, no. 3(Summer 1977): 118–21.

13. "The Unlisted Numbers List Is Growing." *New York Times*, 17 December 1977, p. 35.

14. Alan C. Kay, "Microelectronics and the Personal Computer," *Scientific American* (September 1977): 231.

15. See Seymour Papert, *Mindstorms: Children, Computers and Powerful Ideas* (New York: Basic Books, 1980) for a description of pioneering research on computers as learning tools conducted at the MIT Artificial Intelligence Laboratory.

16. Harold G. Lasswell, "Communications in a Divided World" (1977 Louis G. Cowen Lecture, sponsored by the International Broadcast Institute, London, 1977).

17. Malcolm Muggeridge, *Things Past* (London: Collins, 1978), p. 125.

18. Quoted in Wilson Dizard, *The Strategy of Truth* (Washington, D.C.: Public Affairs Press, 1961), p. 172.

Chapter Two

The American Stake

In considering strategies for the information age, we must be aware of the psychic forces that have created the new environment. The most important of these is the American technological myth, the search for a new Eden through the melding of nature and the machine. This machine-in-the-garden is a persistent vision from the beginnings of American thought. At once utopian and pragmatic, millenial and immediate, it is a view of society as a progression towards an earthly ideal, not, as in older civilizations, an acceptance of unchangeable conditions.

Benjamin Franklin, kite in hand, may be the best-known symbol of the search for an electrically powered paradise. Thomas Jefferson, the farmer/philosopher who distrusted the new industrialism, saw America as sufficiently removed from the evils of European society to be the model for fusing spiritual values with technology-based wealth. A half-century later, the quintessential national philosopher, Ralph Waldo Emerson, wrote, "Machinery and transcendentalism agree well.... Our civilization and these ideas are reducing earth to a brain. See how by the telegram and steam the earth is anthropologized." This is the rhetoric of the "technological sublime," in Leo Marx's phrase, and it runs like a golden thread through the national uplift literature.[1]

This American faith has been a powerful force propelling us toward new forms of post-industrialism. Its focus has changed somewhat as American society has become more complex, and particularly as it has expanded its global interests. However, even the recent lowering of expectations about the United States' role in world affairs has not seriously affected the myth. The lure of the Western frontier has been largely replaced by the lure of the equally elusive global village. This folksy creation of Marshall McLuhan's appeals to our desire to reduce the wide world to familiar proportions. McLuhan is, significantly, one of the best-known of the present generation of believers in the transforming power of electricity. (Others of the faith have included biologist Julian Huxley, theologian Teilhard de Chardin, and engineer Buckminster Fuller.) In a metaphysical flight, McLuhan once declared that the computer "promises by technology a Pentecostal condition of universal understanding and unity."[2]

Social salvation through better communications and information has been a steady promise within the American technological myth. The promise has, moreover, been translated into practice here on a scale never attempted by other societies. The statistical measures of growth toward a new kind of information society are awesome — in numbers of telephones, computers, and other devices. The newly proclaimed information age is, however, less an accretion of machines and techniques than a declaration of faith that electronic salvation may well be within our grasp. The proofs of the faith are found these days in the pea-size products of the microelectronics industry — the stunning range of technologies that began with the transistor in the 1950s and came of age with the integrated circuit, tiny semiconductor devices which are the building blocks of the post-industrial era.

   With all its sophisticated capabilities, the new technological environment includes some stubborn problems. Its initial impact has been to raise the level of social complexity. We try to temper this, often by anthropomorphizing the new machines. Where but in America, to use the old lead-in, would a bank try to sell the services of its computerized teller machines by advertising a mechanical pal named Tillie the Teller — and succeed? "We promoted her personality," says an official of the First National Bank of Atlanta. "She's a bubbly, giggly kind of character".[3]

Tillie the Teller aside, we will have to come to terms with some changing realities in our search for the electronic Eden, the machine-in-the-garden. And here the dark side of the technological myth has to be faced. Henry Adams was one of the early doubters. In *Mont St. Michel and Chartres,* he saw the dynamo, the symbol of technology, as a threat and sought refuge in the Virgin cult of the Middle Ages. Mark Twain expressed his skepticism by having Hank Morgan, the hero of *A Connecticut Yankee in King Arthur's Court,* become trapped by an electrical fence which he had intended to use as protection against the primitive Britons.

In more recent times, an incisive critic of the technological myth has been Lewis Mumford. In his early career, Mumford accepted the optimistic view of technological benefits espoused by his teacher, Patrick Geddes, the Scottish biologist and urban planner. In *Technics and Civilization* (1934), Mumford declared that electricity would be the great instrument of social balance in American civilization. But in his last great book, *The Pentagon of Power* (1970), he attacked easy optimism about the benefits of technology, including those associated with communications and information. Whatever its early promise, he declared, the new technologies were being used to magnify and vulgarize the dominant components of the power structure, making it easier for a small elite to dominate large populations.[4] His conclusions were anticipated some years before by a Canadian scholar, Harold Innis, who challenged the idea that communications would lead to a democratic diffusion of power. Innis saw what he termed the tragedy of modern culture here and in Europe as the influence of print and electronic media undermining space and time in the interests of commercial and political power.[5]

The warnings of Mumford, Innis, and other critics have continued in recent years. Victor Ferkiss of Georgetown University believes American society is at a critical juncture in its inability to understand adequately the political consequences of technological change.[6] At the popular level, Alvin Toffler sees the prospect of social breakdown as the result of uncontrolled information overload.[7] University of California researcher Herbert Schiller maintains that the manipulation of communications and information resources by a military/industrial establishment is undermining the prospects for democratic society in this country.[8] One of the most striking criticisms of the perils of microelectronic technology is found in a study sponsored by an organization with certified establishment credits — the New York–based Conference Board, a business research group. Its report, *Information Technology: Some Critical Implications for Decision Makers,* takes a somber view of our ability to cope with the choices opened up by computers and other information technologies.

We may create and strengthen the power of management elites, cir-
cumscribe the freedom of man, and create a new kind of rich-poor
gap between those, regardless of economic status, who know how to
command information and those who do not.[9]

Although their approaches to the subject vary, these post-
Mumfordian critics concur in their assessment of technology as a
double-edged weapon which is being misused. Their pessimism is
grounded in the dark perceptions of technological consequences outlined by French sociologist Jacques Ellul in the five sobering precepts
listed in chapter 1. None of these critics has stated the case of unintended consequences more sharply than the distinguished American
philosopher, Morris Raphael Cohen. He would propose a dilemma
for his students: If there were an invention that would enormously
increase individual freedom and mobility but demanded the sacrifice
of thirty thousand human lives annually, would you take it? The invention was, of course, the automobile. No one in the early years of
this century could have assessed its benefits and costs. The new information technologies will, if anything, have a greater impact —
although perhaps not involving the direct loss of lives in quite the
same way.

This unease spreads well beyond the problems posed by those
few individuals who ponder the philosophical implications of change.
It is reflected in the ambivalence ordinary men and women feel about
the new environment. The extreme form of this ambivalence is the
Ludditism and other types of defiance exhibited by countercultural
critics of the system. But it is also present, less dramatically, in the
general attitude or feeling that something is wrong, that a ubiquitous "they" is ganging up on the rest of us. This attitude breaks
through in daily irritations about computerized credit card mix-ups,
erroneous bank statements, wrong numbers on the telephone, transportation delays, and shoddy "quality-controlled" products in the
stores. These incidents feed into a vague sense that technologies have
now crossed the threshold into uncontrolled power and consequences
from which there may be no turning back. It is reinforced by the piling up of larger problems, such as diminishing energy resources and
environmental pollution, where technology emerges as cause rather
than cure. Taken together, these problems are seen not as minor
obstacles but rather as the end result of a serious, persistent dis-
equilibrium. As Victor Ferkiss has noted, this attitude highlights the
difficulties of fashioning viable social institutions and processes to
deal with a more complex, technology-driven structure.[10]

If Americans are being currently denied the sunny certainties of onward-and-upward technological progress, we have some sober compensations. These take the form of a greater, if still reluctant, readiness to face up to the situation. Under the pressure of events, there is somewhat less wandering in the meadows of easy assumption about the changed environment of post-industrial society. We have succeeded in shucking off some of the more romantic notions of the technological myth. Hopefully, we have begun to see more clearly the prospects of a free society in which technology can be applied more effectively on a mass scale to serve both material needs and needs for those intangibles that enrich the quality of life. To deny this hope, or not to act on it, would be to erode — perhaps beyond repair — the social mystique holding us together as a civilization that has moved beyond the traditional cultural ties of race or place. The electronic Eden, the machine-in-the-garden, still has a powerful role to play, newly revised to suit conditions that our forebears could not imagine. The question is whether this new reality can be matched with old values in a way that strengthens our prospects for a humanistic democracy.

Here is where the new capabilities of communications and information become critical. They are not simply microelectronic add-ons to the economic structure. They are a controlling resource, the social brain and nervous system holding society together and keeping it in some sort of working equilibrium during a difficult transition. Again, the Wright brothers' unstable flying machine is a useful analogy. It was designed with enough new information input to allow it to move through a turbulent three-dimensional environment under its own power. We have the same problem in our own turbulent times. Do we have sufficient information and adequate communication to navigate this perilous passage? To a considerable degree, the deciding factor will be the effectiveness of our communications and information tools.

Since the focus here is on the American stake in communications and information, we must take the somewhat risky step of separating developments in these fields from those in other technologies. The risk is in trying to factor out the implications of one set of technologies as if they were independent variables. They are not, of course. The cautions are particularly apt in the study of communications and information patterns. These patterns involve fundamental chemistries of change, infusing all other elements of our lives and altering them. Moreover, these patterns are themselves changed as they affect human attitudes, values, and actions, which then feed back into the entire process.

Such analytical pitfalls must be kept in mind in assessing the American stake in a new strategy for communications and information. The task requires triangulating economics, technology, and politics to arrive at an integrated view of the problem. This kind of overall assessment has, until recently, been curiously neglected. The volume of research in communications and information has risen steadily in recent years. It is still largely conducted, however, in tight clusters of academic disciplines — among the graph-riddled economists, the mouse-maze psychologists, the group-dynamic sociologists, and so forth.

One of the pioneers in modern communications research, Wilbur Schramm, reminded his colleagues many years ago that communications is the crossroads where all the disciplines meet. He was trying to tell them that, essentially, they were all talking about the same thing. They duly noted his maxim and turned back to their narrow projects. Fortunately, in the past decade a hardy group of interdisciplinary souls have heeded Schramm's advice and are moving toward more integrative studies. They include Ithiel de Sola Pool at MIT, Anthony Oettinger at Harvard, George Gerbner at Pennsylvania, and Edwin Parker at Stanford. Their respective angles of vision on the subject tend to be different, but they all accept the complexities of a new environment where human communications — and therefore understanding — are increasingly mediated through high-technology machines. They share a fascination for, and an increasing body of research and insights about, the implications of this change.

Meanwhile, real world events do not wait on the promise of better understanding. The new microelectronics-based grid is being assembled without the benefit of clear-cut projections of its many impacts. Even with the most careful studies, the breadth and depth of these impacts make any precision difficult. This should not excuse us from trying to identify where we are now and where we are going in this area. The stakes are too high to justify any Micawberish hopes that something will turn up. A century ago, the historian Jacob Burkhardt warned that the denial of complexity is the beginning of tyranny. The best approach, as proposed above, is to attempt an integrative look at this complexity in communications and information affairs by triangulating their economic, political, and technological aspects.

Microelectronic technology is, for the present, the driving force among these factors, with its active promise of a new era of abundant resources. Economics is next, as industry demonstrates its ability to transform technological capabilities into marketplace realities. The most critical side of the triangle is the political one. Here is where understanding and actions are weakest, threatening the chances that viable strategies for dealing with the new environment will emerge. The choice, in simplest terms, is whether resources adequate to meet our needs can be assured through a linear extension of past political and social practices or whether a new set of strategies is called for. The argument is a common one in discussions of post-industrial problems, but it has particularly sensitive relevance in the communications area.

The dispute runs across the political and social spectrum. At one end are those who would leave present policies and practices essentially alone, adjusting them in small ways as specific conditions change. There is some nostalgia for laissez-faire, muscular capitalism by proponents of this approach. The more compelling arguments, however, involve the recurrent suspicion that, whatever the beneficent intentions of political and/or social actions in this area, such intervention is inevitably counterproductive and even dangerous. The unique American experiment in restraining public intervention in communications and information affairs has worked so far, proponents of this view say. The duplications, confusion, and other inefficiencies of the system, they argue, are a small price to pay, now or in the future, compared to the costs of public actions based on doubtful premises of social efficiency and economic rationality.

At the other end of the spectrum are a small, persistent band of interventionists. Some of them draw their inspiration from various forms of socialism, native to America and otherwise. Another faction is the heirs of a 1930s type of technocratic thinking in which it is believed that the only way through the current rough passage is by applying more rigorous social engineering, based on centrally directed technology.

The answer lies between these ideological extremes. In this society of compromise and deal-making, our real strategic options can be found toward the center of the spectrum. What is clear is that, for all their power, technological and economic forces themselves cannot make the overriding social decisions needed to assure a viable environment in which communications and information resources match our needs. The decisions involve factors well beyond technological advances or marketplace economics. In the last analysis, the issues are strategic and political.

What are the policy choices for the new information environment? Finding out requires the kind of basic assessment that Americans are generally reluctant to make. For all our attachment to efficiency and planning, we are not moving in an orderly fashion into the new environment. We are backing in, with, at best, an over-the-shoulder view of things to come. And there are few junctures along the way that will permit us to get our critical bearings.

In assessing planning efforts in this area, a Harvard study group has declared:

> Decisions of vital importance — national, international, corporate and personal — are being fought out in dimly lit arenas under rules that are not clear even to the lawyers, engineers, economists and bureaucrats who devised them. Rosters and score cards are rare. Some of the players are unnumbered; others wear the wrong numbers. . . . There are many kinds of information technologies, but it is becoming clear that there is really only one information system, no matter how disconnected the parts may seem. Information is a basic resource, fully as important as materials or energy. While materials and energy have not lacked for public scrutiny and policy attention, information resources have developed willy-nilly, their potency overshadowed by their technical details, their pervasiveness so complete they are taken for granted, like the clean air we breathe.[11]

Communications and information policies are a thicket of laws, regulations, administrative decisions, and encrusted practices carried out by hundreds of public entities at the federal, state, and local levels. The pattern is confused and often overlapping and contradictory in both purpose and application. Despite the faults of the system, it reflects — not always clearly — a rough consensus. This includes the agreement that there is a need to limit the growth of a central authority that could undermine First Amendment rights and the wide-ranging interpretation of these rights, both in law and tradition, which has been developed over two centuries.

As a result, no one is in charge, by design. Moreover there is no firm consensus on how to proceed in adjusting the system to new realities, or whether to do so at all. One striking example of this confusion can be seen in the recent attempt to revise the only basic communications legislation ever approved by Congress, the Communications Act of 1934. Simple logic argued that a law which was written almost a half century ago to define telephone, telegraph, and radio broadcasting regulations should be brought up to date in the age of computers, satellites, and other exotic technologies. Congressional hearings on such a revision began in 1976. They have involved millions of words of testimony by hundreds of experts. Five years and many rewrites later, the process continues with no prospect as of mid-1981 of a comprehensive solution yet in sight. Curiously, the debates have not involved disputes over the issue of First Amendment rights. No one has seriously proposed any widening of government controls over communications and information. The vast bulk of the proposals have proposed weakening the public role.[12]

There are many reasons for this policy immobility. In part, it involves a general lack of public discussion of the issues. In a hyped-up media environment which thrives on sensationalism, sober discussions of communications policy attract little attention. The more immediate reason for the legislative impasse, however, has been the inability of the major vested interests to agree on a formula for compromise. If a solution is found, it will be primarily through the interplay of these economic forces.

And there probably will be something missing. The debate over this so-called rewrite legislation (that is, the rewriting of the 1934 Communications Act) has been long on economic arguments. But it has been short on substantive discussion of overall national needs, beyond ritualistic incantations in support of a bigger, better communications system. To a considerable extent, this reflects a lack of firm social indicators that could give direction to a full public discussion of the issue. Such indicators would not be definitive or determining, but they could provide raw material for a more meaningful debate on policy options than has been the case up to now.

The idea of social indicators for communications and information is not new. The Japanese and Swedes, in particular, have been experimenting with such projects for some time. The results have enabled them to identify conditions on a national scale with some precision. The Japanese knew before they started that they had an annual 10 percent increase in the rate of information production. What they found out through their indicators project was that there was only a 3 percent annual increase in the use of this information. Thus, questions were raised: did this mean that more than half of the information produced went to waste because people lacked the time to handle it? What was useful information and what wasn't? The Japanese had no easy answers to these and other issues raised in their indicators surveys, but they did have a new set of questions. In Sweden, there is a similar interest in the day-to-day pattern of information use, especially in the present and potential impact of computer communications on ordinary citizens.[13]

No country turns out more social research on communications and information than the United States. It piles up in mountains of monographs, books, computer tapes, and microfilms — some of it very good, some of it very ordinary, and most of it written in the special corkscrew prose through which social scientists attempt to communicate with one another. The problem lies not merely in its bulk or its uneven quality but in the fact that it is so fractionalized. There is every reason to encourage independent and even adversary research. The question is whether, or how, it can be made more useful and comprehensible in the public policy debates in this field.

Plans for some sort of comprehensive social-indicators system crop up perennially. Numerous proposals for funding such a project have been launched, most of them aimed at the Treasury Department in Washington. In the euphoric days of his Great Society Program, Lyndon Johnson proposed a federally sponsored annual social-indicators index. The idea was promptly rejected by Congress, which did, however, permit the Census Bureau to issue occasional reports. Over and above charges of academic boondoggling, the idea of an annual assessment ran into entrenched suspicions about so-called social engineering.[14] In this area, most Americans have a vested interest in ambiguity. For all our professed devotion to facts and figures, we back away from official attempts to track and measure the conditions of social consensus. In the American version of participatory democracy, with its emphasis on special-interest negotiations, we do not want to be tied down to any plan which purports to codify, under the rubric of objectivity, the social alternatives open to us. As a result, communications and information policies and actions evolve generally without firm indicators of the social conditions involved or the full range of options available.

The lack of a firm consensus on communications and information needs does not excuse us from more precision in defining them. There is a tendency to identify with simple options, from a Pollyanna-ish everything-will-turn-out-fine attitude to the somber scenarios of Lewis Mumford and other pessimists. As noted earlier, Mumford saw American society moving towards a fascistic magamachine future because of the lack of adequate social controls over technology. (His analogy was that of a locomotive, with neither brakes nor engineer, inexorably gathering speed and heading toward a crash.) But he underestimated the role of the web of checks and balances in American society in preventing such an extreme course. This system has worked tolerably well up to now. However, there is serious doubt as to whether it can maintain its resiliency in coping with the information needs of a more complex technological society.

The political implications of this problem were identified almost two decades ago by Karl Deutsch in *The Nerves of Government*.[15] Information is power, Deutsch noted, and — equally important — it is a multiplier of power. In a high-technology society, he argued, control of access to information is more important than control of physical forces such as the police or the military. One of our democratic assumptions is that everyone has equal access to information. In reality, of course, access to information is highly uneven for many reasons. The problem is complicated, Deutsch noted, by an increasing flood of information, which pushes us toward the limit of human capacity to cope. The solution, Deutsch suggests, is a new approach to what he calls "intelligence amplification" through computers and other information technologies that can provide a greater sharing of access to the data we need to survive and thrive.

Intelligence amplification in the service of a democratic society — this is the goal of a strategy for the information age. It is a goal squarely within our national mythos. It identifies and illuminates the psychic bounds of a new kind of post-industrial society whose energies are moving away from the production of things toward the production and distribution of ideas. The objective, after all, is the construction of a national (and eventually global) interactive information grid, capable of connecting everyone on earth with everyone else and with a wide array of information resources. The microelectronic base for the network is essentially proven and available. If a strategy combining technology, economics, and politics can be worked out, this high-capacity grid can be in place in North America well before the end of the century, and in most of the rest of the world early in the new century.

Any such strategy can benefit from lessons already learned in the building of a smaller mass communications grid during the past century — namely, the telephone system. The phone network services 95 percent of the populace directly and most of the remaining 5 percent only at a one-step remove, — that is, with pay phones. A half billion voice calls are made through the system every working day. Only Canada, among major countries, matches the U.S. system in its coverage and use. The phone network offers, moreover, a wide array of communications services over and above what the engineers call POTS — Plain Old Telephone Service. POTS will probably be displaced by data communications as the chief source of the network's revenues before the end of the eighties, and what we now call the telephone system will be called something else because of its extended capacities. (Infonet? Comnet? Or simply, the Network?) The point is that the telephone network exists as an almost universal grid, and that it works very well. More significantly, it is pragmatic proof of the American commitment to the idea of a universal communications system.

However the expanded network develops, it will have the many forms of the present telephone system to use as a reference — technologically, economically, politically, and socially. The new expansion involves upgrading and supplementing an already extensive grid, centered around the Bell System and almost two thousand independent phone systems. There are also an increasing number of independent networks, some of them successors to the old telegraph systems and others newcomers either starting from scratch or as spin-offs from other industries. (The Southern Pacific Railway, to name just one unexpected example, is now a major player in communications networking.)

In chapter 5 we will examine the complex relationship between these many elements, old and new, in the communications and information industries. For now, however, it is useful simply to get an overview of how the expanded network will fit into the new information economy. Although the present network provides some guidelines, these guidelines are inexact when set against the size and complexity of the new grid. The cost of the expanded network will be staggering, measured in hundreds of billions of dollars before it is completed. It will involve technological options on a scale never before tried. Moreover, no one is sure how the system should be configured in terms of its potential use.

Misestimating communications and information usage is nothing new. Alexander Graham Bell thought the telephone network would be primarily an entertainment instrument, transmitting concerts and operas to homes.[16] To his credit, he eventually saw the phone's advantages as a device for personal use rather than for mass broadcasting. The developers of the first modern computer in 1945 predicted that six of the machines would serve all foreseeable world needs. In 1980, thirty years after the fact, the IBM Corporation humbly admitted that in the early fifties it had estimated its market for computers would be limited to about fifty machines.[17] Underestimations of the demand for goods and services has been one of the consistent elements in the communications and information industries since World War II. In fact, these industries are the only areas of the economy which have expanded steadily in recent years, not following the zig-zag course of economic trends.

One result of this has been to confuse the economists. In chapter 1 we looked briefly at a 1977 Department of Commerce report that documented how information related activities now dominate the economy in terms of the gross national product and the work force. The study identifies a fundamental, and still little understood, shift in the focus of American society away from the production of goods to the production and distribution of information. For all its thoroughness — nine eye-straining volumes of it — the report leaves many details of this new economic environment unexplored. However, curiously little in-depth research has been undertaken to follow up on the Commerce Department study.

The apparent reason for this is that economists are generally not comfortable with the intangibles of communications and information. They acknowledge the growing importance of information-related activities, but the subject does not fit neatly into their formulas the way more measurable resources, such as industrial products or energy, do. How do .you put a price tag on a fact or an idea? How is information productivity measured when it involves a scholar ruminating in a library or a scientific researcher manipulating computer data? It is probably true that half of the information produced in this country is underutilized, used only a few times or not at all. Does this mean that too much information is being produced, or only too little of the right kind in the right place at the right time? Who decides what is "the right kind" of information? One question leads to another: how will the information economy change living patterns? What kinds of jobs will be available? Will there be enough work opportunities, and, if so, where will they be?

These are practical questions that go well beyond the difficulties economists may have in providing answers. They involve everyday problems of jobs, family, and community. Deeper down are psychic questions, the doubts of ordinary men and women about the so-called benefits of technology. Here Pollyanna-ish optimism gives way to concerns about the impact of computers and other information/communications machines on prospects for jobs and professional advancement and on personal status in a society where one is identified by what one does from nine to five. These elements have always been present in technological shifts. But they are taking on new force as the United States moves into a period of exponential technological acceleration, particularly in the information and communications fields.

This cycle is just beginning. The fears that computers and other information machines will create hardcore unemployment or downgrade job opportunities are still muted. Information machines have generally created new jobs in roughly the same proportion as they have eliminated older ones. But workers are not economic statistics whose lives can be measured in balanced-out equations. Machines eliminate and create jobs, but the shift is never smooth for the men and women involved.

Nevertheless, even in this early stage of microelectronics the shift is being felt. It is particularly striking in those industries and services that have the financial resources and planning skills to take advantage of the new technologies. A good, close-at-hand example is the Bell Telephone system. After the federal government, Bell is the largest private user of computers and other information machines in the country. Between 1972 and 1977, there was an 18 percent increase in Bell System telephone calls, but the system's labor force dropped from just over 1,000,000 employees to 940,000. Equally significant was the change in the system's mix of employees in the same period. The number of managers, clerical employees, and semiskilled workers dropped, while the number of professional specialists increased by 17 percent and the number of technicians, 50 percent.

The telephone system is an outsized example of what happens when high technology becomes an integral part of an industry. Its experience is being replicated, in varying degrees, across the range of U.S. industrial and service enterprises. The banking business is a typical case. Why have a labor-intensive bank branch, usually in an expensive location, when a customer can go to a machine and use the magnetic tape on the back of his bank card to make withdrawals and deposits directly? This system requires fewer tellers, less paper work, and gives better service. Another increasingly familiar example is the computerized check-out counters in supermarkets that add up purchases, monitor inventories, and order new stock in one operation — again, requiring less personnel and giving more efficiency and better service. These are not futuristic fantasies. The systems are being installed now, and they will become commonplace within a few years. Their advantages are those that have always accrued over the long run when goods and services can be made available to more people with less physical labor. The new information machines will accelerate this process, and the impact on peoples' lives will be more direct than ever before.

Such changes are usually seen as American success stories, modern legacies of the technological myth. The shift to microelectronics can mean more efficient production, lower costs, better products, and a work force with greater professional responsibilities. But there is another side to the story, one which is beginning to be seen more clearly in the light of the economic difficulties plaguing the U.S. economy. Of the nostrums offered to counter economic sluggishness, none has more crowd-pleasing appeal than the idea of "reindustrialization," generally interpreted as the shifting of industrial activity toward more efficient high-technology activities. The fact that this has been happening steadily over many years has not restrained its enthusiasts from proclaiming the doctrine as new and revolutionary. Communications and information rank high on the reindustrialization agenda, since these sectors of the electronics industry have been the leading growth area in an otherwise troubled economy in the early eighties. Reindustrialization is, in fact, a short-term cliché for the longer-range push to adjust the economy to the needs of an information-based, post-industrial society.

Whatever the trend is called, there is growing agreement within the Western industrial nations that microelectronics is a critical area in their economic projections. "The next century's underdeveloped nations," the authoritative London *Economist* says, "will be those industrial societies which fail to harness the explosion of microelectronics technology to all that they make and to the factories that make it."[18] This borders on editorial hyperbole, justified perhaps by the newspaper's discovery of a report which indicated that only 5 percent of British firms were using high-technology electronics. The report was useful in pushing the British government into more effective support for microelectronic research and development — a step taken earlier by the United States, Japan, France, and other industrial powers. Their motivation was basically the same: the hope that microelectronics could overcome some of the constraints on productivity growth that have hurt their economies. A secondary motivation has been the assurance of their shares of the multibillion-dollar world market for these technologies. Microelectronics research and development have boomed at a rate unmatched by any other technology. A new generation of microelectronic circuits has been developed every twelve to eighteen months in this country during the past decade.

The United States holds a commanding position for the present, which would seem to add another chapter to our national success story. However, there are other considerations, involving some negative side-effects. As Colin Norman has noted,

> The nostalgic hope seems to be that microelectronics, along with other high technology industries, will lead the way back to the golden days of the postwar era, when the world economy expanded at a rate that provided high demand that in turn created millions of new jobs. Such a development is at best unlikely . . . . The develop-

ment and application of microelectronics and other technologies will help to stimulate growth, but it will do little to remove the underlying causes of sluggish economic growth.[19]

Norman and other researchers see the need for more effective public strategies to deal with these dislocations. They cite, in particular, the problem of "jobless growth" in industries where production is being automated and workers face layoffs. But the issues are not confined to economics; they will be increasingly political and social as the U.S. moves more deeply into the new high-technology environment.

How will the high-capacity information network evolve? As noted above, it will be, to a considerable degree, an extension of the present grid — the basic telephone network and the smaller specialized networks that have emerged in recent years. These facilities will be upgraded, widened, and in many cases interconnected over the next decade, primarily in response to specific economic needs. The speed with which this is happening has led economists and others to identify the phenomenon as a distinct new structure defining a network pattern in post-industrial America. They see the evolving grid as radically transforming older, slower economic activities by channelling them through high-speed circuits linking buyers and sellers in a vastly expanded electronic market. The concept has been given several nametags, but the one which may stick was developed in the late seventies by a team of University of Southern California researchers led by Herbert Dordick: the "network marketplace." Dordick and his colleagues took a look at the aggregate effect of the many electronics-based information networks being developed or planned and concluded that

> an important industry is rapidly emerging from the marriage of computers and telecommunications. This industry permits users to interact directly with one or more computers, associated data files and problem solving algorithms from remote terminals. It may include access to distributed information systems within and between organizations, remote transaction recording, data base inquiry and computer conferencing. . . . All the usual services of a marketplace can be offered within a large information network. Products and services can be advertised and sellers can be located; ordering, billing and deliveries can be facilitated; and all manner of transactions can be consummated, including wholesale, retail, brokering, and mass distribution. Indeed the entire range of such products and services for business, industry, the consumer and government can be perceived as a marketplace — a marketplace on a communications network or the network marketplace.[20]

This concept of marketplace will be a critical element in the forming of the expanded information infrastructure of U.S. post-industrial society. It will not be the product of a master design, however theoretically efficient such an approach might be. It will develop from a pattern of many decisions, large and small, tied to different (and often conflicting) projections of marketplace needs. This is the reality behind the high-flying predictions of a universal information grid which have become part of the standard scenario of futurists in recent years. Their vision of a plug-in future, of computers in the living room, of global teleconferences, of robotics factories controlled by telepresence techniques, and of a new quality of life based on access to vast information resources is nevertheless too close to possible realization to be dismissed any longer as sci-fi fantasy.

The new network may, however, fail to match these prospects. Its capabilities may be limited to simply providing more efficient communications services to the higher reaches of U.S. business. On the other hand, it can also become a truly universal service grid with a strong economic base, servicing a full range of economic and social needs of both consumers and businesses. This choice will be critical in the definition of American strategies in the new information age. It is useful, therefore, to look at the factors which will determine how, and for what purpose, the new grid will be assembled.

The choice of a mass or elite network can go either way. The grid is now only in the very early stages of development. Its present development is comparable to that of the telephone system after the First World War. Like the phone system of that era, it is a collection of separate networks, large and small. In fact, it was not until the thirties that all the separate — and often competing — telephone systems in this country were interconnected to permit universal subscriber service. Will this serve as a precedent for a new integrated grid of high-capacity communications and information services? There are similarities between the two systems, but many of the details are different. It took a half-century to sort out the economic, legal, and social aspects of a relatively simple integrated phone system. These factors are immensely more complex in the new network, with its expanded capability for voice, visual, and data services. Moreover, in these early years of the grid's development, public policy and pressure from industry strongly favor a competitive system of network diversity.

The U.S. grid, in short, will not be built following any centralized master strategy. It will be the outcome of many competing plans. Consequently, the first integrated national grids will probably be built in Europe and Japan. Although these countries are currently trailing the U.S. in high-capacity networking, their practice of government control over telecommunications development gives authorities greater leeway in laying out a national strategy for an integrated system. They are generally not tied down by the cat's cradle of legal, economic, and social restraints we have imposed on ourselves, beginning with First Amendment inhibitions about government involvement.

The rapid growth of wide-service networking in the past decade has demonstrated U.S. industry's ability to meet the difficult, usually economically based needs of large government and business bureaucracies. Industry's ability to meet the needs of smaller organizations and individual consumers of information is less clear. Herbert Dordick and his colleagues have noted that this can pose a serious problem for a democratic society. As mentioned earlier, we may be moving toward a new and hazardous form of information inequality, well beyond the traditional gap separating those who have the economic and social means to gain access to information resources and those who do not.[21]

Most of the options favoring a full-access grid are still open. For the present, the network is being designed to meet a variety of limited purposes. Will all these purposes add up to a full range of communications and information services needed by a healthy post-industrial environment? Or should we begin to develop some new kind of national strategy that will assure such a range of services, by applying social resources to marketplace economics? For the present, Dordick and his associates point out, "There is not now or in the wings a network policy for the United States."[22]

Right now, there may be no prospect for an all-inclusive national policy in this area, but a network construction boom is in progress, beginning with a series of limited federal government decisions to open the industry to greater competition. Over the past decade, these decisions have exposed a cautious, hidebound industry to new forces — forces that triggered a dramatic expansion of networks and related services in the seventies, which will grow even more rapidly throughout the eighties. Experience to date has confirmed that doing business in the network marketplace can be cost effective, particularly with the rising cost of labor. There are other factors — better overall management control, reductions in energy costs, more effective quality controls over goods and services, plus the intangibles of convenience. However, the ultimate economic prize is the expanded marketplace access gained by buyers and sellers on the network. This will not come automatically; there are still many questions to be resolved as the networks expand. These include pricing of services, public regulatory controls, technical compatability between networks, and capital formation. A number of promising network ventures have already foundered in the midst of such hard realities. A classic case in the mid-seventies was that of the Datran Corporation, a self-styled David that took on the Goliath-like telephone company and, contrary to Biblical form, lost. Many such failures will occur in the series of shakeouts that will inevitably take place before the network marketplace settles into a long-term pattern, a decade or so from now.

By that time, the networks will be adequately serving the needs of the U.S. business and government structure — a major step toward a post-industrial economy. The process, however, will be incomplete if the networks fail to move into the wider field of mass consumer services as the telephone network succeeded in doing two generations ago.

Mass telephone service resulted from a national strategy decision embedded in the Communications Act of 1934. It came about after a hard-fought struggle between industry and government, in which the two sides traded economic concessions for social gains — a process which has been maintained, with some adjustments, ever since. But the conditions required for replicating such a scenario in the future will not be the same. Nevertheless, there are sufficient similarities to suggest that definative policy decisions extending high-technology, full-service networking to mass consumer levels are likely.

This will involve the integration of economics, technological, and policy factors in new and innovative patterns. Two familiar technologies — those of the telephone and television — are already available in most U.S. homes, schools, and other institutions, providing the physical means for consumer access to the network. The high-capacity circuitry to deliver full service is already installed in about a third of these sites via cable TV. This ratio will move up to one half in a few years, with increased use of thin-fiber optic wires in place of expensive copper cables. Other technologies, such as direct broadcasting from satellites and terrestrial multipoint distribution services, will compete with cable systems for the consumer market. This expansion is currently being fueled by the demand for pay-TV films. Increasingly, cable home-delivery systems will provide other specialized entertainment and information services, most of them retrieved from computer data banks.

These "wired nation" strategies have been puffed up for years, only to be deflated by the difficulties of fitting the technological, economic, and political pieces together. The difficulties are still there, but the outlook for overcoming them is more favorable now than ever before. Driven by economic forces, the new networks can expand beyond business and government services into the consumer sector. But the pattern of expansion remains to be seen. Will it be an elite service, aimed at those in the upper income levels, whose information needs are more readily identifiable and marketable? Will it merely reap easy profits from lightweight entertainment services, replicating patterns of commercial television? Will it provide full services to the full range of the population, including people who live in such neighborhoods as Watts in Los Angeles, Liberty in Miami, or East Harlem and Bedford-Stuyvesant in New York?

In their study of the network marketplace, Herbert Dordick and his colleagues suggest that this problem of neighborhood "local loop" services will be the critical one in determining whether mass consumer-oriented services will be available. The economics of high-density business networking is already clearly favorable. The problem will be in so-called "thin route" networking down to homes and smaller institutions, not only in middle-class communities but in inner cities and rural villages. Dordick suggests a 1990s scenario in which Congress is asked to declare a Universal Network Access principle in much the same way as an earlier Congress laid down a similar principle for the telephone system in the 1934 legislation.

The distance between that possibility, a decade from now, and where we are now is considerable. There are too many intangibles, ambiguities, and other surprises involved to predict any firm kind of pattern. Nevertheless, America has too important a stake in the outcome to leave the subject stranded in the belief that everything will turn out all right. It is all too easy to project a flawed strategy in which we may move, in Lewis Mumford's phrase, toward a "megamachine society" in which a self-serving elite uses information and communications resources to control the levers of power. The old confidence, tied to our technological mythos, that it can't happen here is no longer as steady as it once seemed. Social erosion, what Alvin Toffler calls "demassification," is taking place; traditional groups are breaking up, leaving their former members drifting and alienated. Communications and information resources as such cannot stem this erosion. They can, in fact, hasten it. However, they can also supply new linkages between the pluralities of U.S. society in ways that can reinforce communal trust and creativity.

The question is: how can we keep our essential freedoms while developing new information patterns to meet the problems of a more complex post-industrial society. The answer lies somewhere between authoritarian control and laissez-faire drift. It is here that the conflicting pressures of technology and economics must serve the needs of social equity.

Whether successful strategies are designed and followed will depend only in part on technical or economic decisions. The primary decisions are political. They depend on our willingness to adapt basic social institutions to the opportunities of the new information age. How much readjustment must be made, and whether we have the collective ability to make it in time, are open questions for the present. Before examining these policy questions, we will look at the technologies that will shape a large part of the decision process.

Notes

1. Leo Marx, *The Machine in the Garden* (New York: Oxford University Press, 1964), pp. 232–34.

2. The quotation is cited in James W. Carey and John J. Quirk, "The Mythos of the Electronic Revolution," *The American Scholar* (Summer 1970): p. 402.

3. "Banks Promoting a Mechanical Pal," *New York Times*, 8 August 1977, p. 37.

4. Lewis Mumford, *The Pentagon of Power* (New York: Harcourt Brace, 1970), p. 293.

5. Harold A. Innis, *Empire and Communications* (Toronto: University of Toronto Press, 1950), pp. 166–70.

6. Victor Ferkiss, "Technology: The Hidden Variable," *The Review of Politics*, 42, no. 3 (July 1980): pp. 349–55.

7. Alvin Toffler, *Future Shock* (New York: Bantam Books, 1971), pp. 350–54.

8. Schiller has elaborated his theories in a series of works including *Mass Communications and American Empire* (Boston: Beacon Press, 1971), *The Mind Managers* (Boston: Beacon Press, 1973), and *Communications and Cultural Domination* (White Plains, International Arts and Sciences Press, 1976).

9. The Conference Board, *Information Technology: Some Critical Implications for Decision Makers*, report no. 537 (New York: The Conference Board, 1972), p. v.

10. Ferkiss, "Technology," p. 386.

11. *Information Resources Policy: Arenas, Players and Stakes.* (Annual Report of the Program on Information Resources Policy, 1975–76, Harvard University, 1976), p. 4.

12. The hearings on the "rewrite" of the Communications Act of 1934 have taken place in the Senate Banking Committee's communications subcommittee and in a similar subcommittee of the House Committee on Inter-

state and Foreign Commerce. An excellent introduction to the issues debated in both committees can be found in U.S. Congress, House, Committee on Interstate and Foreign Commerce, *Option Papers: Committee Print 95–13,* 95th Cong., 1st sess. (Washington, D.C.: Government Printing Office, May 1977).

13. The excellent Japanese research on this subject is not available in English in most cases. For a useful summary of Japanese views (and American reactions), *see* Alex S. Edelstein and Sheldon M. Harsel, eds., *Information Societies: Comparing the Japanese and American Experiences* (Seattle: University of Washington International Communications Center, 1978). For a useful summary of Swedish views, see *New Views: Computers and New Media.* (Report by the Commission on New Information Technology, Stockholm, 1979).

14. "People Satisfied, Says U.S. Survey," *Boston Globe,* 19 January 1981, p. 10.

15. Karl W. Deutsch, *The Nerves of Government* (New York: The Free Press of Glencoe, 1963).

16. For a summary of Bell's early perceptions of telephone use, see "Bell's Electrical Toy: What's the Use?," in *The Social Impact of the Telephone,* ed. Ithiel de Sola Pool (Cambridge, Mass.: MIT Press, 1977), pp. 19–22.

17. "One of the Great Miscalculations in IBM History." Advertisement in *New York Times Magazine,* 4 May 1980, p. 127.

18. *The Economist* (London), 23 September 1978, p. 91.

19. Colin Norman, "The Menace of Microelectronics," *New York Times,* 5 October 1980, p. G-5.

20. Herbert Dordick, *The Network Marketplace* (Norwood, N.J.: Ablet Publishing Co., 1981). p. ix

21. Ibid., p. 235.

22. Ibid., p. 242.

Chapter Three

The Technological Framework: Communications Networks

In his masterful study, *Empire and Communications*, the Canadian scholar Harold Innis demonstrates how all societies, from Babylon to the present, have been shaped by the production and distribution of information.[1] His emphasis is on the unsettling effects of new technologies. Innis' perceptions apply to our current transition to a new kind of information society. Here we will take a broad look at the technologies involved in this shift and their impact on our future.

Consider a fable about some fifteenth-century citizens faced with evaluating a new technology. In the city of Mainz, Germany, Master Johann Gutenberg has just developed a machine that can reproduce manuscript-like pages in many copies. News of his work has reached the local ruler, the Elector of the Rhineland Palatinate. In the spirit of Renaissance inquiry, the Elector asks a group of scholars and businessmen to assess the new machine's impact on the local economy and culture. Since bureaucracy is just beginning to assert itself as an organizational force, the group is designated the Select Committee to Evaluate Multiple Manuscript Production.

The committee visits Gutenberg's workshop, where the proud inventor demonstrates his machine. The committee is impressed, but skeptical. After considerable debate, the group submits its report to the Elector. The machine is undoubtedly a technological advance, the report concludes, but it has only limited application to Palatinate needs. The committee recommends that the government not invest research and development funds in the project. Its reasons are direct and cogent: (1) a large work force of monks copying manuscripts would lose their jobs if the Gutenberg machine were encouraged; (2) there is no heavy demand for multiple copies of manuscripts; and (3) the long-term market for printed books is doubtful due to the low literacy rate.[2]

It is easy to feel superior to the Elector's select committee and its lack of foresight, but it is wrong to do so. The same errors have consistently been made in our own supposedly enlightened times. One example of such an error is the initial reaction to the wireless radio early in this century. The U.S. Navy installed radio transmitters on ships of the Great White Fleet for its round-the-world voyage and then discarded them in favor of carrier pigeons. In the 1890s, a British publication, the *Electrician*, saw the telephone as a positive menace: "It seems to us that we are getting perilously near the ideal of the modern Utopian whose life is to consist of sitting in armchairs and pressing a button. It is not a desirable prospect: we shall have no wants, no money, no ambition, no youth, no desires, no individuality, no names and nothing wise about us."[3] In our own time, equally wrong predictions about the influence of computers, satellites, and other technologies have been commonplace.

We cannot, in any event, take refuge in the conventional wisdom that "technology is not the problem." In fact, technology is more at the core of the problem than ever before. Until recently, major communications advances could be dealt with on a linear basis. Since they were phased-in gradually, there was time to make the political and economic adjustments needed to integrate them into the existing structure. Forty years separated the inventions of the telegraph and the telephone, another three decades passed before wireless radio came on the scene, and it was still another thirty years before the advent of computers. The time line has been drastically compressed in recent years, with a full range of technologies converging over the entire spectrum of the production, storage, and distribution of information.

The wild-and-wooly situation in microelectronics technology known as large-scale integration (LSI) is typical. Despite its name, LSI involves the miniaturization of electronic circuits. Using LSI techniques, a silicon chip the size of a fingernail can contain the equivalent of tens of thousands of circuits. Properly configured, a chip can have all the attributes of a computer; it is a microprocessor with the computational power of a 1950s wall-size machine. Microprocessor technology came out of the laboratories a dozen years ago; since then it has gone through at least five technological generations, each involving major advances in capacity and efficiency.

The pace will step up in the coming decades, with the introduction of a wide array of innovations. Among them are:

- Josephson junctions, computer circuits that use superconducting metals, which lose all resistance to electricity at very low temperatures. This enables them to handle computations in trillionths of a second, a hundred times faster than existing computer circuits.
- Wave-guide communications channels, carrying the equivalent of a quarter-million telephone circuits on a light beam shot down a hollow tube the width of a car's exhaust pipe.
- Computerized storage systems, now under development, that will house as much information as is in the entire book collection of the Library of Congress in a tabletop container.
- Massive space platforms, structures assembled thousands of miles above the equator, from which will be hung communications satellites capable of beaming signals into pocket-size portable receivers.

Our understanding of the benefits and costs of these technologies is limited by our still primitive experience. But we can now see the possibilities of having a high-capacity, mass access information network much earlier than anyone would have considered realistic even a few years ago. The costs — beyond the enormous economic investment required — are the dangers of building this network haphazardly without fully considering a strategy for long-term needs. Technologists can identify the physical potential of their innovations with impressive accuracy. The political, social, and economic implications are much more elusive. This uncertainty has the effect of intimidating policy makers, both public and private. As an MIT study put it several years ago: "Communications technology is flooding policymakers with options they do not understand, among which they must choose, and which will have profound effects on society." The statement underlines the importance of looking at the new technologies not simply in terms of their capabilities but also in the context of a viable social strategy for their use. This calls for some understanding of the modern evolution of the science of communications and information.

In this chapter, we will look at the development of communications network technology; in the next chapter, the information machines which plug into these networks will be examined.

The so-called communications revolution is, in reality, a succession of three overlapping technological stages that have taken place during the past one hundred and fifty years. The first of these was the Wire Age (1844–1900), the second was the Wireless Age (1900–1970), and the third is the one we are now entering — the Integrated Grid Age, in which wire and wireless technology are brought together in powerful combinations which will form the structure of the future global information utility. The technological advances that occurred between the beginning of the Wire Age and the present are awesome.[4] The early Western Union telegraph machines that opened the Wire Age could relay about forty words a minute. Western Union's first domestic communications satellite, the successor to the old telegraph line, was placed in orbit in 1975 with a capability of transmitting eight million words a *second*. Both machines — the telegraph transmitter and the satellite — nevertheless contributed to the cumulative impact of technology on how we communicate. It is useful to take a brief look at the three evolutionary stages that brought us to where we are today.

The Wire Age was largely the creation of a group of crusty, pragmatic U.S. inventors, beginning with Samuel F. B. Morse and his single wire, which transmitted electrical impulses in code from Washington to Baltimore in 1844. The Morse telegraph was a major technical breakthrough, but it also involved two other innovations crucial in American communications development. The first was the federal government's decision to contribute research and development funds for the Morse invention. It involved modest sums, but set a significant precedent for the hundreds of millions of public research dollars now being invested annually in communications technology. The second innovative decision was that the telegraph system would be developed and controlled by private companies, not by the central government. This pattern distinguishes the U.S. communications structure from that of almost every other nation, whose governments own or strictly control local communications systems. As a result, commercial revenues fueled the rapid expansion of the Morse telegraph system as well as the other major innovation of the Wire Age — the Bell telephone.

A century ago, it seemed inevitable that mass communications networking would be based on wire circuits. Nineteenth-century futurists, looking at the growth of telegraph and telephone systems, would have been safe in predicting that one day all mankind would be linked by wires. They would have forecast, correctly, that wire technology would be improved in ways that would eliminate such problems as fading, unreliable switching equipment, and high costs.

The wire networks were put to many imaginative uses in the late nineteenth century. The telephone was seen as a mass medium for the distribution of services we now associate with broadcasting — news, music, entertainment, and public affairs programming. Within a year after his first successful telephone experiments, Alexander Graham Bell transmitted musical programs by wire in Ontario. Stereophonic music transmitted over the telephone was demonstrated five years later at the 1881 Paris Electrical Exposition. The results encouraged a number of European opera houses to install telephone outlets to transmit live performances to other locations.[5]

The most extensive experiment with mass-media telephone service took place in Budapest. Beginning in 1884, the local telephone system carried a daily program of news bulletins, town happenings, sermons, music, and theater performances through a network that eventually extended 168 miles. The system operated until the late 1920s. Similar experiments on a smaller scale were carried out in other European and American cities. Service was efficient and cheap: a Budapest phone subscriber paid the equivalent of two cents each time he used the news and entertainment network.

The telephone system was not, however, destined to become the all-purpose wired network envisioned by Bell and others. This potential was undercut by another politically and economically powerful technological development — wireless communications, or the transmission of radiant energy in the form of invisible waves moving through the air. The possibility of transmitting without wires had increasingly intrigued inventors during the last half of the nineteenth century: the U.S. Patent Office registered a number of patents for "aerial conduction" of electric signals in the 1870s. But the significant breakthrough was made by Guglielmo Marconi, who began work on the problem as a precocious teenager in the early 1890s. He had the good luck to have a mother, a well-to-do Englishwoman, who took it upon herself to convince the British Post Office that they should pay attention to her son's experiments. Marconi proceeded to demonstrate his ideas in 1896 to a group of British officials, who were intrigued but skeptical. The group may have included some of the same officials who, some years earlier, had dismissed the idea of large-scale use of the telephone in Britain on the grounds that there were enough little boys available to deliver messages.

More astute Britons grasped the potential benefits of wireless communications, both for business and for political links with the nation's overseas empire. They encouraged Marconi to market his invention and to lease transmitters and receiving sets on ships as a monopoly. Other governments, including the United States, quickly recognized the political dangers of such monopolistic control of communications. They convened a conference of the International Telegraph Union in 1903 that approved regulations prohibiting any nation from claiming exclusive control over wireless communications. Meanwhile, Britain and other major European powers equipped their naval ships and military installations with the new technology.

Their experience in the First World War convinced governments that the wireless should be harnessed to strategic national purposes. Its value had been greatly enhanced when voice capability was added to transmission previously limited to dot-and-dash Morse code signals. The result was radio broadcasting and radio telephony. European governments moved quickly to nationalize both techniques, as they had done earlier with telephone and other wired networks. No leader at the time was more perceptive about the potential of radio broadcasting than Lenin. He recognized that radio broadcasting — what he called the "newspaper without walls" — could be a powerful instrument of political and social control. He ordered rapid development of radio stations in the Soviet Union before he died in 1924.

The American response was somewhat different. Given the well-entrenched position of the commercial communications companies, there was no doubt that wireless communications would be part of the private sector. At one point, the federal government encouraged the setting up of a "chosen instrument" company, the Radio Corporation of America, to assure a strong U.S. presence in the field, particularly in manufacturing the new equipment. On the domestic broadcasting front, the American Telephone and Telegraph Company tried to add radio broadcasting to its near-monopoly in telephone services. The attempt failed, and radio networking was eventually divided among a number of companies.[6]

American radio broadcasting was not brought under effective regulatory control until the Communications Act of 1934, the legislation which still defines national communications policy for both wire and wireless services. The law confirmed that both services were to remain in private hands, with regulatory controls administered by a new agency, the Federal Communications Commission. The 1934 legislation legitimized what had become, through commercial pressures, a close relationship between wire and wireless technology. As in

Europe, wire services were confined by law to individual point-to-point messages — telephone calls, telegrams, telex, and the like. Wireless was also used for point-to-point messages, but its greater significance was its capability for centrally directed radio — and, later, television — broadcasting.

Wireless broadcasting was to become, in the words of British communications scholar Anthony Smith,

> the supreme cultural instrument of the nation-state . . . a vast socializing instrument by which all the members of a society could be contacted simultaneously. With the wireless would automatically arrive the possibility of defining cultural policy as deliberately as economic policy; it created national markets for cultural production, national arbitrage for artistic reputation and a new constituency for politics.[7]

The early advocates of controls over wireless broadcasting were sufficiently aware that *wire* transmission could be competitive and therefore had to be restricted as a mass medium. Wire is the carrier of decentralized culture, unmediated by public authorities or commercial firms. Thus it was a threat to the centralized content control which characterized over-the-air broadcasting. This was the motivation behind the controls foreign governments imposed on broadcasting, from the relatively light-handed approaches of the state-chartered British Broadcasting Corporation to the more direct controls imposed by other governments. The United States was an exception to this general pattern. The motivation for broadcasting regulation here was essentially economic and technical, although there has always been a political factor, implicit or explicit, in the process. In any event, the wire/wireless pattern that has shaped communications practices, and a good share of our culture, for the past half-century was set by these policies and reinforced by the enormous profitability of both broadcasting and other services.[8]

This pattern is changing. The decision to separate the functions of wire and wireless technology fifty years ago was based on perceptions of how the technology of that time could be used for political and economic ends. Similar perceptions obtain as we move into a new technological era. A watershed has been reached where the capabilities of wire and wireless are coming together to form a radically different communications pattern. Despite the efforts of vested economic interests to keep them separated on the old two-track system, the distinctions between wire and wireless are being eroded. This melding of capabilities forms the base of a new information environment — the Age of the Integrated Grid — in which messages can move in any form (voice, visual, or print) through an integrated, linked network of wire or wireless channels. Wire and wireless are becoming interchangeable parts of a unitary information utility, the nervous system of post-industrial America. The political, economic, and social impact of the new utility can be understood only in terms of the way wire and wireless technologies are converging after a century of separate development.

First, the wires. Early advances in wire technology generally involved wrapping more wires in bigger cables. There was a limit to this because of the sheer bulk of the cables. In the 1940s, Bell Laboratories developed the coaxial cable, a relatively thin configuration of sheathings and wires with greatly expanded circuit capacity. The new cable could provide a large number of circuits for narrow band use, such as in telephones, telex, and so on, or a smaller number of broadband circuits for such services as television and high-speed data transmissions. Coaxial cable became an important part of the AT&T long-lines network for telephone, television, and other services in the 1950s. Later, such cables provided the technical base for the cable television industry.

The new cables also made possible high-capacity international communications, particularly in the North Atlantic region where telephone traffic was heavy. Although there had been oceanic cables for almost a century, these were limited to simple telegraph message services. Coaxial cable technology expanded this to other services, in particular, dependable voice-telephone links which had previously been limited to unreliable radio circuits. The first transatlantic coaxial cable began operations in 1956, with a capacity of thirty-six telephone circuits. Since that time, five more cables have been strung across the Atlantic, each more technically advanced than its predecessor. The most recent cable, known as TAT-6, has a four thousand telephone-line capacity. Because previous cables were occasionally snapped by the draglines of fishing trawlers, special devices for burying cables in the ocean floor were developed. One of these, SCARAB (Submerged Craft Assisting Recovery and Burial), is a remotely controlled, unmanned submarine that can dig up a cable, return it to the surface for repairs, and then bury it again on the sea bottom.[9]

High-capacity cables will be an important part of the world communications grid for a long time to come, if only because of heavy investments in the present system. The TAT-6 cable, for example, cost $196 million, shared among sixteen European countries and four American firms. This figure masks the economic gains made possible over the years by more efficient cable technology. The first TAT cable in the mid-fifties cost $550 per circuit mile; in the late seventies this cost had dropped to about $10 for an advanced cable marketed by ITT. A higher technology variation of coaxial cables, known as CLOAX, with a capacity for over forty thousand telephone lines has been developed at AT&T's Bell Laboratories. Defining cable capacity in terms of phone calls makes the subject somewhat more comprehensible to laymen. However, these cables can handle any form of electronic communications — voice, visual, or data — in any combination simultaneously.

This capability is shared and immensely magnified by a new type of cable technology — fiber optics — that promises to cause radical changes in the wire communications structure. In fiber optics communication, information is transmitted in optical form (that is, in light waves) along a glass fiber whose thickness is comparable to that of a human hair. The fibers have many useful attributes, the most striking of which is their information-carrying potential. Theoretically, for a given diameter of cable, optical transmission on a single wavelength can carry thirty times more traffic than a coaxial cable.

The idea of using light waves for communications had been understood for a long time. Alexander Graham Bell experimented with what he called a "photophone," a device for sending messages by sunlight reflected from mirrors. It did not work well: sunbeams are scattered by air and rain, and, in any event, the sun does not always shine. Two research breakthroughs were required before optical communications would be practical. The first was the development of a light source that could provide the concentrated, narrow band of frequencies useful for communications applications. That came in the late 1950s with the first demonstrations of the laser, a device that gives off a concentrated beam of light at a single frequency. The second major breakthrough was the development of a suitable optical transmission medium — the channel down which the laser beam travels. As Alexander Graham Bell found out, transmission of light beams through the atmosphere is severely limited. However, wires, or "lightguides," made of pure glass can trap light waves and carry them for m les with little loss in signal intensity. The technical problems of developing a glass fiber with few impurities to impede the beam have been essentially solved in the past decade by scientists at ITT, Corning Glass, Bell Labs and other research groups. Today's fibers are so transparent that light loses more intensity passing through an ordinary windowpane than it does in hundreds of feet of glass fiber. If seawater were as transparent, one could easily see to the bottom of the deepest ocean.[10]

The information-carrying capacities of fiber optic wires are awesome. A pair of copper wires is needed for a single telephone call, but a pair of hair-thin optical fibers can carry nearly two thousand calls simultaneously. Another advantage of the fibers is their potential low cost. The basic material out of which they are made is silicon, which is universally available and cheap. Only five cubic centimeters of silicon is needed to make a fiber a kilometer long. The costs are in the refining of impurities out of the silicon. As this technology has improved, and as volume production of the fibers has increased, the price of optical fibers has dropped dramatically. It may be some years, however, before optical fibers can compete in price with copper cables.

Meanwhile, the fibers have many immediate advantages. They can be installed in tight spaces — a major factor in the new microelectronic devices. They also have high reliability. An optical fiber by itself is a fragile thing, but considerable research has gone into coatings to improve the fiber's durability. Plastic jackets, developed by Du Pont and other firms, allow the fibers to be twisted, turned, and tied in knots. The fibers are unaffected by water, varying temperatures, or corrosion. Their light source, the lasers, may be no larger than a grain of salt and may emit light continuously for a hundred years.

Fiber optic applications have been limited until recently by the short distances a signal can be efficiently transmitted. In the first practical uses, this distance was limited to a few feet, inside the human body. Since the late fifties, fiber optic medical probes, known as endoscopes, have been used like tiny flashlights to examine parts of the body previously accessible only through exploratory surgery. The next step was to use optical wires as substitutes for copper wires in electronic equipment such as computers and telephone switching installations. Now, as their long-distance capabilities are improved, the fibers are being used as high-capacity communications circuits.

In 1980, AT&T announced plans to install a fiber optics circuit between Washington and Boston. At the same time, a British network is being installed on fifteen long-distance routes in England, Scotland, and Wales.[11] These projects are the first tentative steps toward the eventual displacement of many copper-wire networks by optical fibers. Another prospect, though further down the road, is the commercial application of wave guides — highly concentrated light beams carrying hundreds of thousands of messages down a continuous pipe one hundred centimeters in diameter.

Technology is pushing these prospects into realities at a faster pace than even the most enthusiastic fiber optics boosters had imagined a few years ago. Circuit purity remains a drawback. The Japanese have taken the lead in techniques for removing such impurities as hydrogen and oxygen atoms, which impede the passage of light down an optical cable.[12] Their research, subsidized by the government, signals a strong Japanese role in the high-stakes international market for fiber optics technology. Another significant research effort focuses on the replacement of the electronic components at either end of fiber optic circuits with thin-filmed optical equivalents of the electronic devices. These could even be combined on a single microelectronic chip to form a completely integrated optical circuit, performing more complex functions.[13] Even more striking — though still very much in the theoretical stages — is the prospect of using laser beams in a computer to make an optical switch flip on and off at the rate of one trillionth of a second. Such a computer would calculate a thousand times faster than the fastest electronic machines now in service.

Still, it may be unwise to predict a fiber optics "revolution." As noted above, a number of technological restraints remain; another deterrent is the economic loss involved in writing off the billions of dollars now invested in copper cables. Nevertheless, fiber optics technology has a bright future. Arthur C. Clarke, the science writer, confidently predicts that prospecting for cast-off copper wires will be a latter-day version of the old-time gold rush.

Whether they carry their messages by copper wires or glass fibers, high-capacity cables will be major links in the information age's global grid. Their new sophistication is paralleled by recent advances in *wireless* technology. This effort has focused on more effective use of the radio spectrum, the invisible physical resource which makes possible the vast network of wireless circuits. The spectrum is a figurative thing: it does not exist until it is used. Until recently, it has been regarded as an esoteric subject for engineers only. The radio spectrum, is, however, no longer an avoidable technical concern. Its efficient use is now a significant element in defining networking prospects in the information age. These prospects will be influenced as much by political, economic, and social factors as by the work of technologists. These nontechnical considerations were relatively benign only a short time ago. The spectrum was little used, and it was treated as a kind of electrical Wild West frontier with few restrictions.

Today the spectrum, like many other natural resources, is in danger of becoming degraded through overexploitation. This is so despite the fact that the spectrum is not a depletable resource. It is finite but it is always there. The problem is to use it efficiently. At one level, users themselves create interference through their own electronic activities. Noise pollution — the familiar phenomenon of static — is a by-product of the greater general use of electrical power. (Much of this interference comes from automobile ignition systems.) The problem is compounded as more powerful transmitters are designed to punch through the noise, resulting in more noise, particularly if the transmitters are not perfectly adjusted. Most of the other difficulties with the spectrum have to do with the steadily rising number of users and types of uses, all trying to crowd into a finite physical resource. Two decades ago, probably 90 percent of spectrum use took place in a relatively narrow band across the Northern Hemisphere, from Tokyo east to Berlin. The heaviest users are still found within this band, but they must now consider the needs of a hundred or more developing countries, almost all of whom are expanding their use of the spectrum.

The spectrum is therefore a major political and economic concern, not only domestically but internationally. Since the early part of this century, it has been subject to treaty restrictions, under the supervision of the International Telecommunications Union (ITU), which is now a United Nations specialized agency. The ITU was, until a short time ago, an old boy's club composed of the Western industrial powers, the Soviet Union, and Japan. These powers gathered periodically to decide how they would allocate and manage the spectrum for their own uses. This arrangement is now finished; the rest of the world has joined the club.[14]

Under the ITU's one-vote-per-country rules, the newcomers from the Third World have considerable influence on the future patterns of spectrum use. Particular attention has been focused on their needs and demands in a series of international conferences convened for the purpose of reviewing and revising world spectrum regulations to meet changing needs. The largest of these meetings, the 1979 World Administrative Radio Conference, approved major shifts in spectrum use that will affect all communications users throughout the rest of the century. Smaller follow-up conferences are scheduled during the eighties to discuss specific spectrum problems not resolved at the 1979 meeting. In the process it is becoming clear that the radio spectrum is no longer the exclusive province of the technical experts. Given its role as the most important natural resource of the information age, it now attracts the attention of a wide range of political, economic, and social interests.[15]

It is useful, therefore, to take a closer look at the spectrum, noting some of the policy questions involved in each of its major segments. These questions will be cropping up again as we examine the political and economic issues of the information age in later chapters.

The raw material of the radio spectrum is *electromagnetic radiation* — radiant energy in the form of invisible waves moving through space and matter. This phenomenon was identified in theory in 1864 by James Clerk Maxwell, director of the Cavendish Laboratories at Cambridge University. His theories were confirmed in 1888 when a German physicist, Heinrich Hertz, produced the first man-made electromagnetic radiation by sending a strong electric charge across a spark gap and thereby causing a smaller spark — evidence of the presence of an electric field — to jump across a second gap some distance away. The history of wireless communication has been a progressive enhancement of our ability to device equipment for generating and receiving electromagnetic radiation in the radio frequency range and to use such waves for telecommunications.

The usable part of the spectrum extends from 10 kilohertz — roughly the lower limit of human hearing — to 275 gigahertz, a frequency which begins to approach that of light waves. A *hertz*, our permanent tribute to the redoubtable Heinrich, indicates the number of radiated "waves" that pass a given point in a second. One gigahertz is a thousand million cycles per second. The companion measurement is the *length* of each wave; the wavelengths for the usable spectrum run from three thousand meters — almost two miles — down to one millimeter. The spectrum is divided into eight bands, ranging from very low frequency (VLF) to extra high frequency (EHF). Each band covers a "decade" of frequencies or wavelengths. Thus the high frequency band goes from three megahertz to thirty megahertz, or one hundred meters down to ten meters.

Spectrum use has been tied to the development of increasingly sophisticated transmitters and receivers designed to exploit this resource. The progression has generally moved from the low frequencies to the higher ones, with one interesting exception. The U.S. Navy is now conducting experiments at the very bottom (and currently unusable) end of the spectrum — below ten kilohertz, which is so low it is not included in the ITU's spectrum responsibilities. The Navy is interested in the ability of these frequencies to penetrate many fathoms of ocean water and to remain relatively unaffected by upper atmosphere nuclear bursts that can blank out higher frequency communications. These attributes have important implications for communications with nuclear-missile–bearing submarines whose effectiveness depends largely on their ability to avoid detection while submerged. Very low frequency communications with the subs cannot be monitored by a potential enemy. The Navy's plan to install such a system has, however, raised difficult political problems. The system's "transmitter" involves thousands of miles of wires crisscrossing hundreds of square miles of earth. The transmitter site has to have specific geologic characteristics which, in this country, are found in the northern reaches of Minnesota and Michigan. So far, activist citizen groups have blocked the transmitter, despite a public relations campaign by the Navy stressing the national security benefits of what was dubbed, perhaps too coyly, Project Sanguine. In 1981, the Reagan administration proposed dropping the project, replacing it with laser-based technology.[16] Later, it endorsed the original plan.

Just above the low frequencies are the *medium frequencies*, best known for their use in radio broadcasting. The medium wave band has many uses beyond broadcasting, such as long-range navigation devices for ships and aircraft. This part of the spectrum now serves a hodgepodge of uses. It could be better utilized for purposes other than radio broadcasting if there were not such a heavy world investment in radio transmitters and consumer receivers adapted for these frequencies.

The next step up the spectrum is the *high frequency* band (HF). This band has been described as the jewel of the spectrum because of its special capabilities, but it is beginning to look a bit antique. Unlike medium wave, whose transmitting capabilities are very limited geographically, high frequency can have a global reach. When used for this purpose, its frequencies are refracted downwards by charged layers in the ionosphere in a hopscotch pattern, bouncing between earth and sky around the world. Exploiting this capability is a neat trick, but it does not always work. HF's effectiveness varies from hour to hour, day to day, year to year, as well as by geography and the sunspot cycle. The whole band can be crammed down to a very narrow usable section during high points in the eleven-year sunspot cycle.

Despite these limitations, HF channels are in high demand. Before the advent of satellites and large submarine cables, they were used for international telephone service. They are still useful for radio "hams," aircraft and maritime communications, and radar tracking. Another well-known application is shortwave broadcasting. The United States, with its Voice of America network, is only one of over seventy nations operating in this highly competitive field. The Voice of America's transmitters have a total of over twenty million watts of power — the equivalent of four hundred large domestic stations. Despite this, the United States lags behind the Soviet Union, the People's Republic of China, and other countries in total transmitting hours per day.

Some of the pressure in the HF band comes from 'a flamboyant upstart in spectrum use — Citizen's Band radio. CB is electronic populism with its own peculiar customs, language, and folklore. In 1973, there were less than a million CB receivers in operation in this country. In the early eighties, a conservative estimate of operating sets would be over thirty million. CB's forty channels are grouped in a betwixt-and-between area of the HF spectrum — a point at which receivers can be extremely cheap but where the incidence of interference is high. CB receivers interfere with TV and with police radio; they get interference from industrial machines, medical equipment, and even washing machines. Interference is increased by certain weather conditions as well as by the practice of many CB users of installing illegal amplifiers to get greater transmitting range. This electronic free-for-all makes the job of policing this part of the spectrum very difficult; the Federal Communications Commission has long since given up any serious monitoring of CB use. The FCC's reluctance is influenced in part by the fact that CB owners represent a very large voter block who have come to regard the maintenance and expansion of their spectrum space as a natural right.

The next steps up the spectrum are the *very high frequency* (VHF) and *ultra high frequency* (UHF) bands, best known as the location of FM radio and television channels. These bands are also the spectrum home for many so-called mobile services — police, taxi, military, and public service radio as well as automobile telephones. Over 1.5 million two-way mobile stations are authorized by the FCC, not counting CB installations. With expanded frequencies allocated by the 1979 World Administrative Radio Conference, mobile radio will be a major area of communications expansion later in the eighties. Within a decade, mobile services transmitted via communications satellites will be available. In 1977, NASA demonstrated a mobile radio transmitting and receiving device that fit into a small briefcase. The equipment, powered by batteries, sent and received signals from a remote area of Georgia to a Baltimore hospital via a NASA satellite in an experiment designed to test its use for emergency situations.[17]

At the top end of the usable spectrum are the *super high fre-*

quency (SHF) and the *extremely high frequency* (EHF) bands. Here is where the microwaves operate, and where the most controversial advances in spectrum use have taken place. The microwave frequencies lie below the infrared region of the spectrum, with wavelength ranges from about a hundred centimeters, or forty inches, down to a millimeter or 1/125th of an inch. (By contrast, the wavelength distance at the low-frequency end of the spectrum is almost two miles.)

The microwaves are the heavy-duty workhorses of the spectrum. They were harnessed in the 1930s when equipment was developed which could generate higher and higher frequency radio waves with proportionately greater message capacities. Microwave technology was a crucial factor in World War II, when it served as the basis for radar. Microwaves can be focused in directional beams and reflected back by such objects as airplanes. The first radar installations were limited and unreliable. As the military pressed for better definition and accuracy, technologists pushed further up the spectrum, developing equipment that allowed precision targeting by the end of the war.

The microwave revolution got underway in earnest in the late forties. A microwave system, using relay towers, was opened between Boston and New York in 1947; by 1951, a coast-to-coast network was in operation, using 107 towers. (Since microwave transmission is line-of-sight, the towers are placed on elevated points when possible.) Over a quarter of a million microwave relay towers have been built since then in this country for telephone, TV, computer data, and other transmissions at increasingly high capacities. Microwaves also have non-communications uses, such as in surgical operations, in household and industrial ovens, and in agricultural experiments to kill weeds and insects. The "death ray" weapon, favorite of Sunday-supplement editors, remains mercifully elusive, although the military is experimenting with various uses of microwaves in the increasingly sophisticated field of electronic warfare.

If the death ray remains a theory, a more immediate threat from electromagnetic radiation is just beginning to be debated publicly. This involves the concern that microwave circuitry may be responsible for new forms of environmental pollution, a kind of electronic smog that can affect human and animal well-being. In December 1971, a White House task force summed up the possible threat in these words:

> The electro-magnetic radiations emanating from radar, television, communications systems, microwave ovens, industrial heat-treatment

systems, medical diathermy units and many other sources permeate
the modern environment, both civilian and military. . . . This type of
man-made radiation exposure has no counterpart in man's evolutionary background. . . . unless adequate monitoring and control
based on a fundamental understanding of biological effects are insti-
tuted in the near future, in the decades ahead, man may enter an
era of energy pollution comparable to the chemical pollution of
today.[18]

Given political and economic stakes in microwave transmission,
the general reaction to this and other warnings, until recently, has
been to ignore or play down the problem. However, a number of
events have directed greater public attention to the potential hazards
of radiation pollution. The most publicized of these incidents occurred
in the mid-seventies at the American Embassy in Moscow, where
health problems among personnel were attributed to the Soviet practice of aiming electromagnetic beams at the building. Whether or not
this was true, the incident focused attention on an aspect of our post-
industrial communications structure that needs more careful
monitoring.[19]

In the meantime, microwaves are the aerial pathways of a major
space age development —the communications satellite. The satellites
are basically microwave switching stations, the space equivalent of a
ground relay tower. The difference is that a satellite gives the microwave path a line-of-sight capability that stretches across one third of
the earth. Floating 22,300 miles above the equator, the satellites
effectively break the boundaries of the earth's horizon. At that
height, they travel at the same speed as the earth's rotation and
therefore appear to be stationary; they are, in the engineer's phrase,
"geostationary." Since the mid-sixties, the satellites have provided
high-quality communications circuits to nations in Asia, Africa, and
Latin America that would otherwise not have had them for many
more years. By 1981, over a hundred countries, accounting for over
96 percent of all international traffic, belonged to Intelsat, the world
satellite organization which runs the basic network.[20]

In less than twenty years, communications satellites have gone
through five technological generations. The first "birds" were weakly
powered machines, capable of providing only limited services. Later
generations, relying on microelectronic technology, have had progres-
sively more sophisticated circuit capacity and transmitting power. The
current fifth generation Intelsat satellite, *Intelsat V*, can transmit a
combination of twelve thousand telephone calls and two television
channels simultaneously. (By contrast, the first Intelsat generation

had a capacity of two hundred and fifty telephone circuits or one TV channel.) Moreover, the newer satellites have a greater capacity for handling digital data, permitting use of such techniques as data packet transmissions.

The greater capabilities of the newer satellites permits the expansion of services beyond such point-to-point transmissions as telephone calls. They open the way for radio or television broadcasting from space to small earth terminals. Direct broadcasting satellites (DBS) were first tested in the mid-seventies. A NASA experimental satellite, *ATS-6*, beamed educational and other public service broadcasts to remote earth terminals in Appalachia, the Rocky Mountains, and Alaska. *ATS-6* was shifted in 1975 halfway around the world to provide educational transmissions to over two thousand remote villages in India. DBS technology has advanced rapidly in recent years; plans for space broadcast services are underway in Europe, Japan, and this country. DBS technology has also stirred lively controversy in the United Nations, where developing countries are pressing for limitations on broadcasting into their territories without their prior consent. Whatever the outcome of the debate, there is little doubt that television and radio transmissions from space and into homes will become routine in the next decade.[21]

Because they involve a familiar service — television — broadcast satellites are well publicized. However, the range of satellite uses, present and potential, is considerably wider. Two dozen countries now use satellites for domestic as well as international communications. A special satellite network, *Marisat,* provides communications services for ships at sea. Eventually, a similar network will link aircraft to ground traffic control stations. Military satellites are an integral part of the global communications networks of the Soviet and the U.S. defense systems. There is also an increasing number of so-called sensing satellites, which monitor weather and earth resources, returning data to world wide networks of earth terminals.

With so many satellites floating in a narrow corridor above the equator, a unique kind of traffic jam has been created. The choicest frequencies and orbital slots — where the satellites are "parked" — are filling up fast. Given a NASA estimate that there will be a tenfold increase in international demand for satellite circuits between 1982 and the end of the century, the problem of crowded frequencies and orbital slots may soon be critical. At present, the congestion is concentrated in the high-traffic areas over the Western Hemisphere and the North Atlantic region. In early 1980, there were forty-four satellites in the equatorial orbital arc between four degrees west longitude and one hundred and fifty degrees west longitude — roughly from the mid-Atlantic to the mid-Pacific. The satellites are many miles apart in the immensity of space; adding a few more might seem to be as simple as introducing a few more cars on a lonely stretch of highway. However, unless satellites using the same frequency band are kept several degrees apart (about 250 miles), ground stations cannot discriminate between their separate signals.[22]

This has become an international issue in recent years as developing countries insist that the industrialized countries, current near-monopoly of satellite frequencies and orbital slots be ended in favor of a system assuring access to these resources for Third World countries. The issue will come to a head in a United Nations conference in 1985, as will be described in chapter 6.

The solution, at its simplest level, lies in the efficient use of more complex satellites. The current thrust of satellite research and development is in this direction. Whether technological advances can keep ahead of the quickly rising global demands for more circuits is an open question. So far this has been done by providing more transmitting power in the satellites themselves, and by developing techniques for more sophisticated use of frequencies. By the mid-seventies, RCA had commercially demonstrated its *Satcom* satellite's ability to send two signals on the same frequency, thereby doubling circuit capacity. The early eighties have seen a new generation of hybrid satellites, capable of several different tasks. Among these is Western Union's *TDRSS* (Tracking and Data Relay Satellite System), which will operate standard commercial services and also relay data to earth from other satellites operating at lower orbits as well as from NASA's space shuttle. Earth terminals can "see" the shuttle and these low-flying satellites only for a short time before they disappear over the horizon. *TDRSS* will literally look down on them from its position further out in space and will be tracking them more than 80 percent of the time.

The newer satellites also make greater use of digital circuitry, which is capable of moving information — in voice, visual, or data form — at much greater speeds than analog communications. This is an important consideration in the attempt to meet increasing demands for transmission between high-speed computers. It takes several hours to transmit a reel of computer tape at the rate now generally available — 9600 bits per second. At digital transmission speeds of up to 1.5 megabits per second, transmittal time is reduced to three minutes.

Efficient use of orbital slots is complicated by the fact that most present satellites which preempt a slot have a limited purpose. The newer multipurpose satellites — the so-called hybrids — will ease this limitation somewhat, as each will be capable of doing the work of several of the older satellites. Other techniques for easing orbital and frequency congestions are being studied. One of these involves building large space platforms to orbit above the equator. Many satellites could be hung like Christmas tree ornaments from these structures, which might measure several acres in size. Moreover, the platforms would also support large solar-cell arrays to supply power to all the equipment on the platform. The platforms would be assembled in space by work crews using parts delivered by the space shuttle and other transporters. Periodic maintenance checks of the platform and the satellites would be made by space-suited repairmen. The net effect would be to group a half-dozen or more satellites, each using different frequencies, in an orbital slot normally taken up by a single satellite. A prototype platform will probably be built under a NASA research program and be launched in the late eighties.

A less dramatic but possibly more practical approach has been advanced by engineer Paul Baran of Hughes Aircraft. He proposes clusters of separate satellites in an orbital slot, each transmitting its signals through a near-by master satellite. (Satellite-to-satellite communications is quite feasible, thanks to recent research breakthroughs.) A wide range of signals for various purposes could be transmitted, utilizing only one orbital slot. The value of Baran's concept is that it can be realized with currently available satellite technology. Space platform research is still in the theoretical stages; moreover, the platforms will be very expensive pieces of hardware when and if the technology proves feasible.

Other intensive research in the expansion of satellite capabilities focuses on the radio spectrum itself. Here the effort is on techniques for making more microwave frequencies available. Theoretically there is plenty of room in the spectrum for this since, despite the research breakthroughs of recent years, less than 10 percent of the spectrum is being utilized for communications and other purposes. To illustrate this point, let us assume that the total radio spectrum up to 300 gigahertz (Ghz) represents an area the size of the United States. On this scale, one megahertz (Mhz) — roughly the medium wave frequencies — would represent a sixty-foot strip of Atlantic beach. Thirty Ghz — the outer limit of most present applications — would take us three hundred miles inland. Everything beyond would be largely *terra incognita*, or what the spectrum engineers call EHF for extra high frequencies. The halt at 30 Ghz is equivalent to westward migration across the United States that has stopped at the Appalachians.[23]

Any further "migration" in the spectrum is liable to be slow for technical reasons. The 1979 WARC conference allocated specific frequency uses up to 275 Ghz. These allocations in the EHF bands are intended largely for specialized purposes such as radio astronomy. One such proposed use is for a radio telescope to be placed on the dark side of the moon, shielded from earthly radio interference. Another involves sending signals to civilizations beyond our solar system — a favorite project of astronomer Carl Sagan and other enthusiasts of what is known as SETI, the search for extra-terrestrial intelligence.

Meanwhile the technological push is on to open higher reaches of the spectrum for more mundane needs such as TV broadcasts and telephone calls. The most intensive research is in the 20 to 30 Ghz bands — just above the present limits of practical microwave transmissions. The potential rewards of breakthroughs in this area will be vast numbers of new higher capacity microwave channels for satellites and for terrestrial use. The difficulties are formidable; not the least of them are the adverse effects of heavy rainstorms and other weather conditions on transmissions in these higher bands. The very short microwaves at these frequencies can be wiped out by rain or snow drops. One way to overcome this is to establish satellite earth stations in pairs, sufficiently separated and positioned so that such interference will not occur at both stations simultaneously. In 1978, NASA inaugurated a five-year research and development program to open up the 20–30 Ghz bands for communications and other purposes.[24] If the tests are successful, overcrowding in the lower parts of the microwave frequency spectrum could be eased considerably. The Europeans, Japanese, and Soviets are also working on the problem, and all of them are as aware as the U.S. of the economic and political rewards of opening these bands to practical uses.

It is clear that communications satellite usage will expand dramatically during the coming decade. Counting the number of satellites in orbit is not the best way to measure this growth: the satellites come in too many sizes and varying capabilities. A more reliable measure is the number of transponders in use — a transponder being, in effect, a "package" of circuits in a satellite. Taking U.S. domestic satellites alone, present growth rates are impressive. In 1980, there were a total of 156 transponders on these satellites; by 1985 this will have jumped to an estimated 612. Moreover, the satellites will be linking a greater network of earth stations in this country. In September 1980, the FCC reported 591 stations; this is scheduled to increase to 7,500 by

1985; and some predictions for 1990 run as high as 100,000 stations.[25]

In summary, the past twenty years have seen enormous parallel expansion in the range and capacities of both wire and wireless technology. Each mode has its distinctive capabilities. What they share is a greatly enhanced ability to handle most communication tasks interchangeably, carrying voice, visual, or data messages. Sophisticated integrated switching equipment no longer distinguishes between the type of circuitry it serves. Both wire and wireless circuitry will make up the new universal grid, providing a wide variety of high-capacity channels.

Wireless communications — and microwave circuits in particular — were the fastest growth area in telecommunications during the past three decades. However, there will be greater competition in the coming years from sophisticated wire technologies. The present workhorse of high-capacity wire technology is the coaxial cable, the familiar phone-company cable that runs under city streets. However, the future lies with fiber optic cables and with millimeter waveguides that can send fifteen billion bits of information a second down a metal pipe — strange kinds of wires indeed. These developments represent a long technological leap from Samuel F. B. Morse's experiment in transmitting a few coded words a minute over a flimsy telegraph line a hundred and fifty years ago. The Wire Age started by Morse, now technologically compatible with the Wireless Age, has come full circle in the Age of the Integrated Grid.

Notes

1. Harold A. Innis, *Empire and Communications* (Toronto: University of Toronto Press, 1972), pp. 1–11. The work was originally published in 1950.

2. The fable of the evaluation committee for the printing press was proposed by the distinguished American communications scholar, Harold Lasswell. For a comprehensive review of the initial impact of the Renaissance printing press, see Elizabeth Eisenstein, *The Printing Press as an Agent of Change* (New York: Cambridge University Press, 1980).

3. Asa Briggs, "The Pleasure Telephone: A Chapter in the Pre-history of the Media," in *The Social Impact of the Telephone*, ed. Ithiel de Sola Pool (Cambridge, Mass.: MIT Press, 1977), pp. 40–59.

4. Anthony Smith, "The Wire and the Wavelength — An Historical Study," in *Cable: An Investigation of the Social and Political Implications of Cable Television*, a report published by the Standing Conference on Broadcasting (London, 1974), p. 29.

5. Ibid., pp. 31–32.

6. Erik Barnouw, *The Sponsor* (New York: Oxford University Press, 1978), pp. 24–25.

7. Smith, "Wire and Wavelength," pp. 36–37.

8. Anthony Smith, *Shadows on the Cave* (Urbana, Ill.: University of Illinois Press, 1973), p. 351.

9. For a useful summary of international cable developments, see Arthur C. Clarke, *Voices Across the Sea* (London: Luscombe Publishers, 1974).

10. Morris Edwards, "Fiber Optic Links Forge Paths for the Expected Information Explosion," *Communications News*, February 1978, p. 30.

11. "Lightwave Links Form Groundwork for U.K. Digital Network," *Data Communications*, April 1981, p. 36.

12. "Pure Is Best," *The Economist* (London), 4 October 1980, p. 93.

13. Amnon Yariv, "Guided Wave Optics," *Scientific American*, April 1980, pp. 64–72.

14. For a useful description of the International Telecommunications Union, see "How the ITU Works," *Intermedia* (London), September 1979, pp. 1–2; also Delbert D. Smith, *International Telecommunications Control* (Amsterdam: A. W. Sijthoff, 1969), pp. 18–29.

15. The most extensive survey of the political and economic implications of ITU decisions can be found in ten articles on the 1979 World Administrative Radio Conference in *Journal of Communication*, 29, no. 1 (Winter 1979), pp. 143–207. For a description of the technical problems facing the ITU, see Charles Lee Jackson. "The Allocation of the Radio Spectrum," *Scientific American*, February 1980, pp. 34–39.

16. "U.S. Explores Use of Space Lasers to Communicate with Submarines," *New York Times*, 22 April 1981, p. B-5.

17. "Small Radio Could Bring Aid in a Disaster," *New York Times*, 13 November 1977, p. 61.

18. U.S. Office of Telecommunications Policy, Executive Office of the President, *Program for Control of Electromagnetic Pollution of the Environment*, Electromagnetic Radiation Management Advisory Council, December 1971, p. 12.

19. A critical view of radiation pollution is given in Paul Brodeur, *The Zapping of America* (New York: W. W. Norton and Co., 1977). For an industry-oriented response to Brodeur's criticism, see "The Conning of America," *Microwave Journal*, October 1978, pp. 18–19.

20. Joseph N. Pelton, *Global Talk* (Amsterdam: Sijthoff and Noordhoff, 1981).

21. For a summary of the broadcast satellite controversy, see Wilson Dizard, "Direct Broadcast Satellites: The U.S. Position" in *The Cable/Broadband Communications Book*, vol. 2, 1980–81 (Washington, D.C.: Communications Press, 1980), pp. 73–86.

22. "A Traffic Jam in Outer Space," *New York Times*, 26 March 1980, p. D-3.

23. The Rand Corporation, "Radio's Last Frontier," *Rand Research Review*, 2, no. 1 (Spring 1978): 1.

24. Cutbacks in the early months of the Reagan administration threatened this and other NASA advanced research projects. See "Satellite R & D: Washington Moves to Correct a Mistake," *Satellite Communications*, April 1981, pp. 13–17.

25. The statistics on transponders are from *Satellite Week* (Washington), 9 October 1980, p. 9. The projection on earth station installations was made by Sidney Topol, president of Scientific Atlanta, Inc., a leading earth station manufacturer, in "Information Processing," *Business Week*, 6 October 1980, p. 46.

Chapter Four

The Technological Framework: Information Machines

Having looked at the technologies forming the new networks, we now turn to the information machines that plug into the grid. These are the computers, terminals, telex printers and other devices which are the nodal points where human thoughts are transferred into electronic impulses and fed into the system. Their capabilities need to be understood as we try to measure their impact on strategies for a new information age.

We have seen how a convergence of research breakthroughs has revolutionized wire and wireless networks. This pattern of interactive new technology is, if anything, more complex when we take into account the machines that are served by these networks. There are many technological paths leading up to this convergence, and many possible outcomes. There are also significant elements shared by the machines and the networks. The most important of these is their common reliance on microelectronic technology, which provides each of them with new levels of reliability and capacity and new operational functions. Microelectronic products, many of them no bigger than a fingernail, are a key resource in powering the second industrial revolution. Here we will, somewhat parochially, limit our concerns to one part of this process — the post-industrial information structure, a complicated pattern of machines linked to a growing communications grid, all made possible by the commonality of microelectronic devices.

A letter sent across the country by conventional means may involve a typewriter, a postal truck, canceling and sorting machines, an airplane, a pushcart, more trucks and sorting equipment, and finally a mailman walking his route. This is, with luck, a three-day process. A single machine — actually two terminals at either end of a satellite circuit — can deliver the contents of the letter in less than a minute. The technological advantage of this is clear. There are, however, economic, political, and social considerations where the advantages are considerably less obvious. The postal system is more than an institution potentially capable of one-minute mail delivery. It is the friendly mail carrier, Christmas cards, junk mail, and stamp collecting, all of which have to be fitted into, or discarded from, this new one-minute system. The question is relevant to any future information strategies we may devise: to what degree are we willing to modify or even dismantle comfortable ways of thinking and acting in order to accommodate the new technologies?

This accommodation is a tall order for any society. The United States is being pressed to make decisions well ahead of any other country because of its long lead in developing a mass communications system. Competitive economic pressures, in particular, will force decisions either by design or default. We will look more closely at this decision process in later chapters. Here we will survey the present state and future expectations of the new information machines.

The survey begins with microelectronics — the technological common denominator in the new integrated information grid. Its products have, of course, uses beyond communications and information equipment. However, it is probable that half or more of the industry's basic product, semiconductor chips, goes into such equipment. Computers alone accounted for 40 percent of the use of world semiconductor output in 1979. Communications and information applications have set the pace in what has come to be called "the microelectronics revolution." As in most self-proclaimed revolutions, the semantics are imprecise. A more exact, if somewhat less stirring, description would be "speeded-up evolution," with a footnote that the process has not been, nor will it be, a smooth one.[1]

Smooth or not, the evolution is impressive. The primitive era was a scant thirty years ago. At that time, interconnected radio vacuum tubes were the only device for transmitting a current of electrons between electrodes in communications and information equipment. The tubes worked, but they were bulky and fragile. In the early fifties, the process of replacing them began with *transistors*, developed by the Bell Laboratories. In a transistor, the current connecting electrodes flows through solid materials, usually silicon, known as *semiconductors*. The next step, which took place around 1960, was the development of *integrated circuits*, or many interconnected transistors on a single piece of silicon, popularly known as a *chip*. Research has since centered on the progressive sophistication of integrated circuits with larger capacities and expanded functions. The first integrated circuits had ten transistors on a chip. This capacity has been pushed up to one hundred thousand components per chip in recent years. A million-transistor chip is being tested experimentally.

Improvements in circuit capacity have opened the way for the chips to take on new functions. The most striking change has been the incorporation of the *microprocessor*, a complex type of integrated circuit which can function as a computer. A single chip can contain the equivalent of the central processor of a small computer, which performs arithmetical and logical functions, plus some memory. It works in conjunction with *memory chips*, which store information, and with *input* and *output chips*, which are used to get information into and out of the central processor. The technological distance between the old vacuum radio tube and the present day integrated chip is formidable. The pioneering ENIAC computer, developed during World War II, weighed thirty tons, filled a large room, and had seventeen thousand radio tubes, which required round-the-clock replacement maintenance.[2] A present-day chip incorporating a microprocessor the size of a thumbtack can have more computational power than ENIAC. Microprocessors are still a small, specialized part of integrated circuit production, accounting for only about 10 percent of such production. However, this percentage is expected to double within a few years.

In chapter 5 we will take a closer look at the industry that churns out these products. The semiconductor companies were the most dynamic industrial sector of the 1970s, expanding from $1 billion in annual sales at the beginning of the decade to $10 billion by the end. A recent survey by the Boston research firm, Arthur D. Little Inc., predicted an annual market for semiconductors of $40 billion (in 1978 dollars) by 1987 for the U.S., Britain, France, and West Germany alone.[3] This growth is all the more phenomenal considering the average price of a transistor component in a chip is now less than a penny, compared to ten dollars twenty years ago.

Advanced chips will be, in the words of one developer, the jellybeans of the electronic age — plentiful and cheap. They are adapted so quickly to so many uses, from toys to telephones, that they have been in chronic short supply. U.S. firms, which supply 60 percent of global demand, were caught up in delivery delays of up to ten months in 1980.[4] Thanks to the competitiveness of the industry — and particularly the growing threat of Japanese competition — these shortages were made up. Another longer term problem is not so readily solved by production speed-ups. This is the inability of many chip users to get the software they need for the tiny devices. There are still too few trained *software programmers*, the technicians who write the instructions. Moreover, program writing is an expensive operation, and is becoming even more so. A decade ago, two thirds of the cost of integrated circuitry was in hardware, the rest in software. This ratio has since been reversed.

These problems will not seriously delay the shift to microelectronics, particularly in communications and information. Chips are a basic construction module in the upgrading of networks and the machines linked to them. These pea-size devices are already being used to overhaul the network most familiar to us — the telephone system. The end result will be a phone network that will eventually be called something else, since conventional voice service will be only one part of its function.

The transformation of the phone network is taking place now, mostly behind the scenes in exchanges and other system installations. Beginning in the mid-seventies, telephone companies have been replacing their old electromechanical switching gear with electronic equipment. One of the last pieces of equipment to be affected by this modernization program has been the telephone instrument itself. Telephones may be shaped like Mickey Mouse or a plastic doughnut, but the equipment inside most of them is basically the same. The telephone is a thirty-year-old technology; apart from push-button dialing, the design and performance of the standard set has been unchanged since 1953. This will shift in the eighties with the introduction of an all-electronic telephone, complete with chips. In one model, tested in recent years by Bell Canada, about 180 parts of the standard push-button telephone are replaced by three integrated circuits.[5]

The result will be not only a more efficient voice telephone as such but also an instrument better adapted, through microprocessor technology, to plug into other communications and information services, including computers. The days of the phone company's focus on POTS — Plain Old Telephone Service — are ending.

This shift is part of a larger pattern — the restructuring of U.S. communications and information industries. There are complex political and economic reasons for the change, as we shall see in subsequent chapters. However, the determining factor has been microelectronics technology. Given the capabilities of the new devices, it makes less sense to have a single monopoly network dedicated primarily to POTS. Given this political and economic fact of life, the future role of the Bell System has to be decided before the rest of the industry could make a major commitment to the new technology. The decision has unfolded slowly over a decade, and despite the rough-and-tumble politics it has involved, the issue is still not settled completely. However, the basic outcomes are clear: the Bell System has been allowed to enter the competition for the vast communications and information markets beyond telephone service. It will do this under certain restraints designed to limit its ability to overwhelm most of its competitors by its sheer financial and technological power.

Whether the Bell System will be the dominant communications network in this country probably will not be decided for another decade. In its imperial manner, Bell sees itself continuing in this role. Moreover, its current push to upgrade the network is impressive evidence of its ability to be the leader in an expanded market. All of this explains why Ma Bell looks younger and trendier these days, shaking off her dowdy old image. No longer just "the telephone company," the Bell System began advertising itself during the early eighties as "the knowledge business." A strange tag for the phone company, until one realizes that sometime during the next decade the system will earn less from plain old telephone service than from its other services. It is moving in this direction primarily by developing a sophisticated data communications network for linking computers and other information machines. What the new telephone network and its auxiliary equipment share with computers is microelectronic modules, which allow the two to work together as the basic equipment of the information age.

Computers are the main engines of post-industrial power. Like the working group faced with Master Gutenberg's invention in our Renaissance fable, we have trouble getting the computer's measure. The developers of the first electronic computer in the 1940s thought that four computers, more or less, would satisfy the world's needs.[6] Given the state of computer technology at the time, their estimate seemed reasonable. But the fact is that there are now literally millions of machines that can be classified under the broad heading of "computers." After three decades of specialized use in business and government, computers are becoming a mass consumer product. The next ten years will bring widespread use of personal home computers with their own data storage capabilities as well as links to outside data sources.[7]

At many levels, computers are integral parts of the universal information grid. They would be important even if they were only able to store vast amounts of information, like highly efficient filing cabinets, or to serve as high-speed calculating machines. Their great liberating use, however, is their power to extend knowledge, particularly by simulating reality (or even simulating what seems to be unreality) in ways the human brain finds difficult to do or is incapable of doing.

Modern computers and communications circuitry both have their origins among a small group of scientists working on the East Coast and in Britain during the 1940s and 50s. The mention of their names — Claude Shannon, Norbert Wiener, John von Neumann, Alan Turling, and others — causes few knowing nods, even among reasonably well-informed people today. It would be difficult, however, to exaggerate the contribution of these scientists to post-industrial America and, by extension, to the rest of the world. Working in the esoteric area known as "information theory," they understood that they had to define information and its characteristics accurately if their ideas about a more rational organization of information resources were to be realized. Their pursuit of this purpose in seminar rooms and laboratories and in faculty club discussions has had results that put an indelible mark on American society.

The basic orientation of the group was mathematics, and particularly the idea, advanced by Bertrand Russell and Alfred North Whitehead, that logic is the foundation of all mathematics. Russell and Whitehead's 1910 work, *Principia Mathematica*, developed the calculus of propositions, or the solving of problems in terms of statements that are either true or false. As a young MIT graduate student in the late thirties, Claude Shannon demonstrated the practical applications of this calculus in improving the design of electrical circuits. Shannon's initial research, which became his master's thesis, showed that programming an electronic digital computer would be a problem not of arithmetic, but of logic. Later, at the Bell Laboratories, Shannon and his fellow researcher Warren Weaver expanded on these insights to propose a design for a general communications system.[8] They treated information input as a problem in statistics, permitting precise measurement of the amount of information delivered and the efficiency of the devices that handle it. Like computers, the theory deals with information rather than meaning. For the first time, communications and computer scientists had a definitive measure of their commodity — information.

That measure is called a *bit*, a contraction of "binary digit." The bit is the module for the input to most advanced electronic information and communications devices. It can be defined as the lowest common denominator of information, a unit resolving uncertainty or choice between two exclusive alternatives, for example, between yes and no, heads and tails, on and off, one and zero. It is the choice we exercise in choosing left or right when there are no other options, that is, when there is equal probability for each. In choosing, we resolve doubt. By putting many bits together in a computer or communications circuit, symbols (words, pictures, numbers) that transmit information take shape. Whatever form it takes, the information is transmitted onto electrical circuits digitally, that is, it is represented by two digits — zero or one — in patterns that define the information. The letter *A* in a six-bit binary code can be 11001, the letter *P* can be 100111, and so on. The pattern 110001 100111 100111 100011 110101 010010 110001 010100 110011 110101 stored in a computer moves through the circuits and comes out as "applesauce." Trillions and trillions of symbolic ones and zeroes move through communications systems, each a coded part of a message that may be a teenager's telephone call, a credit card transaction, a television soap opera, or a weather report from the Viking space station on Mars.

Shannon also demonstrated how to measure the capacity of a communications channel in terms of *bits per second* (BPS). The channel capacity for a telephone wire used for speech purposes is 60,000 BPS; for broadcast television, 90 million BPS, and on upward to the 15 billion BPS capacity for a millimeter wave-guide system. Shannon's contributions were only part of a convergence of concepts that made possible the new communications and information machines. Britain's Alan Turling had provided remarkable insights into the problem of digital computers in a paper written in 1937 when he was only twenty-five.[9] Another contributor was Norbert Wiener, an MIT mathematics professor and an authentic genius who earned a Harvard Ph.D. in mathematical logic at the age of nineteen. Wiener explored the concept of self-regulating mechanisms akin to the human brain's feedback capabilities. Early work in computers spurred speculation about "thinking" machines and automation. Wiener coined a name for this field of computer control — "cybernetics" — in a book by the same name exploring the uses of such automata.[10] Meanwhile, mathematician John von Neumann at Princeton was developing the *stored-*

program concept, the idea that a machine could control its calculating sequences by modifying its own instructions. Taken together, these concepts moved computer technology beyond storage and calculating functions to electronic, digital stored-program machines, expanding dramatically their creative capabilities as intelligence extenders.

In identifying the logical parameters of information and communications machines, von Neumann and other information theorists laid much of the base for the high-technology advances that have occurred in the last thirty years. Matching their own remarkable insights was the speed with which their ideas were put to practical use. In part it was the result of close collaboration between research and development organizations, both public and private, and American industry. The Department of Defense, pressing for quick military applications of these new technologies, was an important factor in this process. There was intense pressure within the industrial sector to exploit the potentially lucrative opportunities opened up by the new electronics. A production infrastructure developed quickly, with Remington Rand producing the first production-line computer, UNIVAC I, in 1951. By the end of 1953, thirteen companies were manufacturing computers, including IBM which soon became the giant of the new industry.[11]

The first electronic computers were large, free-standing information storage and calculating boxes, with no outside links. Later, computers with stored-program capabilities were developed and connected to remote terminals. These were, however, "slave" terminals, dependent on data and instructions from the main computer. By the mid-sixties, more sophisticated computer and remote terminal patterns, involving interactive networking, came on the market. These terminals could modify main computer instructions and data. More recently, they have been equipped with their own computer memory to handle "local" requirements independently of the main computer. This kind of flexibility has resulted in an explosive growth in computer-based data networks: in 1965 there were fifty thousand installed computer terminals in this country; by 1975, this number had increased to over a million; six million terminals are projected for 1985.[12]

A Harvard researcher, Anthony Oettinger, has suggested that the computer communications phenomenon deserves a new name — "compunications." His elision of the words "computer" and "communications" is more than a semantic trick; the computer and its communications-circuit links to other computers or to terminals constitute an integral information machine. The fact that this "machine" may stretch across continents and oceans is more or less irrelevant. "Compunications" may not make the dictionary, but it describes a reality that has long-range political, economic, and social implications for the information age.[13]

Meanwhile, computer engineers are putting more information power into smaller spaces. Many of the low-capability, room-size computers of the forties and fifties are literally museum pieces. (A number of them are on display at the Smithsonian Institution's Museum of American History in Washington.) Large mainframe computers are not yet passé; they are just shrinking. ICL, the British computer company, has been developing a "giant" computer the size of three filing cabinets able to carry out five billion operations per second. At the same time, the economies of the big machines have been rapidly improving. In the early seventies, it cost twenty-five dollars a month to store a million bits of information in an advanced IBM direct-access storage system. Now, ten years later, the cost has dropped to fifty cents.

Big computing jobs require a special breed of machine — the supercomputers. One example is the U.S. Defense Department's ILLIAC installation in California. Like most supercomputers, ILLIAC has been designed for a unique purpose. One of its tasks has been to track Soviet submarines, which it does by processing data from sensing devices on the ocean floor in order to identify subs by their acoustic "signatures." ILLIAC reportedly handles 300 million instructions a second, and has the potential of being expanded to handle 10 billion.[14] Another monster computer, planned for the mid-eighties, is NASA's Numerical Aerodynamic Simulation Facility, or NASF. By computing the complex equations needed for designing advanced aircraft, NASF will eliminate more expensive (and less reliable) wind-tunnel experiments. NASF's potential for processing information is so advanced that a new word is used to measure its capacity. The word is *flop*, defined as the ability to do a complex operation on two items of data in one second. One *gigaflop* is a thousand million flops. A NASF model proposed by engineers at Burroughs Company has a capacity of over twelve gigaflops, or 12 billion flops a second.[15]

The supercomputers will continue to do big special jobs, but the general technological focus has shifted to smaller machines. The trend began in the sixties with the so-called "minicomputers" — a description that has become almost obsolete in recent years with the debut of even smaller microcomputers and microprocessors. But whatever their names, minicomputers have staked out a significant middle ground between the big number-crunching mainframes and small machines. In addition to performing specialized tasks on their own, they have become the workhorses of the fast-moving distributed data processing field. This involves linking low-cost minicomputers and terminals into communications networks instead of putting everything on a big mainframe. Today's minicomputers have computational powers well beyond the big computers of the sixties. Equally important, their price tag, usually under $40 thousand, makes them attractive to smaller business firms and other organizations. This adaptability to mid-level tasks is reflected in the growth of the minicomputer market. By the late seventies, worldwide sales were increasing at better than a 35 percent annual rate, as against a 15 percent growth for the larger mainframe machines.

With recent advances in microelectronic circuitry, minicomputers and their terminals are beginning to talk and to listen. They can understand spoken instructions and reply with synthetic speech. They can also store speech. One future prospect is voice mail — the storage of voice messages in digital form for delivery at a later time, either as reconstituted speech or as hard copy. In 1980, the Pennsylvania Bell Telephone Company announced a limited voice-mail system that could be the forerunner of a system-wide Bell service.[16]

Eventually, voice mail could be part of an integrated electronic mail system involving telephones, computer terminals, facsimile machines, and communicating word processors. However, it is probable that talking and listening computers will operate alone for the time being. IBM research scientists have used a computer to transcribe speech, composed of sentences drawn from a thousand-word vocabulary and read at a normal speaking pace into a printed form, with 91 percent accuracy. The Orator talking terminal, developed by ARTS Computer Products, can be interfaced with a computer to produce synthesized speech with a full-word capability for use by the blind.

The fastest growth area in the computer market involves smaller machines known as *microcomputers*. These are the so-called "home computers," although most of them are being used for the present by small businesses. When a full consumer computer network is developed, the microcomputer will be teamed up with the telephone in American homes. Already the Radio Shack chain has a software package that can transform its TRS-80 microcomputer into a word processor to compose letters that can then be sent via telephone to a Western Union computer for next-day delivery by Mailgram.[17]

Meanwhile, a new range of technologies is emerging that can

store 100 million bits of memory per square inch on tiny magnetic regions of amorphous metal film. Josephson junctions, now being developed by IBM, use *superconducting metals* (metals that lose all resistance to electricity at very low temperatures) to do sums in billionths of a second.[18]

The chips that led the way to smaller, more efficient computers are themselves going through another change. They were originally identified as LSI, *Large Scale Integration*, technology. The new phrase is VSLI, for *Very Large Scale Integration*. VSLI takes the chips up to what many scientists think may be the physical limits of miniaturization. The progression toward these limits has been swift. The problem, in simple terms, is to etch tinier and tinier circuit lines onto a silicon chip. Every tenfold decrease in the width of the lines leads to a hundredfold increase in the number of circuits that can be put on the chip. Line widths have already been narrowed down to an average two and a half to three *microns* — a micron being a millionth of a meter. The next goal is to narrow the gap to one micron. This would be close to what, for the present, is considered the physical limit of tiny circuit patterns — lines one third of a micron wide. If this limit is achieved, it will be the equivalent of packing one hundred fifty lines within the width of a human hair.[19]

Whether or not this goal is reached, the new generation of chips is already having its impact on computers. The computing power of the new microprocessor chips equals that of a standard minicomputer. These so-called *high-end microprocessors* are faster and easier to program than their predecessors. They completely outclass the standard small computers in price. At about $150 each, they can be produced at a fraction of the cost of the minicomputer. The implication is that the microprocessors will replace the minis. However, there is room for a full range of computers in the new information environment. What will happen is that the bigger computers will increasingly consist of arrays of microprocessors and other chips. But they will shrink even further in size as they increase in computational power.[20]

Computers are the glamor machines of the information age. They are not, however, unique solutions for storing and distributing large amounts of information. There are other methods, many of which rely on the computer and its operations. The old-fashioned book is going through a technological revolution of its own, a sort of Gutenberg revisited. Production of standard books is becoming almost completely automated, expanding production capabilities to thousands of volumes an hour. The next technical step will be direct electronic publishing, a strange new world of paperless books. The first moves in this direction were made a decade ago with improvements in microfiche readers. Existing print books and other publications have been reproduced in microfilm rolls for a long time, primarily for preservation purposes. The problem, as any one who has dealt with microfilm knows, is to eliminate the awkwardness of searching for material through the long rolls. In 1980, Kodak announced a plan for melding computers and microfilm in ways that will reduce search time to a few seconds. The trick is in coding each microfilm "page" and entering the code in a data bank. When a page is sought, its location can be readily identified and the information put onto a microfilm reader. Such devices will probably not be used for standard books but for retrieval of archival materials and for reference publications.[21]

Microfiche — the grouping of many pages on a plastic card — offers greater prospects for direct publishing. In the early seventies, the University of Toronto Press was one of the first publishers to offer all its output in both printed and microfiche form. Some scholarly magazines and publications with small circulations are now being produced only in microfiche form in an effort to cut costs. Another prospect for more efficient print storage is the videodisc, the LP record that "plays" pictures. Best known in its consumer version as a home entertainment device, the videodisc is also a storage bin for print and audiovisual information. One such version, developed by MCA Discovision, provides fifty-four thousand separate "pages" of information on a single disc — the equivalent of the contents of the *Encyclopaedia Britannica*.

The next step is the "book" in a computer. In fifteenth-century Europe, Johann Gutenberg began the print revolution by printing Bibles and other religious works. In twentieth-century California, a computer expert, Bill Bates, may have set off the new print revolution with a cookbook. In 1980, Bates published *The Computer Cookbook*, a work of computer data. The contents are transmitted electronically from Bates's distributor in Ohio to customer terminals without benefit of paper, printing, binding, or other traditional publishing devices. Customers call in, or "sign on", through their terminals and browse through the recipes on their cathode-ray screens at an hourly rate. They can also buy the entire text and have it transferred to a computer disk or even to an old-fashioned hard-copy printout.

Bill Bates, the electronic Gutenberg, sees his project as part of a logical progression towards a new information environment:

Today we can see that every cost associated with traditional publishing — distribution, labor, silver, film, gas, freight, cloth — is going up, whereas every single cost involved in the electronics industry — home computers, word processors, telephone and satellite transmissions, silicon chips — is going down and will continue to go down. At some point, where these two paths cross, electronic publishing is going to become very attractive.[22]

Somewhat further down the technological road is the large-scale use of *holography* — an electronically squeezed-in information storage process that can fit the equivalent of large libraries of data into the space of a table top. Holography uses lasers to record and retrieve information. Its ability to compress prodigious amounts of data into small spaces makes it particularly useful for major archival tasks, from recording birth certificates to logging the massive data output of scientific satellites circling the earth.

These developments may seem strange and even threatening in a literate society that relies on the traditional book for information and for cultural continuity. We are still very much the heirs of Gutenberg's movable-type revolution, despite Marshall McLuhan's unilateral declarations of the end of the age of print in the 1960s. McLuhan hailed the new electronic media as liberators, freeing us from the linear, left-to-right constraints print imposed on our thoughts and culture. He reportedly characterized cultural laggards who relied on books as POBs — print-oriented bastards. McLuhan's prophecies were quickly — perhaps too quickly — rejected by the POBs who read his books. Cultural considerations aside, there is a case for looking to electronic means for moderating the continually rising tide of paper we deal with in this country.

For all our electronic progress, paper is a formidable factor in American information culture. Four out of every ten tons of pulp and paper in the world are produced, and mostly consumed, here. Not all of this paper is used for information, of course, but that is the major use. Per capita annual paper consumption in this country in the late seventies was six hundred pounds. In the Soviet Union it was seventy-five pounds; in India, five pounds. This "paper gap" is one of the little-noticed factors in the information imbalance between this country and most of the rest of the world, particularly the developing countries.[23]

The differences cannot be measured only in pounds of wood pulp. Americans have their own distinct patterns of printed information. There is some truth to the European mandarins' charge that Americans are not serious book readers. Textbooks aside, the U.S. book industry, whose 1979 revenues amounted to $7.2 billion, is geared largely to lightweight recreational or how-to-do-it material. How different from the sober uncut-page products that fill European bookstores or the enormous per capita production of solemn books in the Soviet Union. American scholars can, of course, match their Old World counterparts footnote for footnote; they are also disproportionate contributors to the sixty thousand scientific and technical journals published throughout the world.[24]

But the fact is that long-lasting encapsulation of wisdom is not our national style, for better or for worse. Printed information is, to a considerable degree, a throw-away item. It is the product of a new kind of printing press — the photocopier and the mimeograph. The output of these machines far outweighs that of other publications or even the hundred billion pieces of mail that move through the postal system each year. The paper flow in this country is so pervasive that it cannot be measured with accuracy. In 1975, a Stanford Research Institute study tried to pin down the volume of formal notices and forms used in business, government, and other organizations. The survey concluded that the total may be as high as 800 billion pieces of paper annually — well over three thousand items for every man, woman, and child in this paper-choked republic.[25]

Such statistics are often viewed with dismay, which is probably a mistake. The figures suggest an uncontrollable paper glut, with much waste and duplication. This is certainly a factor. On the other hand, there is a great deal to be said for a society that makes it easier for everyone to have his say through readily available paper resources and reproduction equipment. Even Marshall McLuhan, the scourge of print culture, paid his respects to photocopiers and mimeograph machines for their role in making every person his or her own publisher. This capability will be enhanced in the coming years with the introduction of so-called *intelligent copiers*. Not surprisingly the lead in this area has been taken by the Xerox Corporation. Its new high-technology copiers are actually electronic printing machines that can handle inputs from many sources, such as computers and word processors, store up to a thousand pages of material, arrange it in an appropriate layout, and then print it out electronically, employing up to fifty typefaces. Incidentally, it can also reproduce documents like any traditional photocopier.

Computers and associated equipment will vastly expand this populist possibility of giving everyone an updated version of the printing press. Whether this will reduce the present massive flow of paper is problematical. What is clear is that the potential exists for making a vastly expanded range of information available to more people. The computer will be the critical link; even in its present primitive stage of application, computer technology is changing work patterns and social expectations by doing the drudgery and routine tasks nobody wants to do. These jobs engage the computer at its simplest level. The more important prospect, however, is the information society's ability to exploit the coming generation of intelligent computers. As futurist Arthur C. Clarke notes:

> It's perfectly obvious that the development of such computers would restructure society completely. . . . And they are already doing this in many ways because our society now would collapse instantly if the computers that run it were taken away. And these are very simple, low-grade computers. This raises tremendous social and philosophical problems, not just the question of displaced people. What will the people that were only capable of low-grade computer-type work do in the future? There is the more profound question of what is the purpose of life? What do we want to live for? And that is the question which the intelligent computer will force us to pay attention to.[26]

This leads to subjects dear to science fiction writers: the possibilities of artificial intelligence and of computers taking control. These ideas remain firmly in the realm of science fiction for the present. Dr. John McCarthy of Stanford's artificial intelligence laboratory begins his discussion of the subject with the observation that he never met a computer that was smarter than the dumbest person he knows. Nevertheless, he is careful not to dismiss the prospect of some form of machine intelligence: "One way of putting it is to say that it takes 1.7 Einsteins and .3 of a Manhattan Project, and it is important to have the Einstein first and the Manhattan project second." Even this estimate is challenged by other experts in the field, notably MIT's Joseph Weizenbaum, who dismisses such projections as "simply and utterly ridiculous."

Arthur Clarke, in one of his science fiction stories, puts the issue in human perspective. He tells of the computer failure in a space ship that puts the craft into a disastrous orbit. A Japanese crewman teaches the rest of the crew to make abacuses out of wire and beads which are then used to calculate a course that saves ship and crew. The expectations offered by computers are extraordinary enough without delving too deeply into fantasy. One type of computer use, however, does skirt the edges of artificial intelligence and promises to be a major area of research and application during the coming decade.

This involves robots — or, more accurately, programmable automation. The idea of machines doing human work has fascinated and frustrated engineers for ages. In the eighteenth century the royal courts of Europe were entertained by the Green Lady, a mannikin with hidden machinery under her fancy costume, though all she could do was draw a single picture. Robot research took on new dimensions after World War I with the emphasis on production-line automation. The result was the servomechanism, which could perform relatively simple automation tasks. Today's work with programmable automation is spurred by the possibilities opened by microprocessors. NASA is stepping up its robotics research, for instance, in hopes of lowering the costs of deep-space probes. Its managers think that automated decision-making technology can reduce the need for already scarce trained people to program future missions. The Voyager mission to Jupiter in 1979 required two hundred people over an eighteen-month period to provide its pointing, navigation, power, and experiment control sequences. NASA engineers believe they can cut back on personnel for such tasks by a factor of ten, freeing these employees for work on other space missions.

The big automation push is not, however, in space, but on factory production lines. Here the advantages are more immediate and profitable. Every major industrial country is subsidizing research in this area with the aim of upgrading industrial productivity. The Japanese are the leaders: half of the industrial robots operating in the early eighties are in Japan, a quarter in this country, and the rest in Europe. Most of these robots still do simple mechanical tasks. The next step will be to develop robots programmed to follow optimum paths and assemble complicated products. Beyond that are the prospects for sophisticated remote-control tools, manipulated from across a room or a continent. Simple remote devices have been around for a long time; mechanical arms for handling nuclear materials are one example. However, the new remote-control devices, called *telepresence devices*, would have more humanlike sensory channels involving touch, pressure, textures, and vibration. The prospect has been imaginatively described by Dr. Marvin Minsky of MIT's artificial intelligence laboratory, a telepresence enthusiast:

> You don a comfortable jacket lined with sensors and musclelike motors. Each motion of your arm, hand, and fingers is reproduced in another place by mobile, mechanical hands. Light, dextrous, and strong, these hands have their own sensors through which you can see and feel what is happening. Using this instrument, you can "work" in another room, in another city, in another country, or on

another planet. Your remote presence possesses the strength of a giant or the delicacy of a surgeon. Heat or pain is translated into informative but tolerable sensations. Your dangerous job becomes safe and pleasant.[27]

Given the economic rewards it promises, programmable automation will be a major research and development area in the coming years. It is, perhaps, a paradox that the most sophisticated use of the technology to date has not been in factories but in the telepresence control of robots on the moon and on Mars.

Robots represent only one of the almost infinite ways computers and other information-related technologies can be combined. The remainder of this book will concentrate on the social dynamics involved in bringing these possibilities to full working reality. Politics and economics are critical parts of this process. The balancing factors, however, will be the deeper trends of our cultural patterns and, in particular, our continuing commitment to the American electronic myth.

The myth is still remarkably resilient. Americans moved into the eighties with many doubts about their collective future. Among other concerns, they were uneasy about the effects of helter-skelter technological development. These attitudes were interpreted by editorial-page pundits as signs of a new national maturity or, conversely, as the ending of the optimistic American dream.

Communications and information were remarkably immune from these popular doubts. We may decide not to build an SST transport or to cut back on nuclear plants. However, no one has argued for fewer computers, telephones, or newspapers or more restrictions on the rest of the apparatus of the information environment. This could reflect at least an instinctive belief that this environment is, by and large, exempt from the law of entropy that governs other physical resources, inflexibly causing energy to be degraded or, more exactly, made unavailable. Despite our recent experiences with oil and other depletable resources, we see communications and information in a hopeful light. In these areas, more is better; they seem to be immune to many of our usual doubts about the benefits of technology.

Thus, in the final analysis, technology is shaped by cultural values. In communications and information, these values are based on an equal combination of pragmatism and mythology. The reality is the concrete achievement of democratic freedoms in this society, based in large part on an open information system. The mythology involves transforming U.S. society through technology, moving toward the machine-in-the-garden, the technology-powered Eden. We turn now to the day-to-day realities involved in shaping the strategy of a new kind of information-rich society, beginning with a look at the economic prospects. The stakes involved in this area are critical. They were aptly summarized in a 1979 OECD report thusly: "The electronics complex during the next quarter century will be the pole around which the productive structure of advanced industrial societies will be organized."[28]

Notes

1. For a useful overview of microelectronics developments, see Tom Forester, ed., *The Microelectronics Revolution* (Cambridge,: MIT Press, 1981).

2. Charles and Ray Eames, *A Computer Perspective* (Cambridge, Mass.: Harvard University Press, 1973), p. 132.

3. "Applications Are Chasing the Chips," *The Economist* (London), 24 March 1979, p. 119. See also a special section on microelectronics in *The Economist* (London), 1 March 1980. Much of the material in this chapter on the technical and economic aspects of microelectronics has been drawn from this survey.

4. *The Economist* (London), 1 March 1980.

5. Peter P. Luff, "The Electronic Telephone," *Scientific American*, March 1978, pp. 58–64. See also Charles G. Burck, "Getting to Know the Smart Telephone," *Fortune*, 25 February 1980, pp. 134–46.

6. Robert Noyes, "Microelectronics," *Scientific American*, September 1977, p. 64.

7. Developments in this area are summarized in Alan C. Kay, "Microelectronics and the Personal Computer," *Scientific American*, September 1977, p. 231.

8. Eames, *Computer Perspective*, p. 144. Shannon published his findings in "A Mathematical Theory of Communications," *The Bell System Technical Journal*, 22, no. 3 (July 1948): p. 379.

9. Donald Michie, "Turling and the Origins of the Computer," *New Scientist* (London), 21 February 1980, pp. 580–83.

10. For a layperson's description of cybernetics, see Norbert Weiner, *The Human Use of Human Beings: Cybernetics and Society* (New York: Avon Publishing, 1967).

11. Eames, *Computer Perspective*, p. 136.

12. George W. Sullivan, "Telecommunications Trends and Directions," *Microwave Journal*, September 1977, p. 16.

13. A useful overview of this prospect can be found in Alexander S. Douglas, "Computers and Communications in the 1980's," *Computer Networks* (Amsterdam), 5, no. 1 (February 1981): pp. 9–14.

14. "U.S. Looks for Bigger Warlike Computers," *New Scientist* (London), 21 May 1977, p. 140.

15. "Americans Plan Monster Computer," *New Scientist* (London), 31 May 1979, p. 185.

16. "Talking Terminals and Listening Computers Overcome Toy Image," *Infosystems*, September 1980, pp. 52–56. Also "Next: Machines That Can Talk," *New York Times*, 30 October 1980, p. D-2.

17. "Information Processing," *Business Week*, 12 May 1980, p. 68.

18. "Tinier than a Nerve Fiber, Faster than a Silicon Chip," *New York Times*, 8 January 1980, p. C-2.

19. "Pushing Chip Technology Towards its Limits," *The Economist* (London), 22 February 1980, p. 83.

20. Juri Matisoo, "The Superconducting Computer," *Scientific American*, May 1980, pp. 50–65.

21. "Microfilm Linked to Computer," *Financial Times* (London), 29 September 1980, p. 10.

22. Patricia Holt, "New Ideas from the West," *Publisher's Weekly*, 2 October 1979, p. 32.

23. "The Third World's Paper Gap," *Washington Post*, 1 September 1977, p. 1.

24. For a useful survey of the future of the print media, see "Economic Trends in the Print Industry," a series of six articles on various aspects of the industry, *Journal of Communication*, 30, no. 2 (Spring 1980): pp. 59–103. Also see Anthony Smith, *Goodbye Gutenberg* (New York: Oxford University Press, 1980).

25. The study is described in Raymond Panko, "Outlook for Computer Mail Sunny, but Dark Clouds on the Horizon Also," *Communications News*, July 1977, p. 32. The SRI researchers acknowledged that their paper-flow figures might be off by as much as a half, but their basic point remains valid.

26. Transcript of Dr. Clarke's remarks on the television program, "The Mind Machines," in the Nova series, broadcast by the Public Broadcasting System in 1978.

27. Marvin Minsky, "Telepresence," *Omni*, June 1980, p. 45.

28. "Interfutures Report," Organization for Economic Cooperation and Development, Paris, 1979. Quoted in *The Economist* (London), 3 January 1981, p. 55.

Chapter Five

The Economics
of the New Age

Any strategy for the information age has to reckon with the powerful economic forces organizing and managing the resources of the new global network. This grid may be the largest construction project ever undertaken. Robert LeBlanc, a leading communications finance expert, has estimated that it will take an investment of $50 billion a year over a thirty-year period for foreign countries simply to bring their communications facilities up to current U.S. standards.[1] Meanwhile, the U.S. communications grid will continue to expand both in size and in range of services. Economics will be the driving force, primarily in the form of the network market described by Herbert Dordick and others in their research on future U.S. information patterns.

The communications structure in this country is the result of a complex cat's cradle of uncoordinated, often overlapping decisions going back a century or more. Marketplace economics have dominated this process, with political and social influence playing a secondary role. This point is important to an understanding of the prospects for a more coherent national strategy in this area. Any such strategy will have to recognize that there is no one agency for decision making, public or private, in the U.S. as there is in almost every other country because of their centralized government communications agencies.

The previous chapter described how a convergence of technical innovations points to a new physical structure in communications and information. In the next chapter, we will look at a similar, if somewhat less precise, convergence of social forces that will also affect future decisions in this field. In this chapter, we examine the convergence of economic forces influencing these patterns. The economic pattern was set one hundred and fifty years ago with the decision to allow the original Morse telegraph system to be built and managed by a commercial firm, Western Union. The government's regulatory touch was light until the passage of the Communications Act of 1934. This legislation created the Federal Communications Commission, the regulatory overseer of a large segment of the communications industry, in implicit exchange for a certain amount of freedom from direct governmental intervention in the industry. This arrangement has held for a half-century with some modifications, assuring that the communications sector will remain essentially in commercial hands.

The business of America, said Calvin Coolidge, is business. This may be a narrow view, but it explains a lot. The United States is the only society whose citizens speak unblushingly about the education business, the business of government, the culture business, and so on. The business of communications and information touches all of these, and more. As the 1977 Commerce Department study of the information economy indicated, it may be the biggest business of all — the "premier industry of our times," as *Forbes* magazine identified it at the time in a survey of long-term U.S. economic trends.[2] Reviewing overall economic prospects for the eighties, the *New York Times* singled out communications/information activities as one of the two most promising fields for expansion in the decade. (The other field was genetics.)[3]

Impressive production statistics tell only part of the story. There is a strong case for the proposition that communications and information will determine the economic directions of the coming decade. In part, this reflects the vibrancy of these sectors themselves. The more important element may be their role in overall U.S. economic growth, and in particular, in the new emphasis on reindustrialization, the overhauling of the U.S. economy for more efficient post-industrial tasks. Communications and information are the primary focus of the products and services for this technological turnaround. The changes are already underway: by the end of the eighties, a fourth of all jobs in this country will be dependent on computers. Present-day computers are still relatively conventional machines, isolated from most of the work force in data processing departments. During the next decade, computers will become an integral part of work activities, on assembly lines, in offices, and in other service units. They will not always be the familiar boxes lined up against a wall or on large tables. Most of them will be microelectronic devices built into machines with enormously enhanced production capabilities.

Here is where the opportunities lie for reversing the current declines in industrial productivity. In a 1979 Brookings Institution labor productivity survey of eleven industries, only two sectors showed gains in the 1973–78 period. One was banking, which has turned heavily to automation in recent years. The other, significantly, was communications, achieving the highest productivity gains of any industry largely by applying microelectronic technologies. Although it is difficult to show causal connections in productivity measures, two factors predominate. One is the labor force itself, and here the hopeful element is the growing professionalization of U.S. labor, with its promise of an increasing capability to manage the new technologies. Professionals and managers now hold one out of four of the nation's jobs.[4]

The other factor is the upgrading of the machines themselves. Here is where doubts arise about America's ability to maintain its lead in many areas of technology. Spending on research and development as a share of gross national product (GNP) has slipped from 2.6 percent in 1970 to around 2.2 percent in the early eighties. (The Soviet Union remains the biggest spender on science, as percentage of GNP, followed by West Germany.) Moreover, somewhat over 60 percent of U.S. Government support for research and development — the largest single slice of the research pie — is tied to defense and space research, two areas where technology does not always translate readily into market application.[5]

Funding for communications and information research and development tends to be higher than for other sectors, primarily because the economic payoffs are usually more immediate and tangible. Innovations alone cannot sustain the reindustrialization effort; the industrial structure is too complex for such simple solutions. However, it is clear that the new productivity effort may fall well short of its goals without significant input from these sectors. Historic trends confirm this, with the telephone industry as a useful case in point. In 1910, AT&T handled six million telephone calls with a staff of 120 thousand; that is about fifty calls a year for each employee. In 1979, the system handled 185 billion calls with less than a million employees, or 185 thousand calls per employee. Handling current telephone traffic at the 1910 level of technology and company staff would require forty times the present U.S. labor force.

There are other hurdles to overcome in the reindustrialization effort. Investment policy, and particularly the persistent low rates of capital formation in recent years, are critical obstacles.[6] Another is the high cost of conforming to environmental and other regulations, as well as the impact of inflation on incentive to invest in innovative (in other words, risky) projects. There is also an amorphous but powerful psychological barrier, the fear of change, particularly when it affects pocketbooks and deep-set habits. This is reflected in the bloody-minded Ludditism with which people resist the introduction of new techniques through encrusted corporate practices, union rules, or special-interest laws. There will be a heavy social cost in the reindustrialization cycle, most of it falling on those who are undereducated or otherwise disadvantaged. An important part of any strategy for the information age is to find effective ways of easing social disruption without losing the advantages of technologies that improve productivity and raise overall job prospects.

As noted earlier, the underdeveloped nations of the next century will be those which choose to ignore the implications of microelectronics and other information technologies. There is a curious, and potentially harmful, tendency in this country to suggest that it can't happen here. Recent events forcing us to lower our expectations as undisputed world leader should make us realize that we are not — if we ever were — insulated from the consequences of such changes. Our industrial partners in Europe and Japan are beginning to respond to the microelectronic challenge. Moreover, a significant group of Third World countries — India, Brazil, and Korea, among others — have made it clear that they will not restrict themselves to making the shirts, shoes, and bicycles that the industrialized West can no longer produce economically. There is no reason why they cannot begin to challenge the West in some areas of high technology. The proof is that they have already begun, with small electronics industries that produce an impressive range of communications and information products. These fledgling efforts are useful training grounds for more advanced production projects, and a challenge to any complacency we may have about our long-term economic position.

In summary, the communications and information industries need to be considered not only as strong elements in economic productivity, but also as instruments for shaping the overall pattern of post-industrial society. Accepting these premises as true, one might assume that U.S. economists are engaged in a massive effort to identify the dimensions of the new information-based economy. But this is not the case. Two decades ago, University of Chicago economist George Stigler noted that the study of information resources occupied a slum dwelling in the town of economics.[7] Fortunately the subject has been gradually gaining more respectability in recent years. Since Professor Stigler made his analogy, information studies have moved up from the slums at least to middle-class status, largely as the result of the work of younger economists.

Two pioneering studies identify information factors in the new post-industrial environment. The first of these, conducted by economist Fritz Machlup, was a book, *The Production and Distribution of Knowledge in the United States*, written in 1962.[8] Machlup looked at information activities, which he called "the knowledge industries," and concluded that 29 percent of gross national product and 31 percent of the non farm labor force were involved in such activities during his base year, 1958. Moreover, he added, the overall annual rate of growth for such activities was considerably higher than the industrial growth rate. His conclusion was logical and direct: information-related activities would eventually outdistance industrial production as the major element in the economy.

Machlup's research had a useful impact on scholars' attempts to define the new post-industrial environment. Information and communications activities were classified under the "service sector" rubric in economic analysis until Professor Machlup extricated them from this catch-all category. In documenting their unique, growing role in the economy, he supplied important insights on the shape and content of the new information environment. His approach was broad-brush and did not attempt to analyze the common characteristics of the many "knowledge industry" sectors he identified. It was another fifteen years before a precise analysis of the information and communications sector was carried out, making clear their full impact on the U.S. economy.

This was done in a U.S. Department of Commerce research project the results of which were published in *The Information Economy*, issued in 1977.[9] Primarily the work of a young Stanford-trained economist, Marc Uri Porat, the study is a massive, nine-volume look at information activities in the U.S. economy. It confirmed and expanded upon Machlup's thesis. It also provided a more sophisticated analysis of the characteristics of the new information economy. The report's conclusion was that overall information activities accounted for 46 percent of gross national production in 1967, the base year for the study. In the same year, half the labor force, earning 52 percent of total income, held some type of information-related job.

These conclusions are both dramatic and debatable. In Porat's words, "Information is the data that has been organized and communicated. The information *activity* includes all the resources consumed in producing, processing and distributing information goods and services."[10] Having set up this standard, the study looked at the characteristics of information capital and information workers. Information capital, in Porat's analysis, included the machines, buildings, and other goods and services, from computers to mimeograph machines, that go into the information economy. Somewhat to his surprise, he found the division between information and noninformation activity relatively easy to define: "Most goods are not ambiguous. A tractor is obviously a member of the food activity, and a seismograph is a member of the information activity."[11]

Information workers cannot be divided as readily. All work involves some component of information processing. Porat approached the problem by looking at each of the 422 occupations reported by the U.S. Census and the Bureau of Labor Statistics. He asked: Does income from this work category originate primarily in the manipulation of symbols and information? In many cases, Porat found, the answer came easily. In other occupations there were complications. Doctors presented a problem: to what degree were they in the information business? After considerable investigation, Porat concluded that a doctor's schedule broke down to about half-time in information activity and half-time in noninformation work.

Whether the information-related activities of doctors can be so accurately determined is, however, peripheral to the Commerce Department study's overall analysis of the information economy. The report is most valuable in providing a more accurate picture of the role of information activities. While the Machlup study lumped these activities together in apples-and-oranges fashion, the Commerce study made some important distinctions. It suggested that the information economy is best understood when it is divided into primary and secondary sectors. The distinction between the two can be determined by asking whether information goods and services are exchanged in the marketplace. The organizations and individuals involved in such exchanges are in the primary information sector. The secondary sector includes all the information services produced by public and private organizations for their own internal consumption. These bureaucracies are the repositories of the planning, decision-making, and control apparatus in the economy. By Porat's reckoning, activities in the secondary sector accounted for 21 percent of total gross national production in 1967, almost as much as the 25 percent accounted for by the primary sector.

The long-term evolution of the new information economy is shown in the charts on page 94, reproduced from the Department of Commerce study. The relationship between the agricultural, industrial and information economies clearly indicates the long-term shift toward the primacy of information-related activities. The other chart, tracing the relative standings of the information and noninformation work forces, indicates that the two groups are roughly in balance at the beginning of the 1980s. The significant element to note here is that information-sector employment has leveled off since the beginning of the seventies.

There are important implications here for the U.S. economy during the coming decade. The new information economy has, in a sense, already reached a level of maturity. The time may have passed when the addition of information resources, both people and machines, would automatically have resulted in large productivity gains. Gains may be harder to come by from here on, resulting in a more cautious approach by managers in increasing their information resources. Moreover, there are indications that expansion is slower within the primary information sector — the market sector — than within the secondary sector, the bureaucracy which, whatever its value, does not directly add to the national product. The result may be to reduce the overall efficiency of the information sector, as more resources are siphoned to its bureaucratic component at the expense of more productive elements.

Inevitably, there have been criticisms of the Commerce Department study's methods and conclusions. Some critics have argued that its interpretation of information is overly broad, embracing too many disparate activities. Others have questioned whether information is a commodity that can be as precisely defined as the report suggests. Nevertheless, the study has performed a service in rescuing information factors in the economy from their obscurity in the traditional service industries category. Questions remain, but there is no doubt that the information sector is different from the operation of hotels, dry cleaning establishments, funeral homes, and other businesses lumped together as services.

There will undoubtedly be more rigorous analysis and revision of the Commerce Department study in the coming years. One such revisionist approach has been undertaken by Dr. John Bermuth, a Uni-

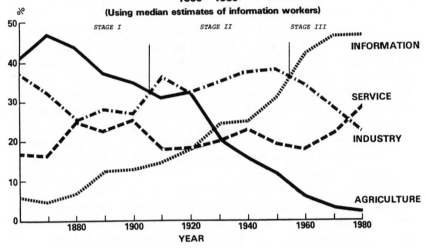

FOUR SECTOR AGGREGATION
OF THE U.S. WORK FORCE BY PERCENT
1860 - 1980
(Using median estimates of information workers)

%

STAGE I   STAGE II   STAGE III

INFORMATION

SERVICE

INDUSTRY

AGRICULTURE

1880   1900   1920   1940   1960   1980

YEAR

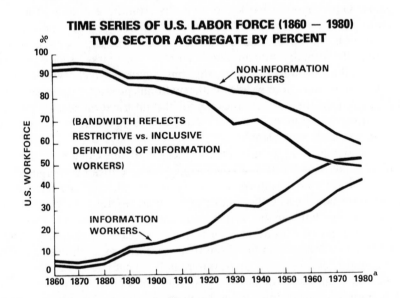

TIME SERIES OF U.S. LABOR FORCE (1860 — 1980)
TWO SECTOR AGGREGATE BY PERCENT

%

NON-INFORMATION
WORKERS

(BANDWIDTH REFLECTS
RESTRICTIVE vs. INCLUSIVE
DEFINITIONS OF INFORMATION
WORKERS)

INFORMATION
WORKERS

U.S. WORKFORCE

1860 1870 1880 1890 1900 1910 1920 1930 1940 1950 1960 1970 1980[a]

[a] 1980 projections supplied by the Bureau of Labor Statistics (unpublished).
Source: U.S. Department of Commerce, *The Information Economy*, 9 vols. Office of Telecommunications Special Publication 77–12 (Washington, D.C.: Government Printing Office, 1977).

versity of Chicago educator studying what he calls "literacy activities." Defining "literacy" as the exchange of information through the written word, Bermuth goes well beyond the traditional stress on language skills. Literacy, he suggests, is a major economic activity, amounting in 1972 to more than a fourth of the gross national product, taking up about 29 percent of the average worker's time on the job and about 17 percent of the average adult's waking hours. Whether Bermuth's literacy format takes hold as a model for clarifying information activities, it and similar new research attest to the continued quest for a more accurate definition of the information economy.[12]

While the academicians debate the meaning and extent of the new economy, its superstructure is being built around them by the communications and information industries. As the 1977 Commerce Department report has shown, these industries are part of the largest single segment of the U.S. industrial economy. Their range extends from the American Telephone & Telegraph Company — an imperial group with annual revenues greater than the gross national products of two thirds of the world's nations — down to the latest hopeful one-room firm, banking on a new piece of electronic technology that may or may not catch on.

The communications industry is complex, profitable, and currently in splendid disarray. After decades of relative stability, communications and information firms are being reshaped by economics and technology. New companies with cryptic names like ITEL, MCI, UTEC, Racal, and T-Bar are challenging the established giants and the giants themselves are changing. The Bell System may be, as one wag has suggested, the closest approach to immortality on earth, but it too is losing some of its eternal aura. Semi-immortal or not, the telephone company will be quite a different institution in the coming years. Its strategy — and that of lesser firms — in adapting to change will be crucial in shaping post-industrial patterns in this country. AT&T and others pass the American pragmatic test — they make things work in exchange for profit. And the profit-oriented market system, battered and berated as it may be, is still a very useful mechanism for dealing with social costs. Despite long-term attempts to wrap itself in the security blanket of government regulatory protection, the U.S. communications industry is being exposed to the winds of competition and change, as technological innovation is forcing massive shifts in its ways of doing business, and even changing the business it does.

This contrasts with the industry's relative stability of only a few years ago. Then it was stabilized around the voice-telephone network, the first interactive mass communications grid. The network's ability to provide nearly universal service was essentially a political achievement, the result of a decision (incorporated into the 1934 Communications Act) to give AT&T a quasi-monopoly in exchange for the development of a full network. This promise was largely fulfilled. In 1934, only 31 percent of the nation's households had phones; today the figure is well over 90 percent. As sociologist Sidney Aronson notes, the telephone's ring is as "ubiquitous . . . as the ever-present tolling of church bells in a medieval village."

Whatever the corporate faults and failings of the American Telephone & Telegraph Company (and sixteen hundred smaller systems), this record of supplying what the engineers call POTS — Plain Old Telephone Service — to such a geographically diverse, economically varied population is unique. Canada aside, no other nation has begun to match it until recent years.

Beyond the telephone grid, the next largest of the old-line telecommunications networks carried data, or "record," traffic — essentially telegram and telex messages. This grid was designed primarily for business use, and it was dominated by the Western Union Company in this country and by a group of "record carriers" internationally — International Telephone and Telegraph (ITT), Radio Corporation of America (RCA), and several smaller firms. The third group of basic grids was the television and radio networks, reaching into almost every home with popular entertainment and news programming. The 1934 Communications Act gave a strong measure of political and economic stability first to radio and, in the postwar years, to television by assuring them government-granted broadcasting licenses that were, for all intents and purposes, permanent. Although the legislation lays down clear public service responsibilities in exchange for renewal of licenses, the Federal Communications Commission, which grants the licenses, has seldom lifted one for a broadcaster's failure to serve the public interest. As one critic of the licensing system, former California Congressman Lionel Van Deerlin, notes, "If a licensee has managed to stay out of jail, he is renewed."[13] Given this kind of stability, the New York–based networks and their local affiliates developed both radio and television into highly profitable merchandising devices for delivering mass audiences to advertisers.

This was the situation with broadcasting and the other major communications networks through the 1960s. Each network was in its own groove, applying technological improvements as necessary without changing its basic operational format. Advanced computers and other high-technology machines based in microelectronics were in the early stages of influencing communications and information patterns. Future historians studying our particular part of the twentieth century will be able to pinpoint more accurately the significance of the technological shift that took place sometime around 1960 in this country, establishing the physical parameters of the new information society. They will see, more clearly than we can at this short distance, a series of converging scientific developments affecting the entire spectrum of communications and information activities. This was quite different from developments in the previous hundred years, when major technical innovations like the telegraph, telephone, and radio appeared one at a time, allowing a cushion of several decades' time in which to sort out their political and economic implications.

For the first time, this adaptation process had to occur all at once. Moreover, the shift involved technologies that provided a quantum increase in quality and capacity of services, as opposed to the slower advances of earlier years. Included among the innovations that came to the forefront during this shift were satellites, high-capacity cables, lasers, advanced microwave techniques, computers, and electronic miniaturization of all manner of technology, from the 1950s transistor to large-scale integration (LSI) technology.

This rush of innovations from the laboratories to production lines two decades ago set the pace for the economic upheaval that has occurred in the communications and information industries since then. The changes are still going on, and no one seems to have a clear view of how a vastly changed industry will look in the future. Indeed, this pace has increased in recent years, creating unsettling implications for decisions on "freezing" the technologies to be used in the industry's hardware. The other ambiguous factor is the effect of a lack of political and social decision making on the overall pattern of the new information society, a situation that also inhibits economic decision making. We will examine these problems in decision making, particularly as they are related to changes in the three key networks — telephone, data, and broadcasting.

We begin with the phone system, and specifically the American Telephone and Telegraph Company. In her telephone operator skits, comedienne Lily Tomlin could tweak AT&T's corporate nose by telling her imaginery customers: "We're the phone company. We can do no wrong. We serve everyone from kings to presidents down to the scum of the earth." Most Americans are prepared to accept the Bell System's oft-repeated claim that it provides the best phone service in the world. (In defending its corporate actions during a 1981 court case, a Bell attoney referred to AT&T unblushingly as "the greatest enterprise on earth.")[14] It is probably true that if a decision had been made twenty years ago to entrust the construction of a full-service information utility in this country to AT&T, the system would be completed by now.

A good part of the technology for such a system has come, in fact, from AT&T's own research arm, the Bell Laboratories, certainly the most productive communications research facility on earth. AT&T has never been shy in claiming jurisdiction in areas other than traditional voice-telephone service. In the 1920s, it actively sought to become a major developer of radio broadcasting in this country.[15] The company was prepared to move into commercial cable television networking in the 1950s until checked by the FCC. More recently, AT&T has sought a dominant role in high-speed computer networking.

In each of these instances a political decision has prevented, or limited, AT&T's expansion into areas beyond its traditional service. Now technology, economics, and politics are combining to create a new set of operational conditions for the vast Bell System and for a host of new competitors. On the one hand, traditional Bell control of long-distance circuits and the right of the company to install its own equipment has been eroded by government regulatory decisions designed to increase competition in these areas. The Justice Department brought a suit against AT&T in the early seventies over alleged antitrust violations, particularly in connection with the company's manufacturing affiliate, Western Electric. On the other hand, the company moved into the eighties with a strong strategy for increasing its share of the data communications market, the newest and fastest growing area in the industry. Several years ago, former AT&T president Frederick Kappel declared that the company's revenues from data communications will eventually be greater than those from its traditional voice-telephone traffic. This seemed to many observers at the time to be a long-shot prediction, but it is now well within the realm of possibility.[16]

Whatever pattern finally emerges, the seventies marks the end of almost a half-century in which Bell's dominance over telephone services was the law of the land. The near-monopoly was raised to the status of dogma by Bell executives and their many supporters. The Bell argument was simple: The telephone system is a natural monopoly, since there has to be a centralized system for connecting phones with each other. Moreover, economics dictate a monopoly since a universal system cannot be built without cross-subsidization between high-density profitable and low-density unprofitable services.

Given the Bell System's generally commendable record in providing telephone services, it can be forgiven its sentimental boasts, usually spoken with a catch in the corporate throat, about getting a phone line up to the last house on the remotest mountain in the nation. AT&T has claimed in recent years that it loses about seven dollars a month on its average telephone customer, a figure disputed by outside observers who suggest that it all depends on who's counting and what's being counted. The facts about telephone economics are very much in the eye of the beholder, an observation raised to high art by the platoons of phone company lawyers, government regulators, and public interest advocates in the interminable round of arguments about AT&T's rate structure. Beyond all the graphs and statistics, Bell's primary argument on behalf of its dominant position has been that it works; the claim is incorporated in a corporate slogan, "The system is the solution," widely advertised by Bell companies.

Whatever its virtues, Bell's case in favor of its quasi monopoly is being passed up by events. A curious but revealing episode in the history of the company's defense of its position took place in 1976 with the introduction of Congressional legislation designed to affirm (or, as far as Bell was concerned, reaffirm) the company's telecommunications primacy. Known as the Consumer Communications Reform Act, the legislation proposed standards designed to avoid "unnecessary and wasteful duplication" in telecommunications. It specifically required Bell's competitors in long-distance services to prove that they would meet these standards. In other words, they had to prove, before introducing a new service in competition with Bell, that they could do better, a regulatory process that would be expensive and time consuming. It is a tribute to the political clout of AT&T and the independent phone companies that the legislation was cosponsored by 175 representatives and 17 senators. The bill never came up for a vote, which was, in turn, a tribute to the collective ability of the rest of the telecommunications industry to stymie it. The subject eventually moved into legislative limbo, following the introduction of more comprehensive proposals to revise the Communications Act of 1934 — a subject that will be examined in the next chapter.

AT&T was looking for political relief from a technological and economic reality whose time had come. The assault on its near-monopoly began in the late sixties with a series of relatively minor Federal Communications Commission decisions which set the tone for what has happened since. In the first of these decisions, the so-called

"Carterphone case" in 1968, the FCC determined that AT&T could no longer bar the use of telephone equipment of which it did not approve or in effect, any equipment not made by its Western Electric affiliate. The Carterphone was just such a piece of banned equipment, used for mobile telephone units. (With imperial *hauteur*, AT&T referred to such equipment as "foreign attachments.") The Commission ruled that customers could use such attachments, provided they did not harm the network technically. For the first time, suppliers could compete with AT&T's manufacturing arm, Western Electric — a major breakthrough that opened the equipment industry to a new range of products and services.

A year later, the Commission allowed a new firm, MCI Telecommunications, to build and operate specialized microwave facilities offering private-line telephone service between Chicago and St. Louis, and gave it the right to connect with the local phone company network within these cities. The service was directly competitive with (and cheaper than) AT&T's long-distance service. The FCC later authorized other specialized common carriers to operate similar networks. AT&T protested that these decisions violated its legal rights and, in particular, threatened the economics of consumer telephone service by skimming revenues from its intercity traffic. In the corporate battles that ensued, MCI brought a suit against AT&T charging it with attempting to undermine MCI services by blocking access to Bell System local phones. In a 1980 verdict that rocked the industry, MCI was awarded $1.5 billion in damages by a federal district court. AT&T's appeal of the verdict will probably take years to settle.[17]

MCI and the other challengers have since pressed hard to expand their services in competition with Bell, but the going has not been easy. At least one company which started off with high hopes, Datran Corporation, went into bankruptcy after several years. Most of the firms challenging Bell were corporate upstarts, new to the business. However, in January 1979, the Federal Communications Commission authorized an industry giant, ITT, to operate a national long-distance phone network linking eleven major cities from Boston to Los Angeles.

The new competition in voice services still represents a very small threat to the Bell System's revenues, which involve profits that have run over a billion dollars quarterly in recent years. The odds against the new firms' capturing a significant share of AT&T's long-distance traffic are still limited. For example, in 1979, MCI's revenues were $144 million as against AT&T's $23.4 billion for long-distance services.

Nevertheless, the age of competition in telecommunications is here. It began with plain old telephone service, but it is rapidly expanding into data networking. The stakes here are massive, affecting the shape and size of the U.S. information utility well into the next century. Given their importance in any strategy for the new information environment, the economic factors deserve a closer look.

The look begins with a quick review of the steps leading to the technological marriage of computation and communications. In simpler days, twenty years ago, most computers were "stand alone" machines; computation and communications were separate operations with no electronic links. In the sixties, they began to merge, with computers that were linked to outside terminals. The result was the rapid growth of *time sharing*, computer power dispersed to multiple users however remote they may be from the mainframe machines. This was the beginning of computer networks, with terminals interacting with a central computational base. However, computation and communications technologists were still essentially separate and distinct.[18]

These distinctions have been steadily eroding in the past decade. Computers are being used to switch both voice and digital messages. Data processing services are moving rapidly toward *distributive networks*, in which the terminals possess memory and logic of their own, placing greater intelligence capability in the terminal rather than concentrating it in the computer mainframe. Thus telephone equipment can be programmed to monitor toll usage and to perform billing and accounting functions.

In other words, computer capabilities are being built into the entire communications system. Microprocessors with memory capabilities are now commonplace in telephone exchange and private branch exchange (PBX) equipment. Digital data transmissions services are oriented toward computer uses without requiring *modems* — the attachments to telephones that permit connections to computers. In these and many other ways, the distinction between computation and communications are being blurred to the point at which data communications are done by computers and network circuits that are, in effect, a single computational/communications machine.

Communiputers? Computercations? Compunication? Whatever this hybrid is called, it will upset most of the old ways of storing and transmitting information. A new kind of business emerged in the seventies, and the rush was on to exploit its possibilities. Conspicuously absent from the initial rush was the Bell System. Critics cite this as another example of AT&T reluctance to shift to more efficient technologies, though many of these technologies were developed in its own Bell Labs. In Bell's defense, it is fair to note that the company is sitting on top of a massive communications network whose upgrading involves complex operational and financial problems. The present equipment is being amortized over a relatively long period of time. Writing it off early could result in higher rates for all Bell services. The arguments and counter-arguments are not simply corporate fiscal games, however. The problem of continually outmoded technologies is a consideration in any information age strategy, not one limited to the Bell System.

Whatever its reasons, Bell moved carefully into the high-technology data network competition. From the mid-seventies on, however, the pace quickened. Bell Labs unveiled the so-called *transaction phone*, a credit card verification unit, among other things, that could be viewed as a type of computation device. AT&T also produced a new generation of telephone-connected data display terminals, beginning with "dumb" terminals and moving toward a sophisticated type called Dataspeed 40-4, which has enhanced computational capabilities. Following a series of legal challenges by other firms, Dataspeed was authorized by the FCC as a legitimate — and regulated — part of AT&T's operations.

The company also began promoting "network processing services," its euphemism for a store-and-forward message switch that IBM and other computer firms claimed was part of the data processing services and equipment market. Continuing their euphemistic course, Bell executives spoke of a dial-up service (for instance, a voice answer-back service for reading bank balances) that, they said, was just delivering a message. Not so, retorted the computer firms. Such a service, they argued, is processing information, which is their bailiwick. Finally, AT&T moved into the satellite communications area, where there was the promise of access to high-speed circuits for data communications. This access turned out to be somewhat less than immediate, however. The FCC delayed AT&T's use of satellites for data networks for several years in order to give other firms a chance to establish their own satellite operations without Bell's overwhelming presence. By mid-1979, the restrictions were lifted and Bell was ready to compete for what it regarded as its destined large share of business in the evolving integrated information utility. With classic simplicity, AT&T christened its project ACS — for Advanced Communications System.[19]

The technology to create the utility was available, but the political and economic strategies for bringing it about were considerably less clear. We will look at the politics in the next chapter; here we will examine the tangled economic pattern — a pattern which may not emerge clearly for a decade. However, the main outlines are already becoming more visible.

The contest will center around two corporate giants — AT&T and IBM, respective leaders in the communications and informations industries. A secondary level of large firms such as Xerox, Comsat, GTE, RCA, and ITT will also be involved. Other communications and information companies are grouped around these major contenders in varying patterns. They all share a common awareness of the risks and opportunities involved, including the prospects of large profits for the survivors of what promises to be a very competitive contest. The end result, hopefully, will be an information utility whose enhanced capabilities can be summarized in a comparison expressed in binary digits. The standard AT&T telephone lines have a capacity of 9,600 bits per second (BPS); the company's data-only circuits operate at 56,000 BPS. A satellite-based network, inaugurated in 1981 by Satellite Business Systems, has a 6.3 million BPS capacity. Bell System engineers have plans for an expanded satellite network, part of which could operate at 600 million BPS.[20] These capacities, and the machines that create them, are transforming the ways in which AT&T, IBM, and the rest of the industry will operate from now on. Meanwhile, the relationship between AT&T and IBM will define much of what happens. Until very recently, the relationship was relatively simple. IBM made large computers and dominated two thirds of the market. The rest of the market was shared among smaller but respectable competitors. (The arrangement was known in the industry as "Snow White and the Seven Dwarfs.") The Bell System sold primarily voice-telephone services, and it had no direct competition. The Bell System and the independent telephone companies (which are very dependent on Bell long-lines circuits) were responsible for over 95 percent of domestic telecommunications revenues. When IBM wanted communications lines to link computers, it went to the phone company. When the phone company wanted a computer it went to IBM or to one of its competitors.

The new integrated communications/computation technologies change this, of course. AT&T and IBM each looked down their respective corporate roads and realized the need for a new strategy to match the change. Bell saw the prospects for computer-based data networking. IBM, looking in the same direction, saw its traditional mainframe market being eroded by smaller computers capable of performing many functions of the bigger machines. It made two decisions: first, to produce the small machines and second, to get into the communications business. Thus, the sight lines of the two firms began to converge. The long-term corporate strategies of both AT&T and IBM are to continue to move down this road, working from their respective strengths in circuits and computers. Each is expanding rapidly into the uncharted areas of sophisticated communications/information equipment and services for automated workplaces — offices, factories, schools, laboratories — and eventually for homes. Their strategies will be complex, since neither firm will be able to operate as a free agent. Each will be limited by political and legal constraints, part of the growing attention to developing a national strategy which will prevent domination of the information utility by IBM and/or AT&T.

Meanwhile, the phone company is on the move. "We are going to draw a bead on the information market," the company's chairman, Charles L. Brown, declared in 1980. The AT&T strategy involves breaking out of the constraints imposed by a 1956 consent decree negotiated with the Department of Justice to settle an antitrust suit. AT&T agreed to confine its data processing activities to the needs of its conventional telecommunications operations. This had the effect of prohibiting it from involvement in "smart" computer terminals or in competing for corporate computer and data processing business. The restrictions, set at a time when such machines and services did not exist, has been overtaken by technological change. The political and legal formulas, for dealing with this change are still being worked out. While waiting for definitive decisions, Bell has been organizing itself for the new market, through a major restructuring of its operations. Its plan provides for a division of the firm into two separate operating entities — one for its older, regulated telecommunications business and a new one for unregulated data communications. The new element, dubbed "Baby Bell," will operate without subsidies from the firm's regulated telecommunications business. This has been a generally accepted precondition for any government actions allowing AT&T to enter the data communications market. Whether the arrangement will achieve its purpose — to avoid giving Bell an overwhelming competitive edge in the new market — remains to be seen.[21]

Meanwhile, the telephone business will still be important to AT&T. It continues to install millions of new phones every year to meet the national compulsion for convenient connections. "To say that the residential telephone market is saturated," says the company's chairman, Charles L. Brown, "is like saying the advertising market is saturated because most of the houses have TV sets. That 'saturation' is precisely what permits the market to grow.''[22] A vast area for expansion in the eighties is mobile telephone service, based on a new technology which will permit millions of such phones using low-powered local radio transmissions controlled by computers.

IBM has, in the meantime, also moved ahead with its own national data communications network. In 1977 it set up a communications company, Satellite Business Systems (SBS), with two other firms, Comsat General and the Aetna Life Insurance Company. With an initial investment of over $400 million, the SBS network began in 1981 to transmit to small unattended earth terminals throughout the country via its own satellites. Initially, its primary customers have been Fortune 500 corporations who use the system for internal office and factory communications. The advantages are both technical and fiscal. The SBS all-digital format permits transmission of voice, high-speed data, facsimile, and video on an integrated basis. Financially, the network provides lower costs by bundling a wide variety of services and, pointedly, bypassing AT&T telephone networks. Significantly, in 1981, SBS announced it would market aggressively for smaller business customers.

Given sponsorship by any group with lesser resources than IBM and its two partners, the project would be an enormous gamble. However, IBM's participation is not a basic departure from its corporate philosophy. Swallowing its natural aversion to government regulation, it saw the need to operate as a regulated carrier (via SBS) rather than run the risk of losing control over an essential element of its long-range computer market strategy by being dependent on AT&T and other carriers. This reflected a hallowed IBM corporate philosophy of having total "end-to-end" control of its operations.

The AT&T and IBM moves to develop national networks have been characterized as a showdown fight between two corporate giants. But this neat journalistic simile does not quite fit the facts. Clearly there is a competitive element involved, but for the present the two networks serve somewhat different purposes. Moreover, the political reality is that stability will have to be maintained during the complex transition period to a new kind of national information utility. This is particularly true of the Bell System's role. Telephone service is the most politically sensitive of all public communications services; good phone service is taken for granted, including its relatively low cost. Keeping the service efficient and its rates down will be the balancing factors assuring AT&T's corporate health during the transition period as well as in its role in the new information environment.

Any changes, therefore, will be formed around the continuing political, economic, and social preeminence of the telephone system. A key factor is that the average person uses a phone only fifteen minutes a day.[23] The many hours of unused capacity can be filled with other services. Everyone, from Bell and IBM down to the latest hopeful entrants into the field, will be concentrating on how to do this with new services for both homes and business.

Bell and IBM will be the largest, but by no means the only, significant players in this contest. There are other telephone companies — including one corporate giant, General Telephone and Electronics (GTE), a respectable second to Bell in both telephone hook-ups and equipment manufacturing. Long considered a solid but lackluster company, it moved swiftly into a full-fledged national data network operation in 1980 with the inauguration of an electronic mail system and the prospect for expanding into other electronic services. At the same time, the fourth largest phone company, Continental Telephone, has been expanding its capabilities for national data services by acquiring interests in satellite communications, data networks, and cable television systems.

Clustered around these industry leaders are scores of smaller companies, each intent on sharing the new network business. The stakes, and the rewards, are high. GTE projects a total intercity telecommunications network of $122 billion in 1987, of which half will be traditional consumer phone traffic, most of it provided by the Bell System. The other half will be business traffic, divided roughly between voice and data services, in which Bell will face intense competition.[24] Here is where the prizes are for the non-Bell sector of the industry. As noted earlier, a number of firms began to challenge AT&T's long-distance telephone dominance in the seventies. Bell faces similar challenges as it moves into the data communications field, following the loosening of legal and political restraints on its operations in this area. The competition promised by IBM's Satellite Business Systems network has been described above.

Another major competitor will be the Xerox Corporation. Following IBM's philosophy, Xerox decided that it had to get into the communications business to make its new computerized photocopying products more accessible and useful to its customers. It has proposed an interactive office network called Ethernet for data communications and electronic document distribution. Meanwhile, the company's new generation of "smart" copying machines are designed to plug into the network. To strengthen its communications expertise, Xerox acquired Western Union International (WUI) in 1979 and assigned to it responsibility for developing future networks.[25]

Bell, SBS, and Xerox are frontrunners in a new kind of information business where technology is erasing the distinctions between telecommunications and computer processing. The decade of the centralized mainframe computer is giving way to a decade of distributed computing networks. The emphasis is on flexible, lower cost processing of information at the point where it is to be used rather than in a distant computer center. The mainframe data business, providing centralized storage and data bank services, is still very much alive. General Electric was one of the pioneers in this profitable business, and sophisticated variations on networking from centralized data bases will continue to develop during the eighties. One prospect, already well advanced abroad, is a "viewdata" service, providing business firms and homes with access, via telephone, to many sources of data material displayed on a modified television set. Such systems are now being offered experimentally to the public in Britain, France, Canada, and Japan. The British system provides access to over a hundred "information providers," or operators of specialized data banks.[26]

Such systems will be common in this country by the mid-eighties. Meanwhile, the industry is concentrating on the immediate prospect of expanding distributed processing networks and services for business. Its goal is the automated workplace, the so-called "office of the future." For all of its oversold future, the integrated electronic office system is on the way. Office-of-the-future enthusiasts are fond of declaring that, while industrial productivity rose nearly 90 percent during the seventies, office productivity went up only 4 percent. Further, they add, average capital expenditure per office worker was only two thousand dollars compared with twenty-five thousand dollars for the factory worker. The figures are slightly suspect, as well as the apples-and-oranges comparison. It is true, nevertheless, that productivity has declined steadily in offices, which are a major part of the secondary, or bureaucratic, sector in the Department of Commerce's study of the information economy described earlier in this chapter. Whether machines can turn around, or even modify, the bureaucracies' devotion to Parkinson's Law on programmed inefficiency remains to be seen.[27] What is certain is that a $15-billion-a-year industry is expanding, with its market focused on sophisticated office word-processing machines, terminals, long-distance facsimile equipment, phototypesetting machines, high-speed printers, and related communications gear. The business is dominated by such old-line equipment manufacturers as IBM, Xerox, and Burroughs, although there are many newcomers, including Exxon.

This equipment, much of it linked to networks outside the office, is actually an electronic mail and storage system. In fact, over 85 percent of all first class postal service mail can be handled electronically. This includes bills and other business forms that now form the largest share of postal volume. The prospects for an electronic postal service are reinforced every time a piece of the new high-technology office equipment is installed. Whether this network will be run by the postal service, by private firms, or by a combination of both is an important issue that has yet to be resolved.

In summary, the economics of the information and communications hardware industry are being transformed by technology. Even IBM, the rock on which the computer industry was built, has not been spared. The firm's share of U.S.-based companies' shipments of computer hardware dropped from 61 percent in 1974 to 50 percent in 1980. The statistics reflect the general shift to smaller minicomputers and away from mainframe products, where IBM has been traditionally strong. The initial minicomputer market was dominated by such innovative upstarts as Digital Equipment, Hewlett-Packard, and Data General. However, at the beginning of the eighties, IBM was clearly not to be counted out as overall industry leader. Following a three-year period in which it invested $4 billion in cash (and another billion from its first bond offering ever), the company came on strong with a new line of small computers and associated distributed data processing equipment that reinforced its position as the major competitor in the field. The changeover was not without cost: in 1979 the firm suffered its first decline in net profits since the early fifties. Meanwhile, it strengthened its hold on the big mainframe market in 1980 with a new product line that included machines twice as powerful as the company's previous large computers.[28]

The strategic industrial focus of the eighties will, however, be on semiconductors, the tiny chips that are the power modules of the new computers and most other information and communications hardware. They are, one industry expert declares, the crude oil of the 1980s: "From a strategic point of view, this industry is sitting on the reserves that are necessary for the future growth of the economy." Semiconductor production began in the late sixties with a small group of innovative companies playing technological leapfrog with one another in the race to develop more efficient products. By the early eighties, the industry has moved into early middle age and many of the pioneering firms are being absorbed into larger corporations dependent on their products. Only seven of the thirty-six semi-

conductor firms that began operations in the late sixties were still independently owned by 1980.[29]

Foreign competition, threatening to cause a significant loss of
U.S. leadership in semiconductor research and production, was an
important factor in this shift. Japanese and European firms, supported by government resources, are mounting a serious effort to dis-
place U.S. research leadership and to erode the two thirds share of
world markets held by American firms in 1980. With their easier access to sources of capital investments, the large firms now beginning
to dominate semiconductor production should be in a better position
to assure continued U.S. leadership.[30] Significantly, however, the
most advanced new semiconductor plant to be built in the United
States in 1982 is owned by Japan's Nippon Electric Corporation.

One area in which U.S. dominance will be maintained for some
time is in the collection and storage of specialized information — the
so-called "data banks." The reason for this is simple: American firms
began to gather up and store such information, as well as to distribute it, usually for a profit, earlier than anyone else. The result has
been to make this country the information bank of the world. No one
knows how many data banks there are, since the industry's definitions
are vague. The banks come in all sizes and purposes. The Medlars
bank at the National Institute of Health provides doctors with sum-
maries of the latest medical research, abstracted from over two
thousand journals. Congress has a data bank to track the progress, or
lack of it, for every bill introduced into the House or Senate. The
National Technical Information Service in Springfield, Virginia, supplies
material on over a million items of research funded by the
federal government in recent years. A Canadian researcher has cata-
logued every known performance of Shakespeare's plays. The list
goes on.

The data bank industry is increasingly dominated by a group of
old-line publishing companies who have in recent years realized that
they are really information handlers. These firms are beginning to put
their print products into computers and to sell them as data. The
New York Times took the lead with its "Information Bank," a computerized version of a newspaper morgue, containing all the information that has appeared in the paper since the late sixties, when the
bank began.[31] The Information Bank has been expanded to include
the contents of sixty other newspapers and magazines, which are also
made available on terminals to customers throughout the country.
And in 1981, The Times added a special Middle East data section to

the bank. Other publishing firms that are moving into data bank operations are Dow Jones, McGraw-Hill, Dun & Bradstreet, and the *Reader's Digest.*

Data banks and other sectors of the information industry will expand rapidly during the eighties. There will be numerous shake-outs as technology and economics combine to challenge the competitive standings of both the old-line firms and the upstarts. The bulk of their business, and profits, will come from sales to other industries engaged in the massive reindustrialization process now underway. A still open question about the future of the information industry is whether there will be a *consumerization* of the market, in which goods and services will be supplied to the home. The answer will have an important effect on a third major telecommunications area — radio and television broadcasting.

Until recently, radio and TV were secure in their dominant positions, supplying news and entertainment to a mass consumer market. Protected from the shocks of outside competition by benevolent government licensing and regulatory arrangements, the broadcasters prospered on their ability to provide advertisers with a range of audiences readily identified by age, sex, and income level in their programming tastes.

The debate on television's beneficent or baleful influences on American life will go on for a long time without conclusive results. What is clear is that the unchallenged dominance of commercial TV and radio is coming to an end.[32] Each will continue to be a powerful influence in its present form for a long time, but at a slowly decreasing level. The reasons for the shift are complex. Contrary to the self-fulfilling prophecies of TV's critics, there are few indications that people are getting bored with television or that their tastes are improving. There are other reasons why they are beginning to spend more time away from the TV screen. One significant element, at least for daytime TV, is that more women are working outside the home than ever before. Another is that competition for audience attention is being challenged by a range of new communications channels and services.

The Big Three networks face growing competition from a range of specialized "fourth networks" that rely on satellite distribution of their programs. The most extensive of these grids is operated by the Public Broadcasting System and National Public Radio which have used satellites since 1978 to provide their member stations with a broad mix of national and regional programs. The result has been to give local PBS and NPR stations more control over their programming choices, a major objective of public broadcasting. Another specialized network using satellites and microwave relays is the Spanish International Network (SIN), serving what will be by the end of the decade the largest ethnic minority in the nation. SIN began feeding Hispanic programming to nine stations in 1977; part of its offerings come from Mexico's national network by direct relay from Mexico City. Another satellite network, the Christian Broadcasting Network (CBN), offers fundamentalist gospel programming from its headquarters in Virginia Beach, Virginia, to hundreds of cable systems throughout the country.

A highly successful "fourth network" servicing cable systems by satellite has been developed by Ted Turner, a flamboyant Georgian who controls, among other enterprises, television station WTCG in Atlanta. Turner has transformed WTCG into a "super station" through satellite transmission of its programs to cable systems throughout the country. Within months after he announced his plan in 1977, over five hundred cable systems in twenty-seven states applied to carry the WTCG signal.[33] By the end of 1980, the network had been extended to over eight hundred cable systems. Cable viewers got a new entertainment channel — mostly old films and TV reruns — while Turner's station extended its audience to several million additional households, with appropriate advertising revenue benefits. In 1980, Turner added the first cable news network to his operation. His success led to a number of other "super station" operations throughout the country.

The most dramatic proposal for new national networking involves direct-to-the-home satellite broadcasting. In 1981, Satellite Television Corporation, an affiliate of the Communications Satellite Corporation, was given approval by the FCC to plan such a service, with entertainment and other programming beamed directly to rooftop antennas. At the same time, thirteen other companies requested permission to develop similar services. Many of these projects, involving readily available technology and considerable programming funds, could be implemented in the latter half of the decade.

A more earthbound threat to the TV networks' ability to attract a mass audience is the range of new machines that can provide alternative news and entertainment facilities in the home. As consumer items, most of these are still in the early developmental stages, but they each represent an alternative to regular TV viewing. The concept of an "electronic newspaper," challenging commercial TV's strong hold on news delivery to homes, was given its first practical experiment in 1980, when an Ohio newspaper, the *Columbus Dis-*

patch began transmitting its entire editorial content to three thousand home terminals around the country on a computer network.[34] At the same time, the Knight-Ridder newspaper chain was experimenting with a system to provide news, advertising, and other consumer services to homes in Coral Gables, Florida. More advanced systems, similar to those already in use in Britain, France, and Japan, are in the planning stages now and should be put into application by the middle of the decade.

After years of big promises and false starts, two other technologies — videotape and videodisc — moved into commercial markets in the early eighties. The early lead for the vast consumer market was taken by videotape machines, which permitted recording of TV programs for later viewing and for showings of the expanding catalogue of old Hollywood movies being recycled once again. With a dozen major electronic companies vying for the business, prices for the recording machines fell below the thousand dollar mark, opening the prospects for mass market appeal, the results of which could revolutionize television and other home entertainment patterns as well as the film industry.[35]

The most important potential challenge to network television has been around, in a different form, for some time. It is cable television — originally known as CATV, for Cable Antenna Television. CATV dates back to the early fifties when hundreds of small systems were installed in suburban and rural areas to provide improved reception of over-the-air TV programs from nearby cities. The equipment was simple: a tall antenna to catch the signal and a cable to relay it to subscriber homes. Broadcasters welcomed CATV, since it extended their audience range and therefore their advertising-revenue base. However, this CATV bonus has turned into a threat as cable operators begin to supply other programming services.

After years of delayed promises of cable programming abundance, cable TV services finally became a significant factor in the midseventies. The first successful national cable programmer was Home Box Office (HBO). A subsidiary of Time Inc., HBO began distributing current Hollywood films and sports events in 1973 to cable systems. It took the firm five years to turn its first profit, but by 1977 it had eight hundred thousand subscribers on more than 370 cable systems across the country. Its success coincided with its inspired decision to distribute its programs by satellite, cutting its transmission costs significantly and allowing it to reach every cable system in the nation.[36] The pay-TV rush was on as other big media conglomerates elbowed their way to sign up cable systems for their films. The boom has propelled the industry into an expansion that would have seemed visionary a decade ago. By 1981, there were over three thousand cable systems with almost twenty million home "hook-ups." This represents a twenty-five percent penetration of all U.S. homes, with the prospect that over half will be cable-connected by the end of the decade. In the competitive scramble for cable franchises and home customers, cable companies will expand their program offerings beyond pay-TV Hollywood films to other programs and services.

The first large demonstration of a full range of cable services was inaugurated in Columbus, Ohio, late in 1977 by the Warner Cable Corporation, one of the largest national cable firms. The project has been a test of cable's ability to merchandise its services in urban areas. Its basic product — retransmission of regular television signals — had not been a big selling point in cities where TV signals are generally satisfactory.

Warner's Columbus system, known as Qube, offered a Chinese menu of services on thirty channels. These included transmission of nine regular TV station signals (five of them imported from other cities), a variety of locally produced community programs, and several "premium" channels providing new movies, sports events, arts programs, and educational courses. The system is interactive; five response buttons on each Qube home terminal allow subscribers to participate in local game shows, vote on referenda, take quizzes, and purchase products from local stores. There is a "home security option" providing fire, burglary, and emergency service connections. The original basic cost to a subscriber was about eleven dollars a month, with extra charges for first-run films and other premium services.

By the end of 1979, after two years of operation, Qube had twenty-six thousand home subscribers and had begun to turn a modest profit for Warner. It also provided the firm with other benefits that could not be measured in bookkeeping terms. Qube proved that there was an urban market for sophisticated cable services. As the first company to demonstrate this, Warner was the frontrunner in the early eighties in the competition for cable franchises in large cities. Within a few months in 1980 it had won franchises in Dallas, Pittsburgh, and Cincinnati, largely on the strength of its Qube experience.[37]

The competition for building urban systems will be fierce in the coming years. Franchises in New York, Chicago, Boston, and Washington, among other cities, have been important prizes. The competitors will include large communications conglomerates such as

Time Inc., Cox Communications, the Westinghouse Corporation, the Times Mirror Company, and the Storer Broadcasting Company. Since cables must be installed underground (rather than on telephone poles) in many urban areas, the cost of cabling city neighborhoods is very high. In the intense jockeying for position, the cable industry has witnessed a bewildering pattern of mergers and amalgamations in recent years, prompted largely by the need for greater financial resources to play the urban cable game. In 1980, Warner Cable, which is a subsidiary of Warner Communications, Inc., strengthened its financial base by sellling 50 percent interest to American Express and changing its name to Warner Amex.

The significance of infusing major financial resources into urban cable projects goes well beyond merchandising Hollywood films or major league sports. The new urban networks can provide the missing links for the development of a full-service consumer-oriented information utility, the network marketplace envisioned by researcher Herbert Dordick and his colleagues in their studies of the economics of information services that we discussed in chapter two. The ability to get high-capacity cable facilities in urban areas is critical to the development of an economically viable national network. Such a network could be a reality by the end of the decade if cable facilities are installed in a significant number of large U.S. cities. It will involve massive funding that will be possible only if the cable industry can continue to attract large investors, in deals like the Warner–American Express agreement described above. American Express not only brought financial resources to Warner, but also its broad merchandising expertise, a key element in the potential success of the new cable-based network marketplace.

Most of these plans for expanding information services to the mass consumer level are still in their early stages. Many of them will fall by the wayside, victims of poor management, financial anemia, or both. However, others will succeed, with high-capacity cable systems offering the greatest hope for realizing the benefits of a full information utility.

Success will depend primarily on economic decisions about the viability of such a system. A new communications and information infrastructure is being built. The strategies for assuring that it will provide a full range of consumer services are still to be worked out. How does a society make wise decisions in this critical area? The answers are not clear. However, as war is too important to leave to the generals, so the future of the information society is too important to leave to IBM, AT&T, ITT, CBS, and the other private communications powers. Political decisions involving public consensus are needed, and we will examine this prospect next.

Notes

1. Robert LeBlanc et al., "Changes and Opportunities in Telecommunications," *Telecommunications Industry Monthly*, issued by Salomon Brothers, New York, 1 February 1978, p. 1.

2. "Communications," *Forbes*, 15 September 1977, p. 139.

3. "Technology — Elixir for U.S. Industry," *New York Times*, 28 September 1980, sect. 3, p. 1.

4. Eli Ginzburg, "The Professionalization of the U.S. Labor Force," *Scientific American*, March 1979, pp. 48–53.

5. "America Tries to Cure Its Innovation Blues," *The Economist* (London), 6 September 1980, p. 83.

6. John Dizard, "The Revolution in Telecommunications Finance," *Institutional Investor*, September 1979, p. 143.

7. George J. Stigler, "The Economics of Information," *Journal of Political Economy*, June 1961, p. 213.

8. Fritz Machlup, *The Production and Distribution of Knowledge in the United States* (Princeton, N.J.: Princeton University Press, 1962).

9. U.S. Department of Commerce, *The Information Economy*, 9 vols. Office of Telecommunications, Special Publication 77–12, May 1977.

10. *Ibid.*, vol. 1, p. 2.

11. *Ibid.*, vol. 1, p. 3.

12. John R. Bermuth, "Value and Volume of Literacy," *Visible Language*, 12, no. 2 (Spring 1978): pp. 118–61.

13. Quoted in Gerald D. Rosen, "Communications Dog Fight," *Dun's Review*, June 1977, p. 18.

14. "Government, AT&T Fire First Salvos at Trial," *New York Times*, 16 January 1981, p. D-3.

15. Erik Barnouw, *Tube of Plenty* (New York: Oxford University Press, 1975), pp. 43–50.

16. Mr. Kappel's prediction is reported in "On the Head of a Pin," *Forbes*, 15 September 1976, p. 32.

17. "High Stakes in Bell-MCI Case," *New York Times*, 13 June 1980, p. D-1.

18. Manley R. Irwin, "Where Do Computers Leave Off and Communications Begin?", *Telephone Engineering and Management*, 15 January 1976, p. 30.

19. "Innovation: Key to Bell's Plans," *New York Times*, 16 July 1979, p. D-1. For a history of the Bell System's research activities, see Prescott C. Mabon, *Mission Communications: The Story of the Bell Laboratories*, published by Bell Laboratories in 1975.

20. "Bell Plans to Increase Capacity of AT&T's Domestic Satellite," *New York Times*, 30 September 1977, p. C-7.

21. "What Restructuring Means for AT&T," *New York Times*, 31 August 1980, sect. 3, p. 2.

22. "Ma Bell Faces Life," *Forbes*, 1 November 1977, p. 52.

23. "A Strategy for the Telephone," *New York Times*, 18 May 1980, p. D-3.

24. "Intercity Network Market Pie Cut into More Slices," *Communications News*, February 1980, p. 28.

25. "Versatile Xerox," *Barron's*, 29 September 1980, p. 9.

26. The problem of technical compatibility between the systems was resolved largely in May 1981 when AT&T announced that it would adopt a standard compatible with the Canadian and French systems. Given the Bell System's economic and technological influence, its standard will probably be adopted worldwide.

27. Jon Stewart, "Computer Shock," *Saturday Review*, 23 June 1979, p. 14.

28. For an estimate of IBM's long-term plans, see "No. 1's Awesome Strategy," *Business Week*, 8 June 1981, pp. 84–90.

29. "Can Semi-conductors Survive Big Business," *Business Week*, 3 December 1979, p. 66.

30. *Ibid.*

31. Anthony Smith, "All the News That Fits in the Databank," *Saturday Review*, 23 June 1979, pp. 18–19.

32. An interesting projection of long-term shifts in television and other mass media can be found in Richard Maisel, "The Decline of the Mass Media," *Public Opinion Quarterly*, Summer 1973, pp. 159–70. See also "Television's Fragmented Future," *Business Week*, 17 December 1979, pp. 60–66.

33. "Superstation Breakthrough," *Broadcasting*, 30 October 1978, p. 25.

34. "First U.S. Experiments in Electronic News," *New York Times*, 7 July 1980, p. B-13.

35. "How a Video Revolution Is Shaping the Future of Film," *New York Times*, 23 November 1980, p. D-1.

36. "The Rise of American Pay-TV," *The Economist* (London), 29 July 1978, pp. 62–63.

37. "Warner Amex — Cable's Winner," *New York Times*, 21 November 1980, p. D-1.

Chapter Six

The Politics of Change

How does a society make wise decisions? How do we determine who we are and what we want to become? How do we organize ourselves and our resources to match these perceptions? These questions are particularly relevant to information and communications policy. A fast-changing society needs access to greater knowledge resources to handle the uncertainties and disruptions that change brings.

Until now our examination of information age strategies has concentrated on technological and economic developments. The United States has already crossed the technological divide into the new age. There are no longer any serious physical barriers to the creation of a full-scale information network utility. We are now crossing the economic divide, as shown in the 1977 Department of Commerce study on the information economy and in more recent research. The major unresolved issues are in the political arena, involving basic decisions on the form and purpose of the new information environment.

This is the most sensitive point in the entire transition. Technology and economics deal largely with immediate problems, focused on particular outcomes in terms of their specific success or failure. As influences on the U.S. information environment, they are powered by their own internal dynamics. Left to themselves, they could create a post-industrial information structure that would be difficult to modify with public policies in the future, if we should wish to do so. On the other hand, reaching consensus in any area of public policy is difficult, especially in communications and information matters. There are strong contending interests involved, together with a healthy First Amendment tradition against government interference in these areas.

Nevertheless we have arrived at a point at which public decisions are becoming imperative. Technical and economic developments are converging in ways that require a clearer definition of their relationships to overall social goals. Until recently, the pace of technical and economic changes has been a linear progression, spread across many years. The transitions from telegraph to telephone, from radio and television to computers and satellites were marked by relatively long pauses, allowing time for us to sort out their economic and social consequences. Today this time-frame is compressed, marked by a convergence of technologies with overlapping decision complexities. As a result, communications and information are being regarded as general political issues, instead of, as in the past, the concerns solely of the industry and a few government agencies.[1]

Public involvement in these policy subjects is still fragmentary, but it is there and it is growing. There is a general recognition of the need for a new information resources design that assures all of us the advantages these resources offer. This goal seemed easier twenty years ago, when many of the early prophets of the information age painted a rosy-hued picture of its prospects. This occurred during what might be called the "first computer decade," roughly from 1960 to 1970. Then, the electronic mythos was in full flower, based on the unfolding promise of computers and high-speed communications circuits. There were visions of a new order of data richness and computer-assisted decision making, a more efficient social competence replacing the old disorderly ways of managing issues and events.

It was a heady goal, spurred by the rhetoric of Kennedy's New Frontier and Johnson's Great Society, together with almost uninterrupted economic prosperity. The literature inspired by this vision evoked memories of the earlier technocracy movement of the 1930s with its engineered solutions to social problems. In the thirties, the great dams of the Tennessee Valley Authority were the prototype for future technocratic success. In the sixties, the model was the Apollo space program and its systems-analysis path to the moon. The new computer-based age would bring similar analytic efficiency to such earthbound problems as education, poverty, foreign policy, transportation, and the cities. Writing in March 1967, a team of researchers studying inner city problems in Detroit declared, "We feel that, in a very real sense, the age of the computer has ushered in a new age of urban planning."[2]

Four months later, Detroit went up in flames, urban renewal projects included. The smoky pall that hung over the city for days was a pungent reminder that stubborn social problems were not amenable to computer printout solutions. Civil disorder was followed by escalation in Vietnam, economic setbacks, and the public scandals that culminated in Watergate. The experience with the new information technologies during the first computer decade, however overblown, had its usefulness in defining the limits of computerized shortcuts. The result has been a more realistic view of the role of communications and information — as important but not cure-all resources in reducing economic and social problems.

If there is now a better understanding of what can be done practically, it is also true that we are still only at the beginning of a consensus on how to go about it. The prospect is still a promising one: providing everyone access to a full range of information resources, allowing every person, as Emerson urged, to produce that peculiar fruit each was born to bear. But this objective forces us to face some fundamental questions. Having reached the point where it is technically possible, is full access to information one of our basic rights in a post-industrial democratic society? Or is it simply a desirable long-range goal, whose attainment will be left to the play of economic and social forces, a linear extension — with some technological flourishes — of what we are now doing, with benefits trickling down largely through the workings of the market?

Choices between these options will reflect our contemporary view of the democratic tradition of open information, which supports our need to know, our right to challenge. We have made many public commitments to these ideals in the past two centuries. Those most relevant to our present situation were the decisions favoring universal free public education over a century ago. Our forebears agreed that this was a necessary democratic entitlement, and so, with some lapses, saw that it was provided. Public education moved from one-room schoolhouses to consolidated schools to our present variegated patterns of learning opportunities. In the post-industrial era, compuers and related information devices can be an effective part of a new lifelong learning cycle quite different in style from traditional classroom practices. To what degree will we extend our concept of education to include greater access to these information resources? The response to this question will signal, to a considerable degree, our willingness to evolve to higher forms of democracy in the new era.

The alternative — restricted access — may push us towards a controlled, perhaps even benevolent, authoritarianism in which an elite has effective control over key information resources and uses this power to manipulate a complaisant *lumpenproletariat*. An amusing, if somewhat chilling, illustration of this possibility was provided several years ago by a Columbia University professor, Alan Westin. It takes place in the early years of the next century, when an authoritarian information elite, working out of National Databank Headquarters in Philadelphia, controls the rest of society. Their plan is temporarily set back by an assault on their computers by a terrorist group known as the Fold, Staple, Spindle, and Mutilate movement. The elite leaders defeat the terrorists, and take the ultimate step of programming every event in each citizen's life to prevent further disruption. Professor Westin's scenario ends with a surprise twist that suggests that human freedom may prevail. We may never have to contend with such a dire situation, but we do have to face up to the future consequences of present trends pushing us towards an information environment where questions of access, control, and privacy are still unresolved.

These are political questions, and the answers will come from the untidy, often frustrating give-and-take of political action. The basic issue is the control and distribution of power, enhanced by the ability of the new technologies to permit massive centralization and manipulation of a wider range of information resources than ever before. This issue was identified by Karl Deutsch in his masterful work, *The Nerves of Government*, published in 1963, in which he argued that control of information resources and communications channels was displacing traditional forces — the military and the police — as the measure of power.[3] This has always been true to some extent, but the new technologies vastly enhance the prospect. This fact argues powerfully against our present inclination to leave major decisions in communications and information to the economic and technological sectors. It is putting a burden on those sectors that they are not equipped to handle, and that may be harmful to their orderly development over the long run.

This point was stressed by a former AT&T board chairman, John deButts, several years ago when he said, "It is not technology that will shape the future of telecommunications in this country. Nor is it the market. It is policy."[4] Mr. deButts made his remarks in the course of presenting his company's ideas on what national telecommunications policy should be. Whatever the details of his advocacy (a unique one, as befits the Bell System's special status), he acknowledged — as many of his shortsighted industry counterparts do not — the need for public debate and decision on the future of American communications.

Participatory democracy, an informed citizenry, a strong economy, technologies that serve human needs — these are the stakes in our consideration of the prospects for viable communications and information policies in post-industrial America. It is well to dismiss at the start any fantasies we may have about a tidy master plan for the new information environment. Such an approach would be unacceptable to almost everyone concerned, since no one would be prepared to suspend his or her negotiating rights in the rough-and-tumble of political negotiation of sensitive issues in the interests of a neat, orderly, and probably unworkable system. A more realistic approach is to define minimum guidelines and goals for the near-term, say the next decade. This will be difficult enough, given the obstacles involved.

Any agreed-upon policies will, for instance, have to be grafted onto complex existing structures, controlled largely by organizations that are generally unwilling to trade the promise of long-term gains for present advantages. The changes will have to be nudged, coddled, and cajoled through a political process heavily influenced by interest groups who settle their differences through complex compromises.

Serious consideration of communications and information issues is hindered by the fact that political leaders generally do not regard them as critical. The issues involved seem too abstruse, too wrapped up in technological and economic complexities to attract sustained popular attention. As noted earlier, this attitude is changing as communications and information impinge more directly on people's lives and interests.

Nevertheless, the present lack of any clear-cut public consensus inhibits the development of strategies for dealing with information age issues. Political scientist Harold Lasswell once suggested that an annual balance sheet of "gross enlightenment outcome" of the nation be drawn up so that there would be a measure for necessary knowledge resources. As yet, however, there are no firm indicators of public needs in this area — a handicap to intelligent planning.

The result is a kind of tinker-toy approach; we are trying to piece together bits and parts of a complex structure without knowing quite what we want it to do for us. The results will inevitably be disappointing unless we can agree on a blueprint that combines economic and technological resources with social goals in a workable fashion.

What are the prospects for such a blueprint? The answer begins with the Constitution, that very flexible document which set down the basic guidelines, in law and in practice, for American approaches to communications and information. The Constitution alludes directly to communications in only one passage, which deals with the powers of Congress "to establish Post Offices and post roads." The document's most abiding influence in this area, however, comes from the First Amendment prohibition against laws abridging freedom of speech and the press. Any discussion of policy on communications or information begins with, and returns to, this fact. These strictures against government involvement explain why the United States is unique in not having a centralized bureaucracy to directly control or heavily regulate communications.

As a result, communications policy is defined and carried out by a large number of public entities at the federal, state, and local levels. The pattern is confusing, often overlapping, and frequently contradictory. Whatever the faults of this system, it reflects a common agreement to limit government intervention in the communications and information field, particularly in those areas affecting First Amendment rights. The pattern has also been shaped by pressures from the private sector against excessive regulations, that is, over and above the numerous laws and regulations designed to protect its own interests.

The limitation of government activities in the communications field was set early in the telecommunications age. The first federal involvement was to provide financial support for the initial demonstration of Samuel Morse's telegraph system between Washington and Baltimore in 1844, although this support was withdrawn the following year. In the following decades, the telegraph and telephone systems developed under private auspices, with government playing a generally benign supportive role.

The same pattern applied internationally. The United States refused to join the new International Telegraph Union, founded in 1865 to provide needed international standards for the new telegraph networks. The United States' refusal was based in part on the fact that it had few international communications links at the time, but more pointedly on a general suspicion about foreign interference in U.S. communications affairs. It was not until the turn of the century, when the British-controlled Marconi Wireless Company attempted to establish a global monopoly over radio communications, that the United States joined the Telegraph Union to protect its interests and, in particular, to thwart the British monopoly.

Technological developments after the First World War forced a stepping-up of government involvement in communications. The Federal Radio Commission was established in 1927 to sort out the chaotic frequency situation caused by an influx of hundreds of new stations. Before the Commission began its work, radio stations gained "authorization" by sending a letter to the Department of Commerce simply notifying it that they were on the air.[5] The Communications Act of 1934 set out more comprehensive legislative standards, including the establishment of the Federal Communications Commission (FCC). The creation of the FCC was an important step in providing a mechanism for sorting out many of the pragmatic problems brought on by the new technologies. However, its authority has been limited to regulating the telecommunications industry. Fast-moving technological developments make it increasingly difficult to define the boundaries of its jurisdiction. A fifty-year-old communications act, designed to cope with telephones and radios, does not provide much help.

The bureaucratic process for dealing with communications and information has developed gradually over the years. Until World War II, government communications matters were handled as a part-time concern of the military. The Navy took the lead in the 1920s in helping create the Radio Corporation of America (now RCA) as a U.S. "chosen instrument" for challenging foreign competition in international communications. The need to set up a worldwide communications network during World War II focused official attention on communications policy matters for the first time. President Truman later appointed a special assistant for telecommunications to deal with the issue. The office and its duties were expanded in a series or reorganizations under presidents Eisenhower, Kennedy, and Johnson. But these changes still left communications policy as a small-fry concern in the bureaucratic fishpond.

The Kennedy administration became more deeply involved in communications policy in 1962 as the result of a technological breakthrough. The technology was the communications satellite, whose capabilities were demonstrated in July of that year when NASA launched AT&T's *Telstar*, the first active repeater satellite capable of switching incoming and outgoing messages in space. (Previous experiments involved passive satellites, with signals bounced off a balloon.) It was a major technical achievement that immediately raised political and economic questions.

The politics involved problems of organizing a system, both domestically and internationally, for exploiting the new technology. Intelligence reports at the time indicated that the Soviet Union was actively engaged in similar satellite research. In that post-*Sputnik* era, the thought of another Soviet space success, and the prospect that the Soviets might take the lead in organizing a global satellite network, was a sharp goad causing Kennedy administration officials and Congressional leaders to move quickly. The result, decided upon in record time for major legislation, was the Communications Satellite Act of 1962, which set up the Communications Satellite Corporation (Comsat) and detailed a plan for organizing an American-sponsored international satellite system. Comsat would be the government's "chosen instrument" for organizing the system and representing the United States in its management.

It was an innovative solution, combining both public and private sector elements, which provided the basic framework for the development of the highly successful Intelsat global system, owned by over a hundred nations. The 1962 legislation was a critical event in focusing American attention on communications policy matters, even though it dealt with only one, albeit an important, aspect of the problem.[6]

A hopeful step toward the development of a coherent policy was taken in the late sixties when the Johnson administration appointed a Presidential commission to study the subject. The commission, headed by Yale law professor Eugene Rostow, made a thoughtful and controversial attempt at the first national overview of communications issues. It defined communications as a critical issue in U.S. society and proposed a series of specific actions for strengthening its role in economic and social development.[7]

Along the way, the commission's report also challenged longstanding government and corporate interests. Given the complex nature of these interests, this was perhaps inevitable, as was the fact that the report was quietly relegated to that special Washington limbo for controversial advisory commission reports. Nevertheless, the Rostow study was important because it did attempt to present a coherent view of the future implications of technological, economic, and social developments in communications. It set a basic agenda which is still valid — no mean achievement.

The Rostow study also influenced the Nixon administration, in 1969, to take a more serious look at the way in which communications policy matters were organized. The result was a decision to upgrade the subject in an enlarged White House unit known as the Office of Telecommunications Policy (OTP) with a charter for coordinating overall government policy and planning on the subject. Setting up OTP was a significant step toward a more rational national approach to communications, but its effectiveness was almost immediately compromised by political controversy. The new office became the Nixon White House's stalking horse for an attack on the alleged liberal biases of the major television networks. Its charges reinforced the fears of the industry and of Congress that the administration intended to use the new office to gain political control over the media in the U.S. This, together with the general distrust of OTP by old-line government agencies concerned with communications matters, effectively ended the hope that OTP would bring a fresh approach to national communications planning. The fact that the office performed some valuable services, particularly in funding policy research projects, was hidden in the black political clouds that surrounded most of its history.

In 1977 it was inevitable that the new Carter administration would abolish the unit. With an eye on the political sensitivities involved, the Carter planners rejected suggestions for a replacement that would have a stronger charter for coordinating policy and planning matters. Instead, they redistributed OTP's functions, assigning the bulk of them to a new agency, the National Telecommunications and Information Administration (NTIA), in the Department of Commerce. NTIA was immediately perceived as weaker than the OTP, particularly because it had no direct bureaucratic entrée to the White House, as did the OTP. However, it is a well-established Washington rule that proximity, bureaucratic or otherwise, to the White House can be an elusive benefit.

OTP's effectiveness was destroyed by the political connotations of its direct White House connection. (On a day-to-day basis, the connection was not all that strong.) In its early years, NTIA demonstrated that a lower political profile was, on balance, a help rather than a hindrance in its work. Like OTP, its most important assignment was to provide a coordinating point for the federal government's own communications and information activities. It is also charged with advising the President on overall national policy in these areas. Significantly, for the first time telecommunications and information have been newly paired as common policy concerns in one agency, a welcome recognition of the technological and economic realities of the information age. With the advent of the Reagan administration, there has been an attempt by some of the more conservative advisers to eliminate NTIA, primarily on the theory that any such federal policy involvement in these areas is undesirable. After some confusion, the administration has retained the NTIA structure with some modifications.

If coordination has been the key word in NTIA's mission, it has also been its most difficult task. The image is of a tidy system meant to bring coherence and order to the federal establishment's far-flung involvement in communications and information matters. The reality is considerably more complex, and less neat.[8] The federal government's involvement is a tangle of facilities and operations — from the White House office that instantaneously provides circuits for the President wherever he may be, to Voice of America transmitters in the Thailand jungles, to the dogsleds used by the postal service to deliver mail in Alaska.

By one estimate, federal communications facilities were capitalized at $67 billion in 1977 and were expected to rise to $100 billion by the mid-eighties.[9] The federal government controls over half of all the radio frequencies assigned to this country under international agreements. It is also by far the world's largest owner and user of computers, though no one is quite sure how many it has.

The agency most heavily involved in telecommunications and information operations is the Defense Department, which uses half of all the frequencies assigned to the government. Although the military has extensive telecommunications facilities of its own, it is heavily dependent on civilian communications. The problems of meshing the two systems came to a head during the 1962 Cuban missile crisis, when serious coordination gaps emerged. This led to the first attempt to develop a strategic-communications plan, centered around the establishment of a National Communications System with the Secretary of Defense as executive agent. The case for such a policy was made at the time by Dr. Harold Brown, then Defense Department Director of Research:

> It is . . . important to recognize that our domestic and international telecommunications systems are critical factors both in our military posture and in our cold war struggle and, indeed, throughout the whole spectrum of conflict. We cannot today consider our communications systems solely as civil activities merely to be regulated as such, but we must consider them as essential instruments of national policy in our struggle for survival and establish policy and organizations consistent with our situation.[10]

The National Communications System charter is limited to assuring government communications "under all conditions from a normal situation to national emergencies and international crises, including nuclear attack." The Secretary of Defense is responsible for the daily operations of the system under White House policy direction. Several attempts have been made to expand the system's scope since it was set up, but these have been resisted by other elements in the government's communications establishment.

There are, conservatively, two dozen civilian government agencies with major communications and information responsibilities. The largest of these is the postal service, a hybrid organization operating in a bureaucratic no-man's-land, heavily dependent on government subsidies. The postal service is, for all its faults, a major element in the national information and communications network. Moreover, its future is the subject of considerable debate, particularly concerning its antiquated methods of using high-priced hand labor to carry pieces of paper to tens of millions of homes and offices every working day.

Besides the postal service, there is a conglomeration of other agencies with major communications and information responsibilities. These include the Department of Transportation, which handles air and maritime communications; the State Department, which handles negotiation of international agreements; the International Communications Agency, operating the Voice of America overseas radio network and other media facilities; the National Aeronautics and Space Administration, handling communications satellite experimentation; the Central Intelligence Agency, seeing to analysis of telecommunications developments abroad; and the National Security Agency, a highly classified operation monitoring foreign communications. Other agencies are also involved, though less obviously. The Federal Bureau of Investigation operates extensive files on American citizens and electronic links to local police authorities. Its capabilities, however, fall short of the computerized national crime information network it and many local police departments have pressed for, despite so far successful resistance by civil liberties advocates who claim that such a system could lead to abuses. Another agency with extensive information responsibilities is the Internal Revenue Service, with its extensive files on what Americans earn and spend. In 1978, as a result of congressional and other pressures, the Carter administration halted the development of an $850 million computer network designed to provide IRS agents with immediate access to the detailed records of taxpayers and corporations.[11] Another government-controlled information base affecting most citizens is operated by the Social Security Administration and contains millions of separate files on almost anyone who has ever had a job in this country since the mid-thirties.

Less known examples of federal information activities are the scientific and professional services provided by the government both for its internal and for general public use. The medical profession relies heavily on MEDLARS and MEDLINE, the National Library of Medicine's computerized compilation of articles published in medical journals throughout the world. Industry and research institutes make extensive use of the Department of Commerce's National Technical Information Service (NTIS), a computer-based source of technical research done by federal agencies. Educators turn to ERIC, the data base operated by the Department of Education, for information in their field. The Smithsonian Institution's Science Information Exchange indexes about ten thousand research projects a month as part of an effort to keep track of research the federal government pays for.

The overall issue of government-held computerized information has been the subject of intense debate in recent years. The technological prospect that previously independent data banks can be interconnected means that information collected by one agency can be made available to many. This led to recommendations that government-held computerized information be centralized in an interconnected data system. The arguments of those stressing the efficiency of such a system have so far been successfully challenged by those who fear its misuse.

The proliferating and jealously guarded division of responsibility over communications and information among so many agencies has at least lessened the threat of Big Brother centralism. But it has also inhibited the development of a workable coordinated policy approach to the problems of the new information age.

The National Telecommunications and Information Administration may eventually be able to play a significant role in improving policy coherence, but it has not yet proved its ability to do so. At present, the most important federal influence on communications and information development is the Federal Communications Commission (FCC). The Commission dates from the technologically innocent days of Franklin D. Roosevelt's first administration, at which time its principal duties were to regulate radio stations and telephone companies. The agency quickly took on the usual bias of such commissions, namely a protective attitude toward the industries it was assigned to regulate. For decades it operated in near anonymity in the grey background of Washington bureaucracy.

This situation changed slowly at first, then rapidly toward the end of the 1960s, for several reasons. New technologies began to intrude on long-standing regulations based on the older techniques. The combination of advanced technologies and more aggressive economic pressures to expand the industry brought communications and information more into the orbit of political controversy. This situation was exacerbated by an increase in public awareness, particularly in the consumer reform movement, about communications and information matters, from childrens' TV programming to telephone company rates. (After decades of being accorded almost reverential treatment by the public, the phone company found itself facing protestors with bell-shaped buttons labeled "Public Enemy No. 1.")

With its restricted mandate, the FCC was in a difficult situation, straining against the limits of outdated legislation (the Communications Act of 1934) that did not anticipate the regulatory problems raised by satellites, computers, high-capacity cable systems, and other new technologies. For many reasons, most of them having to do with the difficulties of appeasing conflicting economic interests, neither the White House nor the Congress was prepared to make controversial policy choices to resolve the conflicts in ways that would benefit the national communications and information structure.

The task has fallen largely to the FCC, which has proved to be an unwieldy agent of change. As an independent regulatory agency, it is not directly accountable to Congress or to the President, although it clearly must take into account signals from both these sources. In the absence of legislated policy, the Commission is a policymaker by default on a wide range of issues. Its failings do not necessarily lie with the Commission or its staff.

The FCC's problem is in coping with the bits and pieces of important communications and information matters in the absence of a clearly articulated national policy. The Commission is less a regulator in the traffic cop sense than a referee without an up-to-date rulebook or even a clear whistle.

Despite these handicaps, the FCC has moved to act on a number of pressing issues in recent years. A good part of this momentum was generated by activist Commission chairman, Richard Wiley, in the early seventies. A lawyer with little previous communications experience (as he once confessed, "I thought digital communications described something you didn't do in polite society"), Wiley took initiatives over a wide range of Commission matters, adding considerable prestige and authority to the agency. However, his activism — which also had its controversial side — could not make up for the absence of overall national decisions by the White House and Congress on the shape and direction of the new information age. Uncertainty continued to hamper the Commission during the Carter years, although important decisions were made to deregulate many telecommunications services and open them up to the fresh winds of new competition. Given the conservative make up of the Commission as a result of Reagan administration appointments, this trend can be expected to continue under the agency's new chairman, Washington lawyer Mark Fowler.

A less known but still significant influence on the formation of national communications policies are the hundreds of federal advisory committees, commissions, boards, councils, and other groups that provide, with varying degrees of effectiveness, outside expertise to federal agencies. They are a particularly strong factor in the communications area, where their membership is drawn largely from industry. One survey indicated that, in 1976, eight of the eleven corporations who contributed the most personnel to all federal advisory groups were in the communications field. In part, this reflects the fact that a considerable amount of expertise — particularly in technical matters — is concentrated in the private sector. It is also an indicator of the outsized role that the industry plays in influencing small parts of a fragmented government policy-planning mechanism, sometimes deterring more effective broader based planning. Although the Carter administration made considerable progress in cutting back the number of advisory groups, the membership of most groups still tended to come from industry. A 1978 survey of advisory group membership showed that AT&T filled 120 positions on such groups.[12]

The absence of overall policy direction in communications and information does not reflect a failure to study the problems in these areas. They have been examined in numbing detail for years. As already noted, the first major study was the Rostow Commission's, reviewing a broad range of policy matters in the late sixties. This was followed by a series of competent research studies sponsored by the Nixon administration's Office of Telecommunications Policy. Throughout the seventies, the independent, congressionally funded National Academy of Engineering and the National Science Foundation sponsored useful studies on the social applications of new communications and information technologies.

Other projects examined the government's role in developing effective technical information networks — a priority concern for the scientific establishment as well as for American industry in its attempt to maintain a technological lead against increasing foreign competition. Important work in setting standards and recommending actions in this field was done by the Federal Council for Science and Technology in the 1960s. One result of this initiative was the setting up of a central source for all research results produced by federal agencies — the National Technical Information Service.

However useful these studies and the actions resulting from them, they have tended to focus on relatively small parts of the total communications and information problem. None of them recommend a general strategy for public policy in these areas. An exception was a 1976 report to President Ford entitled *National Information Policy*, prepared by the Domestic Council's committee on the right of privacy, headed by Vice-President Nelson Rockefeller. The report's major recommendation was that "the United States set as a goal the development of a coordinated National Information Policy."[13]

Although the document stressed problems of access and privacy, it touched on most of the other major political concerns involved in developing a democratically based information environment. Despite its controversial recommendations, the report had little influence, in part because it was issued in the last, lame-duck months of the Ford administration. Nevertheless, the Rockefeller committee's initiative in proposing an overall national information policy provided an important base from which other studies of this subject can be made.

Any moves toward a new approach to communications and information policy will have to consider the role of Congress. The subject is a sensitive one for Congress, involving constitutional issues as well as the relation of Congress with the executive branch and with important constituencies. This sensitivity explains why Congress has not passed a major piece of communications legislation in over forty-five years, since the Communications Act of 1934. Nevertheless, the subject is intruding more frequently on congressional agendas. By and large, Congress shares the long-time executive branch predilection for dealing with communications and information matters in a fragmentary manner.

The exception to this practice in recent years has been the effort, inspired largely by former California Congressman Lionel Van Deerlin, to revise the 1934 Communications Act. Van Deerlin, a former San Diego newsman, headed the House subcommittee on communications until he was defeated in the 1980 elections. He suggested that the committee take a hard look at the 1934 legislation with a view to making it reflect current technological and economic realities.

Van Deerlin's proposal grew out of an effort by the Bell System in 1976 on behalf of legislation known as the Consumer Communications Reform Act. This bill, quickly dubbed "the Bell Bill," was an artful attempt to strengthen AT&T's preeminent position in the telecommunications industry. The legislation in effect reaffirmed the Bell System's monopoly and proposed severe restrictions on the ability of other communications firms to compete with Bell service. The bill was opposed by most of the rest of the industry, particularly by firms whose interests would be affected by any extension of AT&T's quasi-monopoly power. Their lobbying campaign was a well-directed and, as it turned out, effective effort to kill the legislation.

The way was open for Mr. Van Deerlin and his mild-mannered suggestion that it might be better to look at all the issues in the telecommunications field, not just those directly affecting the Bell System, and to determine what changes should be made in the 1934 Communications Act. The result was the most extensive review ever made of national communications policy by Congress. Beginning in 1976, scores of witnesses appeared before Congressman Van Deerlin's subcommittees to present their views. The committee staff prepared a massive "options papers" document, outlining all the issues involved in adjusting the 1934 legislation to current economic and technological realities.[14]

The committee's hearings were a classic interest-group exercise, with all the affected parties bringing different perceptions and pressures to bear on the attempt to review and rewrite the old legislation. The communications industry was split between those arguing for the status quo and those who saw the benefits of a legislative imprimatur for the new economic and technological forces. Government agencies were generally suspicious of legislation that would affect their prerogatives. Public service groups came to the hearings with expectations of a more consumer-oriented approach to communications problems. The conflicting pressures were strong enough to stretch out the process for years, with a renewed attempt in 1981 to develop a comprehensive bill updating the 1934 legislation by the House subcommittee's new chairman, Representative Timothy Wirth, a Colorado Democrat.

Nevertheless, the House (and related Senate) hearings had their effect. They sorted out the problems involved and focused them in unique and constructive ways in a forum — the U.S. Congress — that counted. In particular, the hearings identified many of the very real policy issues involved in adjusting economic and technological factors to new information and communications needs. The process was limited in that it addressed itself primarily to the narrow framework of telecommunications. House and Senate committees were reluctant to address directly the larger issues of the information society, although they heard considerable testimony on this subject. Telecommunications were regarded as a big enough subject, with enough prickly issues to engage the full attention of the committees. Despite these limitations, the committee hearings have performed the singular service of putting national communications issues on the public agenda and providing a unique forum for airing them.[15]

In the absence of definitive legislation, the courts have played a significant role in defining legal aspects of the new communications and information environment and expanding First Amendment interpretations of privacy and other civil rights implications of the new technologies. The Supreme Court's ruling on the Nixon Watergate tapes in 1974 was the most publicized example of this. Other cases have dealt with data protection, wiretapping, and the limits of electronic surveillance.

Any review of communications policy has to take into consideration the parts played by states and localities. States have had a regulatory role in telecommunications through public utility commissions for many years. Many states and cities are now beginning to see telecommunications and information issues in the wider context of their relationships to such local services as education, law enforcement, library systems, and the like. A number of them have organized special units for this purpose: Virginia has had an integrated telecommunications planning unit for public service purposes since the early seventies. Many large cities are following suit: Los Angeles, Portland (Oregon), Boston, and New York City all have commissioned studies on the role of local public telecommunications in recent years.

In summary, policy questions dealing with the new information environment are moving into the public agenda in a variety of ways and at different political levels. The effort is fragmented, discursive, and complex, reflecting the division of power in a sensitive area of national policy. Meanwhile, the communications and information structure is expanding rapidly, largely as a result of incremental decisions and actions based primarily on their immediate utility to commercial interests. The argument favoring a continuation of this approach is that, by and large, it works. The question is whether this time-tested process can continue to cope with the communications and information requirements of a more complex post-industrial environment. The present lack of answers to this question suggests the need for a more accurate guide to where we are going and what policy options and actions are available in developing a workable strategy in this area.

This strategy must deal with the relationship among public needs, available technology, and economic resources. In part, this involves a more precise allocation of responsibilities between the private and public sectors. In the public sector, more definitive guidelines are needed for meeting overall national requirements in the new environment. In the private sector, industry requires reasonable conditions for meeting communications needs in a period of growing demands for increasingly diverse services.

The allocation of tasks between the public and private sectors is clearly a difficult, sensitive job. Kurt Borchardt has suggested a private/public coordination model based on the Atomic Industrial Forum, which is essentially a systems approach for joint government/ industry study and evaluation of the allocations of tasks.[16] There is good reason to question whether this solution would work in the communications sector. It tends to assume that the problem is between bureaucratic policymakers and the industry. There has been relatively little citizen input into the decision making of the Atomic Industrial Forum. This might have been explained — unsatisfactorily, in the view of many — by the esoteric technical nature of nuclear problems. However, a case can be made that more citizen input earlier on in the process might have prevented or modified some of the faulty assumptions made by nuclear planners over the years.

Communications and information policy, by its very nature, requires broad public input. It is a subject that touches everyone at every level. A weakness of our current approach to the new information environment is that decisions are being made, and options closed, every day that should be open to public scrutiny. Despite the advances in consumer rights practices in recent years, decisions on the consumption of communications and information still tend to be the exclusive province of the bureaucracies — public and private — involved. At a time when we need to take actions to strengthen communications and information patterns in this country through the end of the century, an important element in the decision process is often missing — the views of individual consumers.

A good example of the stakes involved is the future of the postal system. This lumbering giant is currently wandering in the limbo between a respectable past and a highly uncertain future. By any slide rule calculation, there is no question about its future: a drastic cutback in its present mode of operations, including daily mail delivery. The old Norman Rockwell image of the friendly postman, slogging his way through snow, sleet, and rain to deliver Valentine messages will fade into folklore. The reason is that 80 percent of all first class mail deliveries is routine business correspondence, mostly bills being delivered or being paid, which could be handled electronically through the telephone system or cable networks at considerably lower cost, according to most experts.

The trouble with this alternative, as we mentioned before, is that the postal system is not just a business, it is a social institution whose value is not totally measurable in terms of profit and loss. The shift to electronic mail delivery already underway may be both logical and acceptable, but the public deserves to have considerably more involvement in the decision-making process than it has had to date. The alternatives need to be presented clearly, including the crucial question of who should pay for maintaining traditional mail services.

The future of the postal system is, however, only a part of the problem of organizing public and private resources for the new information age. Until very recently, the subject was relegated to seminar discussions in a few universities and research institutes. This is changing as more individuals and groups see how their interests are tied to a resolution of the larger public issues involved. For the present, it is largely a sensitizing process, a slow realization that a radically different information environment is taking shape in ways that call for review, and redefinition, of long-standing national goals and purposes.

The need for a broad-based policy debate goes beyond particularistic decisions about computer access, cable television, broadcasting satellites, or the many other issues that have to be resolved. The essential issue is preserving and expanding the sum of two centuries of freedom in increasingly complex circumstances.

In 1787, Thomas Jefferson summed up the case for an open information society in a letter to Edward Carrington during the debates leading up to the adoption of the Constitution:

> The basis of our government being the opinion of the people, the very first object should be to keep that right; and were it left to me to decide whether we should have a government without newspapers, or newspapers without a government, I should not hesitate a moment to prefer the latter.

If Jefferson were debating the principles of a new Constitution today, it is probable that he would have expanded his views on the importance of a free press to include the electronic media and perhaps even open-access computer networks. The principle is the same, whether the technologies involved are eighteenth century flat-bed presses or modern computers that can print out thousands of words a second.

How do we organize ourselves to match Jeffersonian ideals with the opportunities opened by modern communications and information technologies? Given the complexity and sensitivity of the subject, the answer does not lie in any master plan but in a range of general approaches, each of which advances the prospect for making adjustments to the new information environment within a democratic framework. The factor they have in common is the need to establish a workable balance between public and private sector responsibilities.

The facile approach is simply to do more of what we have been doing. This assumes that the public sector will neither take the lead in setting comprehensive national goals nor play an activist role in assuring the orderly expansion of communications and information resources over and above its traditional responsibilities for formal education, library services, and the like. The federal government would continue to act as a regulatory balance, brokering between the major economic interests involved and buffering the present communications structure against the instabilities of too rapid change. Given the hundreds of billions of dollars invested in the present structure and the need to amortize these costs over a long period of time this approach is clearly favored by most of the present managers of the system, as well as by that large segment of the public bureaucracy that has a stake in preserving the status quo. The public argument for continuing the present system is a compelling one, namely, that the system works. A second argument is also compelling, that it would be politically impossible to make any major adjustments in the system, no matter what the theoretical benefits might be, given the political and economic power of its present managers.

Despite the realism of these arguments, they are less and less convincing. There are weaknesses in our present approach, particularly in its heavy reliance on economic cost-benefit standards in determining both the form and pace of communications and information development. We are inclined to be impressed by the very real achievements and to miss the gaps. The assumption is that the gaps will be filled in by a trickle-down process. The question, from a social viewpoint, is whether we can continue to rely on this haphazard approach, given the pressure to bring formerly disadvantaged groups fully into the system.

The second, and more radical, approach is to make the public sector a more active participant in developing and managing an expanded communications and information network. The few proponents of this idea argue that only direct public intervention can create an integrated, full-service network, operated as a publicly owned utility. This would be a major reversal in our national style. The fact that other industrial democracies — those of the Japanese and the British, for instance — have thrived with considerable government involvement at this level would have little weight. There are, in fact, interesting examples closer to home of the workability of publicly managed communications utilities. These involve a handful of cities which in recent years have decided to develop their own coaxial-cable utility networks, providing a mix of commercial and public services to homes. Despite the determined opposition of the cable television industry to public ownership, these systems have been well managed and have generally been much more responsive to public service needs than most of their commercial counterparts.[17]

The problem with this alternative is that it is politically impractical. Comparisons with the experiences of the British or Japanese are irrelevant in considerations of the day-to-day performance of a preponderantly commercial system. Justified or not, the idea raises the specter of domination by government in an area where it has up to now largely been excluded, both by law and custom.

There is a third approach, one that tends to get lost in conflicting rhetoric about the virtues of private enterprise against the evils of socialistic centralized government. It is based on establishing, as public policy, a firm commitment to the evolution of a full-service national information grid, augmenting the present fragmentary system in stages. This would require a more clearly articulated division of responsibilities between the public and private sectors. The basic construction and management of the completed system would be the responsibility of the private sector, which would develop the grid in as many competitive modes as technology and economic considerations would justify. Its performance would be judged by agreed-upon social goals which would be reviewed to reflect the changing communications and information needs of the post-industrial age.

The public sector's role would be limited largely to providing, where necessary, fiscal and other incentives for encouraging the application of innovative technology. The case for such an approach was made several years ago by Dr. Simon Ramo, then Vice-Chairman of TRW Inc., the electronics firm:

> The modifications of the structure of business and the pattern of all other activities needed to exploit the new information technology will involve massive start-up costs. . . . Despite the potential of economic and social gain inherent in the productivity increase and greater flexibility the technology will provide, the speed with which this kind of technology can come into being is greatly contingent on a new organizational teaming of corporations and government. The

government may need to sponsor large-scale experiments to develop the basic ideas, perhaps seeking improved information flow in government operations as the first proving ground, and be willing to allow, even encourage, the setting up of private industry teams to share risk.[18]

Another expanded public sector role would be to assure the availability to individuals and groups of essential communications and information services that might be uneconomic and require public subsidizing. The experience of the Rural Electrification Administration in bringing power and telephone service to the countryside is a classic case in point. A critical element in this process would be cutting back government regulatory restraints whose effect, if not intent, is to inhibit the efficient development of a full-service national information utility. It would foster competitive conditions that would stimulate innovation, flexibility, and responsiveness to overall consumer needs. As John Eger, a communications attorney, has noted, "A regulatory commission can do a pretty fair job of curtailing undue monopoly profits, but it cannot issue an enforceable decree mandating alertness to changing market requirements."[19]

The present regulatory system is based largely on three assumptions, one of them valid and two of them increasingly less so. The valid assumption is that there is a need for public regulation and monitoring of technical standards so that the total system is technologically sound. The second assumption, which has eroded over the years, is that regulation is necessary for the orderly economic development of the system. Originally justified largely by the need to amortize the high capital investment needed for communications, regulation became increasingly an excuse for protecting old technologies from new ones. If any lesson in communications regulations has been learned, in the past decade, it is that the admirable, if somewhat tentative, FCC decisions allowing more competition in the industry have brought new vitality to the industry, not caused its predicted collapse.

The third assumption, which also is losing some of its validity, is that there is need for public controls over the radio spectrum, a valuable but limited resource. For a long time, government's role in mediating industry demands on spectrum resources was essential, given the steady expansion of spectrum use. The difference now is that the scarcity argument is increasingly less convincing, because of technical advances in efficient use of the spectrum and also because of the increased availability of cost-effective, high-capacity systems such as cable and fiber optic circuits that can conserve radio frequencies. Spectrum scarcity has become a considerably less important barrier to the play of market forces in determining which technology, and which segments of the private sector, can supply the most efficient services in developing a full-scale information grid.

In short, many of the old reasons for government regulation of the communications system are disappearing. Given the economic and political stakes involved, the regulatory structure cannot be phased out immediately. But there is no reason why a national commitment, based on a new pattern of public- and private-sector cooperation, could not be made now to carry us through the transitional phase to a full-service information grid providing low-cost, high-capacity services to every sector of American society.

Conditioned by the onward-and-upward rhetoric of the American electronic mythos, we can easily miss the full significance of this commitment. Certainly the most important outcome can be the fulfillment of First Amendment purposes — the right (*and* the capability) to hear and be heard, to see and be seen, to write and be written about, with due allowance for libel and privacy restrictions. For all our gains, we are still well short of this goal. The late critic of the U.S. press, A. J. Liebling, once noted that there is freedom of the press for anyone with $5 million to buy his own newspaper. (The price is considerably higher these days.) Marshall McLuhan has correctly identified the most revolutionary characteristic of the Xerox and other low-cost copying machines: they make everyone his own publisher, if only on a limited basis. The ubiquitous new electronic circuits can expand our information rights in ways we find difficult to imagine, hemmed in as we are by the present limited range of available communications channels and information sources.

The new circuit-rich environment can be dramatically different. Much of our communication will continue to be private and personal, as in the telephone call and its extension to videophone or data communications, either as two-way or as round-robin conference calls among friends and associates. The major changes, however, will come in the way that wider information services are transmitted and received. This new phenomenon might be called "open electronics publishing." It is the logical outcome of the technological prospects opened up by the new high-capacity communications networks and by computers. With the evolution toward channel abundance, supplying a wider range of visual, audio, or print information, competitive electronics publishing will allow any individual or group to offer messages on the new universal information grid. The grid would be a vastly expanded common carrier open to all, no longer restrained by radio spectrum restraints or other circuit limitations.

This approach would represent a giant step toward the realization of Justice Oliver Wendell Holmes's marketplace of ideas. It would be an *open* market, with high-capacity channels available to all comers, big and small, seeking out consumers willing to pay for access to whatever information or services they want for themselves or what they determine, as a social good, should be made available as a general service subsidized by public revenues.

Electronic publishing would be a competitive enterprise on both a large and small scale. Information producers and consumers would be linked in a network operated as an information utility by commercial common carriers. No general laws would be required other than those already governing publishing — copyright, libel, and the like. Public intervention would be limited to circuit rate regulation and to the setting of technical standards for the utility. Meanwhile, much of the present regulatory structure dealing with telecommunications could be dismantled so as to eliminate most of the present restrictions on information access.[20]

There are many reasons — political, economic, and social — why electronic publishing of the type described above is not an immediate prospect. However, there is no reason the concept of an open market in electronic publishing should not be set as a desirable national goal for implementation by the end of the century. The opening up of the information marketplace is beginning to happen already, with the growth of cable television and independent satellite networks and the beginnings of consumer computer grids. This is all to the good: the old-line controllers of limited access, centralized news, entertainment, and other information resources are being challenged. Their instinctive reaction is to seek government protection for their privileged position, drawing on a wide range of self-serving arguments. Media critic Edwin Diamond has neatly summed up some of the more prevalent myths supporting continued government regulation:

> *The myth of spectrum scarcity. Since the wavelengths are limited, government has to ration their use to ensure that everyone is heard.* Cable television will spell the end of that notion, though it hasn't held up very well in recent years in any case. Newspapers also have limited resources — newsprint, delivery trucks, distribution points — but the private market is allowed to operate without Government control.
>
> *The myth that without government, only the monied interest would be heard.* Who's kidding whom? With government now, the

richest people in town — the bankers, insurance-company owners, real-estate operators, what Kansas editor William Allen White called the "country-club set" — own both newspapers and broadcast stations (if the even wealthier chains haven't yet taken over).

The myth that government rules ensure diversity of ideas, the airing of controversy, and the chance for "both sides" to be heard on television. In practice, many broadcasters worry about broadcasting *anything* that might interfere with the nice sounds of their ringing cash registers. They don't like controversy because it gets in the way of profits. Also, where is it written that all issues have two sides, and two sides only? There may be more than two sides, or there may be only one.[21]

Although he does not use the phrase, Diamond is defending the concept of "open electronic publishing." His target is the television pattern in this country, our most visible centralized, limited-ownership information arrangement. It is the medium that could be most radically altered in an open electronic publishing environment. In fact, television's period of automatic onward-and-upward influence is already ending, after a profitable thirty-year run (1949–1979). The reason is that a new pattern of competitive services — new forms of electronic publishing — are cutting into the TV networks' hitherto unchallenged ability to attract huge audiences. Increasingly, the audience is looking at and listening to a new range of attractive alternatives, such as feature films and information services on cable systems and specialized over-the-air television networks. No one of these new electronic publishers is yet a strong challenger to the three big networks. Collectively, however, they are eroding the network audience base, and every indication is that the trend will accelerate in the coming years.

There is enough residual snobbism about television among intellectuals, pseudo and otherwise, to encourage and expand on all reports, however premature, about network television's demise. Their enthusiasm may be somewhat misplaced. The Aspen Institute's Douglas Cater has noted that, for all its faults, network television and its large audiences have been an important element in maintaining social stability during a particularly rocky passage in the American experience:

Is the fractionalization of audiences a net social gain? . . . What happens when each minority group can tune in to its own prophets? When there are no more Walter Cronkites each evening to reassure us that despite all its afflictions the nation still stands?[22]

The real problem may be that television, because of its pervasive influence, has been overburdened by too many expectations. Its natural bent is as a news and entertainment medium, yet it has been charged, under the dubious rubric of balanced programming, with being the electronic surrogate for school, church, town meeting, and other specialized institutions. TV cannot, in fact, serve as the equivalent of these institutions, and it would be wise for us to curtail these unrealizable expectations. By sharing its functions more widely with other electronic publishing channels, network television could be freed up very effectively (and very profitably) to carry out its more natural news and entertainment functions, instead of trying to be the electronic Elmer's Glue binding all our interests.

However, the argument for a new pattern of electronic publishing goes well beyond television and other mass media. Its greatest impact will be in the consumerization of electronic networks, providing a full range of text, voice, and visual information services for the general public. Because of costs and technical limitations, such networking has been the province of big business and big government up until now. The 1980s should see the steady expansion of information networking for smaller organizations and individuals. Two important components of the grid — telephones and TV's — are already in place in over 90 percent of U.S. homes, as well as in schools and other institutions.

High-capacity coaxial-cable lines are already installed in almost 20 million homes and this number will rise to 30 million by the mid-eighties. Until a few years ago, there seem to have been few prospects that another vital element — a low-cost electronic information terminal — would be soon available. However, microprocessor technology makes this possible, either as "black box" attachments to television sets or as separate home terminals connected to telephone and cable lines.

This leaves one significant missing link in the universal grid. It is the consumer-oriented data bases and other services whose product will be useful to the mass audience needed to support a universal grid providing text, voice, and visual services. The grid's full development may hinge on the resolution of a difficult public policy question. A significant group of consumers are clearly identified as a market for any specialized educational and information services. They are the natural information seekers, who are the basic marketing target for commercial electronic information services directed to their homes or workplaces. However, it is a very selective market, one that probably cannot sustain a universal grid. A full network will probably not evolve until there is a clearer definition of responsibilities for educational and information services between the private and public sectors. As long as the grid is limited to commercially saleable information, it will have a limited reach. Its full use may depend on public decisions to develop (or, in some cases, expand) public electronic information services, either as direct government services or through subsides.

Though limited, experience with such public services on cable systems to date has underlined the difficulties involved. Cable system operators and other potential information network entrepreneurs are no more or less altruistic than the rest of us. They are developing the basic circuitry, and the data bases, to serve commercially viable markets. Their circuits will be the infrastructures of what can become a universal electronic publishing network in the coming years. The services provided by the network will depend on economics, and the providing of a *full* range of services will depend on social decisions determining that they are a civic necessity. In the seventies, Edwin Parker and Donald Dunn of Stanford University's Communications Research Institute suggested that the public sector sponsor pilot projects within an overall plan for the long-term development of a national information utility:

> Since most of the funds for this utility will come from the private sector, the principal needs for Federal action are in the areas of coordination, policy analysis and assessment, and the funding of pilot projects and demonstrations designed to stimulate the development of new public-sector education and information services.[23]

Such a proposal is part of a long-standing tradition of public involvement in information resources. The public library system is, of course, the most familiar example. Public organizations are the largest single source of both specialized and general information materials in the country, ranging from the products of the Government Printing Office to the Medlars medical data bank and the National Technical Information Service.

There have been some federally sponsored experiments for public information services on cable systems, along the lines suggested above by Professors Parker and Dunn. Most of these have been funded by the National Science Foundation. One of the most successful was an interactive cable TV information service for the elderly in Reading, Pennsylvania, which demonstrated the social, and emotional, importance of direct access to information for older people, and particularly for those who were homebound. Simple information on Social Security and Medicaid procedures proved to be a critically important part of the services provided. In general, however, government efforts to provide electronic data services have been limited to science and technology subjects, supporting business and professional needs. Such services are, of course, necessary, but they are far removed from ordinary consumer needs.

Efforts to provide consumer services (as in the Reading senior citizen project) have been fragmentary, cautious, and lacking in overall purpose. A good part of the problem is economics: data banks and networking are very expensive operations. A mixed public/commercial coaxial-cable system proposed for the District of Columbia by the Mitre Corporation some years ago put the commercial break-even point for the system at 50 percent of total customers, and the public service break-even point at closer to 100 percent.

This gap is indicative of the economic realities behind the rhetoric that has clogged so many discussions about the new information channels. So-called "free" public services have to be paid for by taxpayers, or through some fee system. Experience with such services on cable systems in the early eighties has been too limited to provide any firm projections of the exact pattern for future services. However, there are indications that they will be tested extensively in the next few years. This will result from the trend requiring that new urban cable systems make specific provision for such services. Systems like Qube in Columbus, Ohio, which provide special information services are being expanded in other major cities, which began awarding new cable franchises in the early eighties. The franchise for cabling Omaha, awarded to Cox Communications in 1980, called for a total of 104 channels. Whether such an abundance of channels will result in a comparable abundance of information and other services, commercial or public, remains to be seen.

The issue deserves considerably more attention than it is now getting. High-capacity communications circuits and data banks are being built largely under commercial auspices. They are efficient, well-managed, and aimed primarily at individuals and organizations who can pay for them. These individuals and groups are the professionals, the information seekers. However, this pattern of development ignores the very large group of people who have neither the money nor the opportunities for access to the new resources. As a result, the gap between the information-rich and the information-poor is likely to widen rather than narrow with the introduction of the new information technologies. The question cannot be begged by suggesting that most people don't need, and don't want, access to sophisticated information resources. This reasoning is demeaning, and not particularly true in an increasingly complex society in which the range of information needed for survival is widening.

Post-industrial America cannot thrive in an environment in which there is a new kind of literacy gap based on unequal access to the resources of the new communications and information technologies. Individuals are not all equal as information seekers, but they all seek information for a variety of reasons. We need to know more about these reasons, the kinds of information services people want, and how the new technologies can be adapted to these needs. The information machines, with their flashing lights and mysterious insides, can be intimidating to many people. These paraphernalia of the new information environment should be developed in ways that make them readily accessible, inexpensive to use, and programmed to provide information people need. This will call for a different kind of public sector involvement in assuring access to the new machines. One researcher has suggested that Xerox-type copying machines be subsidized in ghetto areas, where they are generally not now available, as part of an overall information access program.[24] Whether or not this proposal makes social or economic sense is secondary to the fact that it raises a problem — information access inequality — that has not yet been fully faced in considerations of the role of the new high-capacity circuits and machines.

In the absence of a national consensus on the goals of the new information age, economics and technology are now shaping the future. They are the major forces propelling us into the new age. Experience with earlier, less complex technological advances has shown, however, that at least some of the unexpected, unwanted results could have been modified, and perhaps turned around, by some intelligent prior planning. As *Fortune* editor Max Ways points out:

> The range of possible consequences presented by the new information technologies is so varied and subtle that no society would be expected to have ready-made solutions to the main problems presented. But as the employment of these technologies continues to spread rapidly, it will be disgraceful if policy questions generated by them are not soon identified, discussed and dealt with.[25]

There are sensitive political, economic, legal, and social issues involved in any attempt to develop a viable national approach to information and communications resources. The participants in the debate tend to polarize their positions. On the one hand there are the enthusiasts who exaggerate the influence of the new information machines as solutions, rather than mere necessary supporting resources, for complex problems. At the other extreme are the skeptics who fear, with some justification, that more active public sector intervention is this area could lead to undesirable government controls and erosion of constitutional freedom.

The answer lies, as usual, somewhere in between. The critical issue is whether everyone in this society — both chief and Indian, the powerful and the powerless — has equal rights to the basic information he or she needs to survive and thrive. No society has even come near this goal. The United States has come the closest, and our limited experience has shown us that expanding the information base, plugging everyone in, is the best policy. Moving more rapidly toward this ideal is our biggest challenge in the new information environment.

Notes

1. For a useful overview of interrelated communications and information policy issues, see Glen O. Robinson, ed., *Communications for Tomorrow* (New York: Praeger Publishers, 1978).

2. Harold Black and Edward Shaw, "Detroit's Data Banks," *Datamation*, March 1967, p. 27.

3. Karl W. Deutsch, *The Nerves of Government* (New York: The Free Press of Glencoe, 1963).

4. John DeButts, "Policy, Not Technology, Will Shape the Future of Communications in the U.S.A.," *Communications News*, June 1975, p. 47.

5. Erik Barnouw, *Tube of Plenty* (New York: Oxford University Press, 1975), p. 39.

6. The dispute surrounding the formation of the Communications Satellite Corporation is described in Wilson Dizard, *Television — A World View* (Syracuse, N.Y.: Syracuse University Press, 1966), pp. 263–267, and in Brenda Maddox, *Beyond Babel: New Directions in Communications* (Boston: Beacon Press, 1974), pp. 82–90.

7. U.S. Executive Office of the President, *Final Report of the President's Task Force on Communications Policy*, (Washington, D.C.: U.S. Government Printing Office, 1968).

8. Anne W. Branscomb, "Communications Policy in the United States," in Patricia Edgar and Sayeed Rahim, eds., *Communications Policy in Developed Countries* (Honolulu: East-West Center, 1981).

9. U.S. Executive Office of the President, *The Radio Frequency Spectrum: United States' Use and Mangement*, Office of Telecommunicaions Policy (Washington, D.C.: Government Printing Office, 1975), p. D-18.

10. Testimony of Harold Brown in U.S. Congress, Senate, Communications Subcommittee of the Committee on Commerce, *Space Communications*

and Allocation of the Radio Spectrum, 87th Cong., 1st sess., p. 17. A critical description of the evolution of the National Communications System can be found in Herbert Schiller, *Mass Communications and American Empire* (Boston: Beacon Press, 1971), pp. 63–78.

11. "U.S. Scuttles Plan for IRS Computer," *New York Times*, 7 January 1978, p. 1.

12. "AT&T Continues to Head Companies on Federal Advisory Boards," *Defense Space Daily* (Washington), 28 October 1977, p. 3. Also "Advisers Are Fewer but Expenses Mount," *Washington Post*, 26 March 1978, p. 52.

13. U.S. National Commission on Libraries and Information, *National Information Policy*. Report to the President submitted by the staff of the Domestic Council Committee on the Right of Privacy (Washington, D.C.: Government Printing Office, 1976), p. vi.

14. U.S., Congress, House Subcommittee on Communications, Committee on Interstate and Foreign Commerce, *Options Papers*, 95th Cong., 1st sess., committee print 95–13, May, 1971.

15. For a useful summary of the checkered history of rewrite legislation, see Manny Lucoff, "The Rise and Fall of the Third Rewrite," *Journal of Communication*, 30, no. 3, (Summer 1980): pp. 47–53.

16. Kurt Borchardt, *Structure and Performance of the U.S. Communications Industry*. Division of Research, Graduate School of Business Administration, Harvard University, 1970, pp. 152–56.

17. St. Paul, Minnesota, and Patterson, New Jersey, are cities that have adopted this option. Municipal ownership of cable systems is, of course, strenuously opposed by the commercial cable television industry.

18. Simon Ramo, "Technology and Resources for Business," *Horizon*, U.S. Information Agency publication no. 4, (Washington, D.C.: 1975), p. 32.

19. Quoted in John F. Judge, "The Complexities of Seeking a Policy," *Government Executive* (Washington), June 1976, p. 44.

20. A strong case for electronic publishing is given in Peter Jay, "The Future of Broadcasting," *Encounter* (London), April 1977, pp. 68–79.

21. Edwin Diamond, "Media Myths That Limit Free Speech," *TV Guide*, 5 November 1977, p. 44.

22. Douglass Cater, "A Communications Revolution?" *Wall Street Journal*, 6 August 1973, p. 18.

23. Edwin B. Parker and Donald Dunn, "Information Technology: Its Social Potential," *Science*, 30 June 1972, p. 1399.

24. The suggestion is made in Susan Krieger, "Prospects for Communications Policy," *Policy Sciences* (Amsterdam), no. 2 (1971): p. 312.

25. The Conference Board, *Information Technology: Some Critical Implications for Decision Makers*, report no. 537 (New York: The Conference Board, 1972), p. 6.

Chapter Seven

Exporting the Information Society

Fire fighters in Sweden have an ingenious system for assuring efficient responses to fire alarms. A computer data bank keeps records on each building — its construction features, number of occupants, and any special characteristics (combustible chemicals, for instance) that might be important if a fire breaks out. The data bank also records the quickest route from the nearest fire station. When a building catches fire, this information is instantly retrieved on a computer terminal at the station.

The Swedish fire data bank is an imaginative application of computer power. But the project is interesting in another way: the computer containing the data is located in Cleveland, Ohio. The eight-thousand-mile electronic round trip involved in the transmittal of information to and from the Cleveland computer was not a deterrent in awarding the data bank contract to an American bidder, the General Electric Company. The information can be retrieved as quickly as if its source were in Stockholm or another Swedish city. Similar computer data banks are being developed for American fire departments.

The Cleveland computer's role in Swedish fires is only one example of a new phenomenon — the internationalization of communications and information. When airline clerks make reservations for passengers in Warsaw or Tokyo, they are probably unaware that they are connected to a computer in Atlanta, where a large share of international flight reservations are stored. Nutrition researchers in Rome, searching for technical data in the new European regional computer network ("Euronet") may not know that they are dealing with a data base in Amsterdam. These networks are, in a very real sense, indifferent to time, place, and distance. They have, as anthropologist Edward Carpenter has remarked, made free spirits of us all, not in a Sunday school sense of having wings or being good, but in the sense of being pure spirit, divorced from flesh, capable of instant transportation anywhere.

Free spirits aside, international computer networks are part of a pattern of dramatic changes in global communications and information resources in recent years. To a considerable extent, this pattern was developed first in this country; most of the rest of the world is only beginning to catch up with us. Over and above the effect this pattern will eventually have on our own information environment, the change represents a strategic new element in the American global equation. The United States needs a strong world communications network to support its overseas interests. Economically, the export of communications goods and services is increasingly important. Politically, communications are the nervous system for the interdependent world order to which this country is committed, and particularly important to this world order are improved links between the industrialized and developing nations.

The expanded world communications network will amplify American ideas and values in a more forceful way than has ever been done before. As in the past, these ideas will evoke reactions ranging from admiration to anger — often at the same time. "What makes America unique in our time is that confrontation with the new is part of the daily American experience," Zbigniew Brzezinski notes. "For better or for worse, the rest of the world learns what is in store for it by observing what happens in the United States."[1] University of California communications researcher Herbert Schiller, a critic of American communications practices abroad, makes the point that the United States does not simply export products and services in this field. It exports a *system*, including a heavy ideological bent favoring American values and attitudes which, in Schiller's view, are not in the best interests of other cultures, particularly those in the developing nations. The evidence Schiller cites to support his observation may be debatable, but his basic thesis has merit.[2]

In assessing the American role, three major trends should be considered. The first of these is the pell-mell growth in world communications and information resources, particularly in the last two decades. Accurate statistics are often hard to come by, but taking one measure — volume of global communications traffic — it becomes obvious that growth is occurring at a rate of between 10 and 15 percent annually, roughly doubling every half-dozen years. Whatever measures are used, communications and information emerge as major growth sectors that have been uniquely immune from the economic turbulence affecting other industries in recent years.

The second trend influencing American interests are the changes taking place in the geographic pattern of global communications. Twenty years ago, this was a neat, orderly business, confined largely to the North Atlantic area and a Japanese extension. By present standards, volume was low, consisting primarily of business traffic passing through government owned or controlled networks. Again, the exception to government control was the United States, whose overseas communication circuits were (and still are) owned by several firms operating under light federal regulation. Nevertheless, the American firms worked efficiently with their foreign government counterparts in what was essentially a gentlemanly division of the world market, dominated by American interests.

Today economics, politics, and technology are pulling these patterns into different shapes. The market is becoming geographically more diverse every year, thanks in large part to the 105-nation *Intelsat* satellite network, which provides high-grade communications wherever there is an earth terminal. Among other changes, the satellite network has reduced the importance of the "gateway cities" in Europe, the United States, and Japan through which communications traffic to the rest of the world was formerly channeled. Until the advent of the satellite network, for instance, all international traffic between the east and west coasts of South America was routed through gateway cities in the U.S. Similar changes in Asia and Africa have given Third World countries direct communications with each other for the first time, thus lessening their dependence on the industrialized nations. Another satellite development which promises to change old patterns is the regional satellite networks that will operate outside the *Intelsat* framework. The Europeans are building such a network now. The Arab states are actively planning their system and there are proposals for similar networks in Africa, Latin America, and Asia.

The third significant trend in international communications is the threat of political restrictions on the growth of the world system. The

United States has taken the lead since World War II in advocating the elimination of restrictions on communications flow internationally. In the late 1940s, it used its then-dominant influence in the United Nations to get international approval for the concept of "free flow of information." Our democratic partners approved, while the poorer areas of Asia and Africa were either still colonial states or regarded the issue as irrelevant. Only the Soviet Union and its client states objected, a predictable reaction given the need for tight internal controls over domestic information channels in order to maintain the communist parties in power. Although American advocacy of open information channels reflected deeply held national convictions, it also provided the ideological underpinnings for the postwar expansion of American information influence throughout the world.[3]

Until recently, this influence was welcomed, or at least accepted as a normal consequence of American power and influence. Now it is being questioned in ways that could affect U.S. interests in international communications as well as overall prospects for an open world information order. The reasons for this development are complex, but they center around new perceptions abroad of information as a political, economic, and cultural force. Increasingly, information is being viewed as a strategic resource that, like oil or nickel, is a measurable element in calculations of national strength. As a result, it is a newly contested factor in international affairs. "The battle is for information of all kinds," Andrew Aines has noted. "The battle is to use modern information technology most advantageously. It involves out-and-out espionage, military and industrial. It involves the quest for scientific and technical data of all kinds and for all purposes. It involves the delivery of political information. . . . It involves the United Nations, COMECON (the Soviet economic bloc), the Common Market, military alliances and many other international bodies."[4]

This battle has, in turn, led to a new concept of information sovereignty, defined as the right of a society to protect itself against what it regards as unwarranted intrusion by outside information and communications influences. The concept arose originally during the early seventies when Third World countries complained that their information and communications resources were dominated by American and European interests. The charges originally focused on the influence of Western mass media, particularly film, television, and news agency products. In particular, Third World spokesmen argued that the American free-flow concept did not take into account the massive imbalance in information flows between the West and other parts of the globe. They saw the free-flow thesis as a rationalization for what they regarded as cultural and economic imperialism. The debate went beyond rhetorical charges and countercharges. In recent years, Third World countries have taken a series of steps to gain more control over foreign influences in their domestic telecommunications and information affairs.

The information sovereignty question is also being seriously discussed by European nations, although their perspectives and motives are generally different from those of Third World countries. Confident that they can hold their own in this field, Europeans are considerably less worried about American cultural influence. Their concern is to protect themselves against what they regard as inordinate outside (that is, American) control over their information resources, particularly in computerized data banks and circuits. American companies have been particularly successful in marketing goods and services to industrial nations abroad. Some analysts estimate that between 50 and 60 percent of European *domestic* data records are processed by U.S. companies.[5]

This worries the Europeans, both in terms of the privacy rights of their citizens and the newly perceived strategic importance of information and communications as a national resource. This has led them, as we shall see later, to consider regulations on controlling international data flow. At another level, the Europeans are particularly concerned about the dominant role of American industry in computer hardware. They have taken steps to strengthen domestic computer production through government subsidies and other programs. Through the European Economic Community, they are also developing their own regional computer data network, partly in response to American competition. Taken together, these moves reflect a growing feeling that in the future, as an OECD report on European industry has stated, "information and knowledge rather than capital and production of manufactured goods will become the central issue around which sharp competition will develop."

These world trends toward protectionism and control of information flow across borders have not yet reached a critical stage. However, they are a potentially serious problem for the United States in advancing its political, economic, and cultural interests favoring an open global information pattern. Not only are other countries taking a closer look at their own national interests in this area, but the subject is being debated here. A 1976 Defense Department study suggested that the United States was too liberal in sharing its science and technology know-how with other countries. The report declared that a significant "leak" in this area was created by the large number of foreign students — most of whom are studying technical subjects — in U.S. universities. While it is improbable that the United States would ever adopt general policies restricting information exports over and above longstanding controls on technology flow to Communist countries, there is increasing concern about the rate at which certain technologies are exported, cutting into the competitive edge for American products.

Rapid growth, changing patterns, challenges to American leadership — these are the conditions that will set the agenda for U.S. strategy in the global information and communications field during the 1980s. American decisions in this area will be an important element in determining the future pace and scope of world communications growth. No other country has the technological and economic strength, or the political will, to assume the lead in this area. The Soviets are ideologically incapable of taking a major role, given their own inhibitions about information and communications matters. The Europeans have not been able to develop a consensus, much less take actions, in this area. The Japanese look upon the issue primarily in terms of trade.

If the United States takes on a greater leadership role, it will first have to address the fact that it does not now have an articulated national policy in this area. Its primary interest in the past two decades has been, with good reason, to provide support for the international expansion of the U.S. communications and information industries. Government policy has essentially reacted to commercial needs. In most cases this has been done successfully and in one instance, it was done brilliantly — in the Communications Satellite Act of 1962, which provided the legislative authorization for America to develop a global satellite system. The legislation was a triumph of pragmatism over a formidable list of reasons why it couldn't be done. However, no effective attempts have been made to develop a comprehensive policy approach in other global communications matters since then. One effort to develop such a policy in the late sixties, by the presidentially appointed Rostow Commission on communications which we discussed earlier, was unsuccessful because some of its recommendations clashed with strong communications industry interests in this country.

As in the domestic policy area, international communications responsibilities are divided among a number of federal agencies. The overall responsibility in the executive branch rests with the State Department. Within the department, however, this authority is fragmented among a number of offices. In February 1978, Secretary of State Cyrus Vance took a first step toward improving the department's handling of communications matters by appointing his deputy, Warren Christopher, coordinator for the subject. The coordination role was expanded by the Reagan administration in 1981. Although the Federal Communications Commission's primary responsibilities are in the domestic field, it has become increasingly involved in international matters in recent years as a result of the expanded foreign activities of the domestic companies it regulates. This wider involvement led former FCC chairman Richard Wiley to propose, before he left office in 1977, that the commission be authorized to negotiate agreements on communications matters directly with foreign governments — a function normally carried out by the State Department. The department did not take kindly to the proposal and the matter was dropped.[6]

A dozen other agencies have fragmentary roles to play in overseas communications matters. The Defense Department, manager of its own large global communications system, carries weight in any discussion of the subject involving its many interests. The Department of Commerce, the Federal Aviation Agency, NASA, and the Central Intelligence Agency contribute their particular interests. The International Communication Agency (formerly USIA) has a mandate, under a 1978 Carter administration reorganization plan, to advise the President and foreign affairs agencies on foreign communications matters. The National Telecommunications and Information Administration (NTIA), created in 1978, also has international responsibilities as part of its charter to coordinate overall government communications policies. Its authority is limited in practice, however, by the resistance of other agencies, notably the Defense and State departments, to NTIA activities in areas traditionally assigned to these agencies. NTIA also is inhibited by its bureaucratic location at the second level of the Department of Commerce.[7]

The overall fragmentation of U.S. Government responsibilities was summarized several years ago by Senator Ernest F. Hollings, then chairman of the Senate Communications Subcommittee: "No single agency of the U.S. government has comprehensive authority over international communications, nor was the distribution of functions among several agencies the result of planned allocation. Rather, it grew like Topsy, responding to particular technical or industrial problems as they arose."[8] A significant step to correct this situation was taken by the House of Representatives' Subcommittee on Information Policy in a 1980 report suggesting the establishment of a top level office for communications policy in the State Department, and a White House level interagency coordinating mechanism.[9] Although legislation on this subject did not pass Congress, the Reagan administration adopted a number of the report's recommendations in a somewhat different form.

Meanwhile, the controlling factor in U.S. overseas communications is that these communications are private sector responsibilities, with government in only a minor supportive role. This is unlike the situation in most other countries, where governments control or tightly regulate all international communications. A significant exception to private sector dominance in this country was made in 1962, in a decision to make the Communications Satellite Corporation (Comsat) a government mandated "chosen instrument" to exploit the then-American monopoly on advanced satellite technology. The Comsat exception was a compromise between competing claims within private industry on how best to manage the satellites commercially.[10]

In the absence of any grand design for public policies, the communications industry is the prime mover of American overseas .interests. It is big, wide-ranging, and cockily confident of its capabilities. It has the advantage of operating from a strong domestic base, the biggest market in the world. Almost half of total global communications equipment production is absorbed by the U.S. market. This ratio will drop to about 40 percent by the mid-eighties, still an advantage no foreign competitor will come close to matching. American industry had a running start in the early postwar decades, before competitors in other industrialized countries had geared up. Riding the technological lead provided by their research and development laboratories, U.S. firms dominated most segments of the overseas communications field until the seventies. Competition is more rigorous these days, and the American lead is narrowing in the three key sectors — equipment production, message distribution, and information products and services. Since U.S. industry plays such a dominant role in world communications, it is useful to take a look at its place in these three sectors.

Providing reliable overseas communications circuits has been a complex, risky business since the 1850s when Cyrus Fields attempted to lay the first transatlantic cable — a primitive telegraph wire wrapped in gutta-percha. The cable snapped, and Fields and his associates went bankrupt. A later project was successful, providing the first oceanic link in what has become a cat's cradle of international circuits throughout the globe. The first cables were simple wires that were later supplemented by unreliable radio circuits. This changed in the

1950s with the development of high-capacity submarine cables and, in the 1960s, with satellite microwave links. Thus the technical base for a dramatic expansion in global communications was opened.

American firms were in a strong position to exploit this advantage. In the early 1960s, when expansion began in earnest, over half of all international communications originated in this country. International telephone and telegraph traffic is still a small part of the American communications pattern. A 1976 Department of Commerce report showed that overseas traffic made up 3 percent of total telephone and telegraph service, with a projected rise to about 5 percent in the mid-eighties.[11] These figures do not accurately reflect the quantum jump in American overseas communications in recent years, paced largely by business requirements as American firms expanded abroad. Telephone calls are a good indicator. In 1950, the annual number of overseas calls was one million; by 1975 this had jumped to seventy-five million, and projections for the early eighties are for over two hundred million calls. The increase in data communications, the fastest growing area of international traffic, is even more impressive, with an annual growth rate of over 10 percent.

The U.S. share of the market is split among a half-dozen established firms headed by AT&T. Until recent years, this market was divided between the AT&T monopoly over voice communications and the record (telegraph, telex, data) traffic carried by the other companies. This distinction is breaking down, as will be seen, but it still holds for most overseas traffic. AT&T currently links its circuits to 99.5 percent of the world's telephones, over half of which can be dialed directly. During the eighties, direct dialing will become nearly universal, with the introduction of a worldwide dialing code developed by the International Telecommunications Union.[12] A world telephone number will have up to fourteen numbers, making it possible to reach any dial phone anywhere. Taken together with rapid telephone growth overseas, the result should be a massive increase in world telephone traffic. AT&T will continue to be the dominant U.S. connecting link to this market.

Transmission of American telex and other text and data traffic is largely in the hands of three "international record carrier" (IRC) firms — RCA Global Communications, ITT Worldcom, and Western Union International. The Communications Satellite Corporation serves primarily as a "carrier's carrier," providing satellite circuits for this traffic. Starting out with traditional telegram traffic, the IRCs branched into the telex businesss in the postwar years. Following the domestic trend, the telegram share of the business is headed for extinction in the coming years. The telex business is now the biggest part of the market, and it is currently being transformed from the old-fashioned clackety-clack printer terminal into a variety of high-speed services. The IRCs are playing a high-stakes game in this field, much of it pointed toward the development of international computer-to-computer links.

A transitional step in this direction was taken by the three big firms in the late seventies when they offered roughly similar high-speed terminal-to-computer data transmission services over leased lines.[13] Computer-based links will be the primary growth area in the coming years. A European study found that data processing services will have four times the traffic volume of any other data services by 1985, with a 28 percent annual growth rate projected up to that data. A 1980 American survey of world data communications prospects projected a 16 percent annual growth in the early eighties, with estimated total revenues of $14 billion by 1985.[14]

This growth will be paced by technology and by economic pressures for better international communications. It already affects the way in which international carriers do business. The development of high-capacity cables and satellite circuits have effectively broken down the distinction between voice and data services, the line which divided AT&T from the data carriers for decades. A leased line can be used for both services. The data carriers have been in the telephone business *de facto* since 1964 when the FCC gave them access to what is known as the alternate voice/data service, in which a customer can, with appropriate equipment, use the channel for both voice and nonvoice purposes. The service can provide, in effect, a private telephone line, to AT&T's loss but to the profit of the record carriers, which do about a quarter of their international business in leased lines. The technology cuts two ways however. In 1976 AT&T received FCC permission to begin international data service through its Dataphone system, which operates through the company's normal switched service. In 1980, the FCC took further steps to expand competition among the international communications carriers by giving AT&T and another domestic firm, Western Union, wider authorization to operate international services.[15]

Another significant set of FCC decisions in recent years authorizes domestic specialized data networks such as Telenet and Tymnet to operate internationally, using packet data technology. This will expand public information networks to global proportions in the coming years. The Telenet network, for instance, includes access to the *New York Times* Information Bank, Lockheed Information Systems, and other publicly available data resources. Customers here and abroad can dial into these services from their own private dials or leased line facilities, or they can go to what Telenet calls "public dial ports" — the computer network equivalent of a public phone booth. Telenet has expanded its public dial ports to four hundred and fifty cities. In the early eighties, dial port access was available in thirty-three countries abroad.

The international telephone and data transmission system is clearly in transition from the low-volume elite services of two decades ago to a new kind of mass communications network. The changes have sharpened the competitive edge of the American firms involved, each of them pushing hard for a bigger share of what is, despite all the neat statistical projections, a market whose size and pattern is still unclear. The trends point upwards; the question is how far up? An important part of the answer will depend on the willingness of foreign governments to provide, through the telecommunications structures they control, the facilities the American companies need to extend their new services abroad. During the seventies, government controlled post, telegraph, and telephone agencies (PTT) were reluctant, and sometimes hostile, toward American proposals of new services. Traditionally conservative, many PTT's were generally in no hurry to upset their highly profitable telecommunications services (which normally subsidize postal services).[16] This element was mixed with their governments' information sovereignty fears about the rapid spread of American data processing services in Europe. The result has been to inhibit but by no means to halt the growth of international information networking.

Building a full-scale world information network will require a staggering amount of new machinery, from satellites in space to telephones in African villages. Parts of the network are already in place, but most of it still has to be constructed. One recent estimate puts the construction cost for a minimal world network, with the emphasis on telephone service, at nearly a trillion dollars in the years leading up to the year 2000.[17] In the fast-moving communications and information field, the telecommunications equipment industry will be one of the high-growth sectors. Any growth projections involve educated (and usually conservative) guesses; what is more certain is that the major growth will be abroad in other industrial countries and, increasingly, in the Third World.

Equipment markets were dominated handily by American manufacturers in the early postwar decades. This is no longer true: European and Asian firms are now stiff competitors. The ability of Japan and other Asian countries (Taiwan, Korea, and Singapore, among others) to produce cheaper, quality consumer goods has resulted in a net deficit in the U.S. communications equipment balance of trade in recent years. The American industry's strength is in high-technology products, but even here the advantages provided by innovative research, quality engineering, and patent protections are shrinking. "The world is regressing to the speedy technological transfer of the 15th century, when patents did not exist," the London *Economist* notes. "Electronics, where patenting is nearest to collapse, is recreating that vanished age. In electronics, the technological lead time is usually only 18 months."[18] The result is, increasingly, a global free-for-all as telecommunications firms (and the many governments that subsidize their efforts) scramble for bigger shares of an expanding market.

The market involves a bewildering variety of products, but most of them are grouped around two familiar items — telephones and computers. A century after Alexander Graham Bell's invention, the rest of the world is moving into the telephone age. The phone has been an elite instrument until now in all but a handful of countries — the United States, Canada, Sweden, and several others. Despite its advanced industrial status, West Germany did not have phone service for 40 percent of its families in the late seventies. Moving down the economic ladder, telephone services range from the inadequate to the near-hopeless in most Third World countries. What phone services exist are patchwork systems, often in an advanced state of decay.

The rush is on to build new systems as scores of countries, both the haves and the have-nots, realize that a good telephone system is not only a national status symbol but also an economic necessity. They want their new systems quickly, and they often opt for the latest models, which means expensive, computerized, all-electronic exchanges. (In the case of technology-poor countries, this high initial expense can make sense since electronic exchanges, with fewer moving parts, are considerably easier to maintain with a small trained crew.) Building a minimally adequate world telephone system in the next decade — amounting to roughly a billion phones compared to 1980s half billion — will be one of the biggest telecommunications projects ever undertaken and will cost perhaps $750 billion.

American industry will provide equipment and services for large parts of the new network. The three big equipment firms are Western Electric, General Telephone and Electronics (GTE), and International Telephone and Telegraph (ITT). GTE and ITT are traditional exporters; Western Electric, the manufacturing arm of the Bell System, is reentering the overseas markets it dropped out of in the 1920s. The firm is one of several Bell organizations operating abroad through a new Bell subsidiary, AT&T International. All three equipment companies begin with the advantage of serving a strong U.S. market. Although this country may seem to have become telephone saturated, with over ninety-five phones per hundred households, the market continues to absorb more. In a recent year, 6.5 million new phones were installed, more than there are in all of Africa outside of South Africa.

The overseas market is big, and competition from European and Japanese manufacturers is sharp. Working in Third World countries is difficult. Technicians who are used to neatly phased domestic construction programs find themselves enmeshed in management and technical nightmares compounded by strange political, economic, and cultural customs that, in theory, have nothing to do with building a phone system. One experienced U.S. executive compares the experience to wrestling with a jellyfish.[19]

Although American firms win big contracts (ITT's in oil-rich Nigeria, for instance), they often lose bigger ones. The classic confrontation took place in the late seventies over modernizing the Saudi Arabian system, a project that involved a series of contracts totaling over $4 billion. All of the major American firms were involved in the bidding as were Sweden's L. M. Ericsson, Germany's Siemans, and Japan's Nippon Electric. The struggle was epic in its proportions, involving low intrigue and high diplomacy. The final contracts went to a consortium of Ericsson, Phillips of Holland, and Northern Telecom, a Canadian company.[20]

At the beginning of the eighties, there were growing doubts among some U.S. economic experts about whether American firms were being aggressive enough in the competition for the overseas equipment market. Many of them are still concentrating their efforts on the domestic market, still the largest in the world though its growth rate is slower compared to the offshore markets where there is more pent-up demand. In a 1980 survey of American prospects in this area, *Business Week* noted that the U.S. firms' superiority in technology was offset by weaknesses in the marketing of their products abroad.[21] In 1981, the White House Office of the Special Trade Representative announced plans to give this subject priority.

The economic stakes are equally high for American firms in another equipment area — computers. Here the Americans took an early lead and have kept it. Computer power is a new index of national strength. American dominance is, for the present, formidable. The reasons are not hard to find. Much of the technology was developed here followed by a strong investment program during the fifties and sixties. The major companies have large distribution and servicing organizations here and abroad. The domestic market gave them a strong starting point for what has been, almost from the beginning, a major international market. Finally, American computers have, by and large, set the world standard, making foreign competitors follow in their technical footsteps. As a result, in 1976, U.S. computer equipment firms accounted for 87 percent of the sale of the world's computers, by value. In the early eighties, the American share is expected to be cut to about three fourths of the international market by increased foreign competition.[22]

This is still a healthy lead — but it is also one that will be increasingly challenged during the eighties. No longer can the U.S. computer industry automatically count on its technological and merchandising superiority to win international orders. The industry also has to cope with foreign government policies designed to curb dependence on American computer equipment and to build up national capabilities. The result is a complex series of steps, — involving subsidies, mergers, cartels, quotas, and restrictionist devices — aimed at limiting American computer products and services.

"Watching the movements made by companies and governments in the computer industry worldwide is like watching 15 chess matches going on at the same time," says international computer expert Angeline Pantages. "Every match has one thing in common, though. IBM seems to control both queens on every board."[23] If most computers have a "Made in USA" label on them, they usually also have the clinically efficient IBM logo. The company has its share of the world computer market that starts at more than 50 percent in most major countries; it is almost totally dominant in many smaller markets. Half its sales and half its profits normally come from overseas. With over one hundred thirty thousand employees abroad, twenty-one plants, and ten laboratories, it has a worldwide reach and flexibility unmatched by any other firm. For example, a new model, the 3033, was introduced in 1977 with a $3.38 million price tag for the smallest version and simultaneous production at factories in Poughkeepsie, N.Y.; Havant, England; and Yasu, Japan. The project was typical of the kind of global strategy that has given IBM such a strong lead in research, manufacturing, distribution, and servicing of its products.

IBM may be, as Pantages suggests, the queen of the international computer chessboard, but a more fitting analogy may be that of a Gulliver beset by Lilliputians. The Gulliver image applies to both domestic and overseas markets. IBM's traditional strength has been in the big mainframe computers; it now has to establish its credentials in the growing small computer market against a proliferating number of competitors. Its strategy is complicated by a long-running federal government antitrust suit, designed in part to split up the firm. The issue pits IBM's claims of discrimination on the basis of success against the government's claim that the industry should be made more competitive by reducing IBM advantages in technology, production, and marketing.

IBM faces other similar problems in the future. In Europe and Japan, a combination of government and private strategies have been developed to reduce the company's dominant position. The first moves were made in the sixties in France, prompted by President Charles de Gaulle, who cited both French *gloire* and economic realities as the reasons why IBM's near monopoly of the French market had to be ended. This resulted in a cycle of mergers, licensing deals, and other arrangements, all designed to create a workable domestic alternative to IBM.[24] The results were mixed: IBM's long lead had been cut back, but it still controls over half the French market. In 1976, the newly elected President, Giscard d'Estaing, ordered a comprehensive look at the entire French communications and information structure. (His motivation, in part, was to redeem an election promise to improve the French telephone system, whose condition was summed up in the popular complaint, "Half of France is waiting for a telephone; the other half is waiting for a dial tone.") The resultant government study, the 1978 Nora Minc Report, was a prescription for transforming France into a modern information society.[25] The code word was *télématique*, the integration of communications and information resources into a powerful strategic national utility. The immediate result of the report was a dramatic improvement in the French telephone system. Within five years, subscriber lines were doubled and a host of high-technology innovations were introduced.

However, computers were the main focus of the Nora Report. The future of France as a political and economic power, the report said, rested on decisions in this area. IBM was, predictably, portrayed as the villain, the most formidable factor in American domination of French computer resources and of the data banks on which French industry and research facilities were forced to rely for specialized information. France had to develop its own resources in these areas in order to maintain itself as a healthy society. Although the report concerns technological and economic matters primarily, it includes valuable sections on the cultural implications of the *télématique* society that offer many insights useful for our own American dialogue on the new information environment.

The Nora Report also encouraged a series of French Government initiatives in advanced communications, including increases in subsidies for research and development, and a renewed attempt in 1981 by the Mitterand government to reduce the large American minority share (held by Honeywell) in the biggest domestic computer company, CII-Honeywell Bull.[26] In the meantime the European Economic Community was also taking steps to counter the influence of IBM and other American firms in the Common Market, motivated by the fact that the EEC accounts for only 15 percent of the West's production of computers and 26 percent of consumption in the early eighties. At a 1980 summit meeting in Dublin, the EEC determined that its members should aim for a third of world communications and information resources, both in production and consumption by 1990.[27]

More recently, both American and European attention has been focused on a new competitive force in the high-technology international markets — the Japanese. A more than symbolic turning point in Japan's role as an information power occurred in 1980, when IBM's leading place in computer sales within the country was overtaken by Fujitsu Ltd. The shift also signaled Japan's entry into world markets, competing against the Americans and Europeans both on their home grounds and in the export trade.[28] The aggressive Japanese push in computers will be an increasingly significant factor in the next few years. The more important Japanese impact may involve the basic microelectronic module, the semiconductor chip, with Japanese firms challenging the hitherto massive U.S. dominance of the field, both technically and economically. As noted earlier, the Japanese firm, Nippon Electric, began construction on the most advanced semiconductor plant in the United States in late 1981.

The Japanese challenge has its roots in a 1971 Ministry of International Trade and Industry "white paper" on information and communications.[29] The report set goals for the conversion of Japan to an information-based economy, with due attention given to high-technology electronics. Large-scale government assisted research and development during the seventies paid off in a wide range of technologies. When U.S. manufacturers could not meet the demand for microelectronic chips in the late seventies, Japanese manufacturers jumped in and captured 40 percent of the U.S. memory-chip market by the end of 1979.[30] The Japanese also moved actively into Europe, staking a claim to the growing microelectronics market there. In the process, they forced Common Market economic experts to adapt their strategies to a new non-American challenger.

The U.S. electronics industry has reacted vigorously to the Japanese initiative in the early eighties. Capital spending to expand facilities rose to record levels, as did investments in research and development. Major firms began pooling their research and development efforts, usually under university sponsorship, modifying their previous practice of individual research competition in this area. This shift moves U.S. firms closer to Japanese and European methods of pooling technological resources. The University of Minnesota's new Microelectronics and Information Science Center is underwritten by Control Data, Honeywell, Sperry, and other firms; IBM, Xerox, and Burroughs are among the companies jointly underwriting basic microelectronics research at the California Institute of Technology.[31] In the meantime, the industry was considering political action, in the form of advocating protectionist trade legislation. In May 1981, the Japanese took steps to ward off such a move by agreeing to more liberal trade rules.[32]

These developments reflected the high stakes involved in the future of the U.S. semiconductor industry. Its health, both economically and technologically, will directly affect any American strategy for the information age, since it is essential to a productive electronics industry whose annual output may reach $400 billion by the end of the decade.[33]

Despite challenges from overseas competitors, U.S. electronics equipment manufacturers will continue to have the lion's share of the world market for some time to come. The pattern will change as more competitors enter the field and as the market itself changes to accommodate the new minicomputer, microcomputer, and microprocessor technologies. Not all the competition will come from Europe and Japan. Many ambitious Third World nations want a computer industry in much the same way that they had originally sought steel mills, airlines, and Hilton hotels.[34] Brazil, in particular, has developed firm national policies for building up a computer industry, including protectionist measures against foreign competitors. Other developing countries have invited Western manufacturers in to develop joint venture projects. In some instances, countries have sought to take over majority control of local foreign plants. Almost all of ITT's Latin American production facilities were nationalized or placed under local majority control during the 1970s. IBM pulled out of India in 1978 after refusing to accept 60 percent Indian ownership of its local subsidiary, as the country's government had ordered.[35]

Beyond hardware, there is a new and rapidly expanding export market in information services. Selling (or giving away) information is an old American habit. The United States is the largest information market in the world, a condition that has had incalculable consequences for our political structure, economy, and culture. We have not been shy about sharing this resource with others: until recently two thirds of all international communications originated in this country. Three major changes have taken place in this pattern in the past two decades. First, the U.S. share of this information transfer has decreased as other nations build up their information resources and make them available internationally. Secondly, a larger share of information is moving electronically across borders and increasingly between computers. Finally, the volume of this information is expanding exponentially, probably at an annual rate of 10 percent.

The net result has been the creation of global information networks of all sizes, patterns, and purposes. One of the largest is the World Meteorological Organization's massive world weather watch, which gathers information from thousands of stations on earth as well as from weather satellites in space, analyzes the results, and retransmits them all over the globe. Another is the U.S. Government's Medlars network, a computerized data base of four million research reports from three thousand medical journals and other sources. Medlars is "searched" a million times a year by doctors and hospitals in North America and abroad, either by mail, telex message, or direct on-line access.[36] Another U.S. Government information facility, the National Technical Information Service, makes available reports on all research funded by the government. It is heavily used by foreign governments and institutions for its access to a significant portion of U.S. technological and scientific research.

These and similar public data banks are made available without cost, or for a relatively small service fee. They are an important part of the new electronic information services. Even greater expansion is taking place in the commercial sector. Information is a highly salable item, and this country has traditionally held the lead in making technological data available for a fee. The United States is responsible for almost half of the global trade in the licensing or sale of technical know-how.[37] This is sold in many different forms, but increasingly it is moving as data between computers.

This has spawned a new sector in the information industry that provides access to specialized data resources stored in computers for a wide variety of customers. These include systems operated by such firms as Lockheed, Control Data, Systems Development Corporation, and General Electric. Most of them provide time sharing arrange-ments, where the customer pays by usage, although many variations for obtaining their information have been developed. The General Electric network can be accessed from local telephones in over four hundred cities in North America, Europe, Japan, and Australia. The Swedish fire data system described at the beginning of this chapter operates from GE computers. The network information industry moved up over the billion dollar sales mark by the end of the seven-ties, with international sales accounting for about one fifth of the total.

Another category of networking is composed of private corpora-tion circuits, heavily used by the big multinational firms for their in-ternal communications around the globe. The Bank of America's telecommunications network stretches from Hong Kong to Vienna, involving circuits on three separate satellites. The system provides voice, data, telegraph, and interactive computing services in ways that give the bank's central headquarters in San Francisco instantaneous access to its operations on four continents. About seven hundred of the world's major banks belong to a network known as SWIFT, an acronym for the Society for Worldwide Interbank Financial Telecom-munications. SWIFT's global reach allows its subscribers to.buy, sell, lend, and borrow throughout the world, getting an acknowledgement back five or six seconds after the transaction is made. The process is a big business version of what will eventually be a consumer-oriented electronic banking system in this country, handling similar transac-tions for bank customers in their homes.

Similar services are available to smaller companies, who can plug their terminals into commercial networks for a fee. The best known of these are Tymnet and GTE's Telenet, both of which provide domestic and international electronic mail and other communications services. The future of this sector of the information services business will be determined by the relationship between AT&T, IBM's Satellite Business Systems, and the Xerox Corporation, all of which are de-veloping advanced telecommunications networks that may bring in-formation service grids down to the consumer level in this country, eventually to connect with similar networks abroad.

The rapid expansion of information networks has led to the dis-persal of international business to locations where there are low taxes, good communications and few restrictions on data transfer. Two such locations, popular with banks, are the Bahamas and the Cayman Islands in the Caribbean. The Bahamas has 263 banks, most of them foreign, with assets (in 1977) of $70 billion; the tiny Caymans have 260 banks with assets of $12 billion. Basically, these islands are offshore tax havens, where, thanks to good communications circuits, business can be transacted as easily as if banks were in a traditional financial capital.[38]

But not all international business can be transacted on lush Caribbean islands, whatever the tax advantages. The bulk of it is still done in the old locations, where stricter regulations apply. Foreign governments are becoming increasingly concerned about the vast amounts of computer-based data information moving in and out of their territories, affecting their economies and often their political interests. The result has been a move, particularly in Europe and Canada, toward regulatory guidelines on transborder data flows. The Canadians are concerned that too much information about their economy, and their citizens' private lives, is stored in computers in the United States. In Europe, sixteen countries have developed legislation imposing specific restrictions on the electronic transfer of personal information about their citizens to other countries. The first country to approve such restrictions, Sweden, has a national data control board that must approve all such transfers. On a regional basis, the Organization for Economic Cooperation and Development (OECD) has drafted guidelines for assuring the compatibility of such privacy legislation, and in 1980 it began looking into more general questions of the transborder data flow problem. The United States has been publicly sympathetic to concerns about privacy of information — which it also protects through its own legislation — but is also worried that the expansion of restrictions on transborder data flow may affect American economic interests.[39]

The most controversial area of U.S. information sales abroad involves the mass media — film, television, publications, and news agencies. Here the American information age is made visible to literally billions of people abroad in ways that are brash, colorful, and immensely popular. It will be generations before the impact of contemporary U.S. mass culture on the rest of the world can be measured. Will it be judged as the raucous noise of a flash-in-the-pan society, as critics claim, or will it be seen as the transmitter of ideas and values that created a new democratic world order? For the present judgments are mixed, but there is little dispute about the ubiquitous influence of American mass culture abroad.

In the last century, an English cleric, Sydney Smith, asked, "In the four quarters of the globe, who reads an American book? Or goes to an American play? Or looks at an American picture or statue?" It is a different story now, when American influences have been instrumental in establishing the first world cultural style. There are many sources of this impact, but a large share of it comes from the Hollywood film industry. In the 1920s, the industry produced and distributed most of the world's films, establishing the medium's artistic, technical, and economic standards.[40] This production dominance was cut back in later years as film industries developed abroad, but Hollywood continued to set the pace. It was an envious Stalin who once told a visitor, "If I could control the American film industry, I could control the world." However, entertainment rather than ideological enlightenment was what drew huge audiences to Hollywood films. Even now, when American production is down to 10 percent of the world total, Hollywood films — particularly blockbusters like *Star Wars* — dominate foreign markets.[41]

When film production fell off in the fifties, television programs took its place. As films had done in the twenties, American TV shows provided a large share of world production in the sixties and seventies.[42] Although these products are still a healthy export market for U.S. syndicators, they face increasing competition from foreign producers. In Latin America, once an unchallenged market for U.S. television, Mexican, Venezuelan, and Brazilian producers now have the largest export share. American syndicators also face restrictions in the form of quotas on the amount of foreign programs shown on overseas stations. Many countries now have such restrictions, generally designed to encourage local production as well as to counter criticism that too many foreign (that is, American) programs are shown, with allegedly baleful effects on local cultural patterns.[43]

The other major segment of American media involvement abroad is the news business. The two large U.S. press agencies — Associated Press (AP) and United Press International (UPI) — dominate international news flow, although there is strong competition from European agencies, particularly Britain's Reuters organization. A more uncertain challenge is the prospect that, within the coming decade, one or more large news agencies may be organized in Third World countries. Similar proposals had foundered in the past. In the late seventies, a nonaligned news pool, largely under Yugoslav sponsorship, was set up for news exchanges among Third World countries. The initial results were professionally unimpressive, but the motivation behind the idea was strong enough to suggest that some form of permanent organization might develop.

This motivation was a combination of political and cultural factors. Culturally, it involved a desire to break away from dependence on Western press agencies as news sources allegedly biased against

Third World accomplishments and values. Proponents of this view invoked the concept of "information sovereignty," contending that Western agencies were only interested in reporting political unrest, earthquakes, and *National Geographic* type exotica from their countries. However justified these charges, there was also a strong underlying political motivation to curb Western reports on Third World political and economic troubles. The nonaligned news agency's output in its early years consisted largely of Propaganda Ministry handouts from its member countries. The experiment raised doubts as to whether an indigenous Third World news-reporting system — a laudable enough project — could be developed soon. In the meantime, the American news agencies and their European competitors will continue to be the dominant force in international news flow.

Another influential segment of U.S. international media influence involves print publications — from the *Reader's Digest* to scholarly books and journals. *Reader's Digest* is an international media phenomenon in its own right, with editions printed in thirteen languages and in thirty-one countries. The international editions of *Time* and *Newsweek* reach relatively small but significant elite audiences in every country. The American book industry, with $7 billion in annual sales, relies heavily on its export trade, particularly in the technical field. U.S. publishers have been successful in developing cooperative production and marketing arrangements with local firms in Third World countries since the abrogation in the seventies of a long-standing arrangement that gave British publishers preferential access in large parts of the world.

The weakest area of American media influence abroad is radio. Before World War II, a number of attempts were made to develop commercial shortwave broadcasting from this country, with emphasis on transmissions to Latin America. The war halted these efforts. The only private U.S. stations now broadcasting to foreign audiences are evangelical-type religious stations, most of whose transmitters are located abroad. International radio is largely a government responsibility, with particular emphasis on reaching audiences in communist countries where outside news and information sources are restricted. Three government financed stations — Voice of America, Radio Liberty, and Radio Free Europe — provide almost continuous round-the-clock transmissions to these areas.

In summary, the United States is a major player in the business of international communications and information — from building satellites for the Arabs to selling *Reader's Digest* in Brazil. Although American activities cover a wide range of activities, they share three characteristics. The first is that American firms have a strong position in each sector. The second is that each sector is becoming more competitive each year; the easy postwar days are over. The third is that, in each sector, American products and services face, in varying degrees, threats to their access to foreign markets.

Harvard information resources expert Anthony Oettinger sees information access as a major policy issue for the United States in the coming years. He uses a simple chronological progression to illustrate his point: in the fifties, American strategic interests centered around access to real estate for military bases; in the sixties the emphasis shifted to economic access for the worldwide expansion of U.S. industry and banking. He believes the problem is now shifting to threats to information and communications access, the connectors between an increasingly information-dependent U.S. society and other nations.

One of Oettinger's colleagues in the Harvard information resources study, William Read, has suggested that we may come to a world "information crisis" roughly comparable to the oil crises of the early seventies.[44] This may seem to be a worse-case scenario, given the fact that the trend toward more communications circuits and more information openness is running strong. There is, however, a dark side to this trend, based on the imbalance of world information resources. By and large, this imbalance has favored the United States. As foreign nations begin to perceive communications and information resources as national security factors, American strength in this area is seen in a different light. This shift lies behind the "information sovereignty" argument, or in simpler terms, good old-fashioned political and economic protectionism extended to a new field.

Fortunately, the problem is not yet generally regarded in such rigid, black-and-white terms. Information is not oil, a resource that can be easily bestowed or denied by turning on a tap. However, it would be risky not to recognize the potential of greater political control of information flow. The Soviet Union has demonstrated, over a period of six decades, the relative ease with which a determined authoritarian regime can control information flow for its own interests. The new information technologies, from the computer on down, have no ideology. They can be configured for totalitarian or democratic purposes. The threat is there, and occasionally it surfaces in direct form. In 1978, British telecommunications workers voted not to handle any international traffic to South Africa, in protest against racial policies there. The ban lasted only a short time. It is possible to imagine a similar ban against traffic to this country because of the way it voted on a certain issue in the United Nations, or because of some other political event.

The United States has indicated on at least one occasion that it would be prepared to take such action. Shortly after U.S. Embassy officials were seized as hostages in Tehran in November 1979, the White House ordered a study of the possibilities of cutting off all communications between Iran and the outside world. The study concluded that a complete cut-off, particularly of satellite communications, was not feasible for legal and other reasons, and the project was dropped.[45] The world communications and information networks are fragile instruments, easily disrupted by terrorist attacks. Whereas terrorists and other revolutionaries used to seize radio and television stations, they have now begun to turn their attention to computers and other information facilities as a way of seriously disrupting a society.

These kinds of assaults on electronic networks that link our social and economic activities will be increasingly common events in the coming years. Another, less violent prospect will be the taking of political actions to restrict communications products and information flow. As noted earlier, this is already a problem for American firms in such areas as data communications, television exports, and computer machine exports. In each case, the aim has been to restrict rather than to eliminate American products and services. The initial effects have been economic, resulting in some loss for American industry. This is an important enough consideration, but it should not mask the overriding political issue involved. The United States is in no position — lingering superpower mythologies to the contrary — to impose its will in such matters. It does, however, have a leadership role to play in the evolution of a world communications system whose emphasis is on openness rather than protectionism and outmoded concepts of sovereignty. Clearly this will benefit our trade interests, but the U.S. should not be so preoccupied with short-range economic problems that it does not recognize the need for sharing information and communications resources, particularly in correcting the massive imbalance between industrialized and developing countries.

This will be a difficult, complex job. It will be viewed with suspicion by those with more narrow-minded economic interests as a do-gooder approach, one that limits their options. There is, in fact, no reason why a policy encompassing our long-run economic and political interests cannot be developed. At present, the United States lacks the coherent guidelines needed to undertake this task, over and above a cycle of tactical moves that represent reactions rather than initiatives designed to create a more stable overall environment for global communications development.

Part of the problem, noted earlier in this chapter, is the absence of an effective mechanism within the American Government to coordinate these issues. Policy decisions are spread across a dozen major agencies and departments. The problem is not how to group them in one agency — this would be an impractical and probably impossible venture, given the bureaucratic passions involved. A more realistic approach might be to establish a coordinating mechanism that operates under clear-cut Presidential directives and has strong liaisons with the private and public interest sectors. In any event, both public and private policymakers need to establish better consultative arrangements, within and between each sector, if they are to identify and implement the decisions required for a full American role in the global communications environment. In 1981, during the early months of the Reagan administration, bills authorizing a Cabinet-level committee to oversee U.S. policy and operations in this area were introduced in Congress, but were not passed.[46]

A restructuring of the U.S. Government apparatus remains a prerequisite for handling the more difficult problem of how to improve international consultation on communications and information issues. Any domestic consensus on how to proceed will depend for its success on how it relates to negotiations with other nations, either individually or in groups. Our traditional preference has been for bilateral negotiations, where the problems (and their solutions) are usually more narrow and clear-cut. However, the trend is toward multilateral negotiations as communications and information problems spill over into regional and wider international concerns. This means that the United States will do more of its negotiations through the United Nations and related international organizations.

The number of international organizations claiming stakes in these subjects increases annually. For many of them, communications and information are trendy subjects they can invoke to extend their bureaucratic empires with correspondingly bigger budgets. Other agencies have more legitimate claims. These include such relatively small organizations as the Universal Postal Union, the World Meteorological Organization, and the International Atomic Energy Authority, each of which has performed useful, quiet service in global information cooperation. The two world agencies with the most direct interest in the subject, however, are the International Telecommunications Union (ITU) and the United Nations Educational, Scientific, and Cultural Organization (UNESCO). Most of the critical multilateral negotiations in communications and information during the eighties will be held in these two agencies.[47]

In chapter 3, we examined the ITU's role in developing and administering global standards for telecommunications, including the equitable use of a major natural resource, the radio spectrum. The Union is a one-nation/one-vote organization, and the new nations of Asia, Africa, and Latin America make up the majority of the membership. These nations are prepared to use their influence to seek redress for what they consider, almost without exception, to be an unequal distribution of international telecommunications resources. This pressure comes at a time when the older industrial powers have need to expand their own use of these resources for post-industrial requirements.

These pressures came to a head at the ITU-sponsored 1979 World Administrative Radio Conference (WARC), which reviewed and made decisions on the radio spectrum pattern for the rest of the century.[48] (The conference, which caused hardly a ripple in the world media, was the largest international conference ever held. It had two thousand participants from 145 countries, fifteen thousand proposals to consider, and ran in Geneva for three months.) The 1979 WARC tested the world's ability to deal with its expanding communications requirements within the finite limits of the radio spectrum. This goal is technically reachable. The critical question is whether ITU's members, particularly the new nations-in-a-hurry, can resist confrontational political and ideological temptations in the interests of maintaining an orderly telecommunications framework.

The United States has its own set of temptations in the form of strong domestic pressures from industry and from public claimants on spectrum resources. By and large, the 1979 conference held to its technical agenda, avoiding political confrontation and reaching agreement on most issues. Some of the more sensitive problems were, however, postponed until a later series of specialized conferences to be held during the eighties. This will have the effect of making spectrum issues the subject of almost continuing negotiations throughout the decade. These negotiations will be a stringent test of the ITU's ability to preserve its role of maintaining technical order in international telecommunications, a test it will also be facing at the Union's 1982 decennial general conference as it examines a spate of proposals for restructuring the organization.[49]

The other major international forum for communications and information issues is UNESCO. Founded with idealistic hopes after World War II, UNESCO has a checkered record of achievements and failures. It has settled down to bureaucratic middle age in its Paris headquarters, peopled by an international staff who grind out documents written in a corkscrew international dialect that may, if everything goes wrong, someday become the world linguistic standard. In its early years, UNESCO was dominated by the conflict between the Europeans' esoteric cultural concerns and the Americans' pragmatic interests in literacy campaigns, scientific cooperation, and the like. The organization is now dominated by Third World concerns, reflecting the majority of its members.

Communications and information issues are high on the current agenda. Developing countries see UNESCO as a useful forum for airing policies and programs to correct the communications imbalance. A corollary to this is the effort of underdeveloped countries to curb the "cultural imperialism" resulting from the current heavy flow of Western films, news, publications, and other media to their countries.[50] These concerns fall under the Third World rubric of a "New World Information Order." UNESCO was the spawning ground for the concept of *information sovereignty*, or the right to protect one's cultural heritage from harmful outside influences. This led to a move to overturn UNESCO's long-standing support for free flow of information, a concept sponsored by the United States in the organization's early years, in favor of a new emphasis on the right to communicate and on more balanced information flow. The need to correct the imbalance was acknowledged by the United States and other democratic nations. The debates became sharp, however, when proposals for imposing international restrictions on news flow were put forward under the "New World Information Order" slogan. The subject was extensively documented in a UNESCO-commissioned report by an international committee headed by former Irish foreign minister, Sean McBride, issued in 1980. The report was, from the American viewpoint, a mixed bag. It supported the concept of open information flow and also put forward a number of restrictive proposals which had the effect of compromising this concept. Nevertheless, the United States supported the report during UNESCO's 1980 general conference in Belgrade. At the same time, the American approach has been to urge UNESCO members to call an armistice on the cyclical ideological debates in favor of practical programs for improving Third World information and communications resources. To this end, it sponsored a proposal for a UNESCO project on international communications development programs that was approved at the Belgrade meeting.[51]

Both UNESCO and the ITU are weak reeds on which to build

an international policy structure for communications and information. Each agency is buffeted by pressures that prevent it from acting effectively, even in relatively simple matters. However, both are preferable to any of the occasional proposals for a supranational organization to guide overall global network development — a proposition that would neither serve U.S. purposes nor, in the long run, anyone else's.

There is one limited example of a successful supranational agency in this field. It is Intelsat, the operator of the 105-nation satellite grid that has reshaped global communications in the past 15 years. In 1981, its satellites provided over twenty-five thousand circuits, approximately a hundred times the number of cable circuits that were the only reliable intercontinental connections in 1964 when the first Intelsat *Early Bird* was put into orbit.[52]

Intelsat also represents a significant political achievement, a dramatic step in the exploitation of a major technology through international cooperation. The Intelsat innovation combined profit motives, a pragmatic division of power, and a willingness by its owner-nations to forego short-term political and ideological advantages in the interests of a workable system. Intelsat's owners are diverse, ranging from the People's Republic of China to South Africa to the Vatican State. (The Soviet Union is the only significant nonmember.) Collectively they generate over 95 percent of all international traffic.

The Intelsat system was started by the United States and managed by it, through the Communications Satellite Corporation, for a dozen years. The American voting share, based on system usage, has dropped from over 60 percent in 1965 to below 25 percent in 1981. The surrender of American control was not the result of unalloyed altruism by any means. It was the price the U.S. paid for creating a network management system acceptable to other nations. Intelsat now faces different problems as satellite technology opens new service opportunities and as the needs of its member-owners grow. The organization's success raises questions about its role as a model for other global communications ventures. It is an intriguing idea, but the Intelsat experience is probably not readily transferable to other areas. The organization was a unique creation of its time, involving a technology that would not work without a high degree of political cooperation. The technology was, moreover, a monopoly of one country — the United States — which had the resources, the imagination, and the will to allow its monopoly to erode gradually in the interests of a long-term viable world system. Such circumstances cannot easily be replicated in the foreseeable future.[53]

New technologies like Intelsat's satellites are deceptive in their promises. They encourage visions of instant hook-up, of plugging everyone in. It is a peculiarly American vision — the old electronic myth updated. Why shouldn't there be a princess phone in every Hottentot hut and Eskimo igloo, not to mention a TV set and a table-top computer? Despite the new technologies, however, the world information network is going to be built through the slow, patient activities of a wide variety of organizations, technique, and economic programs.

In summary, we have seen that the United States has a major stake in the development of a strong global communications system. Its own information society can be a general model for a new kind of post-industrial democratic evolution abroad. Access is the measure — access to information and communications resources in terms of their availability, the ability of people to pay for them, and their freedom to use the information for personal enrichment as well as community needs.

Assuring international open access may be the most difficult U.S. information policy issue of the eighties. It is not a new problem, but it will take different forms in the coming years. Many other cultures do not put as much of a premium on open access as we do, including otherwise like-minded societies in Europe. And the Third World is suspicious of our tendency to be aggressive in both giving and receiving resources.[54]

A primary U.S. resource in promoting these interests is its industrial productivity. A world grid will not be built by UNESCO resolutions or other pious incantations. It will be built by good technology, sensible economics, and stable political conditions. This is an elusive combination, in short supply in most parts of the world. American industry has the ability to provide the goods and services needed for the network, as do its European and Japanese competitors and the new communications industries of the Third World. Assuring a reasonably open market for these U.S. products is an important part of overall American strategy. It should complement the major thrust of our strategy — our commitment to an open information order, one in which adequate information and communications resources are available to everyone.

Notes

1. Zbigniew Brzezinski, *Between Two Worlds* (New York: Viking Press, 1970), p. 31.

2. For a summary of Schiller's views, see his *Communications and Cultural Development* (White Plains, N.Y.: International Arts and Sciences Press, 1976).

3. Anthony Smith, *The Geopolitics of Information* (New York: Oxford University Press, 1980), pp. 19–40.

4. Quoted in Jonathan Tourtellot, "A World Information War," *European Community* (Washington), January/February 1978, p. 12.

5. *Ibid.*, p. 14.

6. For a summary of the controversy, see *Telecommunications Report*, 18 July 1977, pp. 2–5.

7. A useful compendium of Congressional and private sector attitudes on government policy and organization in international communications and information issues is given in U.S. Congress, Senate Committee on Foreign Relations, *The Role and Control of International Communications and Information*, Report to the Subcommittee on International Operations, 95th Cong., 1st sess., June 1977.

8. *Telecommunications Report*, 18 July 1977, p. 5.

9. The basic proposals of the subcommittee are summarized in U.S. Congress, House Committee on Government Operations, *International Information Flow: Forging a New Framework*, House Report, no. 96-1535, 96th Cong., 2nd sess., 1980, pp. 55–59.

10. For a description of the debate, see Wilson Dizard, *Television — A World View* (Syracuse, N.Y.: Syracuse University Press, 1966), pp. 263–67.

11. U.S. Department of Commerce, *U.S. Industrial Outlook 1976, with Projections to 1985* (16th ed.) (Washington, D.C.: Government Printing Office, 1976).

12. "International Direct Distance Dialing Offered to More Nations," *Communications News*, November 1975, p. 42.

13. "International Carriers Looking Forward," *Telecommunications*, August 1976, p. 21.

14. "Dataquest Forecasts Worldwide Datacom Service," *Communications News*, September 1980, p. 13.

15. "FCC Seen Acting to Expand Competition Among World Communications Firms," *Wall Street Journal*, 12 December 1979, p. 44. The 1980 decision to permit Western Union entry was opposed by other carriers in the courts. Congressional legislation permitting the firm to compete for international business was introduced by Senator Barry Goldwater (R-Arizona) early in 1981.

16. "Dealing with Foreign PTTs," *Telecommunications*, January 1980, p. 25.

17. "The New New Telephone Industry," *Business Week*, 13 February 1978, p. 69.

18. "Where Are Britain's Capital Venturers?," *The Economist* (London), 23 July 1977, p. 73.

19. "The Great World Telephone War," *Fortune*, August 1977, p. 144.

20. "Blanketing the World with Phones," *New York Times*, 2 February 1980, Special section on international economic developments, p. 12.

21. "Data Communications: A Market Where the U.S. Lags," *Business Week*, 11 February 1980, p. 57.

22. American Federation of Information Processing Societies, *Information Processing in the United States: A Quantitative Summary*, (Washington), 1977, p. 14.

23. Angelina Pantages, "The International Computer Industry," *Datamation*, September 1976, p. 56.

24. For a description of the complex maneuvers involved in the attempt to reduce IBM's share of the French computer market, see "Western Europe's Computer Industry," *Datamation*, September 1976, pp. 65–75.

25. Simon Nora and Alain Minc, *The Computerization of Society*, (Cambridge, Mass.: MIT Press, 1980).

26. Guy de Jonquires, "French Telecommunications — The Wired Society Gamble," *Financial Times* (London), 1 October 1980, p. 14.

27. "Why Europe Is Not an Open Market for Computers," *The Economist* (London), 5 April 1980, p. 83. See also "European Strategies to Fight IBM," *Business Week*, 17 February 1979, p. 43, and "Telematics Are Here: European Community Working on a Common European Strategy," *Europe* (Washington), May/June 1981, pp. 5–7.

28. "Computers: Here Comes Fujitsu," *New York Times*, 11 November 1980, p. G-1.

29. Ministry of International Trade and Industry, *The Plan for an Information Society* (Tokyo: Jacudi, 1972).

30. "Fighting Off the Japanese," *The Economist* (London), 7 June 1980, p. 80.

31. "Joining Hands Against Japan," *Business Week*, 10 November 1980, p. 108.

32. "American Electronics Industry: Fighting to Cash In Their Chips," *Washington Post*, 9 November 1980, p. G-2. Also "U.S. and Japan Plan Cuts in Semiconductor Tariffs," *New York Times*, 12 May 1981, p. D-1.

33. The estimate is from electronics industry expert Warren Davis, quoted in "American Electronics Industry," *Washington Post*, 9 November 1980, p. G-2.

34. Louis Turner and Stephen Woolcock, "Emerging Nations Compete with the Industrialized World," in German Marshall Fund, *Transatlantic Perspective*, no. 3 (September 1980): pp. 21–24.

35. "Computing the Loss of IBM," *The Economist* (London), 1 December 1979, p. 77.

36. In 1980, at least ten countries had full or partial on-line access to

Medlars. See "Information Biomedical Communications — the Role of the U.S. Library of Medicine," *Health Communications Informatist*, 1980, p. 212.

37. "The Trade in Technology," *The Economist* (London), 21 April 1979, p. 48.

38. "A Boom in No-Strings Banking," *New York Times*. 2 February 1980, Special section on international trade, p. 14.

39. For useful background on this issue, see U.S. Department of State, *Selected Papers: International Policy Implications of Computers and Advanced Telecommunications*, Bureau of Oceans and International Environmental and Scientific Affairs (Washington, D.C.: Government Printing Office, 1979). Also "Transborder Data Flow," special issue of *Stanford Journal of International Law* 16 (Summer 1980).

40. William Read, *America's Mass Media Merchants* (Baltimore: Johns Hopkins University Press, 1977), pp. 39–44.

41. For a useful survey of Hollywood's continuing influence on world film markets, see "Hollywood Flourishes, Its Colonies Languish," *The Economist* (London), 4 November 1978, pp. 85–87.

42. Read, *Media Merchants*, pp. 144–79.

43. The point is documented, with some ideological bias, in Jeremy Tunstall, *The Media Are American* (London: Constable, 1977).

44. William Read, *Foreign Policy: The High and Low Politics of Telecommunications*. Program on Information Technologies and Public Policy, Harvard University. Publication P-76-3, February 1976, p. 2.

45. "No Go for Satellite Sanctions Against Iran," *Science*, 16 May 1980, p. 20.

46. "Bills to Establish Review on FCC Clear Hurdles," *Wall Street Journal*, 17 May 1981, p. 6.

47. For a useful description of the international agencies involved in communications and information policy, see Edward Ploman, "The Whys and Wherefores of International Organizations," *Intermedia* (London), July 1980, pp. 6–11.

48. The political and technical aspects of the conference were extensively examined in ten articles grouped under the overall title, "The U.S. Faces WARC" in *Journal of Communication* 29, no. 1 (Winter 1979): pp. 143–207. For a review of the conference results, see Glen O. Robinson, "Regulating International Airwaves: The 1979 WARC," *Virginia Journal of International Law*, 21, no. 1 (Fall 1980): pp. 1–54.

49. A useful survey of proposals for reforming the ITU over the years is contained in J. Henry Glazer, "Infelix ITU — The Need for Space Age Revisions to the International Telecommunications Conventions," *Federal Bar Journal*, 23, no. 1 (Winter, 1963): pp. 1–36.

50. This development is summarized in Jonathan F. Gunter, ed., *The United States and the Debate on the World Information Order* (Washington, D.C.: Academy for Educational Development, 1979), pp. 44–53. See also "Third World News and Views," *Journal of Communication*, 29, no. 2 (Spring 1979): pp. 134–98.

51. Philip H. Power and Elie Abel, "The Third World vs. the Media," *New York Times Magazine*, 21 September 1980, p. 116. For a useful summary of the Third World agenda in communications and information matters, see United Nations, General Assembly, Special Political Committee, *Questions Relating to Information*, Annex to Agenda Item 59, December, 1980. An American-initiated critique of attempts to curb information flows can be found in *Voices of Freedom*, the working papers of the World Conference of Independent News Media, Talloires, France, 15–17 May 1981, published by the Edward R. Murrow Center for Public Diplomacy, Tufts University, 1981.

52. Joseph N. Pelton, *Global Talk* (Amsterdam: Sijthoff Noordhoff Publishers, 1981).

53. Marcellus Snow, "Intelsat: An International Example," *Journal of Communication*, 30, no. 2, (Spring 1980): pp. 147–56.

54. Anthony Smith, *The Geopolitics of Information* (London: Faber and Faber, 1980), pp. 148–73. See also Glen Fisher, *American Communication in a Global Society* (Norwood, N.J.: Ablex Publishing Co., 1979), pp. 141–57.

Chapter Eight

The Open-Loop Future

Having reviewed the overseas impact of American communications and information activities, we now return to the problem of goals and policies for the new information environment here at home. International factors will, of course, influence our formulation of a domestic strategy. Until recently, this global dimension was slighted because of the geographic, economic, and cultural distances separating us from other societies. These gaps, however, are narrowing at such a pace that it is almost impossible for us to perceive the changes and their implications.

We are inclined to be impressed most by the physical components of this international outreach — the satellites, computers, high-speed cables, and other innovations linking us to the rest of the world. But the wider, more significant impact will be on our understanding of our role in a new world order as we touch the minds and emotions of men and women everywhere and are in turn touched by them.

American ideas, resources, and actions will continue to have an outsized influence on what happens abroad, given our progress so far in shaping an advanced information society at home. This does not mean that the U.S. pattern will or should be copied. Nevertheless, the U.S. can set a standard for other societies to consider as they identify their own goals and actions. Our ability to influence these societies will depend on how we develop and carry out our own approaches to the new age. Like the rest of the world, Americans face an open-loop future, in which it will be increasingly difficult to identify guideposts to purpose or direction. As physicist Robert Oppenheimer has noted:

> This world is a new world. . . . One thing that is new is the prevalence of newness . . . so that the world alters as we walk in it, so that the years of a man's life measure not some small growth or rearrangements or moderation of what he learned in childhood but a great upheaval.[1]

Communications and information are driving forces in this environment. Their technologies are no longer constrained by the linear pattern in which innovations were previously introduced over a period of many years. The telegraph, telephone, wireless radio, and other machines evolved slowly, strengthening economic productivity without disrupting social order in an expanding democratic society. In the present age of converging technologies and greater social complexity, the balance between economic productivity and social harmony becomes more difficult to maintain.

The balance is threatened by a dilemma. Technology as a productive force rolls on, while its contribution to social stability, grows weaker. And as the distance between technological promise and social effect widens, confidence in technology is eroded. The situation underscores the warnings of Jacques Ellul on the contrary effects of rapid change. Other observers, like Jay Forrester of MIT's System Dynamics group, suggest that we may have to impose what were formerly unacceptable restrictions on personal and collective freedoms to cope with the consequences of this imbalance. It is a conclusion they reach not because they are antidemocratic but because they see such control as the only alternative to social collapse.[2]

Whether right or wrong, these critics are generally wary of facile post-industrial or information society labels. Their point is valid — but only to a point. The U.S. is not stepping over some imaginary line in time, from materialistic industrialism into a golden epoch of white-collar ease. Such boundary drawing is simplistic, given the still fragmentary evidence of the changes taking place and our own distorting proximity to them. Nevertheless, once we get past the exercise of labeling ages and epochs, we face the fact that the current shift appears increasingly to be a departure from the dynamics that drove our agricultural and industrial past.

Agriculture is still a vital sector of the U.S. economy, but it is no longer a major force for innovation or for shaping social values and goals. Similarly, a loss of inner dynamism is becoming evident in the industrial sector, although this is masked by a continued high output of goods. Less than a quarter of the U.S. work force is now involved in primary industrial production, a ratio that reflects is steady decline in the amount of human energy being put into the production of goods in recent decades. Technological change has profoundly altered the nature and centrality of industrial activity in our society. Growth in agriculture and industry is no longer the major impetus of social development, but is being replaced by a still undefined force. This is an information-based thrust that draws on human resource capital to transfer knowledge into many forms of physical and social activities, to generate wealth in new ways, and in the process, to profoundly alter goals and values.

Is this a permanent shift, or simply a fluctuation in our national energy that will someday subside into a familiar pattern? Improvements in information production and distribution, after all, have been part of all general economic and social advances throughout the agricutural and industrial ages. Then, however, the information factor was subordinate, in terms of applied resources, to physical activities. The shift taking place now, the one we need to know more about, is moving us toward an environment in which information production and distribution will overshadow material production.

This may be a unique moment in human history, one we cannot observe clearly because we are too close to it. Astronomer Carl Sagan has given the concept a cosmic twist with his suggestion that within the past generation we have turned a corner, developing a replication of the information coding and storage capacities of primitive life via the computer. It is, he argues, a quantum leap in the creation and storage of intelligence *exosomatically*, that is, outside the body. For the first time we have machines whose information-handling capacity is roughly comparable to the genetic memory of a living organism — the single-celled paramecium.[3]

This point is sharpened by a comparison of the progressive power of various information storage methods during the past forty centuries. The measure is the number of binary digits, or bits, representing information that can be stored in one gram of each device, beginning with the first permanent information records developed in the ancient Middle East:

Sumerian cuneiform table — 10^{-2} bits or .01 bit.

Paper with typewritten words — 10^3 bits or 1,000 bits.

Electronic magnetic tape — 10^6 bits or a million bits.

Ultrafine silver haloid film on which information is placed with microbeams through a demagnifying electronic microscope — 10^{12} bits or one hundred billion bits.[4]

Such a leap in high-technology information and communications capacities leaves us disoriented. The familiar road markings are smudged or missing. In Marshall McLuhan's analogy, we move into the future looking through a rearview mirror.

Comforting old assumptions can no longer be taken for granted. Heirs to the electronic myth, we like to assume that information and communications factors will continue to raise our level of economic productivity and social progress. There are disturbing indications, however, that such information-based productivity gains may have reached a plateau. The introduction of more resources may not advance the gains of recent years at the same fast pace.

There is growing evidence to suggest that communications and information resources will have to be reassessed if they are to realize their full potential in the current reindustrialization effort. Edwin Parker of Stanford University sees a flattening of growth curves, indicating a point of diminishing returns with respect to investment in information goods and services.[5]

Although the information sector is now larger than the agricultural and industrial sectors combined, the costs of its labor intensive activities may outweigh the productivity gains made possible by more sophisticated technology. In particular, Parker and others have identified the braking effects of a nonproductive public and private bureaucracy, the fastest growing subsector of the information economy despite perennial attempts to control its spread. In the early eighties, office work has accounted for $800 *billion* in annual expenditures in the U.S. economy, 70 percent of which involves salaries and other personnel costs.[6] To reduce the burden of labor intensity in information growth, problems of management conservatism and other obstacles must first be overcome. Better application of existing technologies may be more productive than an accelerated pace of technical sophistication.

Beyond the question of production levels is the matter of social balance in the new information environment. Heavy infusions of information historically have had a disruptive effect on societies. The current flood of new data, increasing at a rate of about 10 percent annually, is unprecedented in any age. It is unclear how much of this is useful information, contributing to social productivity and maintenance, and how much simply adds a potentially unmanageable physical and psychic burden to what Alvin (*Future Shock*) Toffler and other pop analysts characterize as "information overload." In a society that gives the broadest legal protection to the most questionable fact and the most wrongheaded opinion, there is no acceptable way to evaluate information as useful, useless, or superfluous. Justice Holmes's open marketplace of competing ideas remains our ideal, whatever it lacks in standards for selection.

How much information do we need? We began this study with an analogy between the broad information requirements of our evolving society and the specific needs of the Wright brothers in the development of their first successful airplane. Theirs was an unstable machine, designed with barely sufficient information input to allow it to move successfully through a turbulent three-dimensional environment. The analogy remains apt for the perilous passage we have to navigate toward a more complex level of democratic order.

Optimism is difficult to sustain in the face of current trends. One might better take the stance of a pessimist, defined by an anonymous Polish wit some years ago as an optimist with better information. Realistically, the likelihood is that in the near future U.S. society will be marked by higher levels of uncertainty, a blurring of values and priorities, rising mistrust among large sections of the population, and a resulting inability to adapt private and public institutions quickly enough to cope with current problems, let alone adequately anticipate future ones. Expanded information and communications resources will tend, in the short run at least, to magnify these factors rather than reduce them to manageable proportions.

A striking analysis of this prospect is to be found in a 1978 French Government study of the effects of computerization on French culture.[7] Known as the Nora/Minc report after the two civil servants who were its principal authors, the survey was given fairly wide publicity in this country because of its strong attack on the alleged American computer dominance of the French economy. The report's sober analysis of the long-term effects of *informatisation* on French society was largely ignored here. This was unfortunate since a significant point made by Messrs. Nora and Minc was the need to face up to the negative effects of the new computer-based environment, particularly the threat of greater social alienation and erosion of traditional values. The report was a best-seller in France, and the focus of continuing debate there.

We may not be able to replicate the neat Cartesian, and somewhat authoritarian, way in which the French approach problems of orderliness, but we need a better understanding in our own context of the issues raised in the Nora/Minc study. The U.S. faces essentially the same situation — a massive technocratic drive, threatening to go out of control unless its potentially dehumanizing antidemocratic effects are understood and reined in. If this is not done, there is a strong possibility that broad masses of people will be cut off from adequate participation in the technological mainstream, swept along as a kind of information-poor *lumpenproletariat.*

To expect these groups to accept such a position docilely would be dangerously shortsighted. One of the paradoxes of information and communications technology is that, although it seems to benefit primarily those in power, it also provides the means for organizing previously scattered and powerless challengers into strong constituencies.

One example, yet to be adequately documented, is the role played during the Vietnam protest movement a decade ago by a simple technology — the telephone — in organizing groups who reversed a major national policy. Platoons of researchers have concentrated their efforts on the role of television for having "brought the war into the American living room." Though television played a role, it was essentially a passive one.[8] As a readily available two-way technology, it was the telephone that gave politically motivated groups the means for organizing against an establishment that had infinitely more communications resources available for its own purposes. Whether or not the protest groups served overriding national interests is still debatable. Their success, however, is an effective example of the chances a democratic society will have to take in the new information environment in which established power groups may be tempted to limit access to communications channels and information resources to protect their interests.[9]

The risks of open access are substantial. Yet everything in our tradition tells us that the risks are worthwhile, that we must embrace error. A strong reaffirmation of democratic values and actions will be needed to assure social balance and, ultimately, national survival in the new information age. A pluralistic democracy such as America's needs to provide sufficient shared information, beliefs, and assumptions for its members to function as self-governing groups at many levels. "The way to prevent error is to give the people full information of their affairs" — the words are those of an eighteenth-century optimist, Thomas Jefferson. They are a reminder that a fully responsive national communications and information system is not a luxury but an imperative if we are to survive and thrive as a vital democracy.

How can our complex society come to decisions and act to make high-technology communications and information responsive to its goals? We are handicapped by the lack of an overt information or communications crisis or of a coercive fact of the kind that a pluralistic society usually requires to mobilize itself for action. Moreover, we are restricted by a special sensitivity to policy enforcement in this area. A good healthy dose of First Amendment protection buffers us from self-appointed guardians of what is right. British communications scholar Anthony Smith has identified the paradox present in any discussion of the management of communications and information resources in a free society:

> We have acquired a double conundrum: what happens to freedom of communication when the necessary instruments are concentrated inside a small elite of professionals? What obligations has a society towards policing its mass culture when that culture can exercise an influence over the attitudes, the morals, the emotional security of the mass audience? We have already lived with this debate long enough to know that these are not simple organizational questions capable of simple organizational answers. The problems are buried very deep inside our culture and like such problems in past generations they cannot be solved, only replaced with new problems and new formulations of old ones. . . . The only undisputed effect is the dilemma which it poses for all modern societies.[10]

The reality of this dilemma should be a check on any facile approach to a national strategy for communications and information. This caution applies particularly to recurrent proposals for using technocratic methodology to solve sensitive social problems. Such proposals abounded in the wake of the "optimal control" techniques used in the Apollo manned-space-program during the sixties. If computers could be used to identify a path through space that optimized manpower, fuel, and other resources, why not use them to develop policies and programs that optimize the performance of whole societies? The analogy was grossly inexact when applied to a complex civilization whose strengths lie, paradoxically, in an unwillingness to optimize its future by formula. As Nigel Calder notes, it is a wise society that believes the future is too interesting and dangerous to be entrusted to any predictable, reliable agency:

> We need all the fallibility we can get. Most of all we need to preserve the absolute unpredictability and total improbability of our connected minds. That way we can keep open all the options, as we have in the past.[11]

This does not argue against prudent planning. It does suggest hedging our bets against unknown or unforseen factors. If we choose a rigid course and are proved wrong, we all go down. Americans are steadied by a pattern of checks and balances, politically and socially, that in spite of some dangerous tilts, has kept us on keel for the past two centuries. Our stability will be severely tested in the coming years as we adjust our institutions and attitudes to information age realities.[12]

The outcome will depend largely upon decisions dealing with the distribution and use of power. In *The Nerves of Government*, published in the mid-sixties, political scientist Karl Deutsch argued that the new power was in information and communications. The groups that control the nervous system of modern society, the information networks, control the society. Deutsch's thesis was both persuasive and prescient. The proof came in the most dramatic political event of the past decade — the Watergate affair.

The sequence of events in Watergate began with a botched robbery aimed at collecting information about rival politicians. This led to revelations about elaborate White House operations (the "plumbers group") for stopping information leaks and, for good measure, the automated paper shredders and tape erasers designed to destroy information. The critical turning point was the public release of transcripts of tapes from a semiautonomous system of recording devices monitoring offices in the White House. And the highly dramatic culmination came in a televised congressional investigation that made the information available to a vast public.[13]

Watergate exposed the role communications and information played in consolidating political power and also, fortunately, in curbing its abuse. Future attempts at such a major power play will be more subtle, avoiding the stumble-footed flagrance of Nixon's White House. A wide range of sophisticated electronic devices can invade our lives softly and invisibly without, so to speak, leaving fingerprints or incriminating tapes. These devices can be used for benevolent purposes, or for malevolent purposes reminiscent of those employed by Orwell's Big Brother. In between lies a wide grey area, a seemingly innocuous monitoring of routine activities that are carried out in the name of efficiency but are capable of curbing personal rights. Electronic intrusions will be hard to measure and harder to resist, since they will generally involve quiet, discrete functions whose potential threat is not evident.[14]

Such Orwellian scenarios are not all hypothetical. Communications and information technology, unchecked by democratic restraints, can be concentrated in the hands of a distant, anonymous elite bent on containing innovation and protecting its own resources, nominally for some higher purpose. The efforts of any such elite will eventually fail because the new technologies are not that controllable. We have begun to see how modern anarchists, the new breed of political terrorists at home and abroad, can manipulate television, radio, and the telephone system, as well as the traditional print media, for their purposes. Such latter-day guerrilla tactics are, as defense authority Ian Smart has remarked, a lateral evasion of traditional social restraints. This capability is a new form of power, and it can be very effective. The physical fragility of most communications networks — wires, towers, and the like — make them particularly susceptible to terrorist actions which can paralyze a city or an entire region. Terrorist actions will be increasingly directed against computer installations, the newest, and highly vulnerable, form of information resources.[15]

Threats from small activist groups cannot be ignored, but they are peripheral to the problems that have to be dealt with by the majority who accept the premises, and the promise, of the new information age. The central issue is power and its disposition. At this critical time in America, an awesome amount of power is concentrated in complex information technologies and the economic efforts behind them.

Can we handle this expanded power through adjustments in present policies or linear extensions of current practices? Or is a new strategy needed for a different dimension of political power? Are information trends more than a progression of technological and economic adjustments? Do they constitute a fundamental shift in the patterns and purposes of U.S. society? If communications and information resources are in fact pushing us towards a radically different environment, a new political consensus on their use may be needed.

A strong case can be made against a radical change in strategy, for both pragmatic and ideological reasons. The pragmatic arguments stress that the communications and information structure is naturally evolving as an open system through the dynamic interplay of economic forces. In the new competitive environment, the U.S. is moving toward a universal information utility that is accessible to more people more quickly than even the sunniest optimist would have predicted a decade ago.

There is a large measure of truth in that argument, but it is false to assume that technological and economic forces, however dynamic, can by themselves assure a fully accessible system. There will be gaps in isolated geographic areas and among disadvantaged groups who are bypassed for economic or other reasons. Those who are left out will not, in this day and age, be willing to accept second class status until market forces trickle benefits down to them. In a complex, interdependent post-industrial society, the risks of excluding them from mainline benefits may be too high.

The history of communications and information development in this country shows that there has been public intervention at critical points to insure a broadening of benefits. The list is long and distinguished: Congressional funding of the original Morse telegraph experiments, the Morrill Act providing assistance for land grant colleges, federal intervention to assure wireless radio development after World War I. The example most closely paralleling the current situation was public intervention to assure the development of the world's first mass interactive communications systems — the U.S. telephone network — in the 1930s. This decision was incorporated into the Communications Act of 1934, which gave AT&T unique legal protections in exchange for providing universal telephone service, a commitment largely fulfilled. Today more complex decisions are pending, but the need for basic political agreement on a future pattern of communications and information resources is equally pressing.

The ideological argument against political intervention rests on the First Amendment and its protection of individual expression. Rights of free expression, and their support in law and custom, cannot be abridged without compromising the democratic character of the new information age. In simpler times, the definitions of those rights were relatively clear-cut. These distinctions have become fuzzy, however, in the new information environment, with its complex levels of economic and political power wielded by governments and private interests, often in collusion. The line between public and personal rights blurs to the point where civil liberties arguments become a smokescreen for policies and actions that work against individual freedom.

The debate on political principles for the information age is just beginning, as a new sensitivity to the distinctions (and similarities) between public and private interests is growing. "After all," notes communications lawyer Glen Robinson, "interest conflicts do not disappear simply by chanting the words 'public interest' three times, and, indeed the public interest is not something grandly aloof from the amalgam of different private interests that lie beneath it. . . . Yet there must be something more in governance than simply the arbitration and settlement of private conflict."[16] This 'something more' is the elusive and necessary component of a coherent national communications and information policy. Essential personal freedoms must be protected against arbitrary political and economic power without sacrificing the social dynamics that have given this society the most open communications system in the world.

The outlines of a democratic strategy for the new age begin to emerge. These do not constitute a centralized master plan, but a new social compact that will provide the basis for needed policies and actions in the expanding area of information and communications. How can a consensus for identifying and realizing these needs be formed? Agreement will be difficult to bring about in a society in which much of political action is determined by organized interest groups seeking to protect and enlarge group entitlements. New approaches to democratic political strategy are needed, approaches that are not limited to problems of communications and information but recognize their central role in the process. Interest group politics has been given new force by the sophisticated use of communications in ways that often seem to favor direct self-serving actions over the more difficult, slower processes of consensus. Constructive decisions on the future of communications and information may, in fact, be compromised by an anachronistic approach to policy making. It is time for us to reevaluate the ways in which we approach our long-range planning.

The lead has to come from the top. In the U.S. political structure, this means the federal executive branch, and specifically the White House. Communications and information strategies should be put on the priority agenda of critical issues requiring deliberate policy attention. At present, the subject is relatively low on the political list, if only because there is no compelling pressure from major public or private interests. This may be an advantage for the time being. It reduces the prospect that the issue will be "discovered" for some temporary crowd-pleasing purpose. The usual result, in such cases, is to prevent any serious attention to the issue, once the clarion calls for action, the prestigious advisory commissions, and the other paraphernalia for crisis politicking are set in motion.

Long-term strategies for communications and information will be better served by a less frenetic, more deliberate approach, involving the participation of major interest groups. One way of doing this could be a presidentially appointed Communications and Information Policy Council for the purpose of defining problems, goals, and strategies. The council should not have a large bureaucracy attached to it, but it should have sufficient funds to carry out necessary research in preparing its recommendations. A credibly refreshing precedent would be set if the council's funding were shared by federal government, industry, labor, and consumer organizations represented on the council. Participation and funds should also be provided by state and local governments, a generally overlooked sector which has an important stake in communications and information strategy.

The council's primary purpose would be to serve as a sort of communal radar, tracking the implications of communications and information developments out on the horizon and making the results of its deliberations, including those concerning minority views, available to the President, to Congress, and to the public at large. It should strive for consensus, not in the spirit of surface unity, but rather in an ongoing attempt to set the agenda of issues. It should seek cooperatively to identify and address information age realities. No one public organization can encompass all these realities. However, the council could provide a highly visible public forum for identifying and developing long-range national goals and policies in this area.[17]

Meanwhile, certain policies and actions require immediate attention. Priority should be given to the ways in which communications and information matters are now organized within the federal structure. Each administration since the mid-fifties has attempted, with only partial success, to develop procedures for handling communications and information issues within the executive branch. The Carter administration's decision to consolidate many federal programs in a single National Information and Telecommunications Administration brought some order to the subject but did not succeed in providing a strong coordinating point for policy action decisions. At least eighteen federal agencies, plus the independent Federal Communications Commission, remain involved in major communications policy and operational activities. In 1981, the Reagan administration moved cautiously in the face of conflicting recommendations from interest groups to restructure NTIA and other agencies. Nevertheless, there is a strong case to be made for providing a better coordinated approach to both policy making and operational needs in this area.

There are three related areas where policy initiatives are urgently required, whatever new organization structure is developed. The first of these involves both Congress and the executive branch in the problem of modernizing national communications law to reflect information age changes. Significant decisions to move the country in this direction, taken by the FCC and the White House in recent years, have been slowed down by the inability of Congress to pass comprehensive supporting legislation. Until Congress can act on many of these developments, the arbiter will be the courts, which by their own admission are unable to provide clear decisions in the absence of specific legislation. Efforts to bring the Communications Act of 1934 up to date have resulted in legislation only partially responsive to the need. This partial mandate is inadequate; only a comprehensive set of legislative actions can accomplish for the new technologies what the 1934 legislation did for telephone, telegraph, and broadcasting systems.

The second area in need of policy initiatives is the economic sphere. The impact of communications and information as vital industrial sectors in themselves and also as key elements in the current reindustrialization effort must be recognized. The 1977 Department of Commerce study on the information economy discussed in chapter 5 described the dimensions of that impact. Economic policies in this area will be critical in determining the overall growth of the economy through the end of the century.

The third priority policy area involves America's international role, with particular attention to economic factors. Information and communications make up the third largest element in the U.S. export pattern, after agricultural products and aviation. America's high-technology lead in this area gives us a strong competitive edge, an advantage which is being challenged by our industrial allies in Europe and Japan. This is a welcome challenge, in fact, since it is in our overall strategic interest that these countries develop comparable strengths in these sectors. At the same time, we should be pressing an aggressive trade program to capitalize on our present advantage in microelectronic-related products. Specifically, we need to see that increasing indications that we have been slipping, due in part to complacent business-as-usual attitudes, are reversed.[18]

Our international concerns should also extend to the development of more stable policies in the political area. Communications and information have become more sensitive issues as nations identify them as strategic subjects, affecting political, economic, military, and cultural affairs. We have been inclined to ignore, and on occasion denigrate, overseas concerns about the dominant U.S. role in these sectors. Such attitudes, and the policies that sustain them, have to be revised if we are to take a constructive lead in the development of an open global information system. In particular, we need to work more closely with our European and Japanese allies in developing long-range strategies and operations for strengthening communications and information resources in the Third World.[19]

Our responsibilities abroad are a natural extension of the democratic forces that have impelled us to develop an open information society at home. Decisions to continue to support and expand this approach, in a new era of technological abundance, are basically political. We will make them by conscious positive efforts or by default. Either way, they will be made.

The information age is only a convenient phrase to describe the climate of change in which we live. We cannot understand its full significance, however, simply by analyzing the economics, politics, and technology involved, or even by understanding the interaction of these elements. The evolving information environment is part of a larger shift, a shift in the powerful intangibles of values and purposes.

We have gone through two centuries of extraordinary change, beginning in the North Atlantic region and spreading more and more rapidly around the globe under the rubric of modernization. Modernization has many aspects, but its dynamics spring from the scientific revolution. A vision of an inflexible, precise natural order first drove this revolution and then was absorbed into social ideas. The transition was subtle, facilitated by the assumption that, having learned the rules of nature, we had only to apply them to society. Thus the valid precepts of such men as Newton and Darwin were extended beyond their original contexts.

This misapplication of scientific theory pushed us toward the brink of anarchy. We will not survive another two centuries if we continue to pursue the same social chimeras, inspired by myths of scientific and technological certitude. Fortunately, we now sense that something is wrong, and the new perceptions of science confirm our doubts. In physics, Einstein and quantum mechanics shattered the supposed order early in this century. More recently, microbiology has challenged the extremes of Darwinian social views and now offers some hopeful analogs about our human destiny.

Biologist Lewis Thomas has noted, with grace and clarity, the ways in which new studies have questioned older concepts of evolution as primarily a record of open warfare among competing species, with survival limited to the strongest aggressors. "Now," he points out, "it begins to look different. The tiniest and most fragile organisms dominate the life of the earth. . . . [The] urge to form partnerships, to link-up and form collaborative arrangements, is perhaps the oldest, strongest and most fundamental force in nature. There are no solitary free-living creatures; every form of life is dependent on other forms."[20]

These observations from the new biology parallel the realities we face in coming to terms with the information age. The vision of thousands of Einsteins whose talents are liberated by computers, as suggested in chapter 1, will not be fulfilled if computers are used simply as sophisticated storage and calculating machines. Their greatest potential is in creative simulation — not as "artificial intelligence" but as a powerful augmentation of our own imaginations. And this means combining the computer's power with our own power of serendipity — the seemingly formless way in which the human animal arrives at its most enduring ideas, not by proceeding directly and infallibly in doing the essential business of our kind, as other species do, but by leaving well-trodden paths and exercising our gifts for ambiguity.

It is by appreciating this marvelous inherited gift that we can begin to fit the new communications and information resources into a more mature reordering of our personal and collective purposes, not as deterministic evolution but rather as a more harmonious melding of the many-colored strands of our common humanity. British scholar George Steiner has noted the importance of molding communications systems in ways that do not sacrifice diversity to the uncertain benefits of a bland global culture. He cites the role of the world's ten thousand languages in this process:

> Each and every tongue is a distinct window into the world. Looking through it, the native speaker enters an emotional and spiritual space, a framework of memory, a promontory on tomorrow, which no other window in the great house of Babel quite matches. Thus every language mirrors and generates a possible world, an alternate reality.[21]

We may some day shape a world order in which unity not only in language but also in other ways prevails. This prospect, however, is a long way off. For the present, our best interests lie in preserving freedom through competing diversities. This is the objective Americans must keep in mind in shaping our society in a new age. Other cultures will judge us, and identify their own interests, as they see fit. It is, in the last analysis, the one sure path to expanding human freedom, permitting each of us, as Emerson urged, to produce that peculiar fruit we were born to bear.

Notes

1. Quoted in Max Ways, "The Era of Radical Change," *Fortune*, 11 February 1980, p. 201.

2. "Probing Our Future," *Washington Post*, 8 July 1975, p. D-1. For a more optimistic view, see Isaac Asimov, "Communications and the Individualism to Come," *New York Times*, 7 January 1973, special section on direct mail advertising, p. 3.

3. Carl Sagan, *The Dragons of Eden* (New York: Ballantine Books, 1978), p. 25.

4. James G. Miller, *Living Systems* (New York: McGraw Hill, 1977), p. 12.

5. Edwin B. Parker, "An Information-Based Hypothesis," *Journal of Communication*, 28, no. 1 (Winter 1978): pp. 81–83.

6. "Death Sentence for Paper Shufflers," *The Economist* (London), 27 December 1980, p. 56.

7. Simon Nora and Alain Minc, *The Computerization of Society* (Cambridge, Mass.: MIT Press, 1980).

8. Michael J. Arlen, *Living Room War* (New York: Viking Press, 1969).

9. Dallas W. Smythe, "On the Effects of Communications Satellites," *Communications Explosion* (Paper no. 9, Program of Policy Studies in Science and Technology, George Washington University, June 1965), p. 2.

10. Anthony Smith, "The Management of Television in a Democratic Society" (Paper presented at the Symposium on the Role and Management of Telecommunications in a Democratic Society, Munich, June 24–26, 1974),

11. Nigel Calder, *The Life Game: Evolution of the New Biology* (New York: Viking Press, 1975), p. 132.

12. Jon Stewart, "Computer Shock," *Saturday Review*, 23 June 1979, p. 14. Also "Who's Afraid of Video Screens?", *The Economist* (London), 16 February 1980, p. 98.

13. Watergate involved relatively primitive information technology. Computer scientist Martin Hellman of Stanford University has suggested that events would have turned out differently if Nixon and his advisers had relied on more sophisticated technology, such as computer encryption of the White House tapes rather than simple voice recording. "Scientists Urge New Laws to Curb Misuse of Computer Technology," *New York Times*, 23 November 1977, p. D-3.

14. Daniel S. Greenberg, "Molding Behavior Through Electronic Trickery," *Washington Post*, 25 April 1978, p. 22.

15. "Terror by Technology," *The Economist* (London), 19 April 1980, p. 45.

16. Glen O. Robinson, "The New Communications: Planning for Abundance," *Virginia Quarterly Review*, 53, no. 3 (Summer 1977): p. 397.

17. A useful initiative was taken in this area by the White House Conference on Libraries and Information held in October, 1979, in Washington. Its reports recommended a broad series of initiatives for making information available through the new technologies. An interesting proposal for a Temporary National Economic Committee on Computers in America's Future has been advanced by lawyers Harlan M. Blake and Milton R. Wessel in "Time for a National Computer Study?" *Infosystems*, December 1980, p. 12.

18. "The U.S. Lead in Service Exports Is Under Siege," *Businesss Week*, 16 September 1980, p. 70.

19. Recommendations for carrying out such an initiative are contained

in U.S. Department of State, *Toward an American Agenda for a New World Order of Communications*, report issued by the U.S. National Commission for UNESCO (Washington, D.C.: Government Printing Office, 1980).

20. Lewis Thomas, "On the Uncertainty of Science," *Harvard Magazine*, September/October 1980, p. 19.

21. George Steiner, "The Coming Universal Language," *Atlas World Press Review*, October 1977, p. 26.

Selected Bibliography

Bell, Daniel. *The Coming of Post-Industrial Society*. New York: Basic Books, 1973.

Deutsch, Karl W. *The Nerves of Government*. New York: Free Press of Glencoe, 1963.

Edelstein, Alex; Bowes, John E.; and Harsel, Sheldon. *Information Societies: Comparing the Japanese and American Experiences*. Seattle: School of Communications, University of Washington, 1978.

Eisenstein, Elizabeth L. *The Printing Press as an Agent of Change*. New York: Cambridge University Press, 1979.

Ellul, Jacques. *The Technological Society*. New York: Alfred A. Knopf, 1964.

Estabrook, Leigh. *Libraries in Post-Industrial Society*. Phoenix: Oryx Press, 1977.

Evans, Christopher. *The Micro Millenium*. New York: Viking Press, 1979.

Ferkiss, Victor C. *Technological Man: The Myth and the Reality*. New York: George Braziller Inc., 1969.

Fisher, Glen. *American Communication in a Global Society*. Norwood, N.J.: Ablex Publishing Co., 1979.

Forester, Tom, ed. *The Microelecronics Revolution*. Cambridge, Mass.: MIT Press, 1981.

Hammer, Donald P., ed. *The Information Age: Its Development and Impact.* Metuchen, N.J.: Scarecrow Press, 1976.

Innis, Harold A. *Empire and Communications.* Toronto: University of Toronto Press, 1972.

Kuhns, William. *The Post-Industrial Prophets.* New York: Harper & Row, 1971.

Machlup, Fritz. *The Production and Distribution of Knowledge in the United States.* Princeton, N.J.: Princeton University Press, 1962.

Martin, James. *The Wired Society.* Englewood, N.J.: Prentice-Hall Inc., 1978.

McLuhan, Marshall. *The Gutenberg Galaxy.* Toronto: University of Toronto Press, 1962.

Mumford, Lewis. *The Pentagon of Power.* New York: Harcourt Brace Jovanovich, 1970.

Oettinger, Anthony; Berman, Paul; and Read, William. *High and Low Politics: Information Resources for the 80's.* Cambridge, Mass.: Ballinger Publishing Co., 1977.

Phelan, John M. *Mediaworld.* New York: Seabury Press, 1977.

Pool, Ithiel de Sola, ed. *The Social Impact of the Telephone.* Cambridge, Mass.: MIT Press, 1977.

Read, William H. *America's Mass Media Merchants.* Baltimore: Johns Hopkins University Press, 1976.

Schiller, Herbert I. *Communication and Cultural Domination.* White Plains, N.Y.: International Arts and Sciences Press, 1976.

Scientific American, Communication. A special issue, September 1972.

Smith, Anthony. *The Geopolitics of Information.* London: Faber and Faber, 1980.

Smith, Anthony. *Goodbye Gutenberg.* New York: Oxford University Press, 1980.

U.S. Congress, House, *Options Papers.* Prepared by the staff for the Subcommittee on Communications of the Committee on Interstate and Foreign Commerce, 95th Cong., 1st sess. Committee Print 95-13, May 1977.

U.S. Department of Commerce, *The Information Economy.* 9 vols. Office of Telecommunications Special Publication 77-12, 1977.

Wangermée, Robert, and Lhoest, Holde. *L'Aprés-Télévision.* Paris: Hachette Littérature, 1973.

Index

Aetna Life & Casualty Co., 105
Africa, 160
Ahlstrom, Sidney, 3
Aines, Andrew, (quoted), 151
Aircraft communications, use of
     spectrum in, 57
Alaska, 61
Alexandria, library of, 18
American Telephone & Telegraph
     Co.
   size and influence of, 6
   expansion of network, 33
   use of computers, 35
   early role in radio, 49
   long lines network, 51
   use of fiber optics, 53
   role in evolution of advanced
        communications network, 72
   increased labor productivity in, 89
   role in U.S. economy, 95
   quasi-monopoly status, 96
   current evolution of, 97–105

   communications satellite test, 123
   membership on government
        advisory boards, 130
   role in 1976 Consumer
        Communications Reform Act,
        131
   international activities, 156–160
   advanced telecommunications
        network plans, 166
Appalachian region, satellite
     experiments in, 61
Appolo space program, 118, 187
Arab states, 150
Aronson, Sidney, quoted, 96
Artificial intelligence, 15, 82
ARTS Computer Products Inc., 77
Aspen Institute, 141
Associated Press news agency, 168
Atomic Industrial Forum, 134
ATS-6 educational satellite
     experiments, 61
Adams, Henry, 24

"Baby Bell," AT&T subsidiary, 104
Bahamas, 166
Baltimore, Md., 47, 58
Bank of America, 166
Banking industry
  use of electronic equipment, 6, 35
  international data networks, 166
Baran, Paul, 63
Barnet, Richard, 3
Bates, Bill, 79
Bedford-Stuyvesant district in New
  York City, 41
Belgrade, Yugoslavia, 174
Bell, Alexander Graham, 33, 48, 52
Bell, Daniel, 3
Bell Canada Ltd., 71
Bell Laboratories, 51, 73, 98, 102
Benedictine monks, 18
Berlin, Germany, 55
Bermuth, John, 93
Binary digits (bits), 74
Books, changes in production
  methods, 78–79
Book industry, international role of,
  169
Borchardt, Kurt, 134
Boston, Massachusetts, 53, 59, 100,
  113, 133
Boulding, Kenneth, 3
Brave New World, 11
Brazil, 90, 168
British Broadcasting Corporation, 50
British Museum, 19
British Post Office, 48
Broadcasting industry
  regulation by FCC, 96
  early role of AT&T in, 98
  regulatory protection, 110
  critique of, 139–140
Brookings Institution labor
  productivity survey, 89
Brown, Charles L., quoted, 104–105
Brown, Harold, quoted, 126
Brzezinski, Zbigniew, quoted, 149
Budapest, 48

Burkhardt, Jacob, 27
Burroughs Co., 76, 164
Business Week, 160

Cable television systems
  expansion of, 40, 113–114
  challenge to television, 112
  role in consumer information
    networking, 142
Calder, Nigel, quoted, 187
California Institute of Technology,
  164
Cambridge University, 56
Canada, 32
  experiments with teletext, 107
  data banks, 109
  extent of telephone system, 159
  concerns over transborder data
    flows, 167
Carpenter, Edward, 149
Carter, Jimmy, 125, 130, 192
Carterphone decision by FCC, 100
Cater, Douglass, quoted, 141
Cayman Islands, 166
CBS Inc., 6
Central Intelligence Agency, 127, 154
de Chardin, Teilhard, quoted, 5, 23
Chicago, University of, 91, 93
China, Peoples Republic of
  use of shortwave broadcasts, 58
  membership in Intelsat network,
    175
China, Republic of, 159
Christian Broadcasting Network, 111
Christopher, Warren, 154
CII-Honeywell Bull, French
  computer firm, 163
Cincinnati, Ohio, 113
Citizen's band radio, 13, 58
Clarke, Arthur C., 54; quoted, 82
Cleveland, Ohio, 148
CLOAX cable technology, 52
Coaxial cable, 51, 65
Cohen, Morris Raphael, 25
Columbus, Ohio, 144

Columbus Dispatch, 111
COMECON economic organization, 151
Common Market, European, 163
Communications
  effect on democratic development, 24
  open electronics publishing concept, 139
  Communications Act of 1934, 29
  influence on national telephone system, 40, 190
  passage of, 49
  history of, 88, 96, 129
  effects of, 96
  attempts to revise, 99, 131, 193
"Communications and Information Policy Council" proposal, 191
Communications networking
  need for national strategy, 32
  serving network marketplace, 38
  integration of computers and circuitry, 101
  competition between AT&T and IBM, 105
  future growth of, 106
  policy decisions involved in, 117
  cable systems, 142
  international systems, 149, 156
  transborder data flow issue, 167
  Intelsat network, 175
Communications Satellite Act of 1962
  sets U.S. satellite policy, 124
  role in international satellite development, 153
Communications Satellite Corp. (Comsat), 103, 111
  created by U.S. Congress, 124, 155
  "carrier's carrier" role, 156
  manager of Intelsat global network, 175
Communist propaganda, 17
"Compunications," 75, 101
Computers
  creating "Einsteins and Edisons," 9

intelligence amplification capabilities, 14
use by children, 15
expanding uses of, 33
and fiber optics technology, 54
evolution of, 75–80
replacing traditional print, 81
use in international networks, 148
U.S. international domination in, 160–161
The Computer Cookbook, 79
Comsat General Corp, 105
The Conference Board, 24
Congress, U.S., 29
  proposal for universal network access, 41
  action on AT&T legislation, 99
  use of data banks, 109
  role in policy formation, 131–132
  critique of Executive Branch policy, 154
  Watergate investigation, 188
A Connecticut Yankee in King Arthur's Court, 24
Constitution, U.S., 122, 135
Consumer Communications Reform Act (Bell Bill), 131
Continental Telephone Co., 106
Control Data Corp., 164, 165
Corning Glass Co., 52
Cowlan, Bert, quoted, 13
Cox Communications Co., 114, 144
Crozier, Michel, 2
Cybernetics, 74

Dahrendorf, Rolf, 3
Darwin, Charles, 194
Data banks, 109, 148
Datran Corp., 100
DeButts, John, quoted, 120
DeGaulle, Charles, 162
Detroit, 119
Deutsch, Karl, 12, 31, 120, 188
Diamond, Edwin, quoted, 140–141
Digital Equipment Co., 108

Digital transmission techniques, 62
Direct broadcast satellites, plans for, 61, 111
Domestic Council, White House, 131
Dordick, Herbert, quoted, 37, 39, 41, 87, 114
Dow Jones Co., 110
Dun & Bradstreet Co., 110
Dunn, Donald, quoted, 143

"Early Bird" satellite, 175
Economic factors in the information age, 27
  lack of research, 34
  effect on individual lives, 35
  network marketplace concept, 37
  productivity factors, 89
  investment policies, 90
  measured in Department of Commerce study, 91
  international competition, 158–164
The Economist (London), 9, 36, 159
Edison, Thomas Alva, 9
Education industry
  use of communications and information equipment, 6
  role at State and local level, 133
Eger, John, quoted, 138
Einstein, Albert, 9, 82, 194
Eisenhower, Dwight D., 123
Electrician (British magazine), 45
Electronics industry, 70
  role of microprocessors in, 108
  foreign competition to, 109
  international operations, 155–160
  demand for semiconductor products, 163
Electronic mail, 77, 108
Electronic mythos, 22, 84, 118, 139
Electronic publications, 111, 139
Ellul, Jacques, quoted, 13; 17, 25, 182
Emerson, Ralph Waldo, quoted, 22; 119
Empire and Communications, 44

Encyclopaedia Britannica, 18
Encyclopedists, French, 18
ENIAC computer, 70
Environmental effects of microwave communications, 59–60
ERIC data base, 128
L. M. Ericsson Co., 160
Ethernet network, 106
Etzioni, Amatai, 3
Europe, 2
  expansion of videotext services, 8
  role on the "information map," 18
  development of national networks, 39
  space broadcast plans, 61
  spectrum research in, 64
  use of robotics, 83
  microelectronic developments in, 90
  challenges U.S. semiconductor industry, 109
  and American cultural influence, 152
  concerns over transborder data flow, 167
  need to coordinate communications policies with, 193
European Economic Community, 152, 163
Euronet data network, 149
Exxon Corp., 107

Federal Aviation Agency, 154
Federal Bureau of Investigation, 127
Federal Communications Commission, 49
  monitoring CB radio, 58
  report on satellite expansion, 64–65
  and Communications Act of 1934, 88
  licensing activities, 96
  places limitations on AT&T, 98–100
  influences on national

communications policy,
128–30
role in deregulating industry, 138
involvement in international
communications policy,
154–157
Federal Council for Science and
Technology, 130
Federal Radio Commission, 123
Ferkiss, Victor, 24, 25
Feur, Lewis, 3
Fiber optics technology, 52, 65
Fields, Cyrus, 155
Film industry, 112
recycling products for cable
systems, 114
international impact of, 167–168
First Amendment, 29, 118, 133, 139,
187, 190
First National Bank of Atlanta, 23
Flanner, Janet, 16
Forbes magazine, 88
Ford, Gerald F., 131
Forrester, Jay, 182
Fowler, Mark, 130
France, 36
expansion of electronics industry,
70
teletext experiments, 107, 112
concern over U.S. electronics
domination, 162
impact of Nora/Minc report on, 185
Franklin, Benjamin, 22
"Free flow of information" concept,
151
Fujitsu, Ltd., 163
Fuller, Buckminster, 23

Geddes, Patrick, 24
General Electric Co., 107, 148, 166
General Telephone & Electronics
Co. (GTE), 103, 106, 159
Georgetown University, 24
Gerbner, George, 27
German Federal Republic, 70

research and development
expenditures, 89
extent of telephone system, 159
Goldmark, Peter, 7
Great Britain, 7
failure to use high technology, 36
development of fiber optics
network, 53
expansion of electronics industry,
70
teletext experiments, 107, 112
differing policy approaches to
communications, 137
"Great White Fleet," 45
Green Lady, 83
Gutenberg, Johann, 44, 79, 80

Hall, Edward, 10
Harlem district in New York, 41
Harrington, Michael, 3
Harvard University, 27, 29, 170
Health care industry, use of
electronic equipment in, 6
Hewlett-Packard Co., 108
Hertz, Heinrich, 56
Hollings, Ernest F., quoted, 154
Holmes, Oliver Wendell, 140, 185
Holography, 80
Home Box Office Co., 112
Honeywell Corp., 163, 164
Hughes Aircraft Corp., 63
Huxley, Alduous, 11
Huxley, Julian, 23

ICL Inc., 76
ILLIAC computer, 76
India, 61, 80, 90, 164
Information Bank (New York
Times), 109, 157
The Information Economy, (U.S.
Department of Commerce
publication), 4, 88, 91
Industry, U.S. communications and
information, 47

rapid changes in, 95
efforts to maintain technological
    lead, 23
role in policy making, 137
foreign opposition to exports of,
    152
*Information Technology: some critical
    implications for decision makers*,
    (Conference Board report), 24
Information theory, origins of, 73–75
Innis, Harold, 24, 44
Integrated Grid Age, 47, 51, 65
INTELSAT (see: International
    Telecommunications Satellite
    Organization)
Internal Revenue Service, 127
International Atomic Energy
    Authority, 172
International Business Machines Co.
    (IBM), 6
role in development of computers,
    33
entry into computer market, 75
advanced computer designs, 76
development of synthetic speech,
    77
Josephson junction research, 78
current evolution of, 102–106
role in satellite operations, 105
policy on changing technology, 108
international operations, 161–163
underwrites university research,
    164
withdrawal from operations in
    India, 164
advanced information network
    plans, 166
International Communications
    Agency, 127, 154
International Telecommunications
    Satellite Organization (Intelsat),
    activities of, 175–176
International Telecommunications
    Union (ITU)
role in radio spectrum
    management, 55

sponsor of world dialing code, 156
international activities, 172–174
International Telephone and
    Telegraph Co. (ITT), 6, 52, 96
long distance phone network, 100
role in U.S. telecommunications
    industry, 103
international operations, 156, 159
nationalization of Latin American
    operations, 164
International Telegraph Union, 49,
    122
Itel Corp., 95

Japan, 2
location on the "information map,"
    18
use of social indicators in, 30
shift to high technology, 36
development of national network,
    39
fiber optics research in, 54
role in International
    Telecommunications Union,
    55
space broadcast plans, 61
spectrum research in, 64
competition in semiconductor
    development, 71
robotics research in, 83
use of microelectronics, 90
teletext experiments, 107, 112
challenge to U.S. semiconductor
    industry, 109
contrasts with U.S. policy
    approaches, 137
competition with U.S. industry,
    158–159, 162–163
White Paper on information policy,
    163
response to protective trade
    legislation, 164
Jefferson, Thomas, 22, 135, 186
Johnson, Lyndon B., 31, 118, 123,
    124
Josephson junctions, 78

Kahn, Herman, 3
Kay, Alan, quoted, 14
Kennan, George, quoted, 19
Kennedy, John F., 118, 123
Knight-Ridder newspapers, 112
"Knowledge industries," 4, 91
Kodak Inc., 79
Korea, 90

Labor productivity and information, 89
Landsat satellite, 12
Language as preserver of diversity, 195
Large-scale integration (LSI) technology, 45, 78
Laser technology, 52, 57, 80
Lasswell, Harold, 10, 15, 121
LeBlanc, Robert, 87
Lenin (Vladimir Ilyich Ulyanov), 49
Less-developed nations, 55
  industrial challenge to developed nations, 62
  limited use of paper resources, 80
  growth in communications resources, 90, 150
  opposition to "free information flow" concept, 173–174
Liberty district in Miami, 41
Libraries, 80
  involvement in local communications framework, 133
  traditional role in information services, 143
Library of Congress, 19
Lichtheim, George, 3
Liebling, A. J., 139
Literacy as measure of information society, 95
"Local loop" communications, 41
Lockheed Information Systems, 157, 165
Los Angeles, 100, 133
Ludditism, 15, 25, 90

McBride, Sean, 174
McCarthy, John, quoted, 82
McGraw Hill Corp., 110
McLuhan, Marshall, quoted, 23; 80, 139, 184
Machlup, Fritz, 4, 91
Macrae, Norman, quoted, 9
Mailgram service, 77
Manhattan Project, 82
Marconi, Guglielmo, 48
Marconi Wireless Co., 122
Marisat satellite, 61
Maritain, Jacques, quoted, 10
Maritime communications
  use of spectrum, 57
  use of satellites, 61
Marx, Leo, 23
Massachusetts Institute of Technology, 15, 27, 46, 82, 83
Maxwell, James Clerk, 56
MCA Discovision (videodisc technology), 79
MCI Corp., 95, 100
Medical technology, use of fiber optics in, 53
Medlars medical data system, 109, 128, 143, 165
Mexico, 111, 168
Micom Inc., 6
Microelectronics
  as driving force in information age technology, 27
  effects on U.S. business patterns, 35
  role in stimulating growth, 37
  use in information machines, 69
  advanced miniaturization of silicon chips, 77
  effects on national development, 90
  as basis for new computer communications systems, 101
Microfiche books, 79
Microfilm and computers, 79
Microwave networks, 59
Military communications, use of satellites in, 61

Mimeograph machines, 81
Minnesota, University of, 164
Minsky, Marvin, quoted, 83
Mitre Corp., 144
Mitterand, Jacques, 163
Mobile radio services, 105
Modernization theory, 16
Mont St. Michel and Chartres, 24
Morrill Act, 190
Morse, Samuel F. B., 47, 65, 122
Muggedrige, Malcolm, quoted, 16
Mumford, Lewis, 3, 24, 31, 41

National Academy of Engineering,
    130
National Aeronautics and Space
    Administration (NASA), 12
demonstration of satellite-based
    mobile radio, 58
ATS-6 satellite tests, 61
space shuttle, 62
research on radio spectrum, 64
advanced computer use, 76
robotics research, 83
satellite launches, 123
role in U.S. government structure,
    127
international communications
    activities, 154
National Communications System,
    126
National Library of Medicine, 128
National Public Radio (NPR), 110
National Science Foundation, 130,
    143
National Security Agency, 127
National Telecommunications and
    Information Administration, 7
established by Carter
    Administration, 125, 154, 192
role in U.S. policy formation, 128
National Technical Information
    Service, 109, 128, 131, 143
Navy, U.S., 45, 56, 123
Nazi propaganda, 17

The Nerves of Government, 31, 120
"Network marketplace," 37, 87, 114
New International Economic Order,
    16
New World Information Order, 174
New York City, 14, 113, 133
New York Times, 88, 109
News agencies, 168
Newsweek magazine, 169
Newton, Sir Isaac, 194
Nigeria, 160
Nippon Electric Corp., 109, 160
Nixon, Richard M., 124, 133, 188
Non-Aligned News Pool, 168
Nora/Minc Report, 162–163, 185
Norman, Colin, quoted, 36
Northern Telecom Corp., 160
Numerical aerodynamic simulation
    facility (NASF), 76

Oettinger, Anthony, 27, 75, 170
"Office of the future" developments,
    7, 107, 184
Omaha, Nebraska, 144
Oppenheimer, Robert, quoted, 182
"Optimal control" techniques, 187
ORATOR "talking terminal," 77
Organization for Economic
    Cooperation and Development
    (OECD), 152, 167

Pantages, Angeline, quoted, 161
Paper production as measure of
    information level, 80–81
Paris Electrical Exposition, 48
Parker, Edwin, 27; quoted, 143; 184
Pennsylvania Bell Telephone Co., 77
Pennsylvania, University of, 27
The Pentagon of Power, 24
Peoples Republic of China, see
    China, Peoples Republic of
Phillips Electronics Corp., 160
Photo copiers, 81
Political factors in the information
    age, 27

present lack of social consensus, 29
need for decisions, 41–42
choosing technological options, 46
challenge of policy development,
117
lack of clear-cut U.S. approach,
121
White House report on national
information policy, 131
role of State and local
governments, 133
fragmentation of policy making
machinery, 154
international pressures, 164
policy choices in domestic area, 189
Pool, Ithiel de Sola, 27
Porat, Marc Uri, 4, 91
Portland, Oregon, 133
Postal Service, U.S., 81, 108, 127,
134, 135
Post-industrial age, 3
and U.S. technological myth, 23
information structure in, 68
increasing dependence on
computers, 88
lack of economic research, 90
convergence of technological
changes in 1960's, 97
replacing agricultural and industrial
ages, 184
POTS – Plain Old Telephone Service,
32, 71, 96, 101
Poughkeepsie, N.Y., 161
Prestel videotext system, 7–8
Principia Mathematica, 73
Printing industry, historic role of, 5
*The Production and Distribution of
Knowledge in the United States*,
4, 91
Project Sanguine, 57
Ptolemy I Soter, 18
Public Broadcasting System (PBS),
110

Qube cable system, 113, 144

Racal Corp., 95
Radio broadcasting
early history of, 49
use of spectrum, 57
international impact, 169
Radio Free Europe, 169
Radio "hams," 57
Radio Liberty, 169
Radio Shack computer products, 77
Radio spectrum
role in modern communications, 56
applications of, 56–59
need for public controls over, 138
Ramo, Dr. Simon, quoted, 137
RCA Inc., 6, 62, 96, 103
established, 123
role in international
communications, 156
Read, William, 170
Reader's Digest, 110, 169
Reading, Pa., 143
Reagan, Ronald, 57, 130, 172, 192
Reindustrialization policy, 36, 90
Remington Rand Corp., 75
Research in communications and
information, 27, 30
Retailing, effects of new technologies
on, 35
Reuters news agency, 168
Robinson, Glen O., quoted, 190
Robotics, research in, 83
Rockefeller, Nelson A., 131
Rocky Mountain region, satellite
experiments in, 61
Roosevelt, Franklin D., 128
Rostow, Eugene, 124, 130, 153
Russell, Bertrand, 73

Sagan, Carl, 64, 183
Satellite Business Systems Inc., 103,
105
Satellites, communications
initial domestic use, 47
direct broadcasting capability, 61
use in maritime communications, 61

use of geostationary orbital spaces, 61
growth in current circuit capability, 64
for business communications, 105
Intelsat network, 150, 176
Satellite Television Corp., 111
Saudi Arabia, 160
SCARAB (Submerged Craft Assisting Recovery and Burial), 51
Schiller, Herbert, 24, 149
Schramm, Wilbur, 27
Seidenberg, Roderick, 3
Semiconductor industry
    strategic role in 1980's, 108
    foreign competition to, 109
SETI (Search for extra-terrestrial intelligence), 64
Shakespeare, William, 109
Shannon, Claude, 73
Shortwave broadcasting, 57–58
Siemans Corp., 160
Singapore, 159
"Smalltalk" computer language, 15
Smart, Ian, 189
Smith, Anthony, quoted, 50, 187
Smith, Sydney, quoted, 167
Smithsonian Institution, 76, 128
Social indicators, U.S., views on, 31
Social Security Administration, 127
South Africa, 170, 175
Southern California, University of, 37
Southern Pacific Railroad, 33
Soviet Union
    early use of radio, 49
    role in International Telecommunications Union, 55
    use of shortwave broadcasting, 58
    military satellite communications, 61
    radio spectrum research, 64
    submarines tracked by U.S., 76
    satellite research, 124

resistance to free-flow-of-information proposals, 151
role in international information and communications policy, 153
internal censorship, 170
policy toward Intelsat, 175
Space platforms for communications satellites, 46, 63
Spanish International Network, 111
Sperry Corp., 164
Sputnik satellite, 124
St. Louis, Mo., 100
Stalin, Josef, 168
Stanford Research Institute, 81
Stanford University, 27, 82
State and local governments, role of, 122, 133
Stearns, Peter, 3
Stein, Herbert, quoted, 11
Steiner, George, 14; quoted, 195
Stigler, George, 91
Storer Broadcasting Co., 114
Submarine cables, 51, 155
Supreme Court, U.S., 133
Sweden
    use of social indicators, 30
    computerized firefighting system, 148
    extent of telephone system, 159
    government controls over transborder data, 167
SWIFT (Society for Interbank Financial Telecommunications), 166
Systems Development Corp., 165

T-Bar Corp., 95
Technics and Civilization, 24
Technology
    and the American myth, 24
    effects on U.S. society, 25
    American investment in, 89
    U.S. leadership in, 97

foreign concern over U.S. domination in, 152

Tehran, Iran, 171

Telecommunications Policy, Office of, 124–125, 130

Télématique policy in France, 162

Telenet network, 157, 166

Telephone system, 7
unlisted numbers in, 13
extent of U.S. network, 32
and Communications Act of 1934, 40
as Nineteenth Century mass medium, 48
evolution of telephone technology, 71
increased efficiency of, 89
role of independent companies, 96
AT&T dominant role in, 98
introduction of transaction telephones, 102
future role of AT&T, 104
continued importance as basic network, 105–106
international services, 155–159

Telepresence devices, 83

Teleprompter Corp. (Westinghouse Co. affiliate), 114

Television industry, 7
use of satellites, 61
declining influence of, 110
role of "superstations," 111
critique of, 141
international impact of, 167–168

Telstar satellite, 123

Terrorist threats to communications, 171, 184

Thailand, 126

Third World countries (*see* less-developed nations)

Thomas, Lewis, quoted, 194

"Tillie the Teller," 23

Time Inc., 112, 114

Time magazine, 169

Times Mirror Co., 114

Toffler, Alvin, 24, 41, 185

Telepresence, 84–85

Tomlin, Lily, quoted, 97

Toronto, University of, use of microfiche in publishing, 79

Transaction telephones, 102

Transnet Inc., 6

Truman, Harry S. 123

TRW Inc., 137

Turling, Alan, 73–74

Turner, Ted, 111

Twain, Mark (Samuel Langhorne Clemens), 24

UNESCO (United Nations Educational, Scientific and Cultural Organization), 172–175

United Nations
debate over broadcast satellites, 61–62
and free-flow-of-information issue, 151
role of U.N. organizations in international communications and information issues, 172–175

United States
as incubator of information age, 2
and the electronic mythos, 22
leader in communications research, 30
use of shortwave broadcasting, 58
pressures to expand information resources, 69
reliance on print materials, 80–81
commitment to open information society, 119
distribution of information power in, 122
need for broad-based information policy debate, 135
overseas influence in information area, 149
stake in global communications progress, 151

goals for domestic communications
strategy, 182
shift in power structure, 188
need to promote communications
diversity, 195
United States government, general
activities
increasing use of communications
and information equipment, 7
role in funding communications
research, 47
encouragement of wireless radio
industry, 49
organizational changes in
communications policy
structure, 124–125
role of advisory committees, 130
alternative policy options, 136
advocate of international free flow
of information, 150
opposition to foreign economic
protectionism, 152
lack of policy framework in
communications and
information, 154, 172
economic policy planning, 193
United States government, role of
major agencies. (Smaller
agencies are indexed under
their titles.)
Commerce Department, report on
the information economy, 4,
33, 88, 91, 107, 117, 193
Defense Department, 61, 75, 76,
126, 154
Education Department, 128
Justice Department, 98, 104
State Department, 127, 153–154
Transportation Department, 127
Treasury Department, 31
Universal Postal Union, 172
Univac computer, 75
UTEC Corp., 95

Valtech Inc., 6
Vance, Cyrus, 154
Van Deerlin, Lionel, 96, 131–132
Vatican State, 175
Venezuela, 168
Very large scale integration (VSLI),
78
Videodiscs, 112
Videotapes, 112
Vietnam conflict, 119, 186
Viewdate services, 107
Voice of America, 17, 57, 126, 169
Von Neumann, John, 5, 73–75
Voyager spacecraft, 83

Warner-Amex Co., 113
Washington, D.C., 47, 53, 113, 144
Watergate affair, 119, 133, 188
Watts district in Los Angeles, 41
Waveguide communications, 53, 65
Ways, Max, quoted, 145
Weaver, Warren, 73
Weiner, Norbert, 73–74
Weizenbaum, Joseph, 82
Wells, H. G., 11, 19
Western Electric Co., 100, 159
Western industrial powers, 55, 193
Western Union Co., 47, 62
mailgram service, 77
network growth, 96
international activities, 157, 159
Western Union International, 106,
156
Whitehead, Alfred North, 73
Wiley, Richard, 129, 154
Wire Age (1844–1900), 47, 65
"Wired nation" concept, 40
Wireless Age (1900–1970), 47, 54,
65
Wirth, Timothy, 132
World Administrative Radio
Conference (1979), 55, 173
"World Brain" project, 19

World Meteorological Organization
    (WMO), 165, 172
World War I, 49, 123
World War II, 123
Wright, Orville and Wilbur, 1, 26,
    185
WTCG, Atlanta "superstation," 111

Xerox Corp., 15, 81, 103, 139
    underwriting research, 164
    development of advanced network,
    166

Yugoslavia, 168
Yasu, Japan, 161

THE CLIMBING TREE

THE CLIMBING TREE

Carol McAfee

St. Martin's Press

New York

(1)

Design by Holly Block

Library of Congress Cataloging-in-Publication Data

McAfee, Carol.
  The climbing tree.

  I. Title.
PS3563.C264C5 1989   813'.54   88-30545
ISBN 0-312-02560-2

First Edition
10 9 8 7 6 5 4 3 2 1

For Ralph and Kate and the memory of my mother

Acknowledgments

I would like to thank Muffin and Wilma for their love and support, my father and brothers for the shining examples they have set. Tanya, thank you for more than your babysitting. And Claire, for believing in me. I would also like to thank David Reuben and the entire staff of D.R. Associates, International, for their tips on police procedure and Andrea L. Smith and Tim Doory of the Office of the Baltimore City State's Attorneys for their assistance on legal matters.

Finally, I would like to thank my husband Ralph for being my best friend and my daughter Katie for trying to put the rose petals back on a rose.

PART ONE

1

He was the first surprise witness Kate had ever called, and he was on the stand right now. Up until this moment, he had been so brave. He'd sat in the witness box with the endearing, loose-limbed awkwardness of adolescence. He'd spoken clearly into the microphone and had answered all her questions. But when she came to the most crucial question of all, he shrank away from her. His face was ashen. His lower lip trembled.

Kate gently repeated the question: "Who did you see when you crept to the top of the stairs?"

"I saw—" The boy flushed fiercely and stopped.

"Yes?" The slim, copper-haired prosecutor nodded at him.

But Danny only shook his head and stammered: "I—can't."

Kate heard a rustling behind her at the defense table. The boy's eyes darted helplessly to her, and now she understood. Danny wasn't just nervous, he was frightened: the defendant was glaring at him. And worse, the jury couldn't even see because the defendant cleverly held his hand like a visor, shielding his face from the right, where the jury sat.

No longer as confident, her own courage beginning to slip, Kate paced the gloomy, marbled courtroom. She looked at Danny's mother in the front row. Beth Billings sat nervously on the edge of her seat, her fingers drumming on her handbag. Beth was a waitress. Divorced. It must be a lonely life for her sometimes. Lonely enough that she would invite her boyfriends to stay with her and the kids, Danny and Angela. Angela was not present here today.

When Kate thought of Angela, her stomach clenched. She felt anger welling up inside her. She forced herself to turn toward the defense table and look at Clarence Wilbur Carlson, also known as Slick. What a frightening man! He had a soft face with doughy cheeks. His eyes were a chilling cat-green. She always tried to avoid those eyes because they were hypnotic—they trapped her in a world of hatred and violence where no beauty could exist, and no love. She knew she was afraid of Slick. For the seven days of this trial, he had disrupted her life. She thought of him when she got up in the morning and when she walked to work. She thought of him at night over her cooked frozen dinners. Even in sleep she could not escape him, for he invaded her dreams.

Her heart fluttered now as Slick noticed her staring at him. He raked his fingers through the grooves in his black hair and grinned, a smug, arrogant grin. He was so sure he would walk out of here laughing, a free man. She hated his smirking at her. She wanted, more than anything else in the world, to turn away, but she fixed her gaze on him. Her eyes did not blink. They gave him nothing, no flicker of humanity, only her contempt.

She turned back around and there was Danny, sitting not so rigidly in his chair, his eyes bright and alert, his whole body bending toward her. She said firmly: "There's nothing to be afraid of. Don't ever be afraid to tell the truth, Danny. Do you understand?"

"Yes," he said.

"Good." She nodded. "Now I want you to tell the court what you saw when you crept up the stairs and opened the door."

There was a hush in the courtroom. The only sound was the futile whirr of the *Casablanca* fan hanging from the white ceiling. Judge Obermeyer remained studiedly neutral. But the jurors revealed their excitement: their eyes fixed on the young boy.

"I saw *him!*" Danny cried, pointing to the defendant, "touching my baby sister!"

The defense attorney cross-examined Danny but failed to impeach his credibility. There were closing arguments and Maryland jury instructions, then the twelve men and women filed into the jury room. Kate paced the courtroom while she waited for the verdict. She was oblivious to the humidity, which had everyone lining up at the water fountain and she did not notice the admiring gaze of several spectators, who were impressed, perhaps equally, by her talent and her good looks, for she was an attractive woman with startling red hair and indigo eyes.

Kate consulted her watch. The jury had been deliberating for fifty minutes. Already it seemed like forever. She smiled assurance at Danny's mother and continued to pace the courtroom. Once or twice she looked to the oak doors that led to the corridor and the world outside. She wondered what was keeping Reuben, and then suddenly she saw him. He arrived just as the bailiff announced the jury's return.

As the twelve jurors headed back to their seats, tension gripped the courtroom and there was a crescendo of excited murmurings. Judge Obermeyer rapped his gavel. Everyone quieted. Kate held her breath. She scanned the jury. What would their verdict be? It was hard to read juries, but she noted the squared shoulders, heads held high, countenances grave with responsibility, and she had a feeling these twelve men and women were going to convict. She looked at Beth and Danny Billings, then at Reuben five rows back, then she returned her attention to the jury as the middle-aged foreman stood and announced in a solemn voice: "Guilty."

When Slick heard the verdict, he whirled toward Kate and glared at her. The bailiff snapped handcuffs on him, but he still refused to take his eyes off her, and when the bailiff nudged him to get moving, he shouted: "I'll get you for this, bitch! I'll be back!"

Kate was shaken. She watched as Slick resisted the bailiff's hold on him. It took two guards to escort him from the room.

She was still trembling when reporters flocked over to her: "Carlson has a history of violence against women, and he threatened you. Has anyone ever threatened you before?" Kate tried to be polite and answer all their questions, but she did not confess her fears. She only said: "I have complete confidence in our Maryland prisons to keep Mr. Carlson safely incarcerated. And now, I'd like to talk to Danny's mother, please. I think she's trying to get through at the edge of the crowd."

Following her request, the reporters stepped back to allow Beth Billings to rush up to Kate for a tearful embrace. When all the craziness finally died down and the courtroom emptied, Kate returned to the prosecution table and tossed her notes into her briefcase. She felt someone's presence close beside her. She glanced up. It was Reuben. He had waited.

"Hey, kiddo," he said, and there was concern in his eyes. He had heard Slick's threat, too.

"Hey, yourself." She smiled valiantly.

Reuben was a plainclothes detective. He was Jewish, with olive-black eyes, a hook nose, and thatched brown hair. He was not a handsome man, but he was undeniably virile and that made him attractive. She'd met him three years ago, when she first started at the City State's Attorneys office.

Reuben was a sensitive guy, and he saw right through her smile. "Hey, c'mere," he said. He held out his arms and enveloped her in a hug. When they broke apart, he said: "It didn't bother you, did it? What he said?"

"Well . . ." She couldn't lie to him. She shrugged.

"I know what you're thinking, but he won't escape." Reuben smiled affectionately at her. "I promise."

Reuben walked her downstairs. "You sure you're okay now?" he asked.

She nodded to him that she was fine because he was on a case and had to go. But as soon as he'd left she missed him, and even as she returned to the sanctuary of her own office, she felt strangely vulnerable. She felt the withering humidity for the first time, felt the depth of her own exhaustion, but most of all she felt afraid. When everyone came up to her and overwhelmed her with congratulations, she had to force herself to smile. Luckily, nobody noticed. They only wanted to celebrate her good fortune: "Way to go, Riley!" "Good job nailing Carlson." "Can I buy you a drink?" "Whaddya say we tip a few?" The State's Attorney himself, the fair, handsome Peter Coe III, emerged from his inner sanctum and told everybody to clear out, take the night off. "C'mon, Kate." He was beaming. "Let's all go to Moody's, my treat."

———

Moody's was crowded.

Kate arrived late, after the others. She made two stops on the way, one planned, the other spontaneous. Beth Billings's car was in the garage, so Kate drove her and Danny through Baltimore's heavy downtown traffic to their home. On the way, she treated Danny to a double scoop of Baskins and Robbins and was rewarded by the sudden grin on his serious face as he bit into Mint Chocolate Chip. And, too, there was the look on Beth Billings's face as she tousled Danny's hair. Danny had been so good on the witness stand today. Kate knew his mother was thinking: my brave son.

Kate made the second stop on her way to Moody's. She was driving down York Road, the Volvo's air conditioner laboring ineffectually against the heavy July air, when she saw the sign. She slowed, turned onto the old, familiar street, and parked opposite the roomy

7

Tudor house with its beloved mullioned windows. She noted that the new owners had dug up the pink azalea bushes where she and Molly used to play. Along this sidewalk, she used to roller-skate. And, in the back, which she could not see from where she sat idling in the humidity, would be the long narrow driveway and fifty-two rose bushes. Her mother had loved those roses. On some days, their sweet aroma had clung to her hair. Mom wasn't proprietary about her garden, she shared her flowers. She had put them in vases all over the house.

The memory was too painful. Kate squeezed her eyes shut. A door slammed and only then did she look up to see the little girl emerge from the house, a tiny, knobby-kneed creature with red strawberry curls. The little girl scampered toward her swing, which hung from the gnarled old maple tree in back. When she reached it, she jumped on. She pumped her legs vigorously and soon she was sailing through the air, her red hair flying. Suddenly she flung her little body off the swing and hurried to the trunk of the tree. There, she stood on tiptoe and reached for the lowest branch. She got a grip on it and swung a sneakered foot over. Her leg followed, then the rest of her. She disappeared into the tree. And now her mother emerged from the house. She knew where her daughter was, she could see the abandoned swing swaying back and forth on its ropes, but she played the game anyway and pretended to look. Kate imagined the little girl's excitement. How she must love this. And yet she couldn't stand the suspense. She peeked out from behind the leafy branches, and laughed.

Kate's breath caught and tears stung in her eyes. It was time she got going. She urged the Volvo into drive and pulled away, but she couldn't help one last backward glance. As she looked, a shaft of sunlight fell upon the two figures, the swing, and the tree. She would always remember this: the little girl, illumined by that gold patch of sun, pointing so her mother would see, too, how if you tilted your head just right, the green leaves shimmered almost magically and the sky beyond was all blue.

By the time Kate reached Moody's, it was almost dark. The closest parking spot was six blocks away. She walked through a poor neighborhood to get to the restaurant. People sat on porch stoops and fanned themselves and drank beer to fight the humidity. Kate felt the humidity, too.

Once inside, she searched the smoke-clogged restaurant for a familiar face. She felt momentarily cheered when Peter Coe got up to greet her. He had been entertaining a tableful of his fellow attorneys, but he broke off in midsentence when he saw her. He took her by the elbow and steered her to the bar where they could be alone.

"What is it?" he asked.

"Nothing." She tried to smile.

He looked into her blue eyes, watched the lights gleam off her auburn hair. "You're late. Where were you?"

"Just—I had a stop to make, that's all." He wouldn't understand about her visit to her old house, so she would not tell him. That was the trouble with Peter Coe III. The blond, blue-eyed chief prosecutor wasn't very good with emotions. He didn't have time for them. He planned to be Mayor of Baltimore one day, and perhaps, if he was lucky, Governor.

Peter ordered wine for both of them, and when it came, Kate took refuge in it, sipping slowly.

"By the way, congratulations on the Carlson verdict."

"Thanks, Peter. To tell you the truth, I'm relieved the case is over."

"Relieved?"

"Yes, you know, the pressure." The pressure wasn't it, but she couldn't tell him about the dream. That would be another thing he wouldn't understand. She didn't understand it herself.

He studied her. Perhaps he was more sensitive than she thought because he suddenly reached for her hand and held it. Why can't I love this man? she chided herself. He's a good man and he cares for me.

And yet, Peter did not hold her hand to comfort her but merely to press his advantage because he said: "Let's go away someplace."

"Oh, Peter."

"You need to. You didn't even take time off after the funeral." She felt a stab of pain. "My work hasn't suffered, has it?"

"You're the best prosecutor we've got, you know that. You've got the highest conviction rate in Baltimore City. Nobody's better prepared when they walk into that courtroom. But I want you to quit burning the midnight oil. Take a break."

Her heart thudded. Work was her life, her passion, and lately, her escape. Work was where she did not have to think about Kate Riley or turning thirty next month or anything. She inhaled sharply. "Are you ordering me to take this vacation?"

"No."

"Good." She turned away from him.

Just then, Reuben appeared inside the restaurant's entrance. He seemed upset and agitated. Kate waved to him. He immediately hastened over, an anguished expression on his face: "Kate, Jesus, I'm glad I found you. They told me you were here. There's been—"

"What?"

"An accident. Outside Ruxton. Judge Buckner, you know him?"

"I know him," Peter said.

"He—yeah—you know what he did? Got drunk and got into his fancy Lincoln, hopped on I-83 and didn't drive on the right side of the road like the rest of us mortals but crossed the median and hit Jimmy Delorosa in his squad car. Broadside. Jimmy's in ICU at Hopkins right now. In a coma, can you believe it?"

"Christ," Peter said.

Kate didn't say anything. She knew that Jimmy Delorosa was a close friend of Reuben's and what could you say? I'm sorry? She hated it when people said that to her.

"They got Mary with him now," Reuben added. "His wife. They

got a priest in there too." Reuben looked away, down the length of the beer-stained mahogany bar at all the carnival-bright bottles and shiny glasses, then back at Kate: "Spinal cord's all but severed. He wakes up, he'll be a quad. I hope he never wakes up. Jesus."

His voice was cynical, his pose as tough as ever, but Kate knew what to do. She reached out her arms, said, "Reuben, c'mere," and crushed him to her in a hug.

When they broke apart, tears sprang to the corners of Reuben's bright eyes.

Peter, suddenly preoccupied, drummed his fingers on the bartop and said: "Judge Buckner's a loser. This is his second DWI. If Delorosa dies, we're looking at vehicular manslaughter. Believe me, we'll prosecute the hell outta this case."

Kate glanced sharply at Peter. He wasn't seeing the tragedy of the situation—Jimmy's soon-to-be widow, Reuben's grief—he was seeing only his own political opportunity.

Peter leaned confidentially toward Kate and stage-whispered: "This is bound to be a big media case. Naturally I'll need your help. Can I count on you?"

"Of course," she said tonelessly.

Peter didn't notice her reaction. His eyes were alive with excitement as he hailed the bartender: "Joel, switch on the eleven o'clock news, will ya? There's something I gotta see." And sure enough, there on the thirty-six-inch Sony screen were shots of the accident site, the median on Interstate-83 under the wash of white lights. Incredibly, the Judge's Lincoln Continental was barely dented. The other crumpled mass, that contorted confusion of metal, was the remains of a Baltimore City police car.

2

Kate turned the key in the lock and stepped into her apartment. The door was still ajar and her hand was holding the doorknob when she heard the message machine click on. She dropped her briefcase, abandoned the open door, and lunged for the telephone, stopping short when she heard Reuben's voice: "Kate, Delorosa's dead. Just thought I'd let you know. By the way, I'm with Coe on this. I say we bust Buckner wide open." There was a pause on the line, then Reuben's voice cracked: "Jesus, Kate. Jimmy's such a . . . I really loved the guy, you know?" There was a click—Reuben hanging up—then a beep and whirr as the message machine rewound and readied itself for the next caller.

Kate stood still for a long moment. She should have grabbed the phone and offered comfort to Reuben, but she couldn't. The apartment was close and warm, and yet she suddenly shivered. She hugged herself, then hurried to the open door and swiftly bolted it shut, as if Death might come calling on her, too, and she could lock it out.

In the hallway she kicked off her heels, flicked on the switch for central air-conditioning, and padded in her nylons across the champagne carpet to the fridge. She hadn't eaten dinner, just a few pretzels at Moody's, but she wasn't hungry. She reached for the carton of orange juice and poured herself a glass, drank it without really tasting it. Then she walked over to her answering machine and pushed the "play" button. She half-hoped no one besides Reuben had called, she couldn't deal with anything else tonight, but there was another message. It was from Molly, her sister:

"Hi, sweetie. You okay? We haven't heard from you in so long. Anyhow, I'm calling to invite you to supper tomorrow, we'll barbecue, just us, can you come? Say, around six-thirty? Ian keeps asking where's Auntie Kate? And Lily, you've hardly seen her. She's growing up so fast. . . ." There was a long pause in the recording. Kate waited for the beep to signal that the message was over, but there was more. Molly added plaintively: "Kate, please, don't shut me out. I miss her too, you know."

Kate heard the last of the message, turned away to gaze out the sliding glass patio doors at the darkness. She felt so tired, so sad, for a moment she could not move. And now another headache began, starting at the bridge of her nose, a faint hammering. She reached over and snapped off the answering machine. She was off-line now. Her phone would not ring. If anyone else called, there would be nobody home.

Kate took two Tylenol for her headache, then stepped into a hot shower. The warm spray eased the tension in her back. She tried not to think, not about Judge Buckner and the tragic consequences of his drunk driving, not about anything. She slipped into her flowered silk nightgown, climbed into bed, and felt the cool clean of the sheets. She switched off the light and lay there in the dark, staring up at the ceiling. The air-conditioning flowed smoothly through the vents, a soothing sound, and she wondered if she could possibly sleep now. She was exhausted. It had been a long day. She closed her eyes and willed herself to relax. Within minutes she dropped off. Her final thoughts were of Slick. His words echoed: "I'll get you for this, bitch! I'll be back!"

She managed only a few hours of sleep before she had the dream. She awoke in a cold, panicky sweat at 3:05 A.M. She knew from experience that any further attempt at sleep was hopeless so she lay on her back and waited for dawn. She knew she'd made it when the first faint light crept in under the window shades.

At five-thirty she got up and made her bed. Then she walked out onto her patio. Her apartment was on the ground floor so she simply opened the sliding glass door and stepped out. It was a steamy morning; the temperature must be seventy already. She looked at her wind chime hanging by the patio light. It was motionless: There wasn't a breath of air.

She sat in one of her garden chairs and put her head in her hands because she really was tired. She thought about what Molly had said. She was right. Kate *had* been neglecting them. But how could she tell Molly it was just too painful, seeing her and Ian and baby Lily? Whenever Kate was with them, she felt almost happy. But then the shock of remembrance would hit her and she would feel fresh pain and a little remorse, too, for almost forgetting. Their family would never be the same again, never. How could she forget that?

Kate knew she should try to accept her mother's death and go on with her life, but it was difficult. She sighed, got up from the garden chair, and went back inside. She dressed, then headed down the corridor.

Her apartment complex, as always, reminded her of a hotel, with its plush carpeting and high ceilings and lovely interior decorating. She liked living here very much, even though she sometimes felt caught between two worlds. The brick building itself, a renovated high school, was something of a lone outpost. Her fellow tenants were well-groomed, monied professionals who strode confidently out the front door every morning to work somewhere in the popular and upscale Inner Harbor on Maryland's Chesapeake Bay. But if these same professionals ventured out the back door, they would confront the parking lot and then a lower middle-class neighborhood with its cramped rowhouses, broken windows, trash, and abandoned cars. When Kate looked out her back window, she thought of John Steinbeck's Cannery Row.

She used to go jogging through Cannery Row to Fort McHenry. She used to get up early. What a picture of health she must have been.

She reached the building's main entrance. James, the youthful black doorman, clad in a blue uniform with gold epaulets, said: "Morning, Ms. Riley," and handed her a copy of this morning's *Sun,* which she immediately tucked under her arm. Too late, however. She had already glimpsed the front-page photo of the crash on I-83.

James kidded her: "What? No exercise?"

"No," she said. "Not today."

She had said "Not today" for quite a long time now, but he still asked her. It was as if he cared about her and missed her jogging too.

———

Outside, the humidity was oppressive, but Kate pressed on down the cobblestoned lane toward work. To her right was Federal Hill Park. The park had once been a lookout the Americans used to spot the invading British ships in the War of 1812.

She crossed Key Highway, busy with lumbering trucks even at this hour, and emerged on the other side into the cleaner, prospering world of Baltimore's Inner Harbor. She smelled salt air and enjoyed the view of the Chesapeake Bay. Seagulls cawed loudly as they wheeled against a pearly sky, while white-hulled sailboats slept quietly at their moorings.

She stood at the intersection waiting for the light to change, and decided, on impulse, to visit her old haunt: the local pastry shop on Charles Street.

The Buttery was comfortably crowded, even at this hour. Professionals and college kids alike enjoyed the pleasant air-conditioning as they sat in clusters at the wooden tables. There was nothing fancy here. The atmosphere was cozy and democratic; everything suffered equally from benign neglect.

Kate felt a pang of sadness. She hadn't been here in so long, the people behind the counter had changed. And her mother had been on a joking basis with all of them, asking this one about her new baby, that one about the new porch addition to his house. The Buttery had been one of her mother's favorite spots. She'd met Kate here on the mornings she went to school. She was studying for her master's degree in English. Mom had always ordered the same thing, a cup of coffee and a palm-leaf pastry.

Kate was still thinking of her mom when the man behind the counter asked her what she wanted. A lump formed in her throat, and she had to force out the words: "Coffee and a jelly donut, please."

"For here or to go?"

"For here."

Waiting while he fetched her order, she looked around the coffee shop. She was smiling slightly, wistfully, until she spotted a small group of men and women sitting in a corner booth, old friends of her mother's from A.A.

Kate felt the first stirrings of panic. She turned immediately to the man behind the counter and said: "I'm sorry, make that to go."

Outside, there were tables and chairs. Kate took her cheap Styrofoam cup of steaming coffee and sat down in the prickly humidity at the remotest table, where she could be anonymous. She need not be Lily's daughter.

She sipped her coffee thoughtfully, wondering how it could be that she was living her life. She had envisioned a husband and children too, for children brought light and laughter into a house. Would she ever have a child? She would have to meet a man first. Fall in love.

3

Kate entered the old courthouse from the east side. She and the security guard exchanged greetings, then she stepped under the metal detector, retrieved her purse and briefcase, and climbed the well-worn stairs to her office.

The office, which employed one hundred forty attorneys, was called the Baltimore City State's Attorneys Office. The "City/State" appellation proved confusing to everyone. Kate wondered what had happened to the old phrase "district attorney." That was so much simpler. Socially, Kate always referred to herself as a prosecutor. That was a phrase people understood.

At her desk, Kate removed her sneakers and slipped on her more formal heels. She glanced at the mountain of paperwork awaiting her, then at the photograph of her mother. It was an anchor, a calming influence in moments of stress. In it, Lily Riley—auburn-haired, blue-eyed, age wrinkles just beginning to show on her face—was charming the camera, was smiling. She was wearing a brown sweater decorated by her favorite item of jewelry: a gold swordpin. The gold swordpin had belonged to Lily's mother and, before that, her grandmother. Now it was Kate's. The swordpin currently resided in the maroon jewelry box on her dresser. Though Kate loved the swordpin, she never wore it.

Kate studied the photograph a moment longer, then closed her eyes. She felt very tired. Her temples throbbed. She got up from her desk to fetch some Tylenol and water, and on the way, ran into Judith Moore, her secretary. Judith had worked in the office for two years, but had only recently been assigned to Kate.

Austere and slim, an intensely private person, Judith was divorced, in her fifties. She had clear skin, dark eyes, and jet-black hair just beginning to gray. Kate couldn't have been more pleased with Judith's work, but she often wished her secretary would warm up a little. Even on the days when the office was relaxed and people were joking around, Judith remained cool and aloof. And yet, just when Kate was about to give up on her, Judith would surprise her with a sensitive comment, or she would do something thoughtful—bring Kate a cup of coffee on a hectic day or cheer her with a rare smile.

"Good morning," Judith greeted Kate, then said, in a different tone: "I saw it on the news."

"The accident on I-83?"

Judith nodded. "Tragic, isn't it? My heart just bleeds for Mary Delorosa—" she began, then stopped herself. She seemed startled by the intensity of her own emotion, and ashamed. Tears appeared in her eyes. She turned away, but Kate reached out to her: "It's okay," she said. "I've been thinking about her, too."

For a moment they were silent, oddly united, Judith with head bowed, Kate with her hand on her shoulder. Then Peter Coe came bustling in, and the moment was gone. It was Judith who broke away first. "Back to business," she said brusquely and began tapping the already neat files on her desk into even neater stacks.

By ten o'clock the office was alive with attorneys. Television and news reporters waited outside for Peter Coe's formal statement of charges to be brought against Judge Buckner. Peter, always cautious, decided to move slowly. Just now, he was speaking to a group of attorneys and support staff, Kate and Judith included:

"I'll deal with the press, is that understood? Nothing's easy in a case involving a judge. He's a high-profile defendant, and this is a manslaughter case. We can't be too careful. Any questions? Good. You all know what you have to do."

Peter dismissed them, then turned quickly to Kate: "You have a minute?" he asked. "In my office."

Peter Coe's office was a study in luxury. An Oriental carpet pampered the floor while a massive oak desk and thronelike leather chair pampered Peter's ego. He sat down, and motioned for Kate to sit, too.

"Listen, I need to talk to you," Peter began gently. "Slick Carlson threatened you in court yesterday. Why didn't you tell me?"

"Well," she said, "I—"

"I had to hear about it through somebody else. I thought we were better friends than that."

"We are," she protested. "I just—"

"You hurt my feelings."

"I'm sorry."

"Are you?"

"Yes."

"Then you can make it up to me. Are you free tonight? I know you don't care for Moody's, but I'd like to show you the Orchid."

"Oh, Peter, I'd love to, but I'm bushed."

"It's very elegant dining. Romantic candlelight. We'll discuss the case, naturally."

"You mean, Buckner?" She laughed. "We need candlelight for that?" She looked at him, expecting him to laugh with her, but he wasn't even smiling.

And now there was a knock on the door, and Judith poked her head in: "Sorry to interrupt, Kate, but Reuben's on the line."

With an apologetic glance at Peter, she left.

Reuben was all business when she picked up the phone: "This Buckner thing. How's it look?"

"Not good." She sighed. "Even if we get him convicted of vehicular manslaughter, his sentence will be light."

"Yeah, six months of playing Ping-Pong in the city jail and maybe a couple hundred hours of community service, picking up garbage by the highway. Break my heart." Reuben sounded bitter.

"I know," she sympathized. "The sentence is laughable, but I still think we have room to maneuver."

"How?"

"If we can establish lack of remorse on Buckner's part. If we can show that, we can maybe get him disbarred. And he'll have to do more serious time."

"Which means we could use a good psychologist. Someone to interview Buckner and see where he's coming from. I know a guy who used to be on Special Forces. A shrink, name of Fielding. He's terrific."

"Not a hired gun? I don't want him as our expert witness if he's predisposed one way or another."

"No, no." Reuben laughed. "You don't understand. You couldn't buy this guy off with a million bucks. He'll make a good call on Buckner. And if Buckner *is* remorseful, believe me, he'll tell you that too."

"Good," she said. "I'd like to talk to him."

"I'll give him a call," Reuben offered. "Send him down to meet you if he's interested."

"Fine. Thanks, Reuben. You're wonderful."

"I just wanna help," he said, in a changed voice. He was feeling again the pain of last night, when he heard about Jimmy. "Well," he said. He was about to hang up. He would, unless she stopped him.

"Say, listen," she said.

"What?"

She swallowed around a sudden lump in her throat. This was hard for her to talk about. What was the old expression: too close to home? Well, any death hit too close to home now, especially a death mourned by a good friend. "I just wanted to say that I . . . well, I know you miss Jimmy. And I want to let you know that it's okay to miss him. So if you need a shoulder to cry on or just somebody to talk to, I'm here."

There was silence on the other end. Then Reuben said: "You're some lady."

"I mean it."

"I know you do, and yeah, I do miss him. But the best thing you can do for me is nail Buckner. Can you understand that?"

"Yes," Kate said.

When she hung up, Judith was waiting patiently by her side, ready to help. She seemed to know that Kate would need her more than ever.

"This Judge Buckner," Judith said, "he's a criminal, isn't he? I mean, to drink and drive like that. To drink and drive, then kill someone . . ." Judith's voice trailed off. Kate stared at her. Sadness was etched on her face. Kate had never seen her secretary display this much emotion. Maybe Judith wasn't so inaccessible, after all. Kate dared hope that out of all this chaos and tragedy they might actually become friends.

———

Kate had no time for lunch today. Her donut and coffee would have to sustain her. Just now she was busy organizing her cases. Peter had told her to plead out as many as she could. She needed to devote her full attention to the Buckner case. She glanced at her watch. In ten minutes she would meet informally with various defense attorneys in the hall outside. Ironically, more justice was dispensed in that marbled, high-columned hallway than in the courtroom. At precisely two o'clock, she cradled her stack of files in her arms, mustered all her energy, and stepped out into the crowded corridor. She flipped open the topmost manilla folder and announced to the defense attorneys present: "Johnson, Dennis A."

Ed Tucker, a public defender well known to Kate, immediately came forward.

"Kate, Johnson'll pay the fine, but he doesn't want to do time. Let's reduce the charge to a misdemeanor."

"C'mon, Ed," she said, pleasant but firm. "I'm willing to deal, but let's be reasonable." She consulted the yellow rap sheet on Johnson. "This is a 287A, isn't it? Possession of drug paraphernalia. Same charge as two months ago. Our man Johnson shows no signs of reforming . . ."

The chaos of plea-bargaining came to an abrupt halt, and so did, for an instant, her heart, when a tall, ruggedly handsome man touched her arm and said: "Hello, I'm Dr. Todd Fielding."

He was surprisingly youthful, in his mid-thirties. Lean and lanky with careless hair and a shaggy mustache, both nut-brown in color. His eyes were cinnamon. Kind eyes, a little sad. He had dressed casually in slacks and a checked shirt that he wore rolled up at the sleeves.

She didn't mean to stare at him. She didn't realize, even, that she was staring. The sounds in the corridor seemed to melt away and there was just the two of them, gazing at each other, alone, until he frowned suddenly and said, thinking she did not know him: "Reuben asked me to stop by."

"Yes, yes, of course," she said, becoming her lawyer self again as the sounds in the corridor came flooding back. She waved to Ed Tucker, indicating they would talk later, and directed her attention to Fielding: "I'm glad you came. I can't offer you decent coffee, but let's visit the vending machine anyway. There's more privacy there. We can talk."

They traveled in companionable silence down the corridor. In the cramped, windowless room with the tiled floor, they inserted their quarters and banged the coffee machine, which reluctantly coughed up two paper cups of hot, muddy liquid. Now they sat side by side at the wobbly table, alone, save for their vending-machine chaperones and the fan rotating busily on the table. Kate concentrated all her diminishing energy on Fielding. Over the rim of her paper cup, she studied him. She liked his eyes, which were compassionate, yet probing. She liked his mustache, too.

"I've testified as an expert in other criminal cases," Fielding said, "but the attorneys never met with me personally beforehand, we've always just spoken on the phone. I assume you want to check me out thoroughly, and I admire you, Ms. Riley, for taking the time."

"Kate," she smiled at him, "and thank you. I also thank you for meeting with me. I know you have a busy practice."

"Hey, for Reuben," he said, "it's a pleasure."

"Is that the only reason you're here?"

He surprised her by laughing. "Well, I have to admit, the Buckner case has received a lot of media attention, enough to pique my curiosity."

His candor disarmed her. She began to relax. "What are you curious about?"

"Buckner's mental attitude. What possessed him to drink and drive? If he's an alcoholic—okay. Alcoholism's a disease. The question is, does he welcome treatment? Or does he insist on denying his problem at the expense of others?"

Kate was listening closely and she was greatly impressed. She had found her psychiatrist. Fielding knew what alcoholism was and what criminality was, and that they were two separate things. Kate couldn't help thinking of her mom. Fielding would have liked her. Mom had been a living miracle, one of those souls who survived the crucible. She had lived sober as a recovered alcoholic for many years. Yet, during her drinking years, it was possible that she, too, could have killed someone on the highway. It was possible she had just been lucky.

"What would you say," Kate looked at Fielding, "if I told you Buckner had already been convicted of one DWI offense?"

"I'd say I'd still have to talk to the guy. People in need of help hit bottom at different times. We all have different dignity thresholds. Some alcoholics need to lose their jobs or see their marriage break up. Others have to go to prison. Maybe Buckner needed this tragedy to get him to see the light."

Kate liked this Fielding. She liked the way he answered her questions. "I think you'd be the perfect person to evaluate Judge Buckner. If you can spare the time, I'd be grateful."

He smiled confidently. "I can make the time," he said. "I'd be happy to." And now his smile became more personal, and his brown eyes regarded her tenderly; was that possible?

Kate felt a sudden rushing sensation, the room tilted, and her head pounded so fiercely, she clutched it. She felt his arm on her shoulder, steadying her. "Are you all right? Here, relax. Close your eyes. Now breathe evenly. That's right. Good."

She inhaled deeply and opened her eyes. The roaring stopped, the room didn't spin anymore, and he was by her side. She felt immensely grateful, then ashamed. What must he think of me now? she thought.

"Better?" he asked.

"Yes." She looked at him. "I don't know what came over me."

He studied her waxen face, the dark half-moons under her eyes. "My guess is you're exhausted."

"I haven't been sleeping well," she admitted. "I keep having . . ." Funny, she was about to tell him about the dream, just like that, and she didn't even know him.

He prodded gently: "You want to tell me about it?"

"What?"

"What's upsetting you."

She shook her head. "I can't."

There was a long pause. "Okay," he said, "I'll talk to Judge Buckner and get back to you. But listen, Kate, if you ever want to talk to me, as a friend or as a doctor, you know where to reach me."

She nodded. She could not speak.

The bus ride from Baltimore to Hagerstown State Prison was hot and sticky. Slick was suffocating. He complained bitterly about this to the guards but they didn't listen. They were stupid and ignorant and he hated them.

They arrived at the prison in the heat of the afternoon. The place looked ominous: a bleak fortress looming up from behind barbed-wire fences. There was dust everywhere and Slick was coughing, but they had to wait inside the bus and bake some more under the scorching sun. Slick grimaced. His regulation orange jumpsuit was damp, his face dripped perspiration, and he was dehydrated. He had had it. So when the pushy guard with the billy club prodded him out of his seat, Slick took a swing at him, and connected. Stupid guard couldn't take a joke. He cracked Slick over the skull, and then left him to sit on the bus for an extra hour as blood trickled down his face.

When they finally let Slick inside, they took him to the infirmary and sewed some stitches. Then they made him stand in line like everybody else. It was awful. They treated *him,* Slick Carlson, like he was nobody. Strip search, cold shower, change into jeans and a blue cotton shirt, stiff black shoes, and white crew socks. The shirt had a number on it, stamped in black ink: 80962. That was his number. To the guys in charge, he didn't have a name anymore. To the inmates he didn't have a name either, just a reputation. They called him Short Eyes, for child molester. They thought he was some kind of pervert. Jesus! He wanted to tell them he liked chicks of all ages, hadn't he raped one of them to prove it? He'd been lucky, then. His lawyer had gotten him off.

That night, Slick paced his cell. His stints in the city jail were nothing compared to this. This was serious time. He was supposed to rot here for five years.

He cursed and clenched his fists. He hated prison, he hated the guards, but most of all, he hated Kate Riley. This was all her fault.

It was a lovely evening. Molly was grilling hamburgers. Ian was in the turtle sandbox with Superman, Darth Vader, and Luke Skywalker. Baby Lily was sitting propped up in her Fisher-Price rocker. Dave wasn't there yet—he'd be home later. A realtor with Carter and Glynn, he was finalizing the sale of a three hundred thousand-dollar home in Hampton.

Dressed, still, in her navy skirt and white blouse, her copper hair glistening in the sun's fading rays, Kate sat perched on the brick ledge across from Molly and the grill. They were on the back porch. Kate asked if she could help, but Molly, always the big sister, said no, you rest.

Molly swept her bangs out of her eyes, then expertly flipped the hamburgers with a metal spatula. She had black hair and blue eyes, like their father. Molly was a born nurturer: if you saw her in the supermarket, you'd say, there goes a good mother. She looked especially motherly lately. She was nursing Lily and her breasts were overlarge. Her postpartum belly still showed a bit too, so she favored loose-fitting clothes. Tonight she wore a blue-and-white smock. Kate thought she was beautiful.

"I read about that Carlson guy in the paper," Molly was saying. "Did he really threaten you?"

"Yes," Kate said, "but let's not talk about it."

Molly nodded. "I understand." She paused, then asked: "Well, what *do* you want to talk about?"

"Reuben, I guess," Kate answered. "I'm worried about him. Jimmy Delorosa was a good friend of his." She reflected a moment: "You know, this Buckner case really brings out the emotions in people. Even my secretary was upset today, and Moll, you know Judith. She's normally so cold and businesslike, but you should have seen the tears in her eyes. I think she might be lonely. She's divorced and . . . what?"

Molly was shaking her head. "I know somebody else who could use a good cry."

Kate, surprised, said nothing.

"You care so much," Molly said feelingly. "Reuben, Judith, Mary Delorosa. But what about you, Kate?"

"What about me?"

"I love you so much, I just hate to see you suffer."

"I'm not—"

"You look so thin and pale. You eating enough? What's wrong?"

"I . . . I'm confused, I guess," Kate began haltingly. "I love my job, but I don't know if that's enough anymore. I date, but there's no one special in my life. I'll be thirty soon, Moll. My biological clock is ticking. . . . When I see you . . ." I think maybe I want to have kids too, she was going to say, but just then baby Lily flailed her creamy little arms and began to cry.

Molly, busy over the sizzling grill, glanced to Kate.

Kate immediately stepped forward, then stopped. She knew what

Molly expected her to do, but she just couldn't. "Here," she seized the spatula, "I'll take the hamburgers."

"Instead of Lily?" Molly gave her a bruised look. She went to her three-month-old and lifted her to her shoulder. The baby was instantly comforted. "Kate, why won't you hold her?"

"She's hungry. She needs you."

"She's not *always* hungry," Molly said quietly. "And you never hold her. It's as if—"

"What?"

"You blame her for being born so soon after. As if she had something to do with—"

"Of course she didn't," Kate said abruptly. "My God, Molly, she's just a baby!" Kate couldn't bear to talk of this anymore. She watched Ian playing in his sandbox, then she tended the hamburgers, flipped them once more. Finally she turned back to her sister: "I'm sorry, Moll. Let's don't fight."

Molly nodded, but her attention was focused on the baby, who was nursing.

Peering through the acrid smoke rising from the grill, Kate smiled, tears in her eyes, at the precious red-haired bundle in Molly's arms. Molly had gone through labor three months after Mom died. The baby kept growing, every day, stronger, more rosy-cheeked. She could hold up her head now. Her eyes were alert. She would roll over any day. Soon she would crawl. And Kate still couldn't believe she existed. That shock of red hair, those blue eyes. That was the uncanny part: she actually resembled the other Lily, the one who was gone.

Kate felt her heart break and turned away.

Just then, Ian jumped up from the sandbox and came bounding toward her. Did he sense her pensive mood? for he pulled up short, suddenly shy. Ian wore red Adidas shorts, a striped shirt, and sneakers. His kneecaps boasted grainy patches of sand.

"Hey, c'mere, peanut!" She flung open her arms. The exuberant three-year-old gave a small cry of joy before he hurled himself at her and buried his golden curls in her lap. He smelled sweetly of Johnson's Baby Shampoo. She stroked his hair. He was so little, so trusting, she thought of e.e. cummings: nobody, not even the rain, has such small hands.

Kate left Molly's after dark. When she reached the brick building where she lived and turned into the parking lot, she thought she saw headlights close behind. Was someone following her? She parked the Volvo and waited. She expected another car to come driving in, a fellow tenant arriving home after a long day's work, but there were no headlights, no car. Yet, her fear of being followed persisted.

She peered through the car windshield into the shadows. Anticipating what? There was nothing, no one. She could hear the hum of a nearby streetlamp; she looked up and saw moths fluttering in its harsh bright light. Down the street, a dog barked sharply. But that was all.

Kate sighed. Convinced she was imagining things, she climbed out of the car and headed inside. There was no Slick Carlson lurking in the bushes—she was being ridiculous. Still, she was relieved when she gained the front entrance. She said "good evening" to the security guard, then proceeded uneventfully to her apartment.

Kate went immediately to bed. Again she resisted sleep, but she finally dropped off.

She had the dream again.

She thrashed awake shortly after midnight. Her body was drenched in sweat and she was shaking. Her heart pounded. She sat up in bed and tried to collect herself. In the bathroom, she splashed cold water on her face.

As she toweled off, she looked into the mirror. Her face was pale, her eyes haunted. She couldn't go on like this. Tomorrow she would see Fielding.

The next morning she changed her mind.

She showered and dressed for work, and by the time she left the apartment, she had convinced herself that she did not need to see Fielding, she just needed to forget Slick Carlson. It was because of him that she kept having the dream.

At work, Kate found Peter in a playful mood. He idly picked up the calendar on her desk and began flipping through it.

"Hey, I didn't know it was your birthday."

"Next month," Kate confessed.

"I see you penciled yourself in." He chuckled. "August twentieth. Afraid you'd forget?"

"Yes."

Judith happened to be passing by. "Why, this is wonderful. Let's celebrate with cake and candles."

"Oh, don't bother," Kate said, oddly touched.

"Honestly, it's no bother," Judith countered, her voice eager. "I'd like to do it. We'll order up a cake from Grauel's."

"Okay." Kate smiled. "Twist my arm. A cake would be fun, as long as we don't count candles."

"Getting old, huh?" Peter teased. "You're turning what? The big three-oh?"

"Please," Kate protested.

"My daughter will never turn thirty. She's a child," Judith said.

Kate looked at her secretary. "I didn't even know you had a daughter, Judith. I'd love to meet her."

Judith hesitated before answering. "You don't understand." Her voice sounded suddenly hollow. "She's with her father."

"Oh, I'm sorry." Kate met her secretary's gaze and held it for a long moment. Judith seemed to be trying to tell her something, but Kate wasn't sure what.

Peter's question came as an intrusion: "Don't you have visitation rights?"

31

Judith was silent.

Kate sensed that her secretary wanted to drop the subject, so she said brightly, with feigned enthusiasm: "Well, let's get down to work, shall we?"

"Good idea," Peter said, then added casually: "Judith, could you get me a cup of coffee first?"

"Certainly, Mr. Coe," Judith said softly and left.

Peter instantly moved closer to Kate. She could smell his cologne. So that's why he'd gotten rid of Judith. He only wanted them to be alone for a moment. Alone, that is, in a roomful of people, all of them aware that the boss had feelings for her. "Dinner tonight?" His eyes were hard on hers.

"Peter, I can't. We need to get these pleadings ready."

"Tomorrow, then."

"We'll see," she said. She saw the glow of pleasure on his face. Why had she gotten his hopes up? She should have turned him down.

A few minutes later, they were gathered in Peter's office. Judith kept dabbing tissues at her nose while she took dictation. She seemed relieved when Peter was interrupted with a phone call.

"What's wrong?" Kate asked her.

"Oh, it's my allergies. The pollen count is up."

"Anything I can get you?"

"No, thanks just the same." She smiled at Kate, another tentative foray toward friendship. Kate smiled back warmly. She was thinking to herself that Judith could be a good-looking woman if only she weren't so severe. She dressed with the conservative flair of a woman in the Junior League. She had a kind of prep-school classiness about her, and indeed, she had graduated from Vassar with honors. Kate often wondered why she settled for being a secretary.

Peter hung up the phone. "Now where were we?"

"The pleadings," Kate said.

"Right." Peter paraded in front of his desk, snapping his suspenders. "They've got to be done before the press conference tomorrow."

"No problem. I'll stay late," Kate offered.

Judith put her hand up, indicating she would stay, too. She pressed the Kleenex under her runny nose. To Kate, she was looking paler by the minute.

"All right," Peter said. "So, Kate, talk to me. How's the Buckner case shaping up?"

"Well, first of all, we'll have an agreed statement of facts. Judge Buckner tested positive on the breathalyzer test, so the presumption that he was intoxicated is virtually impossible to rebut. The key to litigation will be Buckner's mental attitude. Is the judge willing to reform? Is he remorseful?"

"Right. And obviously, if he's *not* remorseful, that's what we're looking for. We need the shrink in on this. He called you back yet?"

Kate recoiled slightly at Fielding's being labeled a "shrink."

"No, not yet. I'll call him."

"Good." Peter resumed his pacing, but then suddenly he halted. "Hey, I just thought of something. What if we could show depraved heart? We could nail this Buckner for murder. We make a conviction, we'll come off smelling like a rose. We might even make the cover of *Newsweek*."

You mean *you* might make the cover, Kate thought. But she was smiling. Peter's suggestion was so outrageous. "Peter, I hate to disappoint you, but we can't make this a murder case. Even if we can prove malice, we can't ignore Buckner's stature in the community. He's a very powerful man."

"Yeah, you're right," Peter said. "Murder *would* be impossible, wouldn't it? But, dammit, if we just do the usual vehicular manslaughter—"

"You won't make the cover of *Newsweek*," Kate finished for him. "You'll have to wait till you're Governor."

Peter smiled at the thought, then said: "Okay, Judith, elaborate the elements of vehicular manslaughter as defined under the Code. Then type up the lesser-included offenses, driving while intoxicated, et cetera, et cetera. . . . Got that?"

Judith was jotting all this down, then abruptly stopped. Her pen was poised in midair. She shook her head as if to ward off a wave of dizziness.

"Judith," Kate's brow furrowed with concern, "you okay?"

"I'm afraid I'm not feeling well. I assumed it was my allergies, but now I feel like I'm coming down with the flu."

Kate went over to Judith and felt her forehead while Peter watched anxiously. "You don't have a fever," Kate said, "but maybe you should go home, get some rest."

"What?" Peter snapped. "She doesn't want to do that."

"I'm afraid, Mr. Coe," Judith said, "you'll have to get Renée or one of the other girls to type up the pleadings. I simply cannot . . ."

"But Judith," Peter was yelling, his voice shrill and peevish, "we need you! You *can't* get sick!"

Judith looked up at him, helplessly. Peter expected her to be a machine and she wasn't. She was fast becoming as human as the rest of them.

O ver Peter's objections, Kate saw Judith safely off. "You okay to drive home?" she asked her in the parking lot.

"Yes. Only I hate to let you down."

"We'll survive. You just get well."

"I will," Judith said. "I promise." And then she looked right into Kate's eyes. Neither of them said a word. They shared the silence like old friends, then Kate slammed the door for her, Judith gunned the engine, and Kate watched the car pull out of the lot, waved good-bye.

Back in the office, Kate hadn't even reached her desk yet when Renée said: "Kate, line five-oh. Dr. Fielding."

Fielding, she thought, and her heart leapt. She told herself it was the case she was excited about. "Dr. Fielding, hello. Thanks for calling back."

"Kate," he said. And then there was a pause. It was almost as though he had surprised himself with the enjoyment of saying her name and, for a moment, could not go on. "I spoke to Judge Buckner."

"Great!" she said. Her voice never gave her away. She had been mistaken. There was nothing personal between them. He'd called only to talk about the case. "How did it go?"

"Put it this way, I'd be happy to be your expert witness."

"Honestly? You mean he's not remorseful?"

"He's arrogant, Kate. And, no, I don't think he is. I must say I developed an instant dislike for the man."

"You what?" Kate said. The office was suddenly so noisy, she could hardly hear him.

"I say I developed an—"

"I really can't hear you." She put her hand over the receiver and located the source of the disruption. Her fellow attorneys were crowded around an adorable, floppy-eared puppy someone had brought into the office. The excitement wouldn't last long. Still, she found herself saying: "Listen, things are crazy down here. Can I come see you?"

Fielding's modern brick office building was located on a quiet street only blocks from Molly's. Kate parked in the lot in the shade of an old tree. She did not immediately emerge from her car. She needed a moment to work up her courage. She watched the green leaves flutter languidly in the breeze, heard the peal of a church bell and, farther off, the hum of traffic on Charles Street. Then she went inside.

When she entered his office, the tall, lanky Fielding immediately rose and strode halfway across the room to take her hand. "Good to see you, Kate."

"Good to see you, too."

They gazed into each other's eyes. She had forgotten what a warm smile he had and how much she liked his shaggy mustache that almost, but didn't quite, manage to hide the pink scar on his upper lip. He noticed her staring at him. "Football injury," he explained, letting go of her hand and indicating a comfortable chair. "Have a seat. Coffee?"

"No thanks."

"I drink too much of the stuff, but I just quit smoking. One vice at a time."

She sat and watched while he spooned Taster's Choice into a mug of boiling water and encouraged an avalanche from the sugar dispenser. She wondered if he was married, then realized, with a start, that she shouldn't be thinking this about him. To distract herself, she surveyed his office. It was interesting to see Fielding in his own environment. There were lovely prints on the walls and a sprawl of books. The room was clean but littered with papers, magazines, and used Styrofoam coffee cups, complete with lipstick smudges. His office was as comfortable and as unpretentious as he was. Today he was dressed in jeans, shirt, no tie. The contrast with Peter was striking, and she found she liked the difference.

He sat down beside his desk, tipped back his chair, and sipped his coffee. His penetrating eyes fixed on her as he asked: "How are you?"

She shifted nervously in her seat. "Fine, just . . . couldn't, you know, be better."

He looked at her, said nothing.

"Now about Judge Buckner." she said. "On the question of remorse—"

He smiled faintly, ironically, so she stopped.

"What?"

"I'd be happy to discuss Judge Buckner with you anytime. In fact, we could just as easily have spoken on the phone."

Her heart thumped. She felt cornered. "Are you telling me you can't talk now? Because just say so. I understand you're busy." Abruptly, she stood up.

"Please." He waved at her chair. "Stay."

She sat back down, slowly, gripping her purse for some small comfort.

"It's not the Buckner case, is it?" he prodded gently. "Why you're here."

She felt a rush of relief and had to laugh at herself. "God, I'm being stupid, aren't I? Why can't I just be honest?"

"Because it's difficult," he said. "Because sometimes it hurts."

"I guess I don't really know why I'm here. I mean, I didn't. Now I do." She took a deep breath, looked at him. "You said if I ever needed to talk. But, gosh, you probably have a million patients waiting outside. I shouldn't presume—"

"I have a moment," Fielding said. He laced his hands behind his head and leaned back in his chair, the picture of relaxation. "Go ahead."

She tried to sort out her thoughts.

He waited.

She did not feel hurried by him. He did not seem to mind the silence. Because of this she was able to say: "I drove by my old house the other day."

"Oh?"

"Yes. It's on Stoneleigh Road. We had to sell it. My dad lives in an apartment now, closer to the hospital. He's a surgeon at Community General." She paused to watch his reaction. He must be bored by this. But, no, he was clearly interested. Encouraged, she continued: "Dad's so busy, and the house on Stoneleigh's big. He found it too hard to keep up. . . ."

"But . . ."

"But nothing." She frowned at him.

"Come on, something else is on your mind."

"Well, I was thinking, I haven't lived in that house for years and yet I was angry at Dad for selling it. It's as though he robbed me of my childhood. I know it's silly, but that's how I feel." She closed her eyes a moment, then opened them, remembering: "I only intended to stop by the house briefly, but I heard a door bang, then a little girl came scampering out. It was weird. She went straight for my favorite tree. It's this beautiful old maple. Molly and I used to call it the climbing tree. The uncanny part was that she had a swing hanging from the tree, and we used to have a swing, too. The little girl reminded me of myself because she liked the swing and everything, but when her mother came out she went and hid in the tree. God, I don't know how many times I skinned my knees and scraped my palms on those branches, just to get up to my secret hiding place where I would look up at the sky and daydream." Kate's smile was wistful. "It brought me back, seeing the little girl. I fell in love with her. But I was jealous of her, too."

"Jealous? Why?"

"Because . . . she has what I want."

"Which is?"

Kate stared blankly at Fielding. When she finally spoke, it wasn't to answer his question because that would have been too painful. The closest she could come was to say: "I hope that little girl appreciates what she's got because there's just no security. You go along, you're happy, you think you have a handle on things, and then it gets snatched away."

"What gets snatched away?"

Kate hesitated, blinked.

Fielding tipped forward in his chair. "Come on. Tell me. What?"

She exhaled raggedly, gripped the arms of her chair: "My mom, she died."

"I see."

She glanced up sharply. "Aren't you going to say 'I'm sorry'?"

"Should I?" He was watching her now, really interested.

"No, it's just that everybody always says it. 'Oh, I'm so sorry, Kate.' It's so inadequate."

"Then we can live without it, can't we, counselor?" He winked at her.

She found herself, ridiculously enough, smiling. Then the familiar undertow of sadness seized her and swept her away again. "My dad's got a new girlfriend. And Molly's got a terrific husband and two priceless kids. Everybody's doing great. I should be, too."

"Says who?"

"Nobody, everybody. Look, I don't know, It's just . . . she died six months ago. Heart attack. I should be over it by now." Kate looked forlornly at him.

His eyes on her were steady, unwavering. He said gently: "Dying's not a crime, Kate. There's no statute of limitations on grief."

They were quiet a good, long time. He sipped his coffee awhile and she was pensive. Finally he asked: "What are you thinking?"

"Oh, just what Molly said. It's true."

"What?"

"That I never hold baby Lily."

"Why not?"

"Molly said I blame her for being born so soon after."

"And?"

"And . . . I can't help it, I can't love her just now. It's too painful. Sometimes I wonder if I love Ian more just because of his name. Because he can simply be himself. But Lily's named after my mom. How can she live up to that?"

"I don't know," Fielding said. "Does she have to?"

Again Kate was silent. Fielding's attitude was so refreshing. Here she was, unhappily assuming things had to be a certain way when they didn't. She listened to the soothing hum of the air conditioner. She studied the prints on the walls, the books, the cozy rug. She did anything but meet his eyes, for he was regarding her closely now.

"How are the nights?" he asked. "You sleeping now?"

The question made her look straight at him. She thought about Slick and his threat. She hadn't told anyone how afraid she still was, not even Molly. "Actually," she said casually even though her heart was pounding, "there's this dream I keep having."

She had failed to startle him. He said evenly: "Want to tell me about it?"

"I . . ." She could not share this with him. She wanted to, but she was too tired. "Maybe next time?"

"Do you want there to be a next time?"

"Yes," she said. "I do."

———

After she said good-bye to Fielding, Kate should have gone straight back to her office; she had a million things to do. Instead she once again stopped by her old house on Stoneleigh Road. She did not know why she was here.

She thought of Fielding. He said he would try to fit her in once a week. Tomorrow, even, he might have an opening. He would see.

She looked at the house. Five minutes passed, then ten, but no knobby-kneed, red-haired girl came skipping out. There was just the swing under the old maple, hanging forlornly from its two braided ropes, waiting, as if it missed the little girl, too. Remember how she soared in the swing, her hair flying? And remember when she jumped off to hide in the tree? And then she and her mother had played the game, and the sun shone gold on their faces and in their hair. But seeing them was a one-time gift. Kate would not see them again today. And even if she did, it would not be the same.

She took one last nostalgic look, then urged her car into drive. Before she pulled out, she glanced into her rearview mirror. She immediately tensed. Who was that? Somebody watching her? Frowning, she put her foot on the brake and twisted around so she could peer out the rear window. How strange. Whoever it was, was gone. The street was deserted. She stared a good long moment in disbelief, then shifted back around in her seat. She worried about herself. Slick's threat had her imagining things. Or had she simply lost too much sleep? Perhaps there had been no one, after all.

The Volvo purred as Kate rounded the corner. Her old house was in profile. She glanced toward the old garden, expecting to see roses, but there were none. In fact there was no garden at all. They had paved it over to make room for more cars. Now, instead of roses, red and pink and white, there was black tar.

Kate worked late in the office.

She and Renée were the only ones there.

The staff had gone home. This was a government office, so there was no incentive for employees to stay late. The attorneys were absent as well. They'd headed out early for a night of softball, pizza, and beer.

Kate would dictate the pleadings first, then Renée would type them up. Renée dressed like a punk rocker and wore a different wig every day of the week. She was a far cry from Judith, but she was reliable.

Kate sat back in her swivel chair and yawned. She was exhausted, but the pleadings must get done tonight.

The first item of business was the most crucial. She must dictate a charge for vehicular manslaughter against Judge Buckner. She popped a mini-cassette into her dictating machine and picked up the handset, pressed the button to record. She shook off a wave of dizziness and began: "Judith . . . I mean Renée, sorry, . . . this is a pleading in the case of the State of Maryland versus Buckner. First paragraph: The Baltimore City State's Attorneys office, by Peter Coe III and Kate Riley, as and for charges against the defendant Harold Timothy Buckner, alleges as follows. Count One . . ."

Kate worked late to finish her work but also to avoid this: walking into a silent apartment where there was no voice to greet her, no dinner waiting.

She showered and changed, and an hour later, was pacing the living room.

When she first moved in, she'd had such energy and high hopes. She wanted to decorate the place and really make it her own, but she got no farther than her bedroom. In the living room, on the wall, there was a reproduction of the Brontë sisters as painted by their brother Branwell. That painting was it. The rest of the living room was sparkling clean but impersonal. It could have belonged to anyone.

Anxious yet overtired, she flopped onto the sofa, stared at the white walls, and thought of Fielding. She wished she had told him about the dream. Maybe he could have told her what it meant and she wouldn't be afraid, she would be sleeping.

Outside, a car backfired. The noise startled her. She jumped to her feet and strode to the glass patio door, peered out. On impulse, she slid the door open and stepped into the humid night. The air was heavy and there was no breeze. Her wind chimes were silent. She gazed up at a milky-white sky too thick with clouds to allow for stars. A breeze stirred, eerily, from nowhere, just enough to unsettle the chimes but not enough to make them sing. The breeze died, leaving goosebumps on her skin. Shivering, she hugged herself and hurried back into her apartment. She shut the sliding glass door, locked it, then double-checked to make sure. She should have felt safe now that she was inside, but she didn't. She thought of Stoneleigh Road and that person who had been watching her, who, when she turned around, was gone. She thought of Slick Carlson, but of course it couldn't have been him.

An hour later, she was so tired, she was nodding off on the sofa. She reluctantly climbed into bed. She fell asleep instantly.

And she had the dream.

It was the same dream, as always.

She was on a footpath. It was dark and cold, and the autumn leaves rustled uneasily as she brushed past. She headed toward the Tudor house, its windows warmed by flickering candles, their bright orange flames fluttering like angel's wings against the cold frosted panes. Suddenly, she heard a noise in front of her, on the path. Then she saw him. *He* was on the path, a menacing figure, blocking her forward progress. She couldn't go to the house, not now, and wait! no! stop! he was coming after her. Her heart pounded. She turned and fled up the steep, rocky incline. Frantic, she glanced over her shoulder. He was gaining on her! She scrambled hurriedly up the rocks, then she slipped and fell and . . . She was tossing and turning under the covers, her hair was damp with sweat, and it was 4:15 on her digital clock radio.

She lay back, exhausted, against her pillow.

She remembered the stranger in her dream, and she felt afraid all over again. The stranger was Slick, wasn't it? Who else could it be?

7

The press conference was a disaster.

It was held in the ceremonial courtroom, part of the old antebellum courthouse. The room, usually reserved for historic occasions, was musty and dark, with a small bench and bar and a puritanical-looking wooden witness box. Today the courtroom was packed with reporters, photographers from the wire services, and television crews from the three local networks. The *Baltimore Sun, Washington Post,* and *Daily Lawyer* were represented. There was also a vocal chapter from MADD—Mothers Against Drunk Driving.

Kate stood just beyond the glare of the lights, behind Peter, to his right. Even before he spoke, she felt uneasy, perhaps because of this morning. Her day had begun badly. After her four A.M. nightmare, she'd dozed off again. She slept through the alarm to wake perilously late. Hurrying into the hot shower, not testing it, she scalded herself.

Dressing, she got a run in her stocking. At work, she collapsed into her chair, craving a moment's peace. She looked to the photograph of her mom for solace, but it was gone. For a moment she was desolate. Then she steeled herself and began an organized search. She found the photograph easily enough, in the second drawer of her desk. But, oddly, it was facedown. Had someone deliberately done that? Someone who wanted to annihilate her mother's smile? It didn't make sense. . . .

Peter started to speak, distracting her. His blond hair, she noted, was perfectly in place. His suit was perfect. His tie. He had all the right moves, and Kate, at this moment, admired him.

"Ladies and gentlemen of the press," he announced, "charges are being filed today against Judge Harold Timothy Buckner. We expect to prosecute the case in the usual manner—"

"Usual manner?" a reporter interjected.

Kate was instantly alert. She knew the media's power to create and destroy, and she sensed that Peter was in danger.

"Yes, usual," Peter reiterated. "As State's Attorney for Baltimore City, by the power vested in me and my office, I intend to prosecute under the statutes for vehicular manslaughter—"

"Murder, you mean," said the reporter.

"Excuse me?"

"The indictment. I have a copy here, Mr. Coe. And it clearly states murder."

Murder. The word hung in the gloomy air like an accusation. There was a deathly silence. Peter looked baffled. And now all the reporters who had expected another routine statement stirred in their seats and began madly jotting down notes. Some jumped to their feet. This was news.

An assault of rapid-fire questioning began:

"The word 'murder' seems to have startled you, Mr. Coe. You *are* familiar with the crime?"

"Mr. Coe, did you personally review the indictment before having it filed?"

"Judging from from your hesitation, Mr. Coe, you're not at the helm of your own ship. Who's running things down here?"

· "Tell us, Mr. Coe, murder or vehicular manslaughter, which is it? Or don't you know? Perhaps we should ask one of your assistants."

Peter blanched. He didn't know what to do. Wordlessly, he appealed to Kate.

And now the cameras swung toward her. She was blinded by white light but managed to grab a copy of the indictment, scanned it quickly, then strode up to the podium to whisper in Peter's ear.

Peter listened intently. His face betrayed him for only an instant. Consummate politician that he was, he recovered quickly, and said: "Yes, of course I meant murder. This is what happens, gentlemen, when you miss your morning cup of coffee . . ."

There was sporadic laughter, giving Peter time to regain control.

"So you *did* review the indictment, Mr. Coe?"

"Of course I reviewed the indictment," Peter said, fully composed now, straightening his tie. "And I stand by it. The State's Attorneys Office intends to prosecute this case under a murder charge."

"Are you saying Buckner intended to kill Officer Delorosa?"

"No," Peter said. "We do believe, however, that Judge Buckner acted with a depraved heart, which, as you know, also constitutes malice under the law."

"And you have evidence to support this?"

Peter wavered slightly: "I'm not going to discuss the evidence at this time. I'll simply reiterate that we believe we can win this case. And now," Peter paused dramatically, "I would like to introduce the person who is really in charge here. Because this case is so important, involving a prominent judge who by his irresponsibility has cast into doubt the integrity of our profession, I have put in charge my best man, or rather, my best *woman!*" Peter turned to Kate, beckoning to her with a sweep of his arm. She hesitated, then walked to the podium under the hot lights, as cameras clicked and whirred. . . . It was all she could do to smile.

Back in the office, Peter was in a cold fury.

"All right, who screwed up? Kate? Renée? Talk to me."

"I dictated the pleadings," Kate explained. "Renée typed them up."

"For vehicular manslaughter?"

"Of course," Kate said.

"Not murder?"

"No." She shook her head emphatically.

"Then it's got to be you, Renée. You obviously picked up the wrong cassette. Typed the wrong pleadings. That's the trouble with you secretaries—you don't know a damn thing!"

"But Mr. Coe—" Renée tried to defend herself.

"God, I'm so angry!" Peter paced the room. "I looked like a fool up there. Now we've got to prove *murder*. You said so yourself, Kate. We can't possibly win."

Peter continued to fume and Renée was dismissed. He would decide later whether to fire her or not. As Kate sat quietly, waiting for her boss to calm down, she began to doubt herself for the first time. She thought she had dictated those pleadings correctly. She was sure of it. And yet, last night she had been so tired. Was it possible she had slipped?

Because of her own guilt, she didn't blame Peter for his childish outburst. She didn't even blame him for assigning responsibility to her now that the case was hopeless. When he turned to her and said, almost tenderly: "This has been the worst day. Will you help me redeem it? Have dinner with me," she replied against all her better judgment, after weeks of putting him off: "Dinner? Okay. Yes."

———

Everyone was talking about the press conference. Kate couldn't get any work done. The only bright note in her afternoon was a call from Fielding. He had an opening at six o'clock.

Shortly after five, she was driving up Charles Street. She had a few minutes to spare before meeting Fielding. She remembered that

Judith lived nearby and, on impulse, decided to drop in on her and see how she was.

Judith lived in a big old house that had been subdivided into apartments. It was off-white, with black shutters and a small garden. Trees shaded the sidewalk. Kate walked up the marble steps and pressed the buzzer for Moore, Apartment 2B. When Judith's voice came over the intercom and Kate announced herself, there was a long pause, then Judith finally said "Come on up" and buzzed her in.

Inside it was warm—no central air-conditioning, Kate noted. The foyer rug was frayed, the stairs creaked with age. The place was old, but not really run-down. It had a cozy, comfortable quality Kate liked.

Judith was waiting for her at the door. Dressed in a quilted blue bathrobe with knee socks and no slippers, the secretary appeared healthy and fit. Her black hair, graying at the temples, was neatly combed; her bony cheeks shone as if she'd scrubbed them; and her posture, as always, was erect. Her face, so pale yesterday, had regained its color.

"Hello," Kate said.

Judith nodded. She held the door only partway open.

Kate felt like an intruder. "I'm sorry. I should have called."

"No, no," Judith said, opening the door a shade wider. "Quite all right."

"I wanted to see how you were feeling."

"How sweet. Much better, thanks." Judith smiled slightly, then looked away. The tilt of her head was apologetic. "I just finished speaking to Renée. If only I had been there, I could have typed those pleadings myself."

"Don't blame yourself," Kate said firmly. "It's not your fault."

Judith raised her head. Now there was pride in the angle of her chin. Her eyes were bright: "I'll help you all I can."

"Thanks." Kate nodded.

Silence fell between them. Cars on Charles Street ground their gears noisily as they ascended the steep hill outside. The solitary window on the landing rattled.

"Well," Kate said, "I should go."

"Must you?" Judith asked, and the words seemed torn from her, full of emotion, which surprised Kate.

Kate hesitated. It was possible Judith was merely being polite. "No, really I—"

"Please? Just for a minute," Judith pressed, and so Kate allowed herself to be ushered into the relative cool of Judith's modest apartment. The living room lay in the shadow of the tall brick building next door. The furniture was all second-hand. There was a stone fireplace with an empty grate, a bookcase, an old sofa, a rocking chair. Kate looked for photographs of Judith's daughter but couldn't find any.

"I was just fixing myself some tea," Judith said. "Will you join me?"

"Yes. Thank you." Kate smiled.

Judith led her into the tiny kitchen. The radio on the table was playing classical music. On the counter there was a lone piece of carrot cake, a fork placed just so beside it, a flowered china teacup with matching saucer, a teabag, and a spoon.

Judith reached into the cupboard for a second teacup. Kate noticed how few dishes she owned. She probably owned a full set of china, back in the days when she was married.

As if following Kate's thoughts, Judith said: "I used to live in a big house with a garden. I belonged to the Junior League."

Minutes later, they were seated before the barren fireplace, listening to strains of Mozart's "Eine Kleine Nachtmusik" from the radio. Kate nibbled on her carrot cake and pronounced it "delicious." Judith sat in her rocking chair, sipping tea.

Out of nowhere, a marmalade cat appeared. He leapt up onto the table, purring loudly, gingerly pawed his way along the tray, and sniffed the contents of the pewter creamer.

"Mr. Rochester! Down!" Judith commanded and swiped at him. The cat sprang nimbly to the floor.

"Mr. Rochester," Kate said in a quiet voice, looking down at the orange and white cat. "From *Jane Eyre,* right?" She paused, swallowed, and found that she could say the words after all: "That was my mom's favorite book."

"I know," Judith said.

Kate glanced up sharply. "You know?"

"Yes, it's everyone's, isn't it?"

"Oh, right." Kate's voice was flat. "For a moment there I thought you meant—"

"What?"

"That you knew her."

To this, Judith had no reply. Her chilly personality forbade intimacy and this was an intimate moment. And what could she say, anyway? She could not rescue Kate from her grief. Kate sat there sadly with her arms crossed on her lap and wished she had not mentioned her mother at all. Thinking of her was too painful. Even the soothing music of Mozart failed to help.

Judith stirred and poured them each a second cup of tea. It was then she sneezed. "Oh, goodness!" she said, and threw back her head and sneezed again.

"Can I get you anything?" Kate asked.

Judith pulled a tissue from her bathrobe pocket and blew into it. "No, I'm fine."

Kate glanced at Judith's stocking feet. "What about slippers? Have you got—"

"Oh, they're in the bedroom. Don't bother—"

"I'll fetch them," Kate said and started down the hall.

Judith's room featured a twin bed without its twin, a narrow window, and white walls with no pictures. It was an unremarkable room altogether save for the antique wooden cradle beside the bed. The cradle had a blue blanket in it and was mussed as if someone had slept there. Kate stared at the cradle, thinking of baby Lily. She knew Molly could use a cradle like this, but Judith? She wondered what it was doing here.

Judith provided an answer. Judith had glided behind her, ghostlike, down the hall and now stood beside her. "It's Mr. Rochester's," she said.

8

Todd Fielding consulted the calendar on the desk in his office.

He knew, without looking, who his six o'clock appointment was. He didn't know why he played this game with himself, why he needed to see her name penciled in—"Kate Riley."

Since her visit yesterday, he had scrambled to make time for her in his schedule. And although he was one of Baltimore's busiest psychiatrists and had had to skip his lunch hour today, he was glad to take her on as a patient. She was worth it.

People like Kate Riley were one reason why he'd left New York City. New York was saturated with analysts, and he couldn't be of much use there. But Baltimore needed good doctors. Four years ago, they had needed, specifically, a psychiatrist to help the Baltimore City Police, Special Forces. He convinced Sue Ann to leave her Madison Avenue advertising friends and come with him. It had, he thought, been a good decision. He had received hands-on experience and the satisfaction of knowing that he had helped defuse at least two hostage situations, preventing bloodshed. And he had met some good people, like Reuben.

Sue Ann hadn't liked his doing the Special Forces work. Too dangerous, she said, and so he had quit and gone into private practice, which he enjoyed, in its own way, equally well.

His stomach rumbled. He realized he was hungry. Ever since he quit smoking, twelve days ago, he was ravenous. He strolled over to his mini-stove and switched on the kettle for some coffee.

Not smoking was tough. His body had got used to the nicotine. He found himself craving a cigarette at inopportune moments. Sometimes he would break into a cold sweat it was so bad. He had bought himself two pipes, no tobacco. He carried the pipes around in his pockets and toyed with them at his desk, to occupy his hands.

Restless, waiting for the kettle to boil, he prowled the office. He studied the Pat Buckley Moss prints hanging on the walls.

Moss wasn't Amish herself, but the Pennsylvania Dutch influence was evident in her paintings. Her people were simple and lovable. Of the five paintings he owned, his favorites were the family skating on a wintry pond and the couple cuddling under a quilt, whisking through snow drifts in a horse-drawn sleigh. Why was it that Pat Buckley Moss paintings evoked Charles Dickens in his mind? Perhaps because both artists celebrated the family. Since Fielding himself grew up as a rather lonely only child, he had always looked upon large families with the yearning of a little boy standing penniless outside a candy store. Growing up, his secret dream was to have been born, not in affluent Deerfield Park, Illinois, the only son of a banker father, but in some place like The Bronx in a boisterous Italian family, himself only one of a dozen siblings. They would have played baseball together, he and his brothers, and fought at dinner over platefuls of spaghetti.

Fielding straightened the painting called *Skating Joy*.

Sue Ann didn't like Pat Buckley Moss, so Fielding hung all her prints in the office and kept none at home.

He moved to the window, grimacing as he felt pain shoot through his calf muscles. Four miles today. He had gotten up early to avoid the heat. And he'd found he liked being up at that hour. He had the streets, the world, to himself. As he jogged, he thought about things. He thought about Kate Riley rather more than he wanted to.

At the window, he reached into his trouser pocket for his pipe. He gnawed the stem thoughtfully, then pulled the pipe out of his mouth altogether when he saw her drive up in a blue Volvo. She stepped lightly from her car and waved to the parking lot attendant. The gray sky provided a muted backdrop for her shining beauty, her shoulder-length coppery hair. He couldn't see her face clearly at this distance, but he remembered what porcelain skin she had. Soft, unblemished, like a child's. A cute nose she had too. And a kissable mouth that curled impishly when she was amused. She headed inside now—her long, coltish legs striding briskly, her arms and purse swinging, her white chiffon dress swaying with her as she walked—and disappeared beneath the awning of the brick building's main entrance.

He discovered, to his surprise, that he was standing at the window long after she had gone inside. Well, she was an attractive girl.

He frowned, dismissed the thought as thoroughly unprofessional, and hurried to rescue the kettle, which had been wailing for some time now.

At least the water would be hot.

On closer inspection, Kate appeared tired but still beautiful.

She took the chair without preamble as if she was eager to get to work.

He poured himself some coffee. She declined, she'd just had tea, she said.

Fielding laughed. "Most people would have had something stronger, considering the kind of day you've had."

She stared at him. "You heard about the press conference?"

He nodded. "Peter Coe called."

"Oh." She gripped the armrests of her chair. "Does he know I'm . . . ?"

"Seeing me? Oh, no," Fielding reassured her. "Don't worry. Your visits here are completely confidential. He just wanted to discuss the Buckner case."

"I see," she said, relieved.

"But we're here to talk about you," Fielding said. "So tell me, how'd you sleep last night?"

"Me?" She shifted in her seat.

"You," he said, smiling.

She laughed a little, then quickly became serious. "I had the dream again."

"You want to tell me about it?"

She nodded, took a deep breath, and recreated her dream for him. Someone was chasing her, and she fled up a cliff: "On the cliff," she said, "I slip and fall, but I scramble up again. But the stranger is right behind me. I look down at this thunderous, rocky surf below. The stranger closes in. And now I have this dreadful choice. Do I leap to my death or turn to confront this horrible, awful man? At least," she paused, puzzled now, "I think it's a man."

"You think?"

"Well, all along I assumed it was Slick Carlson in the dream. He's so creepy. . . . But now I'm not sure."

"Why not?"

She concentrated hard. "I don't know. Maybe I don't *want* to know who it is."

"Because . . ."

"I'm too scared."

"Tell me, at the end of the dream, what do you do? Jump to your death? Or turn and face your pursuer?"

She furrowed her brow. "I don't know. It never gets that far. I wake up."

"What's that like?"

"I feel hopeless. I can't get back to sleep."

"Because you're afraid you'll have the dream again?"

"Yes." She focused her gaze on him and asked: "The dream—what does it mean?"

"You want me to tell you?" He chuckled softly. "I would if I could. Dreams are messages from the subconscious, Kate. In the final analysis, your dreams mean what *you* think they mean."

Her shoulders sagged. She frowned and looked down at the carpet. He had disappointed her. And he wanted so much to help. But dreams? He wasn't into horoscopes. He didn't read tea leaves. He could, though, nudge her in the right direction, at least in what he *perceived* was the right direction.

"One thing you might think about," he offered.

She looked at him, suddenly eager. "What?"

"Mind you," he cautioned, "it's just a suggestion. But, in your dream, are you being chased or are you running away?"

Her blue eyes were wide and full on him. Finally she said: "I don't know."

"Well, think about it."

"Okay. I will." She half-smiled at him.

They were silent a moment, listening to the steady drone of the air conditioner. Fielding sipped some coffee from his mug. It tasted bitter. He put the mug down, leaned forward, and fixed his gaze on her: "So what else besides the dream? Talk to me. How do you feel?"

She tackled the question head on and his heart surged with fondness for her. She was brave, this one. "I miss my mom. Since she . . . died I'm just . . ."

"Marking time?"

"Yes, even though there isn't much left. I mean, we're all growing older, aren't we?" She paused. "I used to be more active. I jogged five miles every morning."

"That's admirable." His taut calf muscles could vouch for that.

"And also," she continued, "I'm generally an outgoing person, but I've been remiss. Friends call, I don't call back."

"Why not?"

"They want to have fun."

"No, not *fun!*" Fielding gasped. "God, that's *awful!* Surely they don't expect you to join in?"

She smiled, but only fleetingly. Fielding saw the loneliness etched in her face.

"I can't be with friends," she said finally, "because I'm just not up to it."

"I see." He nodded solemnly, no longer kidding around. He tugged thoughtfully on his mustache. "You miss your mom," he said. "Can't you share this with your friends?"

"That's just it." Her candid blue eyes met his. "Whenever I try, I'm disappointed. For instance, this afternoon, just before I got here, I was with a friend, well, she's not exactly a friend—my secretary—and anyhow, I told her about this book, *Jane Eyre,* which was Mom's favorite, then I wished I hadn't."

"Why not?"

"Because, afterward I couldn't deal with it. It hurt too much. No one understands."

"What exactly?"

"How I feel."

"Why not?"

"I don't know. They just don't. Mom and I were very close. And Judith . . . that's her name, my secretary . . . she's got a daughter and I don't think she even sees her. She doesn't even have her picture up."

"So people don't understand."

"Yeah, and maybe they're not interested."

"I'm interested. Tell me about your mom. You mentioned some things. Her name was Lily. She had red hair."

"Yes, red hair," Kate said. She watched him closely: "Did I tell you she was in A.A.?"

Fielding shook his head no.

"Well," Kate sighed a little, having got the worst over with: "It was tough, growing up. When I was in grade school, she was drunk a lot. She had bruises from bumping into furniture. Molly and I couldn't bring friends home, she'd be passed out and snoring. But she joined A.A. and sobered up. She lost all kinds of weight and she was thin, like a ballet dancer. She loved the A.A. meetings just to listen, but she was a dynamic speaker herself. After a while, she was in demand. She traveled to different cities and told her story. When she spoke, people would come up afterward. People would cry."

"Sounds like a great lady."

"She was."

"How'd she die?"

"Heart attack. She was fifty-two."

They fell silent. He thought for a moment, then said: "I'd like you to do something for next time."

"Homework?" She wasn't balking at the idea, just curious.

"Yes. I'd like you to write out a list of your mother's good and bad qualities."

"Okay," she said, not blinking. "I'll try."

This girl was ready to go to work. He liked that. He didn't want to press her, she was doing so well. She loved her mom, maybe idolized her a bit. That could be a problem. They would work on that. But there was something else. All along, he had been listening to what she *didn't* say as well as to what she said. And she hadn't mentioned her father, except to report that he had sold her childhood home and now had a new girlfriend. Fielding got up, dumped more sugar into his coffee, and sat back down. The coffee tasted much better now. He propped his feet up on the desk, let his glance drift over to her, and said, as if the thought had just occurred to him: "You and your dad. You two get along?"

She frowned. "We do okay."

"What's okay?"

"Okay's okay. You know."

"You see him much?"

"Once in a while. He comes to dinner at Molly's. We have barbecues at her place. She lives near here, actually. In Homeland."

Fielding nodded, then said: "Is it a strain?"

"What?"

"Talking to your father."

"I don't know. I've never had a real conversation with him."

"You don't communicate?"

"We never get beyond the polite surface stuff. You know—how's work? Keeping busy . . . ?" She paused, took a deep breath. "Look, he tries hard, but he's a busy physician, he was never there when I needed him."

"And what about the girlfriend?" Fielding said. "What's she like?"

Kate looked as if she'd been stung.

He prodded gently: "She got a name?"

"Blanche. Her name's Blanche."

"And?"

"She lives in Silver Spring where she runs a boutique. She's tall, frosts her hair."

"George Washington wore a wig and had wooden teeth. You going to tell me about her or not?"

Kate didn't reply. She was too confused. She reached up and pressed the heel of her palm against her forehead.

Fielding looked at her tenderly; but he knew, to her he was a million miles away.

———

She intended to drive straight home, but she slowed on Tunbridge, a block from Molly's, and curbed her car. She needed to collect her thoughts. Honestly, she wanted to tell him about

Blanche, but she just couldn't. She didn't like the cool, aloof lady. Her own mom had been such a warm person. But, hey, maybe that was important. Maybe she should have told Fielding that.

Overall the session had gone well, she thought. She found such comfort in his presence, in the sanctuary of those cinnamon eyes. Now, just sitting in the car, she was conscious of feeling good. Good enough, in fact, to stop by Molly's. She hadn't stopped by spontaneously for a long time, not since Mom died.

She pulled out from the curb, and as she did, so did a car behind her. The car looked familiar, but lots of cars looked alike, and Kate was no expert. She continued down the tree-lined, shady street. So did the car, at a discreet distance.

Kate frowned. She wasn't alarmed, yet this car seemed to be following her. What should she do? She remembered that Homeland was crisscrossed by a network of back alleys, once used for ice deliveries. She quickly turned down the nearest alley without signaling. She drove cautiously, as the alley was narrow, and glanced anxiously into her rearview mirror. She was halfway down the alley and just beginning to relax when the car reappeared behind her. Her heart thudded. She urged her car forward and plowed through a gauntlet of overhanging branches that rattled against the windshield. The alley was fairly secluded. If some harm should come to her, if she should scream, it was possible no one would hear. She darted another glance into her rearview mirror. The car was getting closer. She stepped on the gas, and the Volvo shot forward. She didn't dare look behind her now, she was too scared. When she finally reached the main thoroughfare, she swung recklessly out into traffic and cut off another car, which honked at her. She waved an apologetic "I'm sorry" to the driver, then quickly turned to see if she was still being followed. The car was gone.

Trembling, she pulled over and let the other cars roar past. *Had* that car been following her? Or was she imagining things again?

Molly answered the door in her Country Kitchen apron. Her face lit up when she saw her sister: "Kate! Come in!" They hugged each other, then Molly beckoned to Ian: "Guess who's here?"

Kate stepped into the air-conditioned hall. "I can only stay a minute. I'm meeting Peter Coe for dinner."

Ian bounded into the room. He giggled when he saw Kate and thrust a two-inch plastic Superman into her hand. "Play," he commanded.

Molly said: "Ian, Mummie and Auntie Kate need to talk. Here, come with us to the kitchen." To Kate she said: "I'm fixing supper. Lily's napping, but she's due up anytime."

Kate flinched. Then she remembered what Fielding had said. The baby needn't be like Lily; she could simply be herself.

In the kitchen, Kate smelled quiche baking in the oven. On the counter were scraps of pastry dough, a rolling pin, flour, and mixing bowls. She turned to Ian: "Let's get out the Play-Doh."

"Good idea," Molly said.

While Molly fixed the salad, Kate and her nephew sat at the kitchen table and fashioned animals out of Play-Doh with cookie cutters.

Kate took a deep breath. She didn't know how her sister would react, but she needed to tell her: "Moll, I'm seeing a psychiatrist."

"Terrific!" Molly said so genuinely that Kate immediately relaxed. "Is it helping?"

"Too soon to tell, I guess. But, yes."

"What do you talk about?"

"Mom, mostly."

Molly was quiet a minute, then she said: "And the doctor?"

"He's very good, I think. I feel comfortable with him. Funny," she smiled, "he pours more sugar into his coffee than anyone I ever met. It's the kind of habit that, if you didn't like somebody, would really bother you. But when he does it, well, it suits him."

"He's his own person, sounds like."

"He is."

Molly reached into the refrigerator and said over her shoulder: "I don't mean to change the subject, but I've been dying to ask, how was the press conference?"

"Oh, Moll . . ." It was then that Kate told her about the mixup in pleadings and how they had mistakenly indicted Buckner for murder instead of manslaughter. She told her about Judith's being out sick and how she went to visit her: "And, Moll, when I went into Judith's bedroom, there was this cradle."

"A cradle?"

"Yeah, for Mr. Rochester."

"No kidding. She sleep with armadilloes, or what?"

"Cut it out, Moll."

"Well, you've got to admit, it's weird. Like something out of Gary Larson."

"It's not weird."

"It is. A cat's not a baby. A cradle's inappropriate. I bet she never had kids, right?"

"No, she did," Kate said earnestly. "She had a daughter. Only she's with the father. I think Judith misses her."

Molly was amused. She was smiling, shaking her head. "I'm sorry, but that cradle. I still think it's creepy—"

The sisters paused in their conversation as, suddenly, from upstairs, they heard a cry.

Molly didn't even look to Kate for help. She abandoned her salad and grabbed a dish towel to dry her hands.

If Kate didn't stop Molly now, she would be too late. She would lose this chance. It seemed to Kate that she was moving in slow motion, but she strode to the kitchen door ahead of her sister, turned, and said: "I'll get her."

"You don't have to," Molly said, surprised.

"I know. I want to."

Kate sprinted up the hardwood steps.

The nursery was a cheerful room. A rainbow arched the width of the far wall. Under the arch was the baby's crib. Blue-and-white checked curtains decorated the windows. There was an oak changing table, an oak dresser, and a blue bookcase filled with Dr. Seuss books and a colorful assortment of stuffed animals—elephants and tigers and bears. The room smelled sweetly of baby powder and baby oil and of the deodorizer in the diaper pail, but most of all the room smelled of sleep and innocence and peace: of baby.

Kate leaned over the crib and gazed upon her infant niece. Fully awake, Lily lay on her stomach. She was straining with all her might to lift her head off the mattress, and she finally managed it. And yet her head was bobbing, bobbing, and it felt so heavy to her, she had to give it up. With a cry of frustration, she let her head flop to the mattress again.

Lily was so tiny, so powerless. Kate felt a surge of love and pity for her as she reached into the crib and gently lifted her out. Now the baby stopped crying and they looked at each other. Kate was the first to smile, Lily second: her eyes filled with merriment, and she broke into a huge, chubby grin.

Kate did not return downstairs. Instead, she carried Lily over to the rocking chair and sat down with her, cradled her in her arms. The evening sun, shining margarine-gold, fell in rectangles through the Venetian blinds and spilled along the floor, across the chair, and into their faces. Lily's hair, ignited by the sun, created its own fire, and glistened not auburn but orange. Kate ran her fingers through her hair and watched the baby watching her with big bright eyes. She felt so confused. She missed her mom, and yet there was no denying the beauty of this moment or the rightness of this baby here in her arms, as warm as life, glowing and pink. She was such a little miracle. Look at her tiny fingernails, her wrinkled palms, her eyelashes. Kate was filled with wonderment. "Hey, baby bear," she cooed softly. "Well, yes, I *know* you're not a bear, you're Lily, silly. And I'm your Auntie Kate."

9

Peter removed his hand from the steering wheel and laid it suggestively on her shoulder.

They were in Peter's Jaguar, outside her apartment building. It was late, but the July night was still oppressive. Simply walking from the restaurant to the car had been uncomfortable. But now, sitting in Peter's fancy Jaguar, they could feel nothing but cool. Peter had driven them here rather too fast, his quadraphonic stereo blasting vintage Rolling Stones. He was trying to impress her. She was touched by his efforts, but she was not impressed.

She was very conscious of his hand on her shoulder.

He switched off his tape deck and said: "What do you say we continue this conversation inside?"

She smiled faintly: "We weren't *having* a conversation. Not unless you're Mick Jagger."

"Too loud, huh?" He was instantly apologetic. "I just wanted you to hear my new sound system." He pressed closer to her: "Seriously, can I come in?"

She hesitated, reluctant to disappoint him.

"Okay?" he persisted. "Just one drink."

"Oh, Peter, I don't think so."

He withdrew his hand from her shoulder and stared sullenly through the windshield.

The Jaguar's air conditioner hummed smoothly.

"Well," she said, "thanks for dinner and your company." She opened the car door and stepped out into the muggy night.

"Kate?"

She leaned back in.

"Don't you ever get lonely?"

"Of course."

"Well . . ."

"No," she said, "not tonight."

She welcomed the solitude of her apartment. She dropped into the sofa and thought about what Peter had asked her: "Don't you ever get lonely?" She was lonely most of the time. Some days were better than others. Today was a good day. She got to cuddle baby Lily and, best of all, talk to Fielding. When she was with Fielding she wasn't lonely at all.

She slipped off her heels and relaxed into the sofa cushions. Her gaze settled on the painting of the Brontë sisters hanging on the wall. She remembered: she bought the picture in England during her month abroad with Mom, after the bar exam. They had a ball, visiting authors' haunts in London. One day they made a special trip to visit the Brontë parsonage in Haworth, Yorkshire. The parsonage was a sad, bleak house that could never have been much of a home. Next door was the graveyard with its skeletal black trees. Above the tombstones, rooks wheeled against a ghostly sky. The only relief to all the gloom was the purple heather in the fields. But it had been a wonderful day. It hadn't mattered at all that it rained and they got wet—her mom turned the whole thing into an adventure. They ended up in a tiny inn someplace. After a change of clothes, they ordered an extravagant dinner and talked about books, cozy and warm, while the rain pelted against the windowpanes.

Kate could almost smile at the memory.

———

Kate went to bed thinking of her mom and their adventures in England, and the next morning she woke feeling healthy and refreshed. She yawned and stretched her limbs luxuriously. For the first time in ages, she hadn't had the dream.

At work, she was jolted out of her good mood. For the second day in a row, the photograph was missing. She searched everywhere for it and finally found it buried, face down, under a stack of files.

"Kate, what's wrong?"

"Oh, Judith, it's this photograph of my mom. It keeps disappearing. I know it may seem a small thing, but it's distressing."

"Don't you worry," said Judith in a kind voice, "I'll take care of it. I'll write a memo to the cleaning staff immediately."

"You'd do that?"

"Of course."

"Thanks." Kate smiled her appreciation. "By the way, it's good to have you back."

Judith inclined her head.

Kate became thoughtful. Yesterday she'd regretted sharing about her mom and *Jane Eyre,* but today was a new day: she would try again. Only when people made themselves vulnerable did they become friends. "Just for the record . . ."

"Yes." Judith was friendly, open, curious.

"*The Great Gatsby* is *my* favorite book."

"Oh," Judith smiled, "then you're a romantic."

Peter Coe made his grand entrance. He marched into the office, glowering at everyone. The attorneys gave him a wide berth, eyeing each other quizzically. Peter broke stride when he reached Kate's desk. He shot her a pained look, full of meaning. He was angry about last night. And now everybody in the office knew it, too.

Peter turned on his heel and thundered: "Renée, in my office. Now!"

The young secretary cast Kate a look of frightened appeal.

Kate hesitated. Suppose the mistake in pleadings wasn't Renée's fault but her own? She couldn't just stand by and let Renée get fired. She mustered all her courage, got up and hurriedly followed Renée, reaching Peter's office just before he slammed the door.

Fifteen minutes later, she and Renée filed out of that same office. The gregarious secretary was subdued. Only her outfit was loud— her blond wig, leopard jumpsuit, purple ankle socks, and black heels. "Thanks," she said to Kate with trembling sincerity. "You stuck up for me. No one's ever done that for me before."

Kate returned to her desk, looking relieved but pale. That had been a tense couple of minutes. She went into that office intending to inform Peter that the mistake in pleadings was her own fault, but, as it turned out, a confession wasn't necessary: Peter knew that Renée was valuable and had no intention of firing her. Not only that, but more importantly, when the moment for her admission came, Kate knew she was blameless. Her memory told her unequivocally that she'd dictated a charge of manslaughter and not murder. She was sure of it. And she was sure that Renée had done her job, too. The implications were unsettling. Was it possible that someone had tampered with those pleadings? She looked around the office at her fellow attorneys and felt strangely ill at ease. Whom could she trust? For the time being, she would keep this to herself.

She opened the Buckner file and reviewed it. There were witnesses' statements, taken at the scene of the accident and at the Rusty Nail where Buckner had been drinking. Reuben had compiled a biography of Buckner. He was Order of the Coif at University of Maryland Law School, married with two grown-up children, Alice and Samuel. A member of the Maryland Bar for thirty years, Buckner was known as a competent if not brilliant judge, conservative in his views. He had some "heavy" (Reuben's word) political connections and was chummy with his colleagues on the bench. He was fifty-eight years old. Buckner had no police record, save for the notable DWI conviction two years ago.

Kate scanned Reuben's "List of People We Should Contact." She stopped when she came to the name Judge Obermeyer.

Judge Obermeyer would remember her, and she would always remember him. He had presided over the Slick Carlson case. As she thought of Slick, she saw again his menacing green eyes. She heard him shout: "I'll get you for this, bitch! I'll be back!" And she was afraid all over again.

Yet she forced herself to concentrate on the task at hand. She flipped through her Rolodex. With any luck, she would find Judge Obermeyer still in chambers. When she phoned, he answered.

"Judge," she began, "as you know, we're running an investigation on Harold Buckner. If you have a minute, I'd like to—"

His voice was tart: "I have nothing to say."

"You're close friends. You go fishing together, don't you?"

"I've known Harry for years. And as I said, Ms. Riley, I have no comment on the matter. Good day."

Kate slowly cradled the receiver. She was disappointed in Obermeyer, but what did she expect? Just another example of the legal fraternity protecting its own.

Judith said: "Kate, line five-one. Reuben is holding."

She pushed the flashing white button. "Reuben, where are you?"

"Out and about."

"You heard, I take it."

"About the press conference? Of course. I'm an investigator. We know these things." He was kidding around, but there was a catch in his voice. He quickly grew serious: "Tell me straight, what do you figure our chances are?"

"Of proving murder?" She paused. "Not good."

Reuben was silent on the other end. She knew he was thinking of his friend, Jimmy Delorosa. His funeral was today.

"But," Kate continued gamely, "under depraved heart, I think we have a chance."

"What do we need, exactly?"

"We have to show wanton and reckless."

"Well, hell, we've got that!" Reuben cried. "Buckner was drinking like a fish, he goes out on the highway anyway, and he kills Jimmy. Christ, we've even got a history of alcohol abuse. He's got that prior DWI."

"One prior doesn't make a history. Sorry."

"All right." Reuben sounded resigned. "We'll just have to do some more digging. I'm on the road now. Thought I'd drive up to the Rusty Nail, hang out, and schmooze with the locals, the bartender, the waitresses. Everybody's already given their statement to the police, but so far we've come up dry."

"So to speak."

"Dry, right, difficult in a bar." Reuben didn't even laugh.

"Partner," she said, "you okay?"

There was a pause on the line. Finally he said, "You coming to the funeral?"

"You can count on it."

"Okay, Red, I gotta go."

"Bye," she said. Watch out for yourself, she wanted to add. Be careful.

With this Buckner case, Reuben was asking a lot of questions that some people didn't want answered. She worried about him. She reflected a moment, sipped the cold coffee on her desk. She tried to remember when she first thought she was being followed. It was right after the Buckner case began. Maybe she really *was* being followed. Maybe she was in danger, too.

10

They buried Jimmy Delorosa, at noon, in a steady drizzle. As the pallbearers put down the casket, Kate thought of another funeral, another time and place. It was winter, then. The sky was white, the cemetery cold, the ground frozen. Snow drifted against the tombstones and swirled in eddies around their leather boots. Kate couldn't bear to think of her mother inside the casket, that cold, bitter ground. She glanced at the coffin, just once: a spray of roses was lying on top. The wind gusted, the roses fluttered fragilely, and pink petals scattered. . . .

Now back in the office, Kate was eating a sandwich from the vending machines when Judith came in.

"Hello. Mind if I join you?"

"I'd love you to," Kate said, glad of the distraction.

They talked for a moment about the funeral, but there wasn't much to say.

Judith said: "Let's talk of happier things. Your birthday, for instance. What kind of cake would you like?"

Kate laughed. "It's still a few weeks away."

"Humor me."

"Okay. Pound cake and vanilla frosting."

"Fine," Judith nodded, "I'll make a note."

Kate studied her secretary. She wondered why her birthday was so important to her. Was Judith trying to fill the void in her own life? Kate wanted to ask her how old *her* daughter was, maybe *she* was turning thirty, too, but she knew what a private person Judith was, so she didn't.

Kate worked on the Buckner case all afternoon. Peter did not assist her. He was very busy, or else hurt and trying to avoid her. It was after five and the office was quiet. She was poring over the police accident report when she looked up and saw a blond wig and a leopard jumpsuit: Renée.

"I see you a sec?"

"Sure, pull up a chair."

"Alone, I mean."

Kate regarded the secretary closely. So much of Renée was not Renée: the blond wig, the false eyelashes, the orange-sherbet lipstick. Yet under all that makeup there were signs of distress. "Why don't we use the conference room?"

Renee shook her head. "Let's take a walk."

Kate grabbed her raincoat and they went out. It was still drizzling and the streets were wet. They popped open their umbrellas, stepped around puddles, and headed for the pier. They stopped next to the eighteenth-century warship *Constellation.* Kate surveyed the harbor, watched a seagull land on a weathered gray post, and waited for Renée to speak.

"It's Peter," she finally said.

Kate gave her a questioning look.

"It's been on my mind and I . . . well, I wasn't going to say anything, but—"

"What?"

"You know the night before the press conference?"

"Yes."

"And Peter went home?"

"Yes."

"Well, he came back."

Kate absorbed this quietly.

Renée went on: "Naturally, Peter comes and goes as he wishes. Nothing strange about that. But when I saw him, he put his hand up in front of his face and hurried away, like he didn't want me to see him."

Kate frowned. "What time was this?"

"Ten o'clock, a few minutes after."

Kate had finished dictating the pleadings by then. Renée had finished typing them. "After ten? You sure?"

"I'd bet my best wig on it," Renée said.

That night Kate was working late in her apartment. She had spread out her files on the living-room rug where she now sat cross-legged. The tall brass lamp behind her enveloped her in a pool of white light. The rest of the apartment was shrouded in darkness. Even when she took a break to order pizza, she hadn't thought to switch on the lights.

She paused in her labors. Her eyes felt the strain of reading too much, and her neck was stiff. She massaged her neck and thought: Where's that pizza? And then she heard it: the sound from the patio. Something unsettled her wind chimes. She immediately thought of Slick and jumped to her feet. She stood just outside the pool of light, in the darkness, and dared not breathe. The patio door rattled, then the latch gave. She heard the telltale click. Her head swam with fear and confusion. Should she stay and defend herself, or run?

She had no time to decide because the patio doors slid open, and Peter Coe, blond and debonaire, stepped into the room.

"Your order, ma'am," he said, laughing, presenting her with the flat box of pizza. "Sausage and cheese, I believe."

She stared at him. "What are *you* doing here?"

"Dramatic entrance, huh? I met the delivery boy outside." He grinned carelessly, and yet there was a hint of self-consciousness, even of guilt, in his eyes. He had known he would catch her off guard. "I decided to surprise you."

"Surprise? I *do* have a front door, you know. You could have knocked."

"Yes," he said, in a voice so suddenly grave it frightened her: "But would you have let me in?"

I n Hagerstown State Prison, in a badly ventilated classroom with bars on
the windows, Slick Carlson frowned
over his test paper. The teacher had
asked them to spell "picnicking."

The class was called Remedial English. He and Rees were taking
it. The class was stupid. Who cared about grammar and spelling?
But it was better than working in the dairy barn on a day like today.
The manure smelled in the sweltering heat and attracted flies. Slick
wasn't complaining, though. He was happy he drew farm duty. It
was going to be his ticket out of here.

He wasn't taking Rees with him, although Rees would be mad.
Rees was his cellmate, a big blond farmboy, strong as an ox, but
so stupid he exasperated Slick. That's why Slick was going alone.

As soon as he was free, he would go to Baltimore and find *her*.
He thought of her now, and his anger simmered. He tried to distract
himself. He bent over his test paper again, but he couldn't envision

the word "picnicking," he could only see Kate Riley as she stood there in the courtroom, so beautiful, so determined, her contempt shining on her face. He could have loved her, but she had ruined everything, she had made him come to this place. Remembering her now, he seized his pencil and snapped it in half. He was going to escape. He was going to find her if it was the last thing he ever did.

12

K ate spent the morning with reporters, the afternoon on the
phone. In between, she managed one lone vending-machine
sandwich. She'd made little
progress on the Buckner case. People weren't returning her calls.
No one wanted to get involved.

About Peter, she would keep what Renée had told her to herself.
She couldn't believe that Peter would actually tamper with the
pleadings. Or rather, she didn't want to believe it.

At least she and Judith were getting along. Not that Judith
was any less reticent, but she did little things that told Kate she
was thinking of her. Just now, as Kate began flipping through
the day's mail, Judith stopped by on her way home: "Anything
else?"

"No, Judith, thanks. You're a doll." She abruptly quit flipping through her letters and held one up for her secretary's inspection: "Look at this. No one spells my name right. Wiley. Rilly. And I've got a Ridely here."

"I know what you mean," Judith said, suddenly emotional. "You can spell Shepherd so many ways."

Kate put her mail down and looked at her. "Shepherd?"

"Yes. My married name."

"Oh, I see." Kate felt a surge of sympathy for her secretary.

Judith added, in a strained voice: "I use my maiden name since the divorce."

"Of course," Kate said. "I didn't mean to—"

"It's of no consequence," Judith said.

Kate rose from her desk. Only a few days ago she would have been pleased that such a personal comment had slipped by Judith's censors. But now that she knew her secretary better, she felt only sadness. What must it be like, she wondered, to have a family, then lose it? She thought of Molly and the kids. They would always love her. Tonight she was going there for dinner, and the prospect made her glow with warmth. She reached for her briefcase and got ready to leave. Judith didn't seem in any hurry to go home. "Such a lovely briefcase," she said casually.

Kate smiled. "Graduation gift. It's a little worse for wear." She showed Judith the torn strap and was just about to show her the nicks in the leather when she stopped herself. Why was Judith so fascinated with her briefcase? And the other day, remember? Judith had asked about her wallet. And this morning it was her dress: Judith wanted to know where she bought it. Was Judith thinking of birthday gifts? Kate would have to steer her toward something more reasonable.

"You know," she said, offhandedly, "I'm really all set with my briefcase. And my wardrobe's in great shape. But I'm having a devil of a time finding my favorite perfume."

"Oh really?" Judith's intelligent eyes came alive. "What kind is it?" Kate didn't hesitate. She named an inexpensive brand: "Jontue," she said. And she could see Judith concentrate. Jontue, she was saying to herself, so she would remember it.

The phone on Kate's desk rang. She waved Judith away—"You're off duty now. Go on home"—and grabbed the receiver herself.

She spoke to Molly briefly, then hung up. To her surprise, Judith was still there. "My sister," Kate explained. "I'm having dinner at her place."

Judith looked almost forlorn. "I see. Good night, then."

She turned and headed out, walking between the rows of gray desks. She would go home to an empty apartment and watch the sun set on the brick building across the way. She would rock in her chair. She would talk to her cat. . . .

"Hey!" Kate called after her.

Judith heard. She turned and came back.

Judith was incredible with the kids. It was the "witching hour," as Molly called it, that prickly time at the end of the day. Yet Judith had Lily on her lap and Ian seated, enthralled, beside her at the kitchen table. Kate and Molly listened with pleasure from the dining room as Judith read *Winnie the Pooh.*

Molly laughed: "She's so good with them!"

"Maybe you should have Judith over more often," Kate teased. "This is the first time I've seen you sitting down in months."

"I think this *is* the first time," Molly said. "It feels won-der-ful!" She stretched her limbs in pure pleasure and tossed her mane of black curls. Then, as if remembering something, she abruptly rose from the table, and reached into the drawer of her antique hutch. "Happy Birthday, kiddo!" she announced, dropping a bundle of airline tickets on the table. "It's a little early, but I wanted us to make plans."

"Plans?" Kate said.

"Florida, can you believe it? Key Biscayne. Dave got us a great deal. Four weeks from now. Me and Dave and the kids. And you and a boyfriend. How about Reuben? I like him."

"He's just a friend, Moll."

"All right, you don't have to bring anyone. We'll leave Wednesday and return Sunday night so you'll only miss three days' work. What do you say?"

"I'm . . . stunned. What about my trial?"

"It'll be over by then."

"Yes, I suppose . . ."

Molly regarded her closely. She reached out and took hold of her hands. "Please say you'll come. We need to start enjoying ourselves again. This would be a start."

"We?" Kate said, confused. "But you're so happy."

"You kidding? I'm so housebound, I could scream."

"Really?"

"Yes, really."

Kate studied her sister. Molly wasn't leading the idyllic life she had imagined. "All right," Kate said, just like that. "We'll go." She could survive life outside the office for five days, and they could survive without her.

Kate was feeling bold today. Suddenly she found herself saying: "Why not invite Dad and Blanche?"

Molly was startled. "That cold fish!"

"Let's make friends with her."

"We tried."

Kate said evenly, wouldn't Fielding be proud of her now: "Let's try again."

The sisters quickly finalized their plans and decided that Molly would call their father. They entered the kitchen just as Judith laid *Winnie the Pooh* aside.

"Hi, peaches," Molly said as Ian bounded toward her. "We gave Auntie Kate her birthday present. We're all going to Florida on the plane." She paused, looked at Kate. "And Grandpops is coming, too."

"Yea!" Ian cried, and then he surprised them all. He let go of

Molly's leg and hurled himself at Judith. Tugging fondly on her skirt, he insisted: "Dee come too, Dee come too!"

Judith was the first to smile. She tousled Ian's hair.

Molly was the first to speak. "Well, you *are* a terrific babysitter," she said. "*Would* you come? I'd be glad to pay your way."

Kate felt sure Judith would decline, but she said without hesitation: "If you feel you need me, I would *love* to come, I really would."

"That's settled then," Molly said, grinning.

Kate simply stared. She couldn't believe it. There was Judith, so cold in the office, yet here, now, so warm and friendly with the kids. She was like two different people. It was almost scary.

———

The next morning, excited by the prospect of Florida, Kate was in high spirits. Somebody in the office brought in donuts and she joined the crowd, launched an eager bite into chocolate honey glaze, joked, laughed. She had just settled down to work when the phone rang and Judith said: "Kate, line five-oh. Your father."

"Dad, hi!" she said, grinning idiotically. It was the first time he had ever called her at the office, that she could recall.

"Kate, how's Mexico sound?"

"Mexico?"

"Yes. Instead of Florida. We were thinking Cozumel."

We? "We" meant Blanche.

"Gee, I dunno," she said, her heart sinking. "I got really sick in Mexico once, remember?"

"Blanche hates Florida," her father continued as if he hadn't heard her. "Florida is crass and commerical, she says. Too many old people. Mexico is exotic."

Kate closed her eyes, opened them. "Well, what does *Molly* say? That's a long way for her and—"

"She thinks it's wonderful. Anything to get out of the house."

Her father cleared his throat and added: "I'll pay the difference in airfare. Blanche has decided to treat herself and go shop in Mexico City first, pick up some things for her boutique. Then she'll fly on to Cozumel."

"She could fly on to Miami too, Dad."

"I told you, she doesn't like Florida."

But I do! Kate thought. And it's *my* birthday.

"I'll change our reservations, book us a hotel."

Kate said nothing.

"All right?" he prompted her. "You don't object?"

"No." She sighed and pinched the bridge of her nose where the headache began. "Mexico sounds fine, Dad. I'll brush up on my Spanish."

Fielding jogged through the sun-dappled woods. The day was more humid than sunny, with not much of a breeze. As he neared the end of his run, he was sweating. He wore red gym shorts, white T-shirt, tube socks, and his Nikes. He had been running a lot lately. Sublimation, he realized, for what Sue Ann wouldn't give him. No, be fair. What she *couldn't* give him. At least not right now.

He swung rhythmically along the path, thinking: She wants to move back to New York, and I don't. Sue Ann missed her old marketing job, her old friends, the coffee shops, the theater. She still worked with Mystique, International, selling their line of perfume and cosmetics, but Baltimore had been a step down from New York with its invigorating fast pace and sophisticated clientele.

He wanted to make Sue Ann happy. They had been together

since their college days, but he did not want to move back to New York. What was it they called it in chess? A stalemate.

He wiped the sweat from his mustache and began to sprint up the rock-strewn path. He liked this last bit through the woods. His arms and legs pumped in unison. He flew past the last corridor of trees, lungs bursting, and came to a staggering halt on the sidewalk across from his building. That's when he saw her car turn into the parking lot.

He glanced at his wristwatch. I'm late! he thought. It's six o'clock.

Kate emerged from her car. She was swinging along, copper-red hair glistening in the sun, her tall, slender body clothed rather severely today in an executive-style blue skirt and jacket. He felt faintly adulterous, seeing her in the parking lot instead of the office.

"Kate!" he called to her and waved. He felt an indefensible surge of pleasure when she turned at the sound of his voice, and smiled.

They were in the comfortable sanctuary of Fielding's air-conditioned office. He had changed into a sweat jacket and jeans. Now he sat beside his desk, barefoot, while she sat facing him in the leather chair.

His first question was: "So how are you sleeping?"

"I'm still having the dream, but not as often."

"Are you being chased, or are you running away?"

"I still . . . don't know."

"And the stranger?"

"I don't know that either." She paused. "When I wake up, I try to remember the stranger's face. Sometimes I almost recognize it, but . . ."

"But what?"

"I don't know. It goes out of focus." She shrugged. "It's frustrating."

"That's okay," he encouraged her. "You may not see it, but you're making progress."

"And my homework, I feel as though I've failed at that too," she

84

said. "You wanted me to list my mom's good and bad qualities, and I tried, honestly I did, but my list was one-sided. I couldn't think of one bad thing about her."

"She was perfect?"

"No, but—it just seemed wrong, that's all." She hesitated, looked at him: "Are you disappointed in me?"

"No." He smiled. "Maybe we're going too fast. Why don't we try another assignment. You have some pictures of your mom? Letters from her? Good. For next time, I want you to spend time with your memories. Flip through your photo albums, read the letters, okay?"

"Okay." She nodded gravely. It would be painful, but she would do it.

An easy silence fell between them. She felt a deep contentment, being here with Fielding, in his office. She watched him tug on his ragged mustache, and wondered how it would feel, kissing him.

The kettle boiled, and he got up. "Want some coffee?"

"Please."

He stood barefoot at the counter and fixed their coffees.

She said: "I've been seeing more of Molly."

He half-turned. "Good."

"I really enjoy it over there. Her kids give me perspective. Ian has such an active imagination. He can be Ian, or he can be Superman or the Incredible Hulk, it doesn't matter. And Lily, gosh, she's awfully cute, blowing bubbles . . ."

Fielding returned with their coffees and sat down. He did not look at her when he asked: "*You* want kids?"

She hesitated: "I always did. But now the feeling is even stronger. Ever since Mom . . . well," she interrupted herself.

"Ever since she died, you mean?"

Kate's throat constricted. It was all she could do to nod.

Fielding's voice was kind: "Her dying made you realize *you* were going to die, too. And so you'd like to have children who'll survive you."

85

"Yes," she said. She felt the warmth of his eyes on her, felt his gentleness. "Lately, I've been doing a lot of thinking. I've given everything to my career and now I wonder why. I'm thirty years old, or almost, and I've never been in love. Maybe I don't *deserve* to be in love."

"Don't say that," Fielding said, and she stared at him.

His reaction was surprisingly personal for a psychiatrist. He said nothing for a moment. She asked him, without meaning to: "And you? Are you married? Do you have—"

"Yes, I'm married." He got up and went to the window, looked down at the street. When he turned around, his face wore an expression she could not identify. "You're too good at asking questions. I forget it's your profession."

She hardly heard him. She was still feeling the shock, like a blow to the stomach. He was married, as she had known, all along, he would be. His mustache would never touch her lips.

"What are you thinking about?" he asked.

"Nothing, just that you're married, that's all."

He sighed and dropped back into his chair. It was as though he were disappointed, in some way, too. "Perhaps I shouldn't have told you that. We're here to talk about you, not me. Are we talking about what you need to talk about?"

Kate remembered this morning, her father's phone call. "I think," she said, her voice husky with sudden emotion, "I need to talk about my father and Blanche."

And so she told Fielding about the vacation, how Molly had surprised her with Florida, but now they were going to Mexico instead.

"When your dad phoned," Fielding probed, "how did you feel? Here you'd been generous enough to invite him and then he upset your plans. Were you angry?"

"Angry? No. Well, yes, I guess."

"And Blanche? Were you mad at her too?"

Kate pressed the heel of her hand against her temple. "I . . . haven't exactly sorted it out."

"Don't you pay a price for that?"

"For what?"

"You don't sort out your feelings and now you have a headache. See any connection?"

She gripped her chair. Her eyes stung. "If I say any more I might cry."

"So?"

"Once I start, I might never stop."

He tossed her a box of Kleenex. "It's all yours."

She ripped out a tissue and clutched it in her hand. "Molly says Blanche is a cold fish."

He tipped forward in his chair: "Go on."

"It's weird. My dad does whatever she wants. He was never that way with my mom."

"And?"

"And I don't understand. I think Blanche must be this great person, only I can't see it. She can't be cold and self-centered, else why would my dad do all these things for her when he didn't for my mom? I must be wrong."

Fielding said softly: "Is Molly wrong?"

Her heart pounded. She stared at him. "What . . . do you mean?"

"Have you ever thought that you may be right? Maybe Blanche *is* essentially cold and egocentric."

"Then how come she's allowed to live and my mom's dead?"

Her question reverberated in the still, quiet room. She shuddered violently, once, then choked on a sob. Fielding watched her with those warm, cinnamon eyes. Then he came over and stood beside her and put his hand on her shoulder.

She knew her crying didn't solve anything, and yet she felt better. In her mind, she saw her old house on Stoneleigh Road. The maple's green leaves shimmered against a cloudless sky, and the wooden swing waited eagerly for the little girl to come out.

PART TWO

PART
TWO

14

K ate knew this courtroom well. And she knew this feeling, too, of waiting. In a moment she would stand and give her opening statement in the case of *The State of Maryland* v. *Harold T. Buckner.*

She had devoted herself to the case these last two weeks. Two weeks were all they had because they had moved for an expedited trial. Judge Buckner was generating too much pretrial sympathy, and the sooner they acted, the better.

Next to Kate at the prosecution table sat Peter Coe. He was attired in his best gray suit, his blond hair impeccably combed. He would be sure to take the credit if she won her case, and he would be the first to desert her if she lost. Behind Kate, in the crowded spectators' section, sat Reuben and Judith, for moral support. She smiled at them now, but her smile abruptly faded as her attention shifted to the defense table where Chip Doolittle conferred with his client. Buckner was tall and imposing, silver-haired. He looked like a prosperous man who was pleased with himself. He did not look like a man on trial for murder.

Kate was still staring at Buckner, wondering how he felt about Jimmy Delorosa, if he felt anything at all, when Judge Greenhill asked: "Is the prosecution ready?"

Kate found her voice easily, spoke with confidence: "Yes, your Honor."

"Then proceed."

Kate stood and walked toward the jury. She liked the twelve who had been chosen on *voir dire*. She felt they would be fair. Facing the jury, she began:

"Ladies and gentlemen, this is the story of James Delorosa, how he lived and how he died. James Delorosa was a police officer, fifteen years on the Force, decorated twice for bravery. James Delorosa was not only a fine police officer, he was a husband and father, too. He and his wife Mary were high-school sweethearts. They married after Delorosa completed his training at the Police Academy. They had two children, Joey and Tess.

"Joey and Tess used to have a nightly routine. Their mother would bathe them and get them into bed, then their father would read them a story. The other night, Tess began to cry when her mother started to read to her. She said she wanted her father to do it. So her mother tried to explain that their father wouldn't be reading them bedtime stories anymore. Not tonight or tomorrow night or the night after . . ."

Kate paused to look at the jury. They were feeling the children's and their mother's grief.

"James Delorosa once said that nothing—not even a bullet— could stop him from getting home and seeing his kids. Well, he was wrong. This defendant stopped him. On the night of July fourteenth, this defendant, knowing of his weakness for alcohol, visited a roadside tavern, consumed several glasses of Scotch on an empty stomach, and then, intoxicated, climbed back into his car. This defendant floored the gas, rocketed onto the highway, and swerved into the median strip and crashed into James Delorosa's squad car, mortally wounding the detective, who died three hours later.

"On the night of July fourteenth, this defendant committed murder.

"Now, murder is a word we should define. We all know what murder means in everyday usage. But the legal definition of murder is a bit different. Murder is when a person kills another person with malice aforethought. There are four types of malice. The kind of malice you are probably most familiar with is intent to kill. The prosecution is not seeking to prove this. We are not trying to show that Harold Buckner intended to kill James Delorosa or that he specifically intended to do him any harm. What we *are* seeking to prove is another type of malice that is called 'depraved heart.' By this we mean to prove to you, beyond a reasonable doubt, that Harold Buckner, by drinking and driving under the circumstances he did, acted with an unjustifiably high risk to human life. . . ."

When Kate finished her opening remarks, she made eye contact with each individual juror, then sat back down. The jury was watching her with rapt attention. Peter Coe leaned over and whispered: "You've got 'em in the palm of your hand."

She nodded at his praise.

"Will the defense proceed," Judge Greenhill said.

Chip Doolittle approached the jury box and gave his opening statement. Kate listened attentively and jotted down notes on a yellow pad.

When Doolittle finished, Judge Greenhill addressed the jury. Greenhill was one of Baltimore's most respected judges. Black, in his fifties, he was liberal in his politics, a man of unimpeachable integrity. Ten years ago, two unidentified street thugs had stormed into the courtroom and shot him. Today he wore an artificial arm.

It moved stiffly and the metal prosthesis poked out from beneath his black robes. Kate wondered, whenever she saw that arm, if Judge Greenhill was in pain.

"Ladies and gentlemen of the jury," Judge Greenhill said, "you have just heard opening statements in the case. Let me remind you that the opening statements are *not* part of the evidence for you to consider in your deliberations. The evidence will come to you from witnesses who testify on the stand and from certain documents and photographs that will be marked as evidence during the trial." The judge looked to the prosecution table. "All right, Ms. Riley, let's continue. Call your first witness."

"Yes, your Honor. The State calls Lynette Parker to the stand."

The bailiff escorted Lynette Parker into the courtroom. A waitress at the Rusty Nail, Lynette was the prosecution's star witness. She was the only person, of all the people Kate and Reuben had interviewed, who was willing to testify against Judge Buckner.

Lynette was petite, in her early thirties. She had a rough, throaty voice as if she'd inhaled too much cigarette smoke in the ginmills she'd worked at. Her hair tried to be blond but tended more toward brown. Her eyes were tired, gray. Lynette had dressed simply and modestly, as Kate had instructed her, in a skirt and blouse. Yet her flamboyant personality still asserted itself in her silver fingernails and spangled bracelets.

While the jury watched, the clerk administered the oath to Lynette, who seemed calm and in control. If Lynette could just be herself, Kate was convinced, the jury would believe in her.

Kate approached the witness box. She looked reassuringly at the waitress, then began: "Please give us your full name and address for the record."

"Lynette Parker!" Lynette's voice boomed over the microphone. "Six-five-one Eastern Avenue! Dundalk, Maryland!"

"Lynette," Kate said as some spectators snickered, "just relax and speak as if we're in your living room, okay?"

"Okay," Lynette said, somewhat subdued.

"Tell us, please, where are you currently employed?"

"Nights I work at the Rusty Nail."

"And what is the Rusty Nail, Lynette?"

"Restaurant and tavern near the intersection of Route six-ninety-five and Reisterstown Road." "We open for dinner at five P.M. And our doors close at two A.M."

"How long have you been employed at the Rusty Nail?"

"Five years now. I'm a waitress."

"Five years? That's a long time in your line of work."

"Sure is. Mr. Grimes, he just promoted me."

"Mr. Grimes is your manager?"

"Yeah. I'm head waitress now. Get the best benefits and vacation time."

"It's nice to hear you're such a valued employee."

Doolittle stood. "Objection, your Honor. The comment assumes facts not in evidence. We don't *know* that Ms. Parker is a valued employee."

"Mr. Doolittle, let's not nitpick," said Judge Greenhill. "It's obvious that Lynette Parker's employers think she's a good waitress or they wouldn't have kept her for five years. But Ms. Riley, don't editorialize. Continue your interrogation."

"Thank you, your Honor." Kate resumed: "Lynette, were you working the evening of July fourteenth?"

"Yes."

"At any time during that evening did you observe anyone in this courtroom at the Rusty Nail?"

"Yes, I did."

"Can you point that person out for us?"

Lynette pointed her finger at Judge Buckner, seated at the defense table. Kate walked over and stood behind Buckner. She knew full well that this was a dramatic moment whose impact would not be lost on the jury.

Kate said: "You are identifying the defendant, Harold T. Buckner."

Judge Greenhill said: "Let the record show that the witness has identified the defendant."

Kate knew she had momentum. She pressed on: "At what time, Lynette, did you observe the defendant enter the Rusty Nail?"

"Nine o'clock. Something like that."

"Was the defendant alone?"

"Yes."

"And where did he sit?"

"At a table near the bar."

"I see. Did he order a drink?"

"Yes. Dewars and a splash of water."

"Dewars is an alcoholic beverage, is it not?"

"Yeah, it's Scotch."

"So the defendant ordered a Dewars and water."

"Yes."

"At what time?"

"Right after he came in."

"Did you serve him that drink?"

"Yes, I did."

"Did the defendant *pay* for that drink when you brought it to him?"

"No, ma'am."

"Why not?"

"He said he wanted to run a tab, which is okay by me 'cuz that usually means a tip. Or better still he uses a credit card to pay."

"Did the defendant order any other drinks?"

"Yes."

"How many?"

"Four more Dewars and water."

"So how many drinks is that?"

"Five."

"Did the defendant order anything to eat while he was drinking?"

"No."

"At what time did the defendant leave?"

"Eleven or thereabouts."

"Eleven o'clock. And the defendant began drinking at nine o'clock, you said."

"Yes."

"And he ordered four additional drinks after the first drink?"

"Yes."

"Which makes five alcoholic beverages within a two-hour period on an empty stomach."

Doolittle threw down his pencil. "Objection, your Honor. Ms. Riley is assuming facts not in evidence. My client could have had a ten-course meal before entering the restaurant."

"Let me rephrase," Kate said. But she had spoken deliberately. The jury would remember her choice of words: "on an empty stomach." "The defendant drank five glasses of Scotch but didn't order anything to eat, is that right, Lynette?"

"Yeah, he didn't even eat the pretzels sitting there in front of him."

"Did you observe the defendant's condition just prior to the time he left the Rusty Nail?"

"Yes, I did. Judge or no judge, he was four sails to the wind, let me tell you—"

"Objection!" A furious Doolittle leapt to his feet. "The witness is *not* responding to counsel's questions! And, what's more, she's *totally* unqualified to provide an opinion on the defendant's condition!"

"Sustained as to your first point, Mr. Doolittle," Judge Greenhill ruled. He turned to Lynette and cautioned: "Keep your answers brief and responsive to counsel's questions." Judge Greenhill faced Doolittle again: "Overruled as to your second point, sir. The witness may testify as to her observations of the defendant's condition. Proceed, Ms. Riley."

"Thank you, your Honor." Kate knew this was a golden opportunity. Lynette had already told the jury that she believed Buckner was intoxicated. But now, because of Doolittle's objection, Kate could reemphasize this point. "Lynette, what *was* the defendant's condition, as you perceived it?"

"Condition? He was drunk as a skunk. Like I said—"

"He was intoxicated?"

"Yes, ma'am."

"Were you concerned about the defendant's intoxicated condition?"

"Yes."

"What, if anything, did you do about his condition?"

"Well, I wanted him to have some coffee first, sober up, but he wouldn't, so I asked him for his car keys."

"You asked him for his car keys. Why?"

"Because I knew he was going out to his car. And stumbling around like that . . . I mean, he could hardly stand up from the table. I figured he might hurt someone. . . ."

Lynette's words echoed in the silent courtroom. She didn't need to say anything more.

"Thank you, Lynette," Kate said. "Nothing further, your Honor."

Judge Greenhill nodded, turned to the defense: "You may inquire, Mr. Doolittle."

Doolittle seemed reluctant. He was slow to stand, slow to button his suit coat. Even the arrogant Buckner appeared shaken as his attorney approached the witness box to begin Lynette's cross-examination.

Flushed with success, Kate returned to her seat. The jury was one hundred percent behind her, she could feel it. Lynette had been a terrific witness, genuine, convincing. Lynette believed Buckner was drunk and now the jury would, too.

Peter Coe leaned over and whispered in her ear: "Dynamite, Kate, just dynamite."

She nodded, searched for Reuben behind her. He grinned and gave her a thumbs-up. She herself was smiling faintly as she turned to watch the defense attorney. But her smile vanished, as she saw, in action, the cool ruthlessness of Chip Doolittle.

As a trial attorney, Doolittle cut an imposing figure. His was a shrewd, predatory intelligence, and Lynette was immediately intimidated. Kate had warned her witness that cross-examination would be stressful. She had told Lynette to take her time, to choose her words carefully. Lynette had done very well when they had role-played, but now, under Doolittle's formidable gaze, she became flustered—and vulnerable.

"Now, Ms. Parker, you've testified that you work *nights* at the Rusty Nail."

"Yes, that's right."

"You began work that evening at what time?"

"Four o'clock I punched in."

"Four o'clock in the afternoon."

"Yes."

"What did you do before you arrived at the Rusty Nail?"

Lynette hesitated.

"You were *working,* weren't you, Ms. Parker? At another job."

"Yes," Lynette said.

"And what is this other job?"

"I work at the Hair Cuttery."

"You cut hair?"

"Yes."

"And what were your hours that day, July fourteenth?"

"Seven to three."

"I see. So, on the day in question, you were working in the Hair Cuttery from seven o'clock in the morning until three in the afternoon, is that correct?"

"Yes."

"You must cut a lot of hair in that amount of time."

"Yeah, I guess."

"How many customers, would you estimate?"

"Twenty-five heads, something like that."

"Twenty-five *heads*," Doolittle repeated loudly. "You call them 'heads.' I guess it's hard to see them as people."

Kate longed to object but knew it would only emphasize Doolittle's point.

"All those customers," Doolittle went on. "And this was *before* you even *started* to work at the Rusty Nail?"

"Yes," Lynette said quietly.

"Okay, so you got off work at the Hair Cuttery at three, then you drove to the Rusty Nail, which is your second job, correct?"

"Yes."

"So it would be fair to say that by four o'clock, you had already been up since six A.M., worked eight hours, and you were a little tired?"

"Objection." Kate stood up. "Your Honor, there's been no testimony on that point whatsoever."

"I'll allow it," Judge Greenhill said: "Answer the question, please."

"Were you tired?" Doolittle repeated.

"A little, I guess," Lynette said, in a subdued voice.

"So by nine o'clock, when you say you observed the defendant, you'd already been up fifteen hours, so you were *more* than a little tired at that point, were you not?"

"I . . . I'm used to it."

"That's *not* the question, Ms. Parker. The question is *were you tired?*"

"Yes, but—"

"You were tired, that's established. You've testified that you served the defendant his first Dewars and water at nine o'clock. Is that correct?"

"Yes."

"How do you know it was a Dewars and water?"

"I remember."

"You *remember*." Doolittle's voice reeked with doubt. Then, abruptly, he became friendly again: "The Rusty Nail is quite a popular place, isn't it?"

"Yeah, I guess."

"How many tables are there?"

"Forty or so."

"Forty or so. Plus there is a rather large bar area, is there not?"

"Yes."

"How many waitresses work at a time?"

"Three of us."

"Just three of you? Estimating conservatively three people per table, plus twenty more at the bar—that makes three waitresses serving one hundred forty people. Would you say that's a fair estimate?"

"I don't know."

"Do you dispute its accuracy?"

"No."

"Then it's a fair estimate."

"I suppose."

"Do you know how many people you served on the night of July fourteenth?"

"I have no idea."

"But we've just estimated that it must have been quite a few, wouldn't you agree?"

"Yes."

"You and only two other waitresses serving, at any given time, close to one hundred and forty people, and this is *after* you'd been cutting hair all day, correct?"

"I . . . yes."

"Now you've testified that you served the defendant a drink at approximately nine o'clock. A Dewars and water, you said."

"Yes, he ordered the Scotch and drank it."

"He drank it, you say. But did you see him drink it?"

"What?"

"Did you see him drink it?"

"Well, I *know* he drank it 'cuz he ordered another."

"That's not my question. Did you actually *see* him drink it?

"No. The bar was busy, okay? I got lots of other things to do besides watch a guy drink his drink."

"Precisely!" Doolittle interjected. "You were *busy* that night, weren't you?"

"Yes, we were."

"In fact, Thursday is one of your busiest nights."

"Well, yeah."

"In fact, it was so crowded, can you be sure you remember the defendant coming in that night?"

"Yes, of course."

"You remember everyone who came in that night?"

"No, but—"

"Do you have a good memory, Ms. Parker?"

"Yes, for faces, I do."

"You do? A good memory for faces, you say." Doolittle's tone was neutral, with no emphasis at all.

He looked smugly at Kate, then returned his attention to Lynette.

"Ms. Parker, you've identified the defendant as being in the bar. I'd like you to take another look around this courtroom and see if *anyone else* was at the Rusty Nail that night."

Kate was alarmed. She jumped up: "Objection, your Honor! Defense counsel and the State both agreed to exclude witnesses from the courtroom until they're called."

"I'm not calling this person as a witness," Doolittle countered. "I'm simply trying to establish the veracity of a prior statement."

"All right, I'll allow it," Judge Greenhill said. "But let's stay on track with this."

"Thank you, your Honor." Doolittle faced the rear of the courtroom. He beckoned to a man in the back row to stand. The man was dark-haired and very ordinary-looking.

Doolittle turned back to Lynette: "Did you observe this man at the bar on the night of July fourteenth?"

Lynette hesitated. "I . . . can't remember."

"You can't remember." Doolittle shook his head. "I thought you said you had a good memory for faces."

"I do, but—"

"But *what*, Ms. Parker?"

Lynette was frustrated. Doolittle was making her feel like a fool. Helpless, she struggled to defend herself: "You expect me to . . . Look, I'm not some genius, all right? I can't remember *everybody*. It was so *crowded!*"

"So *crowded*," Doolittle repeated triumphantly. "Exactly!"

Lynette appealed to Kate, her eyes asking: Did I say the wrong thing?

But it was too late.

Doolittle, in his deliberate, insidious way, had destroyed her credibility. The jury would never believe Lynette Parker now.

"C'mon," Reuben said gently. "It's not your fault. Lynette fell apart. There was nothing you could do."

"I could've done something."

"Well, I can't think of anything, and I'm an extremely bright guy, right?" He laughed.

Kate raised her eyes to him. But she did not smile. She sat glumly at her desk where he'd found her. It was late. The office was empty, except for them.

"What can we do to cheer you up?"

"Win this case."

"Hold on! I figured you'd want a cup of coffee, maybe, I could handle that. I'm no magician."

"I keep feeling like we missed something."

"Like what?"

"You still running a check on Buckner?"

"Of course. Nothing helpful so far."

"He's hiding something."

"I think so too," Reuben said. "Hey, whad'ya say we go to the Rusty Nail?"

She shook her head. "No one will talk to us. Be a waste of time."

"Oh, really?" He was teasing her now: "You so sure of everything, Riley, wanna buy me a lottery ticket?"

She looked at him, and, for the first time all evening, smiled.

There was a surprise for her at the Rusty Nail. Her friends were waiting at a table by the bar. Peter Coe had arranged it. He grinned mischievously when she walked in.

"What's this?" she asked.

"A little party," Peter said. Blond and confident as always, impeccably groomed in his tailored gray suit, Peter stood up from the table and took charge. "Here, have a seat. We'll do a postmortem on today and figure out where to go from here."

Peter sat her down beside him and left Reuben to fend for himself. Seated on the other side of Kate was Judith. Kate knew what an effort this must be for her. Judith was used to her solitude, her rocking chair, and her cat. Kate smiled warmly to her and pressed her hand: "Thanks for coming."

Peter beckoned the waitress over and they began ordering drinks.

Kate thought: This isn't right. This is just what Buckner did. He came here, he ordered drinks too, and then he went out on the highway in his car. And so, when it came her turn, she ordered a Sprite.

They talked and nursed their drinks. Peter was drinking rather more than was good for him. His handsome face was flushed. He spoke in a loud, brash manner and laughed aggressively at his own jokes. He monopolized Kate until Reuben rescued her. The country-western band was playing a Patsy Kline number when he came over and asked: "Wanna dance?"

The Patsy Kline number ended as they reached the dance floor.

The guitarist stepped up to the microphone and started crooning Willie Nelson's "Always on My Mind." It was a slow dance. Reuben put his arms around her. She liked the feel of him, he was a good dancer, but, as she held on to his neck and swayed with him, she found herself thinking of Fielding.

When they sat back down, Peter was silently fuming. He was so possessive of her. When this case was over, she would have to tell him she did not love him. It wasn't fair to either of them to continue this way.

She consulted her watch. It was already after eleven, they'd be leaving soon. She kept wishing someone would come up to them, a waitress, the bartender, or maybe a patron who'd been here that night, but no one approached them.

She scanned the room, as if looking for a clue. Her eye was caught by something moving on the opposite wall. With a start, she realized it was a security camera with a roving eye, the kind you see in a bank.

She studied the camera intently.

Reuben asked: "What is it?"

She pointed, and now conversation at their table quieted, and everyone looked up. The camera was trained on the cash register and the surrounding bar area.

"I wonder," she said aloud.

"What?" Peter was curious.

"The night he was here, Buckner sat near the bar."

"So?"

"Don't you see? He might be on tape. But do they keep them or erase them?"

"If they keep them," Reuben grinned, "I *will* have you buy me that lottery ticket."

She couldn't believe their good fortune.

Management *did* keep the tapes. They kept them for three months.

Charlie Grimes reluctantly let them into the back storage room.

A stooped, dour man with balding hair, Grimes was Lynette Parker's boss and the manager of the Rusty Nail.

After an hour of digging, they unearthed the VHS cartridge, the one marked: "Week of July tenth." They set up the video screen, turned on the recorder, and fast-forwarded the tape. When they came to the right evening, they slowed the tape down. Kate held her breath and watched. The camera swept in front of the cash register down the length of the bar. No Buckner. But on the backswing, the camera lighted on a cluster of tables. "Freeze it!" she said, and there he was. He was sitting alone, just like Lynette had said, and there was a glass in his hand.

The rest of the tape bore out Lynette's testimony. Through the camera's neutral eye, they witnessed Buckner's deterioration as the evening progressed. They saw Lynette serving him drinks, and him drinking. In the end, they saw Lynette try to take his car keys, in a nice way, but he angrily snatched them back. Finally, he lurched from the table and stumbled out of view.

There was a moment of stunned silence, then Peter stopped the tape.

Everyone was staring at the now-vacant screen except Judith. She was looking at Kate: "Does this mean we'll win our case?"

Kate was about to reply, but Peter didn't let her. Laughing, he flung his arms around her neck. She stiffened, she smelled alcohol on his warm breath, and then he kissed her.

It was after midnight.

Judith and the others went home. Kate and Reuben and Peter stayed to talk to Charlie Grimes. They were trying to convince him to come down to the police station.

"But why do you need me?" Grimes asked.

"Because," Kate explained, "we don't want any chain of custody problems with this tape. If *we* take it downtown, the tape is in our control, and the defense might accuse us of tampering with the evidence."

"What's in it for me?" Grimes asked cynically.

Reuben stepped in: "This is a big trial. If you're our witness, we can't guarantee you'll be on TV or anything, but you'll make the paper."

"No kidding," Grimes said, pleased. He was thinking his friends would be impressed. "Okay, what do I gotta do?"

In the parking lot, Kate insisted that Reuben drive Peter home while she and Charlie Grimes took care of the tape. She was thinking of Buckner and what he'd done, and she did not want Peter behind the wheel.

Downtown, the rookie on duty was sleeping. She and Grimes jostled him awake. Yawning, smiling apologetically, he took her treasured VHS cartridge and deposited it in a big manilla envelope. The envelope was marked in bold red letters: "Exhibit 18." The rookie yawned again. He was about to toss the envelope on a pile.

Kate frowned. "Aren't you going to seal it?"

"Oh, right," he said.

She watched like a hawk as the rookie produced a red adhesive seal and folded it over the envelope's seams. No one could get into the envelope without breaking the seal.

As soon as the rookie was finished, he started yawning again.

Kate felt reluctant to leave her prize with him. "Don't lose this, okay?" she told him. "It's important."

"Hey," he protested, "I'm on top of it."

Kate had Grimes drop her off at her apartment.

She climbed out of the car, then leaned back in: "Tomorrow, nine o'clock sharp."

"Okay," Grimes said. "I'll be there."

Happy, her confidence soaring, Kate danced up the steps to her building. She did not notice the car idling in the parking lot, engine running, headlights dimmed.

16

Exhibit 18, under police lock and key, was delivered to the courthouse promptly at 8:00 A.M. The manilla envelope was given to the court clerk, Mrs. Babcock. At 8:05 A.M. Mrs. Babcock placed the envelope in Locker C in the court evidence room. Mrs. Babcock was a gray-haired veteran at her job, conscientious as well as efficient. She gave the lock on Locker C an extra twist, then tested it with a nice hard tug. The lock held. Mrs. Babcock was very busy today, there were a lot of trials going on. She forgot about Exhibit 18 and went about her other duties.

Kate was already in the courtroom. She had been here since six-thirty. She had watched the sun come spilling through the windows onto the hard-grained floors, bathing the judge's bench in golden warmth and making the varnish on the Maryland and American flagpoles gleam. She sat in the wooden pew in the spectators' area and listened to the silence. Once in law school, she'd visited her contracts classroom after the class was over. The empty room had possessed an aura, still, that inspired reverence. Today this courtroom gave her the same feeling. She looked at the jury box and thought of all the jurors who had searched for truth. She thought of all the lawyers, felt their presence, and heard the echo of their impassioned eloquence. This was hallowed ground.

She thought, finally, of the evidence she would produce this morning. Because of it she would win their case. Justice would be done. Soon the courtroom would be invaded by spectators, court reporters, and clerks, but she relished this moment of solitude. For the first time since she became a trial attorney, she felt she belonged here. She felt worthy.

It was nine o'clock, and the courtroom was humming with excitement. Kate and Reuben set up the video equipment while the jurors watched with bright, curious eyes. Doolittle and Buckner began to look nervous.

At 8:55 A.M., Mrs. Babcock brought out the box of exhibits and took her place at the clerk's desk. One of the fattest envelopes in the box was the manilla envelope marked in bold red letters Exhibit 18.

Kate looked at Peter Coe sitting next to her. His choirboy's face betrayed no signs of a hangover. She glanced behind her at Reuben and Judith. She smiled, her eyes saying: It won't be long now. Reuben smiled back and Judith crossed her fingers for good luck. And now the uniformed bailiff barked: "All rise." Judge Greenhill strode in in his formal black robes, his artificial arm stiff at his side. He took his seat of honor and the trial resumed.

"Ms. Riley," he began, "you have newly discovered evidence that you wish to show the jury at this time?"

"Yes, your Honor, I do."

"Judging from the equipment you've assembled, am I to deduce that your evidence is some type of audio-visual recording?"

"Yes, your Honor. We have a VHS video cassette tape we wish to play."

"I don't need to remind you, counselor, that such evidence is hearsay."

"Yes, your Honor. But the prosecution seeks to have the videotape admitted as a business record."

"You have a testimonial sponsor?"

"Yes, your Honor."

"Very well. Proceed, Ms. Riley. However, I must warn you"—the jurors were listening keenly now—"I'll be keeping close watch on you. Your evidence better be probative. I won't allow any undue prejudice here."

"Yes, your Honor." Kate was delighted by the judge's instruction, which only served to heighten the jury's curiosity. In a loud clear voice, she said: "The State calls Mr. Charles Grimes to the stand."

Charlie Grimes had dressed appropriately in suit jacket and tie. He took the oath. And now he sat comfortably in the witness box, respectful yet relaxed. He was going to make a fine witness.

Dispensing quickly with the preliminaries, Kate cut right to the heart of the matter:

"Now that you've explained the Rusty Nail's security stystem, Mr. Grimes, and how the cameras operate, can you tell us, are these tapes maintained in the ordinary course of business?"

"Yes."

"Fine. I'd like to call your attention to last night and the tape that attorneys for the prosecution located. Did the tape remain in your control at all times?"

"Yes, it did."

"Objection!" Doolittle leapt to his feet. "She's leading the witness."

"Your Honor," she said, "I am merely trying to establish an unbroken chain of custody."

"All right, counselor," Judge Greenhill ruled. "I'll let you proceed."

She turned back to Grimes: "What happened last night after we located the tape?"

"I drove down with you to the police station."

"Did the tape ever leave your sight?"

"No, I held on to it."

"What happened at the police station?"

"We gave the tape to the custodian of the evidence room. He put the tape into a big envelope, and put a red seal over it."

"Did he mark the exhibit?"

"Yeah. Eighteen."

"Thank you, Mr. Grimes." Kate's pulse quickened as she walked over to the clerk's desk where Mrs. Babcock sat. This was the moment they had all been waiting for. The jurors sat forward in their seats. The room became absolutely still. Kate kept her voice calm, but she was secretly thrilled: "Mr. Grimes, I'd like to show you what's been marked as State's Exhibit Eighteen and have you identify its contents." She took the manilla envelope from Mrs. Babcock, cradling it like a bouquet of flowers. She walked over to Mr. Grimes, then turned and faced the jury. She announced officially: "I am now breaking the seal." She broke it, flipped the envelope on its head, and gently, almost tenderly, let the evidence slide out onto the table.

The jury gasped.

Kate recoiled in horror, as if she'd touched something repugnant. But it was just an ordinary book, a slim paperback, from the Scribner Library collection: *The Great Gatsby*

What kind of joke was this?

She looked at Judith. The secretary sat frozen in her chair, her face ashen. She was as shocked as Kate was.

And Peter? He looked stunned too.

But Buckner? Of everyone in this room, he appeared the least surprised. His smugness, if anything, only intensified.

She stared at Buckner for a long, hard moment. She felt anger welling up inside her. She turned to Judge Greenhill. "Your

Honor," she said, trying to repress her indignation, "the tape, it's been stolen!"

"Objection!" Doolittle cried. "Misplaced!"

The court recessed.

Judge Greenhill directed the custodians of the police evidence room to conduct a full-scale search. In the meantime, Kate and Doolittle were to submit briefs on how to proceed if the tape continued missing.

Kate was not optimistic. Whatever wrongdoing Buckner was guilty of, and she was sure he was the one who'd arranged for the tape to disappear, she could not prove it. Without evidence of bad faith on the defense's part, Judge Greenhill would have no choice but to assume that the police were slipshod in their handling of exhibits. The case would proceed without the tape. And, without it, Kate would lose.

Outside the courtroom, cameras were rolling. Kate spoke gracefully to reporters but quickly escaped to the sanctuary of her office. There, she collapsed at her desk, buried her face in her hands. People who came in left her alone. She squeezed her eyes shut at the memory of what just happened in the courtroom. A shudder ran through her body. But, gradually, she collected herself. She thought of her mom. Mom would say: "Well, it's bad, all right, but you can't sit here forever. For one thing, you'll get a backache." Kate smiled. She opened her eyes and sat up.

She was beginning to feel like her old self again when her glance fell on the floor beside her desk. There was the framed photograph of her mother: smashed. Mom's face, her smile, were obliterated under a jigsaw puzzle of broken glass. Kate tried to rescue the photograph, clear the glass away, but she pricked her index finger. She gazed despairingly at her mother's image, at all the shattered glass, and found herself thinking that this was her life, shattered too.

A week passed.

It was evening now, and Kate was in her apartment, drinking.

She was dressed in her lacrosse T-shirt and an old pair of cut-off jeans. She had been gazing out the window at Cannery Row, waiting for the sun to go down, but it wouldn't, so she grabbed the bottle of cheap chardonnay and walked in her bare feet over to the couch. She preferred to drink in the dark but daylight was fine, too.

The bottle was half-empty. She filled her glass again, let her head loll against the cushions. She held the glass in her hand, tipped it back, and drank. After this round, she hoped to be, finally, numb.

This last week in trial had been a nightmare. After a ten-hour, item-by-item search of the police evidence room, the tape was still missing. Kate submitted her brief, but Judge Greenhill ruled as expected. He had no evidence of bad faith. He had to assume that the police were negligent and that Exhibit 18 was lost, not stolen. "However," he told both her and Doolittle in chambers, "if I *do* find evidence of bad faith, I will come down with the wrath of an avenging angel, am I clear? In the meantime, counsel, let's proceed with our trial."

And so Kate had concluded, in a palpable atmosphere of anti-climax, the case for the prosecution. Fielding testified as her expert, but his remarks were necessarily of a general nature and did little to help.

When the prosecution rested and the defense presented their case, Buckner took the stand. He was smooth and convincing. Kate failed to shake him on cross-examination. Buckner remained throughout the picture of a well-bred, cultured gentleman, falsely accused. He maintained he'd only had one drink on the night in question and that he was by no means intoxicated. The breathalyzer test administered by the police fell under suspicion. Even the missing tape seemed a fiction, a desperate ploy by the prosecution. To the jury, it all began to look like a clumsily staged frame-up.

The defense was drawing to a close. All that remained was Kate's rebuttal argument. But that would be a mere formality. She had no new evidence to disclose, nothing to add.

The sun was low on the horizon now, a pale orange ball about to disappear into gray haze. Kate sighed. She had given up everything for her career, a career somebody was trying to sabotage. Someone had tampered with the pleadings, someone had stolen the tape, and as a result, she was forced to argue an impossible case with inadequate evidence. She knew she should be outraged and fight back, but she was too tired. She drank more wine, seeking to anaesthetize herself, but it wasn't working; she felt remarkably clear-headed.

The phone rang and her message machine clicked on. It was Reuben: "Kiddo, are you there? C'mon, partner, it's been two days now. Come to the phone, I wanna talk to you." He paused on the line. She did not move from the sofa. "All right, if you won't talk to me, I'll talk to you. God, I feel like an idiot speaking into this machine. Anyhow, I've been busy. Done some digging and I've come up with something that might pay off. . . . Come on, kid, aren't you curious? Don't you want to know what I found? All right, you won't come to the phone, you won't answer your door, I'm forced to play my trump card. Kate, think of your mom. If she saw you holed up in your apartment, would she be proud? Think of what she stood for."

Kate sat up at that, stared at the glass in her hand.

Reuben sighed audibly. "If you're listening, I gave it my best shot. I guess, well, I'll call again tomorrow . . ."

He was about to hang up.

She leapt from the sofa, grabbed the phone.

"Reuben," she said. "It's me."

"You okay?"

"I will be, soon's I pour out this wine. Hold on."

"He has a mistress," Reuben said. "Name of Melanie Day."

"Oh!" Judith said, taken aback.

"Melanie Day," Kate repeated, trying to imagine her.

"She's thirty-five. Single. A model, but she just quit recently."

Kate nodded, quietly absorbed the news. She and Reuben and Judith sat in a corner booth in the Buttery. Kate didn't mind being here, thinking of her mom, her two creams in her coffee and her palm-leaf pastry. It was a terrific bakery, and she wanted to share it with her friends. "A model. Hm. Why'd she quit?"

"Don't know." Reuben shook his head. "Maybe she didn't need the money. Although *now* she does. According to her neighbor, she's behind on her rent. Until two months ago, guess who was footing her bills? Harold T. himself."

"He cut her off, you think?"

"Yup. Her neighbor also told me that Melanie and the judge were real tight, lots of partying going on, but lately nothing." Reuben leaned forward on his elbows. "There's more. She's got a car. A Cadillac. I ran her license through DMV, and guess what? Three months ago, on a Saturday night, she was ticketed for speeding. Apparently she was involved in an accident in Ocean City."

"What kind of accident?"

"That's just it," Reuben said. "The police report seems to have disappeared."

The chain was still on the door and the door was open only a few inches, but there was Melanie Day, like a dream, standing before them. My God, she's beautiful, Kate thought, noting the creamy skin, the sculpted cheekbones, the long blond hair, those velvet eyes. But then Melanie turned slightly and Kate saw the scar: the jagged slant above her eyebrow. No model could have a scar like that. Was that why she quit?

"I know you from the newspaper. You're here about *him,* aren't you?"

"Yes, Melanie. I'm Kate Riley and this is my assistant, Judith Moore. Can we come in and talk to you? It's important."

"We aren't seeing each other anymore. So I really have nothing to say."

"But you know him," Kate said. "You could help us."

"Why should I?"

"To keep him off the highway. From drinking and driving. So what happened to Jimmy Delorosa doesn't happen—"

"Stop it!" Melanie protested.

"Why, does that disturb you?"

"No," she said, then, "Yes, of course it does. I read about his kids, all right?"

"And don't forget his widow. She'll have to survive on Jimmy's pension."

Melanie relaxed her hand, let it drop from the doorknob. Kate didn't want to press her too much, but she sensed the ex-model was willing to talk, at least a little. "Did Buckner drink a lot when you were together?"

"Sure. What of it?"

"Did he ever take the wheel when he was inebriated?"

"What do you mean?" Melanie's tone was hostile.

"Was he with you when you had that accident in Ocean City?"

Melanie's hand instinctively went to the scar on her face, and suddenly Kate knew: "That's how you got your scar, isn't it?"

Melanie was about to reply, then stopped herself: "Look, I don't know anything, okay? I'm sorry, I really am." Her eyes were brimming with tears. She cast Kate one final anguished look goodbye, then slammed the door.

Connected to the Harbor Place Apartments where Melanie lived was a five-story concrete garage. Kate left Judith behind while she descended to the garage to look for Melanie's car. Here, in the basement, her footsteps echoed eerily in the perpetual gray twilight. The air was stale and muggy. Each of the parking spaces was numbered in yellow paint. She reached parking space number 2501, the same number as Melanie's apartment. She wanted to take a look at that Cadillac. But as soon as she stepped near the car, a voice rang out: "I help you?"

She glanced up. She saw a middle-aged black man in blue overalls: the parking lot attendant. He had a friendly face, but just now he wasn't smiling.

She thought fast: "Oh, hello. I don't know if you *can* help me. Melanie just asked me to fetch her sunglasses, and I stupidly forgot to get her keys. You wouldn't have a spare pair, would you?"

He smiled ironically. "No, I wouldn't." He didn't trust her, and she didn't blame him.

"I'll just run back up and get them. Dumb me. Well, so long."

She was poised to leave when he said: "Yeah, she wears those sunglasses a lot now. Surprised she left 'em in the car. She don't drive much."

"You mean, since the accident?"

He looked at her strangely. "No. I mean ever. Beautiful car like this sitting here day after day. I's supposed to wash it once a week, keep it clean. Only time it leaves this space is when Mr. Bradford comes."

"Bradford?" Kate said, puzzled.

"Yeah, hey, listen," he was eyeing her suspiciously now, "I thought you was a friend o' hers."

"I am." Kate thought a moment and decided to take a gamble. It could be that Buckner saw his mistress under an assumed name. "Sure I know Bradford. Tall, silver hair. Imposing guy."

"Yeah, that's him." The garage attendant nodded, the doubt vanishing from his eyes. "Yeah, it's a sad story. She never took to driving, then the one time she does, she gets hurt bad. Man, you shoulda seen the bandages. Oooh-ooh, *painful* to look at. She wore 'em for weeks. Then she takes 'em off and there's that scar. And she was such a pretty thing too."

————

Judith unlocked the door to her apartment and let Kate in. Kate carried the box of files into the kitchen and set it down. On the counter there was an item that caught her interest. It was a bottle of Jontue perfume.

She didn't want to ruin Judith's birthday present to her, so she pretended not to see the perfume. She let her secretary bustle into the kitchen and start dinner while she started down the hall in search of the bathroom. The closed door to the right looked like a good bet. She seized the doorknob and began to turn it, she could feel the lock shift, the door began to swing open . . . but before she could see inside, she felt a hand clamp over her own. And, with a savage yank, the partially opened door slammed shut.

Alarmed, Kate stepped backward.

"You *mustn't* go in there!" Judith snapped.

Kate was bewildered. What could warrant such secrecy? But Judith had a right to her privacy. "I'm sorry," Kate said, seeking to make peace with her secretary. "I was looking for the bathroom to wash my hands."

"It's this way," Judith pronounced, pointing. "Here, let me bring you a guest towel." Her voice became friendly again, as if her outburst a moment ago had never happened.

Kate soon forgot about the incident and it seemed Judith did too, as they ate dinner and then put the kettle on for tea. While they were waiting for the water to boil, Kate picked up *The Great Gatsby* from the box of files. "You know, it puzzles me. If Buckner stole the tape, why did he substitute this? How could he know it was my favorite book?"

Judith produced two teacups from the cupboard and said: "Maybe he didn't. Maybe the book is there for some other purpose."

"Like what?"

"A calling card."

"You mean, Buckner is telling us something?"

"Yes." Judith nodded, pursed her lips. "That man is so arrogant, he's laughing at us, Kate, playing games."

"What game are we playing?" Kate asked.

But Judith only shook her head.

The kettle wailed and Judith fixed their tea. Mr. Rochester was curled up on the floor, sleeping. Seated once again at the kitchen table, Kate wondered aloud: "Where is that police report of Melanie's accident? Did Buckner arrange for that to disappear too? And you know what else bothers me—what the garage attendant said—Melanie *hated* to drive. So, assuming Buckner was with her, why wasn't *he* driving that night in Ocean City? Was he too drunk? No, unless . . ." Kate's voice trailed off. She remained perfectly still a moment, then her eyes widened. She jumped up and grabbed *The*

Great Gatsby from the counter, shook it excitedly in front of her: "Don't you see? It's just like in the book."

"What?"

"We assume Melanie was driving because she got the ticket, and it's on her license. But maybe she wasn't driving. Maybe *he* was. And maybe, just maybe, they switched places."

"**M**s. Riley," Judge Greenhill said, "does the State wish to present a rebuttal case?"

"Yes, your Honor."

"All right let's get this trial wrapped up."

Kate looked at the judge. He was talking about wrapping things up. Even he believed her case was lost.

She returned to the prosecution table where she had been sitting alone. Peter was not with her today. He assumed things were still going badly, and did not want to be present when the jury announced their verdict and the press arrived. Behind where Peter would have sat, however, were her loyal friends, Reuben and Judith.

"Proceed, counsel," Judge Greenhill said.

"Your Honor, the State recalls the defendant to the stand."

The silver-haired, smoothly handsome Harold T. Buckner took

his seat in the witness box as if he owned the courtroom and everyone in it.

Even Judge Greenhill felt the power of the man's presence. He said, in a subdued, overly polite voice: "Mr. Buckner, a reminder that you're still under oath."

Kate approached the front of the courtroom. She alone was not awed by the witness, and, she hoped, by the time she was through here today, no one else would be either. Today she would help the jury look beneath Judge Buckner's veneer of education and breeding into his soul.

"Mr. Buckner," Kate began, "you've testified that you had but one previous conviction for DWI, is that correct?"

"Yes, a fact that I admit," Buckner directed his words to the jury, "and deeply regret. I'm sorry that that happened. And I'm saddened as well, truly saddened, by Jimmy Delorosa's unfortunate death."

Kate ignored Buckner's attempts to sway the jury. She pressed on: "Other than that DWI conviction and the accident involving Jimmy Delorosa for which you are currently on trial, have you ever driven your automobile or another's automobile while under the influence of alcohol?"

"No."

"Have you ever been involved in a car accident while you were under the influence of alcohol?"

"No, I just told you . . ."

"But, in fact, you *have* been involved in an accident, a very serious accident, while under the influence of alcohol."

"That's totally untrue."

"Is it?" Kate frowned skeptically. The jurors, for the first time, gave her their full attention. "Isn't it true that on Saturday night, April eleventh, you were involved in a serious accident in Ocean City, Maryland? An accident that nearly cost the life of your passenger?"

"Absolutely not. I haven't been to Ocean City in months. I have been far too busy with my official duties as circuit court judge, a position that I—"

"Mr. Buckner, on the date in question, were you or were you not driving a nineteen eighty-six Cadillac Seville registered to Ms. Melanie Day of Baltimore?"

"Objection!" Doolittle pounded the table. "Your Honor, this line of questioning is completely collateral to the case."

"Overruled. Proceed."

"Thank you," Kate said.

Harold Buckner did not answer her question. He was looking at her strangely. She saw the faintest glimmer of fear in his eyes.

"We're waiting, Mr. Buckner," Judge Greenhill said.

"Melanie Day," Kate repeated. "Were you driving Melanie Day's car?"

Buckner appealed to Doolittle for help. Doolittle, looking puzzled, only shrugged: You're on your own. Buckner chose to remain defiant. He shook his head: "I'm not familiar with anyone by that name."

"You're not?"

"No."

"And you deny being with Melanie Day on Saturday, April eleventh, in Ocean City?"

"Yes. I don't know what you're talking about."

"Mr. Buckner," Kate said sternly, "let me remind you of the penalties for perjury. Isn't it true that not only are you acquainted with Melanie Day, but that the ex-model was in fact your mistress?"

"No! That is a total untruth."

The jurors sat bolt upright in their seats. They were hanging on every word.

"Isn't it a fact that you and Ms. Day frequently went to Ocean City for the weekend?"

"No."

"And that in April of this past year, you went out for dinner with Ms. Day, during the course of which you became intoxicated?"

"Absolutely not."

"And while you were driving the two of you back to your hotel—because Melanie hated to drive—you, due to your intoxicated condition, ran a red light, causing the Cadillac to collide with another car?"

"No," Buckner said, but he shifted in his chair. He rubbed his neck where his shirt collar was chafing him. He was visibly uncomfortable.

"Mr. Buckner," she said, "have you read *The Great Gatsby?*"

"Objection!" Doolittle cried. "Irrelevant."

"Your Honor, this question is highly relevant as you will see in one moment."

"Counsel, I'll indulge you. The witness will answer the question."

"I believe so," Buckner said.

"You believe so," Kate repeated. She turned to the jury: "In *The Great Gatsby,* the climax occurs when Gatsby is with his love Daisy and they are driving together. They've both had too much to drink. Daisy takes the wheel and runs over a woman, her husband's mistress. But Gatsby is blamed for the woman's death. Do you know why, ladies and gentlemen of the jury? Because, before the police arrived, Gatsby and Daisy switched places, making it appear that Gatsby was behind the wheel." Kate gave Buckner a stern look. "Mr. Buckner, you must see where this is leading, sir. I give you one last chance to redeem yourself and admit your wrongdoing."

"I have no wrongdoing to confess. Though I admire Mr. Fitzgerald's writing tremendously, I still fail to see its relevance here."

Kate regrouped. She had given Buckner every chance to tell the truth. Now she would be as ruthless as necessary: "You are telling me, sir, you do not know Melanie Day?"

"No."

"You were never in Ocean City with her?"

"No."

"You did not drink too much and then get behind the wheel?"

"No."

"You never ran a red light?"

"No."

"You were never in an accident?"

"No."

"Come on, admit it, isn't it a fact you *were* in an accident?"

"No!" Buckner was exasperated now. He was shouting at her.

"And isn't it a fact that, as a result of this accident, Melanie Day suffered a serious head injury, and also received multiple contusions and abrasions on her face, which created ugly scars, which, in fact, ruined Ms. Day's career as a model?"

"No! I told you!"

"And isn't it a fact that, after this accident, even though your passenger was seriously injured and moaning with pain, all you could do was think of yourself? And that's why, *knowing* of your DWI conviction, *knowing* that your license would be suspended if you got caught, you convinced Ms. Day to switch places with you, convinced her to pretend that *she*, not you, was behind the wheel?"

"No," Buckner cried. "Dammit, I said no!"

At that, Kate became very calm. She said the words with slow deliberation. "You're lying, sir, aren't you?"

"No!"

"You're a liar, and I'm going to prove it."

"Objection, your Honor!" Doolittle was furious.

But Kate turned to the back of the courtroom. "Okay, Melanie, you can come in now."

Astonishment, then sympathy washed over the jurors' faces as in walked the beauty that was once Melanie Day. She was blond and gorgeous, tall and leggy, a perfect ten, except for her face, except for that angry jagged scar.

———

Kate put Melanie on the stand. When she told about the accident, everyone had tears in their eyes. And when she left the courtroom, so did truth. The jury looked to Buckner, sitting at the defense table, and they knew without a doubt that he had lied to them. He had lied about Melanie and the accident in Ocean City. So what was to stop him from lying about the night he killed Jimmy Delorosa? It was beginning to look like murder, after all.

Kate understood how betrayed the jurors felt. There was no need for her to prove anything to them anymore. "That's all, your Honor," she announced. "The State rests."

After that, things moved very quickly. Judge Greenhill gave the jury instructions and Kate and Doolittle gave their final arguments.

The jury filed into the jury room, where they would be sequestered until they rendered their verdict. Kate gathered her papers together. Judith was by her side as they both stepped into the corridor. They were instantly overwhelmed by reporters. Cameras clicked and whirred. Lights flashed. Microphones were thrust in Kate's face: "Ms. Riley, that surprise appearance by Melanie Day stunned the jury. Judging by their expressions, they don't think much of Buckner now. Are you confident of a prosecution verdict?"

"Brilliant strategy, Ms. Riley. Did you save the model till the last minute?"

"Since when did you know about her affair with Buckner?"

To all this, Kate said: "The jury's out. I have no comment until they give their verdict. I'll talk to you, then, ladies and gentlemen. Thank you." She was about to move on when she saw Peter Coe across the hall, looking cross and dejected because the press had left him to rush over to her. Seeing Peter made Kate remember something she had promised herself—that if she ever had the opportunity, she would thank the people who worked with her. She turned back to the reporters and the microphones. The lights were hot on her face and in her eyes, almost blinding her, as she said: "I can't comment on the trial's outcome, but if we do have a victory, it will be largely due to help from my associates, notably, my secretary Ms. Judith Moore." She turned to reach for Judith's hand and bring her forward, but Judith, who was standing right by her side just seconds ago, was gone.

Was Judith publicity shy? Kate wondered. Or maybe she was

saying that she didn't need accolades to feel good about herself. If so, she had Kate's respect and admiration.

But look at Peter down the hall. He was Judith's opposite. As the covey of reporters left Kate to surround him, he instantly became energized. In the wash of white lights, he was glowing and handsome. His boyish face was almost radiant. But behind his photogenic smiles there was, she sensed, a certain ruthlessness. When Peter wanted something, he generally got it. She remembered the night he broke into her apartment and told her with a grin that he would not be kept out.

The jury had not yet reached a verdict, but Kate was optimistic. She stood at the sliding glass doors to her patio and admired the evening. Pink spread itself against the sky as the sun descended. There was no humidity. The light was soft, the air sweet.

Kate felt restless. What should she do? She smiled to herself. She might regret it in the morning, her muscles would complain, but it would be worth it.

Not wishing to lose this mood, this unaccustomed hopefulness, she hastened into her bedroom and threw on her running shoes and an old T-shirt. She laced up her sneakers and thought that it didn't matter now that someone had tampered with the pleadings and stolen the tape. It didn't matter because she would win her case anyway. Buckner would go to prison.

There was another man already in prison because of her, but she would not think of him. This was her night, her celebration. Just for tonight she would pretend that Slick was part of her past but not her future.

She went into the living room and did some stretches. Then she headed for the door. Now she was a figure jogging along the city streets. She moved fast and fluidly. She was surprised at how good she felt. When she crested the paved hill, she became part of the pink horizon. There was a boy on a bicycle who had climbed the hill beside her. He joined her, as in a painting, and became pink too.

128

"Ladies and gentlemen of the jury," Judge Greenhill said. "Have you reached a verdict?"

"Yes, your Honor," the foreman replied. "We the jury find the defendant guilty."

The verdict still rang in Kate's mind as she drove up Charles Street toward Molly's. Buckner really would go to prison now. Of course Jimmy Delorosa was still dead and Mary was a widow, but maybe there would have been another highway accident, another widow: at least they had prevented that.

Molly opened the door with Lily in her arms and Ian giggling behind her skirt: "Kate, what're you doing here! You should be off celebrating."

"Are you kidding?" Kate laughed. She looked at her sister, so cool and summery in her white blouse and sandals; at Ian, taller now, no longer wearing his Superman cape; and at Lily, the little princess: "You guys *are* my celebration. Honest, Moll, there's no place I'd rather be."

Inside, she and Molly shared a cup of coffee and talked about Mexico. "Can you believe we're leaving day after tomorrow?" Molly said. "I'm so excited, I can't stand it."

"Me too."

"Is Judith still coming?"

"Yes. *That* and my birthday are all she talks about."

"Great." Molly sipped her coffee and appraised her sister: "You look terrific. Not so thin. The psychiatrist. Fielding, is it? You still seeing him?"

"With the trial, I haven't been," Kate said, "but I have an appointment tomorrow." She kept her voice carefully neutral. Even with Molly, she could not reveal the intensity of her emotions. Fielding was married, after all. She had no right to the feelings she had for him.

"Kate?" Molly was calling her back. "Daydreaming?"

"No, I—" She shrugged, smiled.

Molly understood. She let it go.

The sisters' talk ended there. Ian was restless and Lily needed a nap. So while Molly took the baby upstairs, Kate took Ian into the backyard where they played in the swimming pool. Ian had her sit next to him while he squatted in the grass, his knees muddied and scratched, and watched, with wide-eyed fascination, as black beetles, ants, and spiders landed in the pool. "Look, spidey!" he cried. Kate hardly heard him. She was staring at the car across the street. The car was partly obscured by trees, but the driver's window was open. She squinted her eyes. All she could see was a gray shape. The driver might be anyone, but she had a sudden horrible thought, and her heart froze. Suppose it was Slick?

She immediately stood up, feeling chilled: "Come on, Ian. Let's go see your mommy."

She reached her hand out to the golden-haired boy and he took it. They headed inside, and all the while, she was acutely aware of

Ian's tiny hand in hers. She felt very protective of him. She didn't care that she might be in danger, she was only thinking of him. But when she opened the screen door and saw him safely into the house, she felt afraid again. She glanced toward the car. She was surprised. It was already gone.

And yet her fear persisted. She left Molly's and went shopping. She bought a new bikini, sunscreen, and sunglasses for Mexico but couldn't stop thinking about Slick. When she returned home to her apartment and the phone was ringing, she had a bad feeling even before she answered it: "Hello?"

"Kate Riley?"

"Yes."

"Walt Schumaker. I'm the warden at Hagerstown State Prison. I hate to tell you this, but one of our inmates, Slick Carlson, escaped from the prison grounds this morning, and he's currently at large."

"Oh, no . . ."

"Carlson's threats against you are on record here with our prison psychiatrist, so that's why I'm calling. I tried you earlier, but—"

"I've been out all day."

"I suggest you get police protection as soon as possible. Just as a precaution, mind you. We've got a manhunt underway, and I think we'll have this thing wrapped up in no time. But just in case . . ."

Kate swallowed dryly. "Where was he last seen?"

"Hitchhiking on I-Seventy."

"Toward Baltimore?" She held her breath.

"Yes."

Still in shock, she hung up the phone. She was about to dial the police when there was a knock on her door. She looked through her peephole and saw two detectives, friends of Reuben's.

Ten minutes later, Kate and the two detectives were watching the six o'clock news. The Channel 2 newscaster was saying: "The explosion at Hagerstown Prison created a veritable inferno. Arson is certain, and evidence strongly points to the fugitive, Clarence Wilbur Carlson. Those who know Carlson point to his warped sense of humor. The rigged explosion, they say, along with his escape, is Carlson's way of laughing at authority."

Kate turned away from the television. She couldn't listen anymore.

She started for the kitchen in search of some Tylenol when there was another knock on her door. The detectives quickly unholstered their guns. Skip, the thin one, signaled for her to stay beside him while his partner answered the door.

Kate counted off ten tense seconds, but nothing happened. And then, of all people, Reuben walked into the room. She ran to him.

He enveloped her in a warm hug: "It's okay. They found him. He was robbing a 7-Eleven."

"Really?"

"Darn it," Skip said. "And I just ordered pizza too."

Kate looked stricken.

"Sorry," he apologized. "Cop humor."

Now the other detectives were gone, and it was just her and Reuben alone in her living room. The phone rang. She hesitated to answer it. Would this be more bad news? But it was only Peter. "I heard," he said. "You okay?"

"I'm fine."

"Stupid jerk. Who would rob a 7-Eleven in broad daylight?"

"I guess he did," she answered.

"I thought he was smarter than that." There was a pause on the line, then Peter asked, in a changed voice: "Listen, can I come over? I can be at your place in fifteen minutes."

"I appreciate the offer, but I'm fine. Really."

"I *want* to come over. Will you let me?"

"Peter, tonight's not a good time for me."

"Why not?"

She hesitated, then said: "Reuben's here."

"Oh."

"Okay?" she said. "Another time."

"Sure, sure." But Peter was angry with her; he hung up.

If Reuben had overheard, he didn't let on. He waited for her on the sofa. When she came back over, he stood up.

She said: "He's really in custody?"

"Yes."

"He's not out there somewhere?"

"No. They've got him, Kate. You're safe now."

She nodded. She was only a few feet away from Reuben now. His bright olive eyes were watching her. He seemed to know just how she felt. She gave him a small, self-conscious smile. Then she averted her glance and said: "You ever been here before? I can't remember."

"Just when you had that party a while back. And to drop you off."

He was still looking at her, and now she couldn't keep her eyes off him. She drew back a coppery strand of hair and tucked it behind her ear.

He cast her a yearning look, stepped forward, then stopped: "I have to go."

"Why?"

"You're tired, and . . ."

"Is that the real reason?"

"No. It's just . . . you look too good. You're beautiful."

"I'll wear curlers next time, I promise." She tried desperately to smile, but now all she could think of was how cold she felt and how lonely.

A look of pain crossed his narrow face, and he said: "You're shaking."

"No, I'm—" She was about to deny it, but she couldn't. She gave him a small smile of surrender.

They reached for each other at the same time, and when they touched it was electric. Still, when their lips met, when he buried kisses in her neck and she clung to him, it wasn't Reuben she saw with her eyes closed: She could only see Fielding.

20

Reuben didn't stay the night. Maybe he was afraid of the morning after, or maybe he really did need to leave like he said. Either way, she understood. There was still a tender mood between them as she pulled on her bathrobe and he sat on the edge of the bed and wrestled on his cowboy boots. They were both thirsty. Before he left, they shared orange juice right out of the carton. Light spilled in from the open refrigerator, and they smiled into each other's eyes.

The next morning, she woke early. She pulled up her blinds and looked out. The sky was white, and the sun was just gaining in strength, glinting in the windows of the rowhouses and glancing on the treetops like golden fire.

She decided to pack for Mexico, then take a shower. An hour later, she walked into the kitchen in shorts and bare feet, her wet hair glistening and uncombed. She fixed scrambled eggs, realizing that she hadn't made even a simple meal like this for herself in a long time. Not with the trial. She was glad it was over now, so she could get on with her life.

Tonight she would see Fielding. It had been three weeks. How much would he have changed? How much had she? She remembered their last session. What a pleasurable shock, seeing him come charging out of the woods in his running shorts, all sweaty. He said he had lost track of the time. Upstairs, he dressed but he didn't bother with shoes and socks. He remained barefoot. She wondered if other psychiatrists were that unorthodox. Probably not.

She ate her eggs and toast with enjoyment, then wondered what to do with herself. She was taking the day off, and tomorrow she was going to Mexico. She thought she would dread this vacation, but it felt wonderful. She cleaned up her dishes and decided what to do. Fielding had told her to look at family albums and read old letters. She would dig out Mom's diary and cuddle up with that.

She found the diary in a U-Haul box in her study. She sat cross-legged on the carpet and opened the diary to the first page, almost reverently, as if this were a hymnal and she was in church. She became oblivious to her environment, the sprawl of family albums and momentos around her. . . .

Twenty minutes later, she came upon the first in a series of startling passages penned in her mom's angular script. Stunned, she reread the diary entries, hoping each time they would end differently, but they always came out the same. She didn't understand how this could be, that her mother hadn't told her. But her mother had been in love. She'd had an affair with a man Kate had never heard of, a man named Anthony Reed.

The sun was high in the sky. Its harsh light hurt her eyes as she looked toward the window. Her mood had changed utterly since this morning. She hugged herself and felt small and alone. She would see Fielding at six o'clock. She didn't know if she could make it until then.

"Hello, Kate. Good to see you!"

"You, too," she managed to say.

The room was charged with emotion as the two of them stood there, gazing at one another. The problem was, Kate thought, Fielding had not changed in three weeks and she loved him no less. She longed to wrap her arms around him, feel his arms around her.

"What is it?" he asked.

She couldn't tell him that being here with him was painful, to be near him but only for a little while. The time would slip away so fast, she almost couldn't enjoy his company. But, no, she had to remind herself, she mustn't think this way, she was here to get better and he was here to help her, so she told him about her shock this morning, reading the diary.

When she was through, he regarded her compassionately: "You seem upset but not angry. Why is that?"

"What do you mean?" The knot in her stomach loosened. He was so matter of fact. Maybe her world hadn't crumbled, after all.

"Your mom had a lover," he said. "You're letting her off easy, don't you think? She committed adultery."

"Adultery? C'mon! Scarlet letters are so nineteenth-century. No, I can understand her affair with Anthony Reed. They were both in A.A. They had something in common. At home, what did she have with my father? Theirs was a cold marriage, and I know she was lonely." Kate paused. Her throat was so tight she couldn't swallow. "But still . . ."

"You're upset," Fielding prompted.

She nodded.

"Why?"

"Because she didn't tell me. And I thought we were best friends."

"Maybe she thought you'd be hurt. She wanted to spare you."

"I'm hurt *now!*"

Fielding was silent a moment. She watched his eyes travel to the Pat Buckley Moss painting called *Skating Joy*. A man and woman in black coats and blue scarves glided on the frozen pond while their children frolicked behind them. What did the painting remind him of? Because he became wistful and sad. When he looked back at her, he said, "Everyone has secrets, Kate."

She studied him and pondered his words. She supposed her mom had a right to her secret, to her own life, but she still felt betrayed. "I loved her," she said finally. "I wouldn't have stood in her way."

"I know." Fielding nodded. His eyes were gentle on her. "When I gave you this homework, to spend time with your memories, I intended it to be therapeutic. I didn't expect you would have to deal with this."

"I wouldn't have read the diary if I'd known."

"I know."

"I feel as though I've trespassed on sacred ground. I wish I could go back to before, to when I hadn't read it. I don't know, I feel like I need to do something. I can't talk to Molly, I don't want to hurt her. Oh, I wish I could talk to my mom!"

"She might be a tough connection," Fielding said. "But there *is* someone you could talk to."

"Who?"

"Anthony Reed."

Outside in the parking lot, Kate hesitated before she climbed into her car. She deliberated a long moment, then hastened to the phone booth across the parking lot and looked up a name. When she got the number, she began dialing right away so she wouldn't lose heart. It was a difficult call, but she made it.

———

Anthony Reed was dying.

His wife Jesse, a pleasant brunette with country-club breeding, told Kate as much while they traversed the wide expanse of green lawn to the swimming pool. Behind them was the Reed estate, an antebellum brick mansion nestled between two spreading oaks. To the right was a red clay tennis court, and beyond that, a woods where birds were singing. Jesse added, looking right at Kate: "I knew your mother. She was a lovely woman."

"Yes, she was," Kate replied tentatively, wondering how much Jesse knew.

Jesse smiled and seemed to read her thoughts: "I was jealous when I found out. And self-righteous, too. I almost left Anthony because of it. But here I am, as you see."

"Yes," Kate said, smiling back at Jesse, liking her.

They arrived at the deep end of a large rectangular pool. In the pool, a silver-haired man with a silver goatee did laps while a male nurse in white pants and white short-sleeved shirt looked on.

Jesse turned: "I'll leave you now. You must promise not to tire him."

"I won't," Kate said. "And thank you."

In the pool, Anthony Reed struggled bravely. He was doing the crawl, but he was tiring. His kick lacked power and his arm strokes were feeble. He began to slap the water with his arms. He cast about with his head. He lost all smooth forward momentum each time he bobbed up for air. As he touched the pool's side, the male nurse knelt and shouted encouragement to him: "Fifteen. You can do it. Five more!"

With an aching heart, wishing she could swim his laps for him, she watched Anthony complete his regimen. The last two laps, he thrashed ineffectually at the water, his arms not obeying his instructions. Moaning with every stroke now, he willed himself down the length of the pool and back. Finally, exhausted, Anthony finished. In the shallow end, he drew himself up on his elbows and hung breathless over the side. His upper torso twitched with spasms and his face was ashen and twisted in pain. Yet, between lungfuls of air, he managed to gasp: "Don't forget, Borges. Tomorrow we race. Double or nothing? I've got a mean sprint."

When Anthony Reed said that, she loved him.

Borges helped the warrior out of the pool and into a terrycloth bathrobe and his wheelchair. Anthony was just relaxing when he looked over and saw her. "Kate Riley," he said softly, just as he had on the phone. He smiled. "Please, join me." She went over to sit in the lounge chair next to him. When Borges left, he took her hand and pressed it. "I'm glad you called, glad you came."

"I am too," she said, meeting his level gaze, reading both pain and hope in his eyes. She had so many questions. They still seemed important, but not as important as when she first decided to come here, before she knew he was dying.

"You look like her and you don't," he said, stroking his silver goatee. "Same red hair. Different eyes. Yours are bluer, I think. Lots of compassion in you, Kate Riley."

She laughed. "You can tell from my eyes?"

"No. I know because you're here. And you're not angry. Our silence was a betrayal of sorts. Maybe you should be a little bit angry. Jesse was. She left me, for a time, when she found out."

"She . . . told me."

"Yes, I can see that." He chuckled. "You're the kind of person people tell things to." He paused, gazed into the aquamarine pool. "Your mother and I . . . it just happened. God, I loved her!"

"So why didn't—?" Kate began.

"We get married?"

She nodded.

"We didn't want to disrupt two households. We had you and Molly to think of. And I've a daughter and two sons."

"But we're grown up! We would have understood." She said this, but as soon as the words were out, she knew the real reason for their silence.

He was watching her. "We fell in love three years ago," he explained. "Shortly after that, I found out I was dying. It didn't seem right, you see, to unsettle all your lives." He became dreamy. "Also, we didn't trust what we had. We were so passionate. Like adolescents."

Kate took a deep breath. Tears brimmed in her eyes. She was glad when Borges interrupted them with drinks.

"Wonderful!" Anthony said. "Lemonade, Kate?"

"Yes."

The lemonade tasted cool in the humid August evening. They listened to the birds. Then Anthony continued: "Darndest thing, I was at work—I sell computers—and I suddenly felt this terrible twitching in my left leg. Well, the leg got worse and I went to see a specialist. Amyotrophic lateral sclerosis, they said. Lou Gehrig's disease. Attacks the nervous system. Funny thing is, I never did like baseball."

She had to smile. What a courageous man. Understated, too. In that way like Fielding. When he said "I sell computers," she realized who he was. He didn't merely sell computers, he designed them. He was Reed of Reed Enterprises, Inc. He created The Buddy System, computers specially geared for elementary-school students and used nationwide.

Anthony's wrist and hand trembled in a sudden spasm as he held the glass of lemonade to his lips. She feared he would drop the glass and it would shatter. She longed to take it from him, but she knew he had to try. It took him several moments of fierce concentration to get his motor skills to cooperate and enable him to return the glass to the table. When he finished, he chuckled: "Straws were invented for less."

They sat in silence on the lawn by the pool.

Anthony clumsily stroked his goatee, an old habit that had become awkward. He waited patiently because he sensed, rightly, that she had something on her mind. She sorted through her memories and finally said: "I still miss her. I feel like there's nothing I can do, to be like her. She helped so many people. I guess that's why I studied criminal law and became a prosecutor. I wanted to do some good. But it doesn't compare, what I do." She looked at Anthony and told him something she had never told anybody: "Do you know, the night she died, I prayed to God to put her back on earth and take me instead."

Anthony's eyes filled with sympathy: "I used to idolize her too, Kate. But it's not good. You must learn to appreciate yourself. You too have a purpose." There was a rustling in the lawn behind them and Anthony looked up. "Yes, Borges?"

Borges had reappeared and now stood before the wheelchair. "Dr. Parker is here, sir."

Kate rose immediately. "I'm sorry. I stayed too long."

"No, don't apologize." Anthony reached for her hand once more. "Will you come again? There's something I need to show you. I think, under the circumstances, Lily would have wanted you to see it."

21

The lock was candy.

Slick eased back the sliding glass door, brushed the drapes aside, and stepped into her living room. He snickered. Here he was, in her apartment, and he was supposed to be in prison. They would sort things out eventually, realize they had arrested the wrong guy, but in the meantime, he was free to do whatever he wanted. And what he wanted to do was to hurt *her*.

He paraded through her apartment like he owned the place. He was thinking of his escape today and gloating. He had wired the dairy barn with plastic explosives and stayed to watch it blow. What a kick! He only wished more people had gotten hurt.

Of course Rees wanted to come too. He would be mad at Slick for leaving without him. Slick hoped he wouldn't be too mad, but he didn't really care. Rees couldn't touch him now.

He turned on the lights and the air conditioning, made himself at home. He wouldn't mind if she came walking in the door right this minute. In fact, he wanted her to. He wanted to see the surprise on her face: Remember me? I told you I'd come back.

He stopped in the kitchen. In her refrigerator he found mayonnaise, turkey, and cheese and fixed himself a sandwich. He uncorked the bottle of wine. He gulped the wine straight from the bottle and devoured the sandwich standing up. It tasted good. He thought he just might make himself another when his glance settled on the kitchen table and her open leather briefcase. He strode over. Her briefcase was full of files and papers. Next to the briefcase, all by itself, was an airline ticket. He plunked the wine bottle down and picked up the ticket with both hands. Eastern Airlines—Baltimore to New Orleans to Cozumel.

Cozumel was in Mexico, wasn't it? And she was leaving tomorrow!

He excitedly absorbed this new information. In the United States, Kate Riley was a prosecuting attorney. In Mexico, she was nobody at all.

He stood there in the kitchen a moment without moving. He changed his mind about the apartment and what he would do here tonight. He finalized a new plan. Before, he'd intended to leave her his calling card, let her know it was *him.* But now he washed and dried the kitchen knife he'd used, screwed the top back on the mayonnaise jar, corked the wine bottle, wrapped everything up and put it away.

He remembered what he had touched in the apartment and wiped his prints off. He knew he should go now, but he couldn't resist a visit to her bedroom. She did not disappoint him. She had it done up very pretty and feminine. Flowered wallpaper, delicate curtains in the windows, and a soft white down comforter on the bed. Also on the bed was an open suitcase full of clothes.

Her clothes intrigued him. His heart pounded as he walked over to touch them. He inhaled sharply as he reached for her sweater, her sunglasses, her perfume. He sifted gingerly through the suitcase, his pleasure increasing with each item he touched. And then he sighted her bikini, and it was almost too much to bear. An all-black bikini. His heart skipped a beat and his throat went dry. He lifted the bikini top and held it, swaying, before him. He laid the bikini top gently back down on the pile of clothes and reached feverishly for the black bikini panties. He clutched the panties close, pressed them to his face. Just think, she wore this. He sniffed inside, searching for her scent. He pictured her on the beach in Cozumel, under a sun hat, her skin coppertone, her silky body clad only in this.

Imagining her, he could feel his excitement stir. But excitement became frustration. What good was touching her things? He wanted *her*.

Dissatisfied, irritable, he cast about him for some way to wound her. That was when he spotted her jewelry on the dresser—the gold swordpin with the diamond setting. He grinned. The police would never know that he was the one who'd ripped her off, and he would so love to hurt her feelings.

He swiftly pocketed the swordpin and headed out. He was in the living room when he heard the sudden, unmistakable sound of a key rattling in the lock. He dove for the patio doors, muscled them open, and was about to plunge outside when his ankle got tangled in the drapes! Struggling to free his foot, he cast an anxious glance at the door. He prayed it would not open.

———

The door opened.

Kate walked in with Peter Coe at her side. She had just returned from Anthony Reed's, and he had surprised her in the lobby.

"I thought you'd stop by the office to say good-bye," Peter said, "but since you didn't, well, I wanted to give you this." He handed her a heavy, rectangular box that was clumsily wrapped and tied with a lopsided bow.

She was touched by his efforts to wrap her gift himself. The fact that he had labored with Scotch tape, scissors, and wrapping

144

paper meant more to her than the gift itself. "Peter you didn't need to—"

"Come on," he urged, "open it."

She tore into the shiny blue paper and opened the box. Inside she found a snorkel, face mask, and fins. "Oh, Peter!"

"For snorkeling, you know?" he said eagerly. "I heard it's great down there. Incredible tropical fish."

She smiled at him, letting him know how much she appreciated his gift, but he watched her doubtfully: "You really like it?"

"I *love* it!" she said, putting more enthusiasm into her words than she felt. An awkward silence fell between them. They were both standing there in the lobby. She was holding the big box, with its jumble of fins, face mask, and snorkel. She was tired, it had been a long day, but she felt obliged to invite him in.

Now, as she stepped into the apartment and set the box down, she sensed immediately something was wrong.

"What is it?" Peter asked.

"It's just . . . I don't remember leaving the air conditioning on. Or the lights. In fact I'm sure I—" Her eyes widened, and her white fingers fluttered to the haven of her neck like startled doves. Over by the sliding glass door to her patio, the ivory drapes were twisted. The patio door was open and the drapes shifted with the breeze.

"Wait here," Peter said, and before she could stop him, he strode across the room and plunged bravely onto the patio. In a moment, he stepped back inside and slid the door shut. "Nobody there," he said, but then he examined the lock on the sliding glass door and saw that its flimsy lock had been tampered with. He went to her.

She was shivering.

"You okay?"

"I'm . . . fine."

He put his hand on her shoulder: "Look around. See if anything's missing. I'll call St. Claire." St. Claire was Reuben's superior and Peter's personal friend.

While Peter phoned the police, Kate toured the apartment. At first, she found nothing out of place, everything seemed normal, and she began to be hopeful. But at the threshold of her bedroom, she paused. She had an eerie sinking feeling, instantly validated when she looked at her jumbled-up clothes in the suitcase on the bed. She had packed neatly. Who has been here? she thought. Seeking what? She found her answer when she inspected the jewelry on her dresser. Her mother's gold swordpin was gone. She gave a moan of despair.

Peter appeared instantly. He opened his arms and beckoned to her, and she came to him with tears in her eyes. She laid her head against his shoulder, seeking comfort there, but she instantly regretted it because, just at that moment, Reuben walked in with his partner Woodie and Sergeant St. Claire. When Kate saw Reuben, she stiffened in Peter's arms. Peter felt the change in her. He looked across the room, and now he saw Reuben too. But Peter did not relax his embrace or let her go. Instead, he held her tighter, his act a boast he had no right to make: *See? She's mine.*

I'm not yours or anyone's, Kate wanted to say, but she could not do so gracefully. Instead, she extricated herself as quickly as she could. She went up to Reuben, took his hand, and thanked him for coming, but he would not quite look at her, and so she knew that, without meaning to, she had hurt him.

Sergeant St. Claire was brief and businesslike. He and Woodie dusted for fingerprints and inquired of the neighbors if they had seen or heard anything, while Reuben and Peter sat with her in the kitchen. She studied them appraisingly. They were so different. Peter, stylish and formal in his tailored Brooks Brothers suit, and Reuben in his faded jeans and blue polo shirt.

St. Claire and Woodie learned nothing from the neighbors, and they were doubtful about the prints. They told Kate they were sorry and then said good night. But Reuben and Peter stayed on. Before Kate realized it, it became a contest. Neither would leave before the other.

"I don't think you should be here alone," Peter said to her.

"He's right," Reuben agreed. "I'd be glad to stay."

"Or I could," Peter offered.

She hesitated. They were both watching her. Reuben was cool, scuffing his boots on the kitchen tiles. Peter was more obvious. He stared straight at her, his face an open appeal. They were forcing her to decide between them, but she wouldn't. She thought of a way out: "Tell you what, guys," she said, smiling. "Why don't you *both* stay here, because I'm going to Molly's."

At that, Reuben laughed.

Peter, though, didn't even smile. He said: "Okay, but one drink before we go?"

He didn't really want a drink, she knew. He just wanted an excuse to stay a little longer. She thought of herself and Fielding. That's how she felt about him, their time together just slipped away, so she took pity on Peter and said, despite the lateness of the hour and her exhaustion: "I don't want anything, but you go ahead."

"Reuben?" Peter turned to the detective. "Join me?"

"Sure," Reuben said.

Peter reached into the refrigerator, searching for beer, and found wine.

When Kate saw the bottle of chardonnay, she said: "Funny, I don't remember opening it. Honestly, I'd swear I didn't."

"Really?" Reuben said, suddenly thoughtful.

Molly greeted her with a warm hug, fixed her a mug of cocoa, and settled her into the guest room. But even after their cozy chat, even with the glowing comfort of knowing that Ian slumbered in the next room, Kate could not sleep.

Toward daybreak she finally dropped off. After weeks of undisturbed sleep, she had the dream again. She was walking toward the house, the stranger came and chased her. She fled. She clambered up the rocks to the precipice. There, on the cliff, the stranger reappeared. He loomed before her, huge and menacing. And the worst part of all was, she could not appeal to him for mercy. He had no eyes, nothing, just a blank face. Desperate, she cast about her, but there was no escape. She glanced at the crashing surf and rocks below. If she jumped, she would die. And yet, if she turned, she would have to confront the stranger, and she couldn't do that. . . .

22

The airport was busy, the terminal at Eastern Airlines crowded. The only place Kate could think of to meet Fielding was the balcony coffee shop. The waitress came by and she ordered coffee, but she didn't drink any. Instead, she toyed with her silverware and shredded her napkin. Every so often she would look up, hoping to see Fielding, but each time she was disappointed. She didn't like sitting here alone. Ever since she'd sat down, she'd had the strangest feeling. It was just like the day she was playing with Ian in the backyard and she knew she was being watched.

Fielding found her in the airport coffee shop, just where she said she'd be. He spotted her instantly: Who could miss that copper-red hair? She had dressed for Mexico in white slacks, sandals, and a silk blouse the color of her eyes: indigo. He noted circles under those eyes, though. "Kate!" He called her name with a surge of inward joy.

When he tucked himself into the booth across from her, she reached impulsively for his hand and he felt a shock of pleasure. They were together for an instant, smiling at each other with their eyes, then she suddenly looked mortified as she realized she was holding his hand, and drew back. "It's so good of you to come," she said. Then her lip trembled and she fought back tears.

She was so brave. He wanted to wrap his arms around her. Instead, he gave her his handkerchief. "You can cry, you know," he said gently. "It's allowed."

She cast him an agonized glance. "Look at me! I'm falling apart."

No, you're not. You're lovelier than ever, he wanted to say. But he only remarked: "You're distraught. The jewelry belonged to your mom. It was very special to you. That's perfectly normal, Kate." He paused. "Maybe it's too much for you to go to Mexico right now. What do you think?"

"Oh, no! I've *got* to get away! I can't wait."

Her enthusiasm to leave him behind was wounding. He must have winced because she was quick to add: "Of course, I don't mean I want to leave *you*, I meant only—"

"I understand," he said brusquely. He tugged on his mustache and looked away so she couldn't read his eyes. What was happening to him? When had it started? He was acting like a lovesick teenager. He had canceled two appointments to rush down here and be with her; he was seeing her outside the office, which he shouldn't be doing; and now he was sad to be saying good-bye. He was her *doctor*, for chrissakes! He was supposed to be helping her.

They talked. She told him about the burglary, how scared she was, and all he could think was: I wish I had been there to comfort you, I wish I could get your swordpin back.

She was looking to him for guidance, but he found he had little to say. She was going away. He was going to miss her. Already he felt numb.

It was time for her to go. He watched her leave while he paid for their coffees. She descended the stairs from the balcony, then emerged below. Immediately her nephew Ian came bounding toward her. She hugged him and he hugged her back, but then he dropped his toy truck. She bent down to retrieve it for him. When she pressed the truck back into his tiny, eager hands, was she smiling? Fielding couldn't tell. He wished she would turn around and look for him, see if he was still there, but she didn't. She didn't turn around, and he couldn't see her smile. He could see the little boy Ian's smile, though. A little boy with tousled blond curls. Cute as a button. If Fielding had a son like that, he would count himself the luckiest man in the world.

———

Slick stood behind her in line. The people ahead of her put their purses on the conveyor belt and stepped through the metal detector. You had to go through it to get to the gate.

Slick scowled. He'd spent all the appeal money his mother sent him from New Jersey. He'd gone to a place where they took him out back and they had everything—cameras, appliances, men's suits, passports, you name it. They'd even suggested he dye his hair blond. So now here he was. A blond dressed like El Touristo, in baggy pants and Hawaiian print shirt. So, sure, he didn't expect Kate Riley to recognize him. Still, shouldn't she have felt something? It was *him*, after all. She should know he was here.

God, it was so infuriating. He was so close to her, after all this time, and yet he couldn't touch her. He couldn't watch her eyes fill with fear.

She walked through the metal detector and started walking toward the gate.

Slick was impatient. He wanted to clear the metal detector, too. But, then, he saw the cop standing there. Why hadn't Slick noticed him before? The cop was searching the crowd. When he came to Slick, his eyes stopped. Jesus! Slick patted his forged passport for reassurance and ducked his head. When he glanced back, the cop was still checking him out, like he was saying to himself: That guy looks familiar.

Slick was so angry! He had come this far, and now this stupid cop stood in his way. But there was nothing he could do. He had to get out of here. He pretended he'd forgot something and stepped out of line. Even as he left, he could feel the cop's eyes on his back.

Outside in the humidity, Slick hailed a taxi. The driver asked, "Where to?" and Slick almost told *him* where to go. But then he tried to think. He couldn't follow her to Mexico, what was he going to do now? First, he needed some money. Then he needed to lay low for a few days. He would find a chick to shack up with. The woman had to be a certain way. It was good if she was single, better if she was divorced, and best of all if she was lonely.

And as to *her?* What would her punishment be for going to Mexico and leaving him behind? Well, he would just have to surprise her, wouldn't he? With a nice little gift: Welcome home.

"So, what'll it be?" the cabbie asked.

"Laurel racetrack," Slick said. "And make it snappy."

———

They were safely airborne. Kate gazed out her window at a heaven of blue sky and cottonball clouds. In the seats ahead of her, Molly and Dave were talking. Baby Lily was asleep. And Ian was sitting on Judith's lap.

Beside Kate sat her father, Dr. Riley. Just now, he perused his medical journal with perfect concentration. She considered telling him about the burglary but then decided not to. She didn't want to interrupt him. Maybe later. She studied him. It wasn't often she had a chance to be alone with him, without Blanche. Blanche was flying in from Mexico City. She would meet them at their hotel.

Dad had a clinical air about him. She often wondered if strangers could tell he was a doctor. She'd heard from people that he had a warm bedside manner. She found that incredible as well as wonderful. To her, growing up, he had been remote and cold, a busy man with more important things to do than be with her. She supposed he must have bounced her on his knee, read her bedtime stories, and listened to her prayers, but she had no recollection of any of this. Still, he was her father. Maybe one day he would be her friend. This trip could be a fresh start.

As the plane soared higher, Kate began to relax. She felt happy to leave Baltimore and the burglary and her fears of Slick Carlson behind. Here, sailing through the clouds at twenty-five thousand feet, she was free. She envisioned Cozumel: sandy beaches, palm trees, and a turquoise sea. That hot, buttery sun would feel so good. When her skin got too warm, she would go snorkeling. She imagined herself swimming toward the coral reefs when she drifted off to sleep. In her dream, Fielding glided through the water beside her, tanned, sleek in his red swim trunks and fins. They swam together, holding hands. They saw a clown fish and followed it. . . .

———

The night Kate's plane touched down in Mexico, Fielding reached out to touch his wife.

"Mmn?" Sue Ann murmured sleepily. She was curled up under the covers and shivering because the room was cold. She had the air-conditioning on high. She lay on her side, turned away from him, but now she rolled over on her back. "What is it?"

He sighed. There was a time when she wouldn't have asked that question, she would have known. There was a time before that when she would have reached for him.

"Honey, what?"

"Nothing." He climbed out of bed and nosed into his slippers. He wore only the slippers and a clean pair of running shorts. "You roll over. Get some sleep."

Downstairs he peered into the refrigerator. There was wine. He poured himself a glass. He shut the refrigerator door, hesitated, then went over to a kitchen drawer by the stove. He opened the drawer and rummaged through it. When he found what he was after, he closed his eyes a moment, as if in pain. He considered slamming the drawer shut, but he didn't. He grabbed the pack of cigarettes, got his wine, and plunged outdoors.

He sat on the porch swing at the side of the house. He had skipped his run today. Not in the mood. Now his back and legs felt stiff. He swung back and forth on the swing, sipped his wine, and reflected that the lawn needed watering. It hadn't rained in weeks. He really must remember to turn on the sprinkler tomorrow.

He continued to rock back and forth on the swing. On the red-checked blanket beside him, in a place where Sue Ann would have fit nicely, the pack of cigarettes lay in wait.

He thought back to the airport and Kate Riley. He wondered if he would have found her so attractive if last summer hadn't happened. He supposed she would have been equally attractive, but he wouldn't have noticed. That was the difference.

But who was he kidding?—it was more than an attraction. At odd moments he'd catch himself thinking of her. He would remember how the setting sun caught her red hair and set it on fire. Her bewitching blue eyes. Her laugh. At the airport he had yearned to stay and watch her plane take off, make sure she was safe, but he'd had to get back to his patients.

He studied the cigarettes beside him and began to perspire. He had been good for so long, but now the struggle didn't seem worth it. With trembling fingers, he tapped out a cigarette and lit up. He coughed at first, like a teenager. Then the cool menthol hit him, all at once, in an exhilarating rush. That was good. He had forgotten. He took another deep, luxurious drag and exhaled. The cigarette smoke hung thick in the heavy humidity, but this time he didn't even cough.

She would be back Sunday. She would come for her session, as usual, on Tuesday. So why did he find it unbearable, that she was gone?

He should take advantage of her absence. Tomorrow maybe, he

would call Gilberti, a brilliant psychiatrist and his mentor. Fielding had done his dissertation with him at Columbia. Gilberti would lecture him, sympathetically, about transference and countertransference. He would advise him to refer Kate Riley to another doctor.

But God, he couldn't give her up. Could he?

He sat on the porch swing and wondered if she liked it in Mexico. Was it muggy like Baltimore, or nice, with an ocean breeze? She was probably in bed by now, sleeping. Did she dream of him? No, of course not. He smoked his cigarette. Its tip glowed orangely, sentry against the dark, humid night.

It was very late when the two sisters rode up the elevator of the elegant Mayan Plaza Resort and Beach Hotel.

"Too bad for Dad," Molly said. "Her getting sick."

"I know. I wish he could stay at least one day."

There had been no Blanche to greet them at their hotel. Only a telegram, from Mexico City. Blanche wasn't terribly ill, but she had some kind of stomach virus. Tomorrow, first thing, Dad would fly on to be with her.

The sisters got off the elevator and traveled down the corridor toward their rooms. They reached the door to Kate's room first.

"Well," Kate sighed. She looked at Dave, further down the corridor. He put the hotel key in the lock and opened the door to his and Molly's room. Judith was with the children in the room adjacent. Molly and her husband would get to spend the night together, alone. Kate did not want to keep them. And yet it was hard for her to say good night.

Molly understood this. And did she understand Kate's feelings for Fielding too? Because she suddenly said: "Fielding looks like a nice man. I only caught a glimpse, mind you."

"He *is* nice. And kind. He's helped me a lot."

"I can see that. You seem happier."

Was she really happier? Yes, she was, despite reading her mom's diary and finding out about the affair. But that had turned out all right in the end; she had got to meet Anthony Reed. She would tell Molly about him some time, not just now.

"I should let you go," Kate said. "See you tomorrow."

"First thing," said Molly.

Once in her room, Kate walked outside onto the balcony. The moon was low. The breeze swirled her cotton skirt around her knees and caressed her face. What a view! She overlooked the white sandy beach and the emerald Caribbean sea. In the courtyard below, men in sombreros played mariachi music while couples swayed in the moonlight under the romance of palm trees. She felt a stab of loneliness. She had no Fielding to dance with.

But, no, she shouldn't think of him. He had a life all his own, a world where she did not belong. She imagined him doing family things, cooking frankfurters over a grill, lighting the Christmas tree, raking leaves, playing touch football with his brood of handsome, lean, loose-limbed kids. Making love to his wife . . .

She turned from the balcony and went back inside.

The sun was mild, the breeze gentle, and the day was perfect. They were at the beach, a delightful chaos of bold, bright towels, striped umbrellas, adults reclining in canvas lounges, and children chasing after waves, squealing, carrying buckets of water up from the sea, scooping up sand, losing their bathing trunks.

Under the shade of the umbrella, Judith read Dickens's *Bleak*

House while Dave and Lily slept. Ian played in the sand and Kate lay on her back in her aqua bathing suit, her sunglasses on, her eyes closed. Molly was glad to see her relax.

But Kate didn't relax for long. Soon Ian wanted an ice cream and Kate kindly volunteered to take him to the snack bar further up the beach. On their way back, Molly watched. Ian skipped along and licked his vanilla ice cream cone. Kate followed close behind, looking sleek and beautiful and even like a movie star in those sunglasses. Judith must have noticed Kate's beauty too because she suddenly said: "She's got everything, that girl."

Molly stared at her. It was so fleeting, just a fraction of a second, but she saw a look of passionate envy cross Judith's face. The look was there, then it was gone. And then Judith gave Molly a totally innocent and friendly smile and went back to her book. Molly began to doubt herself. Was she mistaken? She must be. Your eyes could play tricks on you in the sun.

———

The longer they were in Mexico, the better Kate felt. Every day she felt her strength returning. She felt refreshed and restored. Every morning she woke early to jog along the beach. She went down by the water and ran along the undulating shoreline where the sand was firm and cool and wet. She would look at the waves and the horizon and let her mind drift as her arms and legs swung rhythmically along. She thought about her life back in Baltimore and decided to make some changes. She would work fewer hours in the office and spend more time with her friends. She wanted to get back in touch. She was glad she felt this way. She knew it meant she had reached a new stage in her grief.

They spent afternoons in Cozumel as typical tourists, shopping and sightseeing. They went to the Aquarium to see the sea turtles, rented bicycles, and flew to Chichen Itza to visit the Mayan Ruins.

Evenings they retired each to their own room to rest before dinner.

Kate would write a few postcards, then shower and change into a cool summery dress. She would sit on the bed and buckle her sandals. And she would think: This is when I miss Fielding the most. When I'm doing the everyday things—showering, dressing, sitting on a bed. Because if we were married, we would share these things. In the morning, I would watch him shave and put on his running shorts. And, at night, he would watch me undress. . . .

But even this time of the day, when she missed him the most, was special to Kate. Everything was special this vacation. It felt so good to be away.

The days flew by, and now, too soon, it was Sunday morning and time to leave. Kate stood alone on her balcony and looked out over the ocean. Already she felt nostalgic. Already she missed this place. She would miss times like last night when Dave kept the kids and she and Molly and Judith made farewell toasts with their pineapple drinks at the bar. And she would miss times like yesterday afternoon with Ian. They were in the fresh-water pool. She was helping Ian practice his floating, but then he stopped to take a rest. That was when he suddenly giggled and splashed water in her face and asked: "Does Kate love Ian?" He had never used the word "love" before, not that she'd ever heard. She had laughed and said, "Yes, Kate loves Ian very much," and then splashed him back.

But they would not go swimming today. There wasn't even time for one last jog on the beach. She sighed and went back inside. She zippered her suitcase, picked it up, and headed for the door.

On the flight home, everyone was quiet. Even Ian, normally so active, fell asleep in Judith's lap. Kate looked out the window at nothing but clouds. As they drew closer to Baltimore, she missed Fielding more than ever. When she was in Mexico she could daydream, but the time for daydreams was over. She would never share that paradise with him, or any paradise. Back in Baltimore, it would be the same torture all over again. She would take her longing to bed with her, that and the knowledge he was married.

Peter Coe III strode briskly through the terminal toward Eastern Airlines Flight 202, arriving at Gate 10-K. Peter wore his best tailored suit, white linen by Giorgio Armani, with a pastel-blue silk tie. His blond hair was meticulously groomed and his cheeks had been splashed with cologne. In his hands, he held a dozen long-stemmed roses.

The roses were for Kate.

Peter realized now that the scuba equipment had been a dumb present. But roses. Roses were romantic.

These last days at work had been a torment without Kate. He missed her. But now he felt so happy, almost giddy. Her plane was landing any minute. He couldn't wait to see her!

———

Baltimore greeted them with gloomy skies and thundershowers. The plane taxied to a halt on the runway. There was a delay and then they were allowed to disembark. With a feeling of anticlimax, they headed down the jetways, but at the gate, they met with a surprise. Reuben was waiting.

"Welcome back!" he said. "How was Mexico?"

"Wonderful!" She smiled, but her smile vanished when she noticed his haggard face, the lines about his eyes: "What is it?"

"The wine bottle from your fridge. I took it to the lab."

"And?"

"They found fingerprints." He hesitated, then added: "They're Slick's."

Her heart thudded. Panic welled up inside her and for a moment she could not breathe. "But he was arrested!"

Reuben shook his head. "Kate, they got the wrong guy."

She could say nothing. She and the others looked at each other. And then the chill hit her. She felt so cold, she thought she would never be warm again. She raised her eyes to Reuben and said: "Hold me, will you please hold me?"

They were locked in an embrace when Peter Coe appeared, in his white linen suit, flourishing a dozen long-stemmed roses. "Buenos dias—" he began, and stopped.

He didn't acknowledge Molly and Dave and Judith and the kids. He only stared at her and Reuben. His face was ashen. But he didn't say anything. He abruptly turned and left the gate.

"Peter!" she called after him.

But he never came back. She watched him disappear into the crowd, and felt a stab of pity. The roses that were meant for her were lying on the carpet, their red velvet petals scattered, their green stems snapped.

They emerged from the airport luggage area into the oppressive mugginess. It had rained recently and would again soon.

"Well," Kate said to Dave and Molly. "I guess this is good-bye."

"Will you be all right?" Molly was anxious.

"She'll have around-the-clock protection," Reuben assured them. "I promise."

"But where will you take her?" Judith asked. "Surely not to her apartment." She turned to Kate and offered: "Why don't you come to my place? Slick would never expect you there."

"Oh, Judith," Kate said, "that's so kind of you. Reuben?"

"I think it's a good idea. Why don't I drive you home, Kate? You can pick up a few things, and we'll meet Judith there."

She and Reuben drove in silence as the thunder rolled and the skies opened. Rain drummed on the car's roof and fell in slanting sheets on the sidewalk and streets. Pedestrians put up their umbrellas and fought the sudden gusts of wind. Reuben turned on the radio for a weather report, but got a news bulletin: "Police have still failed to locate Hagerstown prison escapee, Clarence Wilbur Carlson. Information leading to the fugitive's whereabouts . . ."

"Sorry," Reuben said and switched the radio off.

By the time they reached her apartment building, the rain had stopped. Reuben parked the car but he did not cut the engine. She was surprised to find that he was trembling. "Before we go in, I . . . well, I just wanted to say . . . I missed you."

"I missed you too," she said, but not with the same intensity and depth of feeling, and he noticed.

"There's someone else, isn't there?"

She looked at him. She could not speak.

"I thought you said you and Peter—"

"No, not Peter."

"Who, then?"

She shook her head.

They sat side by side in the car, not talking, and then Reuben must have seen how close to tears she was because he said gently: "You really love him, huh? This other guy."

She didn't answer. She had been keeping this secret for so long, and now Reuben's kindness was almost too much to bear.

"Do I know him?"

She said, very quietly: "It's . . . Fielding."

"But, Jesus, Kate, he's married!"

"Yes," she said. "That's just it."

"Does he—"

"Oh, no! I'd never tell him. He'll never know . . ." Her voice quivered and then broke. She was so unhappy, she didn't know what to do. She cast Reuben an agonized glance.

"Aw, c'mere, kiddo." He leaned away from the steering wheel and let her bury her face in the sanctuary of his shoulder.

He comforted her, and for this she was grateful. She drew away from him and pressed his hand: "Thanks," she said, "for being my friend. I'm ready now. Let's get my things."

He was right behind her when she turned her key in the lock and swung open the door to her apartment. In shocked silence, she numbly set down her suitcase and surveyed the destruction.

24

P lants had been separated from their pots and then hurled against the wall. Her ficus tree was lying in the corner, in wounded repose, gnarled roots exposed, leaves crushed, branches broken. And next to the ficus tree was her picture of the Brontë sisters. The glass covering the poster lay in splinters and the poster itself had been slashed with a razor blade. Now Charlotte and her two sisters looked out at Kate with scarred, contorted faces, and Kate felt a wrench of anguish. She sank to her knees by the poster. She thought of the smashed photograph of her mom in the office, and now this. One by one, it seemed, her memories were being taken from her. Full of grief and despair, feeling outrage at Slick that he had done this to her, she began trembling all over. She raised her eyes in appeal to Reuben: "Help me. Please. I don't know what to do."

Reuben took care of her. He called the crime squad and waited with her until they came. While they were waiting, he fixed her a glass of iced tea and let her work up her courage before she faced the bedroom. There was something she had to see.

When she was ready, he led her into her room. It was a shambles. The overturned dresser drawers, scattered clothes, and slashed and torn wallpaper all bore mute testimony to Slick's fury and frustration. And yet, there was one spot that remained, curiously, untouched. Her bed was still neatly made, the white comforter smooth and unwrinkled. Everything was as it should be, save for her pillow. The pillow had been stabbed clear through by a sharp object that held a note in place. The note was handwritten, from Slick. It said: YOU'LL HEAR FROM ME SOON. MEANWHILE SLEEP TIGHT. DON'T LET THE BEDBUGS BITE.

Kate was terrified by the note, but even amid this tragedy there was some happiness to be found. The sharp object that held the note was slender and vertical. Its shaft was plunged deep into the down of the pillow, but its gold hilt and the diamond embedded there sparkled in the room's dim light. It was her mother's swordpin.

25

It was Sunday evening. Fielding knew he shouldn't go, but he went just the same. How many times had he made this trip, last summer? He didn't know. So many, he had lost track.

The air was sticky and humid. The rain had abated, but the skies still threatened. Fielding stepped around puddles to get to his car. He tossed his suit jacket onto the backseat, fired up the engine, and headed south. Sue Ann didn't know anything about this.

His car hummed along the highway and his thoughts went to Kate. She was coming home today, she would be safely settled back into her apartment by now. She had probably had a wonderful trip. Had she missed him at all?

He had missed her terribly. Now that she was back, he missed her still.

He never did call Gilberti about her. He had been putting it off.

He had also been smoking. That night on the porch, that one cigarette, and now he was hooked again. He was fighting it, though. Just now, as he parked his car and strode toward the doors of Community General, he carried a pipe in his hand for moral support. In his pocket, he had a pack of cigarettes for later tonight when his willpower would weaken and he would give in. Between the pipe and the cigarettes, he felt like a walking tobacconist.

He swung through the doors of Community General and walked to the elevators. The hospital hadn't changed one bit. He noted the same salmon-pink corridors, the same arrows on the floor directing people this way, that way.

He and Sue Ann had made love last night. "Made love," he supposed you could call it that. More like two lonely souls groping in the dark. He had finished too soon and Sue Ann not at all. Afterward they had rolled over to their separate sides of the bed, not touching, each pretending the escape of sleep.

He rode the elevator to the fourth floor where he was momentarily confused. Still not certain which way to go, he headed for the north wing. Was this right? He opened a heavy door, strode into the room, and stopped. Next to a bed with a respirator hookup, in a chair, a mother was hugging her frail, sick daughter. He knew they were mother and daughter because they looked so much alike. The mother was in her fifties probably, the daughter was . . . in her teens? in her twenties? It was hard to tell. A nurse stood beside them. The mother stroked the daughter's lank sandy hair while the daughter's chest heaved with the effort of breathing. The girl wore a glazed expression, she could have been retarded. Fielding wondered if she knew where she was. But the mother. She was like a madonna, he thought. What love shone on her face, and what agony. "Sorry," he said. "Wrong room."

It took him two more tries to find the right place. This disconcerted him. He should know the way. But perhaps he was getting lost on purpose, delaying the inevitable?

Finally, he found the nursery. He stepped up to the glass window and peered inside. Look at the tiny faces, little clenched fists, bodies bundled in soft blankets, heads warmed by blue and pink knitted caps. From inside, the nurse on duty approached the opposite side of the glass. The room was soundproofed so she mouthed the words, "Which one?" She thought he was a father. She was going to show him his baby. He smiled at her sadly, shook his head.

He didn't break down until he got to his office and made the call to his old mentor. As soon as he heard Gilberti's gruff voice: "Hello, Fielding! What's cooking?" his throat went dry, his eyes stung, and he began to sob.

"It's all right, boyo," Gilberti said. "Let it out."

M ost people saved up their emotions, like gold coins, and spent them on the week-ends with their lovers and their husbands. But Kate would save hers up for Tuesday, when she would see Fielding. She was thinking this as she stood alone at Judith's living-room window and watched the night fall. She was trying not to think of her ransacked apartment or the fact that Slick was out there, somewhere, waiting. She forced herself to think ahead and plan. Tomorrow she would go to work. Tuesday she would see Fielding. And Wednesday. Well, Wednesday was her birthday.

Looking out at the brick building across the way and at the lonely sky above, she thought of Reuben. It made her sad to know that Reuben loved her while she loved Fielding who loved somebody else, his wife. In life, could you ever love someone and have them love you back?

Well, she loved Molly and Ian and baby Lily. Her mom, she had loved her too. And they loved her back, so the answer was yes. But romantic relationships were more difficult, she supposed. A different kind of love, more intense, and both people had to feel it or you had nothing at all.

Fielding's eyes, Kate recalled, were brown as cinnamon. They were eyes you could tell anything to. On Tuesday she could tell him about coming home to her vandalized apartment, how that felt, and how the worst part of all was finding the poster of the Brontë sisters, their faces razored to ribbons. What would her mom have done if she'd seen Charlotte's face? She would have cried.

Outside the window, the gray sky grew grayer. Night was coming on quickly now. These last few moments of light would soon be gone and then there would be only darkness. Judith was out grocery shopping. Kate wished she would come back. Of course, Woodie was here. He was downstairs in the lobby, settling in for the night. He would protect her, should anything happen. Reuben, though, wasn't with him. He was following up a lead. He knew that Slick was into gambling, and there was that felony murder down by the Laurel racetrack.

Murder. Well, she wouldn't think about that.

She would keep her mind on Woodie, downstairs. Detective Theodore Woods was only five-feet-seven, bespectacled, with thinning wisps of blond hair. He looked more like an accountant than a detective, but he was a good cop. Next to Reuben, Woodie was the best marksman in the precinct. Earlier tonight, she had fixed him a thermos of coffee in Judith's kitchen. She'd asked him: "What do I do now?"

"You go about your business."

"I go to work tomorrow?"

"Yes."

"And socially?"

"That, too."

She headed for the kitchen now. Judith's air conditioner was laboring fitfully against the humidity. Kate was thirsty. She opened the refrigerator and got out the pitcher of iced tea. As she walked toward the kitchen table, she bumped into an object on the floor. She looked down and saw, with surprise, a brand-new leather briefcase. Not only that, but the briefcase had her initials, KLR, inscribed on it. Another birthday present? This was too much. Judith had already bought her the perfume.

Kate didn't know what to do. For now, she shoved the briefcase further back into the corner. When Judith returned, should she confront her about this or let it go? It was clear Judith was taking her birthday too seriously. She didn't have the money to spend on gifts like a briefcase. Kate would have to talk to her about that. Kate returned to the living room and her post by the window. Now it was total darkness outside. And the apartment, though she had not noticed it, was shrouded in shadow too. As dusk ebbed into night and the blackness became absolute, her surroundings became faintly sinister. The upholstered sofa had an ominous hooded presence; the bookcase and chairs became creatures with malevolent intent. Alone in the gloomy, haunted room, Kate suddenly shivered. Still, she did not turn on the lights. If Slick was outside looking in, and she stayed in the dark, he could not see her.

Kate found she couldn't stop shivering. She hugged herself with her arms and thought: I don't like it here, I wish I were home.

She was so frightened, she resolved to turn on the lights, after all, when she heard, from down the hall, a scuffling sound. She tensed. She did not move for some seconds. She prayed the sound would go away, but, after a brief silence, there it was again: more scuffling. What should she do? Call downstairs to Woodie? But suppose it was a false alarm? She crept soundlessly across the room. She had decided to get Woodie and was heading for the front door when she heard the sound again, much louder. In her fright, she grabbed the nearest object, a broom, as a weapon. And now the sound stopped. She knew she should run for the door, escape, but the sudden silence made her curious. Clutching the broom, she stole down the hallway. The sound, she felt sure, had come from the room to the right, the room Judith had forbidden her to enter.

Heart pounding, Kate stepped up to the door. She held the broom poised, then with her other hand slowly, ever so quietly, turned the doorknob. The door creaked open, and then, for one horrible instant her heart stopped, as, out of the darkness, Mr. Rochester sprang at her, hissing, his claws bared. And then, before she could even catch her breath, Judith was by her side, her arms laden with groceries, fixing her with a hostile, accusing stare.

"The cat," Kate said. "He was—"

"You have no business in that room! Did you look inside?"

"No. I—"

"Good," Judith said. She slammed the door shut before Kate could see into the darkened room. Then Judith said sweetly, as if nothing had happened, nothing at all: "Now, then, what shall I fix us for supper?"

———

It was early Monday morning. Kate walked to work with Woodie by her side. Despite the detective's presence, she darted anxious glances around her. She was suspicious of every pedestrian who brushed against her, of every car that innocently drove past. At one point she felt sure there *was* a car tailing them, but she didn't say anything. She had the oddest feeling that whoever was in that car was after her, but it wasn't Slick. Was she paranoid?

She remembered that time in Stoneleigh, that stranger watching her as she visited her old house. And that time in Homeland when someone chased her down those back alleys in the car. And that afternoon with Ian when she had felt a malevolent presence and looked up and there was that car across the street. It wasn't Slick in that car. He had only just escaped that morning; he hadn't reached Baltimore yet. So who was it? Somebody else hated her too. . . .

Feeling more frightened than ever, Kate stayed close to Woodie as they made their way through the city. They reached the courthouse

171

steps in safety, but there they were ambushed by reporters. Kate clutched Woodie's arm in desperation while he forged them a path through the crowd.

Slick was furious. He had a knife, he was all ready to rush the bodyguard when the flock of reporters came swooping down the courthouse steps. Damn the press! He couldn't get to her now.

Pocketing the knife, he cast angrily about him. He was suddenly so hungry he couldn't think. He searched the street for a place to eat and decided on the sub shop.

He stood in line and ordered his submarine, a special. Then he sat down. He took out his knife and used it to slice up the bread. He couldn't stop thinking about *her*. Wouldn't he just love to press the knife up against her flesh and feel it pulse against her neck. She would want to scream, but with the knife there, she couldn't. Well, soon, soon . . . first, he would have to come up with a new plan.

He gnawed on his salami and cheese hero. The window next to him was greasy with palm prints. Behind him, two juveniles were losing quarters to the pinball machine. The pinball machine was ringing every two seconds and it was noisy on the street too, some kind of construction, which irritated Slick. But then his glance fell on a copy of today's newspaper. The headline read: PRISON ESCAPEE STALKS FEMALE PROSECUTOR.

He read the article from start to finish. Pleased with himself and with all the attention he was getting, he was snickering, until he came to the part about Rees: "Rees Samuelson, who has been so cooperative with authorities in the statewide manhunt for his former cellmate, was released yesterday. In exchange for his testimony, the governor commuted his sentence and granted him an immediate pardon."

Rees pardoned! Slick spit out his mouthful of salami and cheese. Rees might have been pardoned, but he would still be mad at Slick for escaping without him. Rees should *thank* Slick, but he was so crazy and stupid, he wouldn't see it that way. He would only remember Slick leaving him behind. He would come after him. He was probably already on his way.

Slick shoved his sandwich aside, got up from the table and hurried out.

The streets were steaming in the humidity, and the hammering from that construction site was nerve-racking. Slick was more irritable than ever.

Up until now, he'd been sitting pretty. The racetrack had worked out just fine. He'd got plenty of money off that old man, and he had a sweet setup with that hairdresser Trish. But now, with Rees in the picture, things were different. Slick couldn't afford to wait anymore. He had to act.

He headed down the street, frowning in concentration. He seemed unaware of his surroundings, he was so preoccupied. But when he came to the construction site, he stopped.

He gripped the chain-link fence overlooking the excavation. They were constructing a new Public Safety Building, the sign said. That meant more holding cells for guys like him. He winced. The only joints he liked were the ones you smoked.

He watched the men and their machines. The metal clam bucket scooped up fill while the dump trucks stood by, and all the time, the pile hammer smashed the tall steel girders into place. *Bam! Bam! Bam!* Slick covered his ears. He couldn't stand the noise. It reminded him of that time he was between casino jobs. He had worked a six-month stint as a batch man, delivering cement, and he never got used to the noise, not even then.

He hung around the site until a big guy in a T-shirt and green hard hat walked by. "Howdy," Slick said.

The big guy ambled over.

Slick smiled. "I see you got most of your forms up."

"Yup. We're gonna start pouring concrete first thing tomorrow."

"Tomorrow, huh? No kidding," Slick said.

27

Monday morning, close to noon, Fielding sat in his office, feet on the desk, smoking a cigarette. He had a ten-minute break before his next patient. For these next ten minutes he could be alone.

He gazed out the window. It had rained all day yesterday and was supposed to rain again today. The leaves on the trees were wet, the lawns were lush and green. Rain meant fertility, didn't it? He thought of Sue Ann. It may have been raining out, but they didn't make love anymore. Didn't *really* make love. The last time, two lonely souls groping in the dark, didn't count.

He swiveled in his chair and regarded the paintings on his walls. Lately his Pat Buckley Moss prints depressed him. Too much celebration of family, too much happiness.

He stabbed out his cigarette, got up, and went over to *Skating Joy*. He studied the picture for a long moment. In the foreground, a man and woman glided on the pond together, blue scarves flying, eyes sparkling. Behind them were their children, the little pink-cheeked girl sprawled out on the ice, the little boy bent over her, asking: Are you all right?

At least that's what Fielding imagined him asking her.

If Fielding had a little boy, he would buy him ice skates. He would take him out on Sundays to the park and watch him race beneath the trees as fast as the wind.

Fielding sighed, reached up, and eased the large painting off its hinges. He rotated the frame and lowered it to the carpet. Now the skaters faced the wall. He wouldn't have to look at the little boy, the little girl, or the man and woman anymore.

He went back to his desk and sat down. He reached for another cigarette and lit up. Of course he was worried about Kate. He'd read about her in the papers. He hoped they would catch Slick, he had put in a phone call to Reuben to see if he could help. From his Special Forces work, he had some experience in these kinds of cases, and he would do anything for her. He didn't allow himself to wonder whether she would come tomorrow for her six o'clock session. He assumed she would. He had to believe he would see her again, and soon, or he could not make it through the day.

The phone jangled, startling him. He collected himself, then lifted the receiver: "Hello. Todd Fielding."

"Hey, buddy, it's Reuben."

"I'm glad you called. How is she?"

"She's tough. She's a fighter."

"Any leads?"

"I'm working on it, I think I got something. And, hey, I got your message. Thanks for the offer. I'll let you know if we can use you. But, listen . . ." Reuben paused. "That's not why I called."

"No?"

"I have something to tell you. You're her psychiatrist, so I thought you should know."

"Know what?"

"I mean, I think it affects her therapy."

"Okay." Fielding was patient, waiting.

Reuben sighed. "She's in love with you, man. She told me. Tell you the truth, I'm half in love with her myself."

"I see . . ." Fielding couldn't think straight, his head was spinning.

"Maybe you should talk to her."

"I'll do that," Fielding said.

After they hung up, he sat perfectly still in his chair. He felt so fragile, he was afraid to move. Would his world come crashing down on him? But finally he shifted slightly and reached for his pipe on the desk. And now he was joyfully incredulous. His beloved office remained the same—his coffee pot, his books, his paintings—and yet he felt different. For the first time in weeks, he had hope. If she loved him, if she really loved him . . .

―――――

Kate didn't know what to do. She was surrounded by people when it was solitude she craved. The office was humid, the air conditioners weren't working, and there was a loud hammering from the construction site across the street. She almost immediately had a headache, plus she kept thinking about those reporters who'd rushed her on the courthouse steps. She was so frightened! Even with Woodie by her side, she had been frantic to search each of their faces, praying she would not find Slick among them, armed not with a camera but a gun. And now, in the office, she hardly got a chance to sit down. Everyone wanted to know about Slick. She tried to be friendly and polite and answer all their questions, but she was feeling rather desperate by the time Fielding's phone call came. As soon as she heard his voice, her heart found the sanctuary it needed.

"Hello, Kate."

"Oh," she said, "hi." She swallowed around the lump in her throat. She hung on to the receiver. She could scarcely breathe.

"Tell me, how are you?"

I feel sick, I'm so in love with you, she thought. I can't sleep at night, not just because of Slick but because of you. But she couldn't tell Fielding this. He was married. He had his own life. "I'm . . . fine," she said. "Considering."

"Listen," he said, "Reuben called."

"He did?"

"Yes. Kate, we need to talk."

There was an endless silence between them. She was wondering how much Reuben had told him, how much he knew.

"Kate?"

"Yes, I'm still here."

"Can you make it until our session tomorrow at six?"

"Yes," she said, "I can."

"Good. Tomorrow, then." His voice cracked, became gravelly: "You . . . take care of yourself."

"I will," she said lightly, thinking: Was it possible? *Had* his voice cracked? No, she must have imagined it.

She replaced the receiver slowly. Her mind was still on Fielding when Judith approached her desk and said: "I bet you haven't had time to think of yourself. Here, I brought you a donut and coffee."

"Oh, thanks, you're so sweet." Kate had been thinking she had no one in the office who really cared, but that wasn't true. The one person in all this craziness who treated her like a human being was Judith. And if the ex-Mrs. Shepherd, living alone, robbed of her former identity and perhaps some of her old married friends, had grown solitary in her habits, even secretive, Kate could forgive her that. Judith was her friend.

Just now, Judith was studying her with concern. "Holding up okay?"

"Oh, I'm trying." She smiled bravely. "Not succeeding very well."

Judith hesitated, then said: "It's hot, it's noisy, everyone's coming up to you every five seconds. . . . Why not take the day off? You're always welcome at my place."

"Oh, thanks," Kate said, but she did not want to stay at Judith's again tonight. If she went anywhere, it would be home. "I guess I'll have to face my apartment sometime. Maybe the sooner the better, huh?"

"Are you ready emotionally? It will be a shock."

"Yes, I think I am."

"Then, please, let me help you," Judith offered.

Kate looked at her. She felt more grateful than she could say.

She began packing up her things and that was when she noticed the photograph of her mom. It was where she had left it, in the drawer. She remembered the Buckner trial and finding the smashed photograph under her desk, pricking her finger on the shards of glass; the trickle of blood; and all those tears she'd kept inside.

If she hadn't been convinced before that she needed to go home, she was now. She couldn't do any work here. Not after seeing the photograph. She stood up to leave and, just then, Peter Coe arrived. She had not seen Peter since the airport, and she felt certain he would still be angry with her, yet, surprisingly, he wasn't. "Kate, good morning." He strode right over to her and gave her a big smile. "Can you step into my office, please?"

She followed him in and sat down.

He looked as handsome as always in his navy suit and maroon silk tie, and as always, he failed to move her.

"Kate, I'm so sorry. I acted like a jerk. You have the right to see Reuben or anybody else . . ."

She nodded. He *was* a better man than she'd thought.

He went on: "Right now, that is, you have the right to see Reuben. In the future, I hope things will be different."

"Oh? Why?"

"Marry me, Kate. Be my wife."

His words would not penetrate. She said nothing. She simply stared.

"Am I too blunt? Should I be more romantic? It's just that I have no words. But here . . ." He reached into his coat pocket. With trembling hands, he produced a small object and slid it across the desk to her. It was a jeweler's box. "Open it."

She sat mute in the desk chair, unable to respond.

He thought he had simply overwhelmed her, that she needed more time. He came around his desk, pressed the tiny box into her hands, gently opened it for her to see. The diamond ring sparkled against the blue velour, but there were more lights in his adoring eyes as he said: "I know your birthday's not until Wednesday. But I can't wait. Besides," he chuckled, "there's Reuben and who knows who else, and I'm afraid I might lose you. Kate, will you marry me?"

"Oh, Peter . . ." She bowed her head. She knew too well the pain she was about to inflict and she wished she could spare him. Finally she raised her eyes: "You'll make somebody very happy one day. I'm just sorry it can't be me."

He stared at her in disbelief, then turned away. Not soon enough, though. She had already seen the stinging tears in his eyes. Was he hurt or simply angry? She couldn't tell. "Get out!" he said sharply. "Just get out!"

She shut the jeweler's box, smiled sadly at his proud back, and left.

I n the morgue, Reuben looked at the body of Harry Weber. A good man, from what Reuben had been able to ascertain in the last few hours. A widower, he had always fondly mourned his dear Bessie and never remarried. He adored his daughter and took great pleasure in baby-sitting his grandchildren. He liked fishing, poker, salted peanuts, and beer. He died at sixty-two. He wasn't young, sure, but he kept fit. He could have lived longer.

Weber had suffered a heart attack in the front seat of his Dodge. Bruises and scratches about his head indicated a struggle of some sort, and he had been robbed. The healthy Harry Weber had, in a way, died of fright. Perhaps he had lost his faith in humanity. Now he was a thin, reedy body laid out in a drawer, his toe ticketed to identify him.

"Thanks, that'll be all," Reuben told the coroner.

Minutes later, he walked out of the building into the humidity. He could find no fresh air.

The man who'd caused Harry Weber's death was Slick Carlson, Reuben was certain, though he couldn't prove it. Not yet.

He went back to Laurel racetrack with Slick's photograph in his pocket.

The racetrack wasn't busy today. It was unbearably muggy and the skies were an ominous gray, threatening thundershowers.

Reuben showed the photograph, but at first, he got nowhere. No one recognized Slick. No one, until the janitor and the fat lady who sold jumbo hot dogs. The janitor recognized the face, but that was all. The fat lady remembered more. She said she saw Slick talking with an old man. The old man she described sounded like Harry Weber.

Reuben was grateful to the lady for remembering, but what she remembered wasn't very helpful. He needed leads on Slick's current whereabouts. So far he had none. Reuben sighed. He was no quitter, but he began to despair. He was hot, sweaty, and tired. His feet were throbbing. If he had to go up to one more person, produce the photo of Slick, and say: "You ever see this guy before?" he thought he would scream. But he pushed himself. He went to one more person and one more person after that. Then he came to Earl, the black bartender.

"Sure thing, I know him," Earl said when he saw the photograph.

"You do?"

"Yeah, he had himself a lady. Puttin' on the ritz for her, so he slipped me a tip."

Reuben felt a surge of excitement. A lady friend. That was Slick's M.O. When he wanted to lie low, he would pick up some lonely lady and go home with her. "His lady friend. Seen her before?"

"Not that I recall."

Reuben leaned close to the bartender. "He gave you a tip. What else?"

"Let's see," Earl said, thinking hard. "He was bragging. He said

181

he won big on Count-My-Love and then . . . oh, he called her Mama. That doesn't help much, does it?"

"Not much," Reuben said, disappointed.

"Yeah. He said, 'Trish, you just like my mama.' "

"Trish? You sure?"

"Yeah."

Reuben suddenly grinned.

He took a break, then, and bought himself a soda to celebrate. While he was drinking the cool liquid, he thought about Kate. He wouldn't have been good for her, not in the long run. He loved women, but he always left them. Relationships with him were a night, scrambled eggs in the morning, and that was it. He was sorry he hurt the women he loved, but that's partly what made him a good cop. He carried around all this guilt. And the one thing that made him feel better was to nail guys like Slick. It made him a good guy, at least for a while.

―――

The apartment was worse than she remembered. Woodie and Judith had to steady her when they came in the door. She felt the same shock and outrage all over again. How could Slick do this to her?

It wasn't just that he had slashed her curtains and toppled her plants and overturned her furniture. And it wasn't even that he had slashed her Brontë poster with a razor blade. She was prepared to face that. Today what she wasn't prepared to face was the *mess*. Her kitchen was almost unrecognizable. He'd thrown eggs against the cabinets where they had splattered and dried. He'd emptied her copper canisters of coffee and flour, and now a fine white powder lay over her countertops, and coffee grounds crunched underfoot as she stepped into the kitchen. Worst of all, he'd raided her refrigerator and poured the contents of half-gallon cartons on the floor and carpet, and now the rancid odor of sour milk and orange juice made her gag.

She was trembling as they surveyed the wreckage. Then, when the first awful moments passed and she could find her voice again, she said, with a rueful smile: "Well, I didn't have anything to do this afternoon anyway."

"Me neither," Judith said, patting her shoulder. "We'll help you, dear."

And so Kate changed into a pair of old khakis and a T-shirt and tied her lustrous hair back in a ribbon, and the three of them set to work. They borrowed a heavy-duty vacuum cleaner from the building superintendent, also rug shampoo, brooms, and sponge mops. They righted the furniture and took down the torn drapes. All the while, Kate kept a running list of new items she would need.

Judith and Woodie concentrated on the living room while she tackled the kitchen. She got down on her hands and knees and scrubbed the milk and orange juice from the carpet and tiles. She felt dizzy from the ammonia and her eyes were stinging red, but she persisted until she finished the job.

Two hours later, the kitchen was in good shape, but she was exhausted. Judith said: "You look pale, why don't you take a break?" And so while Judith, a tireless worker, continued with the vaccuming, Kate retreated to her bedroom for a shower and a change of clothes. Before she could even shower, though, she had to fish clothes from her toilet and bathtub where Slick had thrown them all in a heap. That she couldn't even take a shower without picking up after him upset her the most. Her rigid self-control cracked, and all the feelings she had suppressed welled up inside her. In the privacy of the shower, the sound of her grief muffled by the spray, she cried in harsh, wrenching sobs.

After her cry, she felt better. She let the warm spray soothe her aching shoulders and back, then she toweled off and dressed. She was on her way to see how Judith was doing when the phone rang. She let Woodie answer it, as she had been instructed, but it wasn't Slick: It was Molly.

"Kate, how are you? I've been worried sick. They told me at the office you went home."

"Yes, well, I wasn't doing any good there. I couldn't concentrate."

"But your apartment, Kate? Do you think it's safe?

"Safe as anyplace else. Besides, Woodie's here. And Judith. She's helping me clean up. You know, for all her quirks, she's a loyal friend. She really is. She's the only one in the office I can trust."

"What do you mean?"

"It's not just Slick, Moll. Remember what I told you in Mexico, how someone is trying to undermine my career? When I went back to the office this morning, there was that photograph of Mom staring me in the face. I have to buy new glass for the frame. It's all broken. . . . I guess when we were on vacation, I could forget, but now that I'm back, seeing that picture, I'm reminded that someone else doesn't like me."

"But who?" Molly asked. "The same person who tampered with those pleadings?"

"I don't know."

"Someone jealous of your success?"

"Maybe," Kate said.

"Is there anyone you know who *is* jealous?"

"No, not really," Kate said. But she was thinking of Peter Coe. It suddenly struck her, what *was* his motive in wanting to marry her? She assumed he loved her, but maybe he was only trying to eliminate his competition. Realizing she must be upsetting Molly, Kate tried to reassure her sister: "Please, Moll, don't worry about me. Judith's being a peach. And Woodie, too. I'm fine, really." She tried to sound hopeful and not depressed.

But Molly knew her too well. She said: "Sounds like you need some cheering up, and I have just the trick."

"What?"

"Dad called. He offered to take you and me out to dinner, just us girls. He's worried about you too, you know."

"He is?"

"Yes."

Molly had to go, Ian needed her, so the sisters said a hurried good-bye and hung up. The happiness Kate had felt at Molly's invitation quickly disappeared. Woodie and Judith were in the next room, but even so, she felt alone and vulnerable and afraid. She decided to join the others, fix them both a well-earned sandwich, but suddenly she was so tired, she thought she would lie down for a minute. She kicked off her sneakers, flopped back in bed, and gazed up at the ceiling. She was looking forward to dinner tonight: That was her one bright hope. That, and the promise, tomorrow, of Fielding.

She blamed Slick for her depression, but it wasn't only Slick, was it? She'd told Fielding she was marking time, and that was weeks ago. She had been talking about her mom. When Mom died, that's when the feeling began, of not going forward with her life. But why hadn't she? What was stopping her?

She didn't know. She had no answers, only questions. Then she yawned; she felt herself slipping away, but she was powerless to resist, and so she slept.

She had the dream.

It was the same dream, as always, only this time she did not wake up before the end but kept on dreaming. She ran, stumbling, up the cliff. Chasing after her, panting heavily, was the stranger. When she came to the edge of the cliff, she trembled. She was petrified. Should she leap to her death or confront her pursuer? She felt cold skeletal fingers grip her shoulder and nudge her toward the rocks and the thundering surf below. Frantic, she resisted, but the stranger was too strong! She began to lose her footing and slide off the cliff, but then, no, she wouldn't let this happen, she summoned all her strength and thrust him away: "Stop!" she cried. "I don't want to die! It's not fair!" Shouting this, she stared at the stranger. And now the stranger suddenly became less horrible and more human. He stood and watched her, and then he sat down and put his face in his hands and began to weep. When he looked back up at her, his blank face, for the first time in all her dreams, came to life. Awestruck, filled with wonder, Kate saw before her the chameleon flickerings of people she knew until the face settled into repose and became, finally, itself.

The face in the dream she had fled for so long was her own.

When she woke up, the dream remained with her. She lay still in bed for a long moment, absorbing her new knowledge, flexing her feelings. And how *did* she feel? She felt okay. More than okay. She felt restored. She had found, in some deep core within her, in the rhythmic beating of her heart, peace.

When Reuben called an hour later, she sensed he would have good news and he did: "Listen, I've got a name. Trish. A woman he met at the track. I'm working on a last name right now."

"Terrific," she said.

"So how are things? You sound up."

"I am, I guess."

"You going out tonight? Tell me your plans."

"My plans?" She laughed. "I'm getting on with my life. First, I'm visiting a dear old friend and then I'm meeting Moll and my dad for dinner."

"Okay, but take Woodie with you."

She laughed again. She felt such a sense of well-being, not even the threat of Slick could darken her bright mood. She thanked Reuben for all his help, then they hung up. She went immediately to her dresser, and her jewelry box. She opened the second compartment and took out her mother's gold swordpin. She studied the swordpin a long moment. Now that Slick had returned it, she had been given a second chance. She would wear it tonight.

29

The dear old friend Kate went to visit was Anthony Reed.

She had hoped to find him in the pool. Instead, she found him in bed, or on a sofa, actually, propped up by pillows and with a blanket tucked over his legs.

The sofa was upstairs in a luxuriously appointed bedroom with oak floors, Persian rugs, exquisite antiques, and Impressionist paintings. Kate recognized a Renoir—a picture of women in white dresses, bathed in sunlight, parasols flung over their shoulders, traipsing off to a picnic.

The sofa faced floor-to-ceiling windows beneath a vaulted cathedral ceiling. The windows overlooked a lush green expanse of lawn and pine woods. You could not see the swimming pool from here. You could, though, see the clay tennis court where Anthony's wife Jesse, in whites, battled Borges, the male nurse.

Anthony did not see Kate enter the room or pause to marvel at the view. His eyes were closed. He was listening to music floating out from hidden stereo speakers. Kate instantly recognized Rachmaninoff's third piano concerto, one of her very favorites.

Dressed in a blue velvet smoking jacket that hung loosely on him, Anthony appeared thin and haggard. His face was wan and narrow, his hooked nose pronounced. Even his goatee failed to hide the hollows in his cheeks. His proud mane of hair remained, but the silver in it had lost its luster and had dimmed to gray.

Next to the sofa was the wheelchair. She stepped around it to get to Anthony, reached for his hand and gently pressed it. His eyes fluttered open. They were filled with pain. It took him an instant to recognize her, but when he did, he smiled. She leaned over and kissed him on the cheek. "No swimming today?"

"Oh, these doctors. They say the pool needs a rest, so who am I to argue?"

She smiled briefly and took the chair by the sofa. "How are you, Anthony? Really?"

"Well enough to perk up when a pretty girl comes into the room."

Now she grinned. "I'm glad to see you too."

"I've been worried about you, Kate."

"Me?"

"Yes, my doctors are strict, but they *do* let me watch the news."

"I see." She had decided not to tell him about Slick, but he obviously knew. The three local TV stations had aired segments on her.

"The man accompanying you, who's waiting downstairs?"

"That's Woodie. My . . . bodyguard."

Anthony stroked his goatee. "Listen, I've an idea. Why don't you stay here until they catch this fellow—Carlson, is it? We'll keep the estate under lock and key. I've got the manpower for it."

"Oh, thanks, but no. I couldn't do that. I would feel worse putting you in danger. Can you understand that?"

"Yes, I can. All right, I promise not to mention it again, but the offer stays open."

Kate studied Anthony and thought of her mom. She got up, then, and crossed to the window. The peace she'd felt after her dream was still there, but it was muted now, transposed to a minor key. She gazed out at the lush green grass and rich green pines and watched the moody storm clouds conquer the sky. Rachmaninoff played in the background, the adagio passage, poignant and lingering. Tears appeared in her eyes.

"What are you thinking about?" Anthony asked. "Death?"

"No." She kept staring out the window because she couldn't look at him. "It's Rachmaninoff. Rachmaninoff always makes me sad."

"Your mother was no great liar either."

"All right." She turned, at last, to face him. "I was thinking I'll miss you."

"I'll miss you too. But I'm not going anywhere yet. Jesse's fixing her veal cordon bleu tonight so I plan to stick around, at least through dinner and dessert. Chocolate mousse. Will you stay?"

"I'd love to, but I have plans. Another time?"

"Yes. Good." Anthony winced as he tried to raise himself higher against his pillows. His arms had so little strength, they were shaking like a gymnast's would during a long routine on the parallel bars. He inched himself up, little by little, and at last he collapsed back against the pillows, a bit more comfortable than before. "Before you left last time, I told you I had something to show you, remember? About Lily."

"Yes. I've been wondering—"

"Got your curiosity up, did it?" He chuckled. The chuckling released the phlegm in his lungs and he doubled over in a coughing fit. Finally, he caught his breath and proceeded as if nothing had happened: "Well, now, what I want you to do . . . reach into that dresser drawer there—yes, that's the one—and bring me the manilla folder you'll find. Thank you." He flipped through the file she had fetched and pulled out a yellowed clipping from the *Baltimore Sun*. "Here. Read this."

She pored over the article.

The room was silent save for Rachmaninoff.

When she finished, she turned to him, perplexed: "This has to do with my mom?"

"Yes."

"Am I missing something?"

"Tell me what you know."

"According to this article, dated twelve years ago, there was a car accident. A girl named Sandy, an honors student, eighteen years old, was driving to St. Paul's Church one night when a drunk plowed into her. A Mr. Rubetti, with a point twenty-five blood alcohol."

"Go on."

"The girl suffered severe spinal and head injuries, and there was massive hemorrhaging. I still don't see—"

"What else?" Anthony was patient.

"Let's see, Governor Mandell, then governor of Maryland, got wind of the accident. He jumped on the bandwagon and urged stricter drunk driving laws, stiffer penalties."

"Right." Anthony nodded, satisfied. "That's what you know. Now let me tell you what you don't know."

"Please."

"There's an irony at work here: Sandy herself was an alcoholic."

"You mean, the girl who got totaled by a drunk driver was drinking herself?"

"No. At the time of the accident, she'd been sober three weeks."

"She'd been going to the Program?"

"Yes. That's where your mom met her. They became friends. In fact, Lily was her sponsor."

"But she was so young to have a drinking problem!"

"Kate, you should know age has very little to do with it. The girl was a heavy drinker. She'd even had blackouts."

190

"But it says here she was an honors student."

"She was very bright. Her grades, though, were starting to slip."

Kate nodded. "But what about my mom? What does all this have to do with her?"

"On the night of the accident, you see, Lily planned to pick Sandy up at her house. But at the last minute, this was a Friday night, Lily got a call from Herb Feldman. Herb is very senior in the Program down in Annapolis. He needed Lily to address a large meeting, three hundred people, because their main speaker was sick and had to cancel. Well, Lily phoned me up. She was in a state, you know how she got sometimes. She knew Sandy was shaky and needed her support, but she had to weigh that against the needs of those three hundred people—"

"And she decided to speak at Annapolis."

"Yes."

"And Sandy?"

"That's just it. Lily arranged for someone else to pick her up and take her to the St. Paul's meeting here in Baltimore. The trouble was, the arrangements got boluxed up. No one went to fetch her." Anthony's eyes grew sad now, as he remembered. "So . . . Sandy decided to drive herself to the meeting."

"Did she have one for the road?"

"No."

"But Mr. Rubetti did," Kate finished.

There was a moment of heavy silence. No Rachmaninoff to soothe them now. The concerto had long since ended.

Kate finally said: "And what happened to her? She didn't—"

"Die? No. But she's still in the hospital. She's severely retarded, Kate. She needs a respirator to breathe."

"Oh, how awful."

"Your mom never really forgave herself."

"Why? It wasn't her fault. She was thinking of those other three hundred people."

"That's what troubled her. She really wasn't. She knew Herb

191

could have found another speaker, but Sandy needed *her*. And yet she went to Annapolis anyway."

"Why?"

"Well, she thought a lot about her motivation. Yes, she thought about it . . . and she didn't like what she learned about herself."

"Which was?"

"That she craved recognition. She wanted to speak in Annapolis that night because she loved it when everybody clustered around her afterward, told her how moved they were, how wonderful she was."

"Really?" Kate was incredulous.

Anthony nodded.

Kate reflected on all this for a moment, and frowned. She felt a faint hammering between her eyebrows, the beginnings of a headache. She was surprised by her own vehemence when she asked: "This thing with Sandy—why didn't Mom ever tell me?"

"Good." Anthony studied her. "You're a little bit angry now, aren't you? That's good." He paused to cough. His frail body shook. "I suppose she didn't tell you because she was ashamed. She didn't really consider Sandy's needs. Just her own."

"But that's human! That's understandable. That's—"

"Exactly, but it's not something to be proud of. We try hard, Kate, and sometimes we fail."

Her lip trembled and tears brimmed in her eyes. "Why are you telling me all this?"

"So you'll let yourself off the hook and stop comparing yourself to her."

"I don't compare—"

"Oh, yes you do." He waved a feeble hand at her. "But you're a fine person in your own right. Take some credit once in a while, will you do that?"

She nodded, sniffled a little. "Okay, I will." It was curious, but the dream, and now what Anthony had told her, seemed to fit together somehow, parts of a whole.

"Promise?"

"Promise," she said and reached for his hand. Anthony didn't have much of a grip now. His fingers trembled uncontrollably. But she held on tight, tight enough for both of them. They sat there together and looked out the window at the green lawn, green pines, and pearl-gray sky.

"Tomorrow," Anthony said, "I'm going swimming."

S
lick watched her leave the Reed estate, but she didn't see him. He was pulled off the road in a shady grove of pines, suffering in the humidity, sucking on the straw of a sweaty milkshake, eating a wilted Big Mac. He tossed the half-eaten cheeseburger onto the seat beside him, fired up Trish's Pinto, and followed. He couldn't get too close, though. Because her body-guard stuck right behind her. He drove a separate car.

Slick was grumbling to himself, wondering where they were going, when all of a sudden she pulled into the parking lot of this fancy restaurant, L'Escargot. When Slick saw the restaurant, he knew instantly it would be perfect. He was so excited! Soon he would have her all to himself.

In the meantime, though, he had things to do. He nosed his car back onto the road and left L'Escargot behind. He would go to Trish's place to get his stash from Count-My-Love. He called it *his* stash but really it was old man Weber's. The old man had won big on Count-My-Love on a lucky bet, and Slick just couldn't let all that good money go to waste. What would Weber have done with it anyway? Probably wallpapered his bathroom.

Slick thought of tonight and of *her,* and he became impatient. He scowled at the Baltimore traffic. The longer he had to wait, the more worried he was about the money. What if it wasn't there? He started leaning on his horn and the guy next to him said, "What's your rush, buddy?" That made Slick really mad. He *hated* it when people told him what to do.

———

Trish was worried about the money.

She had spent the evening darting glances at the door, chain-smoking Camels, and sipping rum and Cokes. She couldn't even concentrate on *Soap Opera Digest,* she just flipped the pages.

She heard a sound in the hall and jerked upright on the sofa. No, it wasn't Slick. Just Mr. Alberts, next door.

She got up, flicked the TV on, and padded barefoot back to the sofa. She tucked her knees up, drew her ratty bathrobe around her, and reached for another cigarette.

Two days ago, she stumbled onto the money. It was in the drawer where Slick kept his camera case, underwear, shirts, and socks. He said he'd won big on Count-My-Love, but since she'd never seen the money, she figured it was just talk.

It wasn't just talk. It was three thousand two hundred dollars.

Until today she hadn't gone near that money. It wasn't hers, and she was no thief. But today she got a tip on a three-year-old filly, Frankie's Girl. Post time at Pimlico was one P.M. Twelve noon her bookie, Enzio, called. She told him her usual bet, twenty dollars. But then, she was rinsing out Mrs. Blume's perm when she spotted Slick in the parking lot. She couldn't believe it. He stole her car. He didn't ask her or anything. He just peeled out in her Pinto like he owned it, like he owned *her.*

She thought of her car and Slick's attitude. Then she called Enzio back, told him put thirty-two hundred on Frankie's Girl, she was good for it.

She heard the race on the radio. Frankie's Girl was a real strong runner, but around the clubhouse turn, her jockey took a spill. The horse Trish had put all her hopes on didn't even finish.

Trish smoked four more cigarettes. The ashtray was full.

Outside, it was getting gloomier by the minute. The air was thick with humidity. Trish felt all prickly with sweat and would have hopped into the shower, but she was too anxious.

She heard footsteps in the hall. The lock on the door rattled and the door swung open. She was so sure it would be Slick, she was almost relieved to see it was a perfect stranger. He loomed above her, he was a giant. He had massive shoulders and hands. "Hi," he grinned wickedly, "I'm Rees. Slick around?"

31

Fielding stood in his yard and stared up at the sky. Moody black storm clouds were rolling in and the air was heavy with humidity. It would rain within the hour. There would be even thunder and lightning, too.

Children were afraid of thunder and lightning. If Fielding had children, he wouldn't mind a storm because he could gather them up, cuddle the littlest one in his arms, let the independent older one sit on his knee. He would tell them he loved them, that it was all right, they were safe.

He sighed and went back inside his eighty-year-old house with the wraparound porch and porch swing. The house had four bedrooms, which was three too many.

Dressed for dinner in jacket and tie, he leaned on the banister and yelled up the stairs: "Honey, you ready?"

Sue Ann swept down the stairs, blond and untouchable, cool in her summery blue dress. "We've got to talk."

"Fine, let's stay home."

"No," she said. "We'll go out."

"You sure?"

"Yes." She pursed her lips in that definitive way she had. He would not be able to change her mind.

"All right." He sighed. "Where are we going?"

"L'Escargot. I made reservations."

———

At L'Escargot, the maître d' led Kate across the exquisitely appointed dining room. Kate did not notice the elegance of her surroundings; she was thinking, still, of Anthony Reed and wondering if she could ever tell Molly about him. She was so close to Molly that not telling her seemed, in some way, like lying, and yet, to tell her might be hurtful. She was thinking, rather sadly, that she might *not* be able to tell her when the maître d' halted by the corner table and Molly stood up and flung open her arms. "Kate!"

As they took their seats at the table, Molly said: "Dad phoned. He'll be late."

"Oh." Should I tell her, while we're alone? Kate was thinking. I should tell her, only I can't.

Her distress must have shown on her face because Molly said: "You're so quiet. What's wrong?"

"It's just . . . Moll, there's something I need to talk to you about, but I don't know if I *should*. Does that make any sense?"

Molly nodded, was listening.

"Before I came here I was at . . . a friend's. A friend of Mom's actually." Kate was tentative, groping her way.

Then Molly shocked her. "This friend of Mom's. It wouldn't be Anthony Reed, would it?"

Kate stared at her sister. Of all the scenarios she had scripted—how to best spare Molly's feelings yet tell her the truth—she had never dreamed of this, that Molly would know, too. She stuttered: "I can't believe . . . how do you know?"

"I read her diary after she died. Last winter. I was feeling low, I missed her, and I thought her diary would bring me close to her again. It was a shock, reading it. Afterward, I wanted so much to tell you, but then I got to thinking—was it right for me to alter your perceptions of her? So I didn't. I knew Dad gave you the diary, so I knew you'd come to it when you were ready. I thought that was best."

Kate nodded solemnly.

"So this Anthony," Molly said, after a long pause. "How is he? Do you like him?"

"Moll," she said feelingly, "he was *worthy* of her. He's warmhearted, bright, funny. I love him so much, I almost wish I hadn't met him."

"Why do you say that?"

Kate's eyes grew misty. "Lou Gehrig's disease. He's dying."

"Oh," Molly said, in a low voice. "Did Mom know?"

"Yes. She did."

The sisters gazed at each other in the candleleight, an exchange full of love and wonder and sadness, and Kate said: "It's funny, you know? I thought Mom was perfect. But she was braver than that. She was like us, Moll. She had faults, but she tried hard. And another thing. I don't tell you this enough, but she would be very proud of you. How you're bringing up Ian. And she would just *love* baby Lily. She wouldn't have been above bragging how cute she was, how she looked just like her with that red hair. . . ."

Molly nodded and tried to speak, but her lower lip trembled. She sniffled and reached for a Kleenex in her purse. "This grief thing. It catches you up by the ankles, doesn't it?" A tear rolled down her cheek and she dabbed at it with the tissue. "You know what? When Mom died, I thought you took it the hardest. But now I feel like you've climbed out of your shell. I mean, look at you, you're even wearing her swordpin tonight, don't think I didn't notice. You're doing so beautifully, you really are, you don't need me anymore. But now, well, I guess . . . I need you."

"I'm here," Kate said. She felt a surge of affection for her sister, she felt protective, as if *she* were the older one now. She draped her arm around Molly's shoulder as Molly began to cry.

"Stop the car. We've got to talk," Sue Ann said.

They were two blocks from L'Escargot, but Fielding curbed the car and parked.

Sue Ann swept her blond hair back off her face. In the wash of the streetlights, he could see her classic high cheekbones. He could also see that she was nervous.

She didn't speak.

He gazed out the window and thought of Kate. He couldn't wait to see her tomorrow. They had so much to talk about.

"You're thinking of her, aren't you? The redhead," Sue Ann said. "Kate Riley."

He stared at his wife. He had never shared this with her.

"You talk about her all the time, Todd. You don't realize it."

"Oh," he said. He stared at the dashboard.

"Hey, don't tune me out."

"I'm not."

"I have things on *my* mind, too!"

"Oh, really!" he snapped. It surprised him, that he was suddenly so angry. "Tell me about it. *Your* life's in danger, is it? Hers is, you know."

"Not *my* life. *Our* lives. *Our* marriage."

"What's that supposed to mean?"

"Why do you think I had us stop? I tried to tell you, lots of times, but you're so preoccupied lately, I—"

"All right, all right." He turned to face her. "I'm sorry. Now, tell me, what is it?"

She became, even more obviously, flustered. She twirled a blond curl around her index finger: "I shouldn't be critical of you. God knows, I'm not perfect." She took a deep breath, as if to steel herself. "I've been so lonely these last months."

"You have? But every time I've touched you—"

"I pushed you away. I know."

"You do?"

"I can't help it, Todd. I don't want to try anymore. I can't. I think you blame me, and I can't live with that. I look in your eyes and I see pain." She paused, bit her lip. "But I still have my needs. And I need to be loved."

"What is it you're saying?"

She smoothed the pleats in her dress, fumbled with her wedding ring: "You know how I've been traveling a lot lately?"

"Yes."

"Making commercials, selling new ads?"

"Yes."

"Well," she took a deep, shuddering breath, "I *have* been traveling, but it hasn't been strictly business."

There was silence, save for the drone of the air conditioner. Several seconds ticked by.

"Who is it?" Fielding finally said, his throat dry.

Sue Ann shook her head. "You don't know him. Besides, it really doesn't matter, does it?"

"No," Fielding said, "I suppose not."

After an endless moment, Sue Ann finally said: "We have reservations. We'd better get going."

"You want to *eat?*"

"Honestly, I feel so relieved I finally told you, I'm famished."

Fielding felt sick to his stomach. "Well, I don't think *I* can eat."

"Are you telling me you're angry?"

"No, it's just . . . maybe . . . I don't know. I don't know *how* I feel yet. It's too soon."

"I think we should go to the restaurant. It's neutral ground. If we go home, you'll retreat into your study."

Fielding looked at his wife. She was right. If they went home, they wouldn't talk. "Okay."

She gave him a tentative smile and lightly touched his hand. She was showing him they could still be friends. Could they? He didn't know. It was too hard, just now, to see through the veil of pain. His emotions in tumult, he concentrated on the mechanics of getting them to the restaurant. He noted that it had begun to rain. He flicked on the windshield wipers, methodically eased the car into drive, and continued to L'Escargot.

32

At L'Escargot, Kate looked across the table at her father. Bespectacled and remote, he had his usual clinical air, and yet, she could tell, he was really trying. He was not as warm as her mom would have been, but he was, for him, friendly and talkative tonight. And, though he didn't express it, she knew he was concerned about her, too. Every so often, she would catch him glancing toward Woodie, who sat perched on a stool at the long mahogany bar, keeping watch. That her father worried for her safety touched her deeply. This could be a new beginning, she thought. And so she said, feeling oddly hopeful: "What a wonderful idea, bringing us here."

"Yes," Molly said, and in unison, they smiled at their father.

He did not smile in return, he said brusquely, "My treat." But his eyes behind his glasses softened, as he added, in a gentler voice: "I only wish . . . well, we should do this more often."

Kate was surprised at the depth of her father's feeling. She longed to say something, but the timing wasn't right, not with the waiter hovering over them. But she promised herself she would not let her father remain a stranger. If, in the past, they had neglected each other, they could change that; it wasn't too late.

They ordered dinner and, by candlelight, they talked, sipped their wine, and listened to Vivaldi's *Four Seasons* playing softly in the background. Kate was glowing. She had dressed simply and elegantly in a white silk dress and her mother's swordpin, and she looked beautiful. She was enjoying herself and the company of Molly and her dad, but then she observed the fourth chair at their table, the empty chair, and she thought: Mom should be here. Yet even this sad thought did not defeat her because an image suddenly came floating into her mind: Mom, auburn-haired and laughing. Kate embraced the memory, cherished it, and afterward, she felt no pain, just contentment and a feeling of connectedness to the past. She could remember her mom and feel happy, and she *was* happy, when she chanced to look up and see the couple being escorted to the table across the room. The couple wasn't just any couple. It was Fielding and his wife.

It seemed to Kate that everything altered, after that. She no longer felt a part of things. Her father and Molly were still talking, but their words sounded foreign to her. And the room—wasn't it warm and stuffy in here? She felt faint; she could not breathe. Gradually, bit by bit, she began to recover herself. She looked across the room once more, as if to make sure Fielding was really here, and he was. Oddly, he looked very sad, forlorn even, and his wife sat angled away from him. Was something wrong between them? Fielding seemed to sigh as he tapped out a cigarette. A cigarette, when he didn't smoke anymore, he had given them up.

Molly had seen him come in too, and she had seen Kate's reaction. Now she was studying her sister. "Fielding, isn't it?"

Kate managed to reply, her voice just above a whisper, "Yes."

That was when Molly knew, if she hadn't guessed before, that Kate was in love with a married man: Kate could see the knowledge in her eyes. Yet Molly cared for her so much, she immediately forgot her own surprise and thought only how to rescue her. "Delicious salad," she said, hoping to change the subject, but their father was staring at the newcomers. "Todd Fielding," he observed. "The psychiatrist?"

Kate could not speak, so Molly volunteered, "Yes."

"I know him. Or rather, know *of* him. He's well respected. One of the best . . . A tragedy, what happened to his son."

Kate blinked, found her voice. "His son?"

"Yes, one of our nurses used to work in the neonatal unit. Even after she came to work with us, she used to visit him. Baby boy born six weeks premature. They had him in an incubator in intensive care. Cute little guy. Everybody was rooting for him, but he didn't make it. Their firstborn, too."

Kate was stunned. It seemed to her that the walls of the restaurant were closing in on her. "When . . . was this?"

"Last August, I think." Her father sensed her distress now, he was watching her closely. He knew in some way he had wounded her and he hadn't meant to. "What is it?"

But Kate could not answer. She gripped her napkin and twisted it around in her fingers. She felt desolate. Fielding had had a son, and he'd never told her. She wasn't angry at him, she understood that he was her doctor, but as her friend, couldn't he have told her? Oh, she was so confused! And now, seeing him across the room with his wife, it all became too much.

She put her napkin on the table and abruptly stood. "Excuse me, Moll, Dad. I need some fresh air." With that, she left them, Molly looking upset, her dad looking sorry for whatever it was he'd said. At the bar, she told Woodie, "I'll be right back," and plunged through the oak doors into the rainy night, alone.

* * *

205

Fielding saw her for the first time when she rose from the table.

How beautiful she looked! Her copper-red hair. Her white silk dress that outlined the soft curves of her body. High points of color flared in her cheeks. She was excited. No, agitated. He watched, mesmerized, as she flung down her napkin and ran out.

For a moment he wondered what might be wrong, but then he knew. It was him. She had seen him. She had seen him with his wife. He reached for the ashtray across the table and stabbed out his cigarette. "Sue Ann, I'm . . ." Sorry, he was going to say, but he decided he wasn't sorry at all. "Go ahead without me. Order whatever you want."

In the parking lot, Slick was watching the entrance to L'Escargot. He was waiting for *her* in the backseat of her Volvo. He was soaking wet and in a very bad mood. That he had broken into her car successfully was the only good thing that had happened to him tonight. Back at Trish's he found out Trish stole his money from Count-My-Love. He could have killed her, except she asked him, did he know somebody named Rees? Jesus! He just stood there, open-mouthed. Then he told Trish thanks for all her help, slapped her hard, and split.

Now back at the restaurant, he sat huddled in the Volvo, chilled and wet, and tried to organize his thoughts. Okay, so the money was gone. He had been without money before. The important thing was *her*. He could still get to her. He would hurt her, and after he did, everybody would know who Slick Carlson was and that he was boss.

Grinning to himself, not in such a bad mood after all, he peered intently through the rain hammering on the windshield. He stared at the front entrance, wishing *she* would appear, and suddenly there she was! She came out through the big oak door and stood under the awning, where it was dry. She looked shining and glittery in her long white dress, her mane of red hair tossed back like she was angry or something, defiant.

He was excited. She was more beautiful, even, than he remembered.

C'mon, c'mon! he thought. Ask for your car.

The valet said, "Can I get your car, ma'am?"

And Kate, who had not thought of going home or anywhere else, hesitated, looked at the valet and said, "Yes."

She stood under the awning, shaking uncontrollably. Woodie came sprinting out. "Jesus. Don't run off like that," he said.

"I'm sorry, I'm just—" Upset, she was going to say, but she turned and there was Fielding, tall and handsome in his black suit and tie, his nut-brown hair in tousled disarray. Oh, why did he still have this effect on her? Her heart fluttered at the sight of him, but then she remembered what she had learned tonight and tears gathered in her eyes.

Fielding asked Woodie: "Can we be alone for a minute?"

"Sure," Woodie said. "Kate, you need me, I'll be right inside."

Alone with Fielding, she peered into the dark night, into the pouring rain, and shivered. She couldn't look at him, but finally she said: "Your son."

"What?"

"Your son. You had a son."

The pain of his loss made him grimace.

Instinctively, she reached out to him, gently grabbed hold of his arm: "I wish you'd told me. Because of my mom, I would've understood. Maybe I could've helped."

He shook his head. "Hey, I'm the shrink, remember? *I'm* supposed to be helping *you*."

"You're a doctor, but you're a father too, and you lost your little boy. You must miss him terribly. Tell me about him. What was his name?"

"Kate, don't—"

"Please! Share this with me. It would mean so much. *What* was his name?"

"Just listen, Kate, there's more going on here than you realize. Have you heard of transference and countertransference? It's very common."

She stared at him. He was changing the subject. "We were talking about your son."

"Well, I'm talking about *us*. Will you come back inside? Woodie's waiting. Inside, we can straighten this out, okay? We'll talk."

He was about to put his arm around her and urge her back into the restaurant, but she stepped back. A minute ago, she cared only about helping *him*. But now her own feelings came rushing back and she felt overwhelmed. "Go back? I . . . can't. Seeing you with your wife, finding out about your son, I need to be alone for a while, to think."

"Kate, please."

She gave him a look full of anguish: "You called it transference. A big word we can all hide behind. But my pain is real, don't you see? It hurts me just to be near you . . . Oh, you don't understand!"

"What?" he asked. "Understand what?"

But she didn't answer. Her Volvo swung up to the curb, valet at the wheel. She and Fielding had to dance away from the spray of rainwater. The valet hopped out and held the door open for her. She cast a longing look toward Fielding, then dashed over to the driver's side. She didn't jump in immediately. Her copper hair glistened in the rain and her body trembled as she put her hand on the roof and leaned toward him: "Jesus, God," she sobbed, "I was in *love* with you!" With that, she ducked into her car and the valet slammed the door.

"Wait!" Fielding hollered. He ran out into the rain and rapped on the passenger window. "Kate. Kate!" She saw his face pressed close to the glass, his mustache, his brown cinnamon eyes. She saw Woodie appear beside him. Woodie was pounding on the window too, telling her: "Wait! You wait till I fetch my car."

She put her foot on the accelerator and eased forward into the rain while tears streaked down her face. She had been so happy tonight, until this. She'd felt she was making progress, getting better, but how could she have been, if she could feel as badly as this? Her equanimity was so fragile a gift, so easily destroyed.

Everything that could go wrong, she thought, *has* gone wrong. But she had forgotten something, or rather, someone, hadn't she? How eerily appropriate to feel the cold metallic blade of a knife pressed against her flesh, to hear the familiar creepy voice say: "Remember me?"

———

Kate did not scream.

He was in the backseat but pressed forward, indecently close. He held the knife just so. She could feel her pulse beating against the blade. If he leaned into the blade a fraction more, it would break her skin and draw blood.

She did not dare turn her head, but out of the corner of her eye, she could see him. How dreadful he looked with his fat, doughy cheeks and dyed blond hair. And his eyes were fixed on her, glittering greenly.

She glanced desperately into the rearview mirror. Her car was already at the edge of the parking lot. Could Fielding and Woodie see her, in the rain? Would they know she was in danger?

"Drive!" Slick hissed.

She blinked at the command. Her heart hammered in her ears.

"I said drive!"

She nodded obediently and let the car creep forward.

"Turn left," he ordered.

She swung out onto the main road. There was absolutely no traffic, no passing cars she could alert by honking her horn. She drove as slowly as possible. Peering into the dark, rainy night, she thought she discerned headlights behind them, but she must have been mistaken because endless seconds ticked by and nothing happened. No one came to rescue her.

"Speed up!" Slick snapped.

"If I go any faster—"

"Just do it!"

She reluctantly stepped on the accelerator. They barreled down the slippery, rain-washed road. The windshield wipers worked frantically, but visibility was poor. Kate concentrated fiercely, squinted her eyes, but she could barely see into the dark night.

"Make a right at the next corner."

"Where are we going?"

"Just drive!" He pressed the knife against her neck and with the flat of the blade scraped her skin. She bit her lip but did not cry out. She was so afraid now, she could hardly drive. Her body quivered.

"Hey, stupid. Red light. Slow down."

"Okay," she said, trying to sound calm. Her pulse was racing as they came to the intersection and she braked. Rain pummeled the roof of the Volvo and thunder crashed overhead. But there was nothing more terrifying than his voice, close to her ear, saying: "Soon, I'll have you all to myself."

A shiver ran down her spine.

One last time she looked into her rearview mirror. There was no Fielding and no Woodie, and suddenly she knew there wouldn't be. No one could follow her in this storm. She was on her own. Slick had the knife, he would hurt her if she didn't do what he said. She was his prisoner. She was helpless. Unless . . .

When the light switched from red to green, she floored it. The car lurched forward, knocking Slick off balance. His arms flew up and he tumbled backward against the seat cushions. She jammed on the brakes now and lunged for the door, but he was too fast for her, he seized her arm and yanked her back, hard, and pinned her against the headrest. He was choking her. She twisted to push him away and, as she did, she lifted her foot off the brake pedal. They were on an incline. The car began to roll. They continued their struggle, and meanwhile the car was still rolling, picking up speed. She let go of the steering wheel and now the car veered sharply left toward a row of parked cars. "Grab the wheel!" Slick cried, too late. The parked station wagon leapt into view as they thudded into it. The jolt flung Slick backward, freeing her. There was a grinding sound of metal against metal, but Kate didn't even wait until they were stationary. With a final burst of energy, she thrust her door open and scrambled out.

Trembling, breathless, she fled down the sidewalk, purse flapping at her side, high heels slipping on the wet pavement. The rain dripped from her hair and streamed down her cheeks. Her silk dress clung to her. Where was she? She could barely make out the tall dark buildings, the deserted intersection. She didn't realize she was even with McKeldin Courthouse until she blundered against the fence that overlooked the construction site for the new Public Safety Building. With a moan of victory, she staggered across the street. She cast an anxious glance behind her into the dark rainy night and then, seeing no one, pressed on through the familiar courthouse doors. The doors were unlocked—as usual you didn't need a key to get into the building—but where was security?

A guard should be on duty, she thought. Where is he, on a coffee break?

Darting another desperate glance behind her, she hastened up the marble stairs to her office, fumbled for her keys, unlocked the door, and stumbled in.

She was gasping for breath and she felt faint. She struggled to calm herself. *It's okay,* she told herself, *you're okay. The thing to do now is call for help.*

The first desk she came to, she reached for the phone, but she stopped herself when she thought she heard a door creak. She held her breath and listened. She heard nothing more, but still she was afraid. The room was bathed in dark shadows; she could hardly see.

She was facing the door, fully expecting the attack, if it came, to be from that direction. Consequently the blow to the back of her skull took her by complete surprise. A guttural cry of protest rose in her throat and died there as she felt an instant of blinding pain, then spun into unconsciousness.

33

Back in the parking lot at L' Escargot, the detectives were drinking coffee. Someone offered Fielding some, but he declined. He didn't need any. His guilt kept him awake. They couldn't find Kate, not in that rain. He and Woodie went in search for her in Woodie's car, but it was no use. They couldn't see three feet in front of them.

When they'd first returned to the restaurant, Fielding gave Sue Ann the car and told her to drive home. Then he asked to take a look at Slick Carlson's file, which one of the arriving detectives had brought. Clarence Wilbur Carlson was a very disturbed individual, but he could appear normal in social situations. He grew up in a lower-income household in New Jersey. There was an incestuous relationship between Slick and his mother, and the father, apparently, surprised them in bed together. He beat Slick so severely, the seventeen-year-old had to be hospitalized. Fielding paused in his reading, and for an instant he pitied Slick. And yet, if the teenage Slick inspired sympathy, the adult Slick inspired only contempt. Women were the frequent victims of his sexual frustration. His rap sheet showed numerous sex-related offenses, but Slick had always managed to get off lightly, until Kate prosecuted him in the Angela Billings case.

The more he read about Slick, the less Fielding understood him. Slick was an intelligent man, but emotionally scarred and very volatile. It was hard to predict how he would behave in a hostage situation. Fielding knew only one thing for certain. Slick Carlson hated authority. A supreme egotist, he needed to be the one in charge.

Fielding absorbed the contents of the file and handed it back to Woodie, then he joined the other detectives. They shared cigarettes and Hershey bars—but they all felt useless. It was after midnight and she was out there, somewhere, with Slick. And here they were, because of the rain, doing nothing.

Thank God for Reuben, because when he arrived, things changed. Fielding felt his optimism. Reuben refused to give up, he was thinking, always thinking. While the other detectives were filling him in, he noticed the rusty Pinto in the restaurant parking lot. Nobody else had noticed it, not in all this time.

They ran a check on the car. The DMV came back on Reuben's car radio: the Pinto belonged to one Trish Jackson, 1815 South Charles Street, Apartment 3C.

"Trish," Reuben said. "That fits. Let's roll." He jumped into his car then flung open the passenger door. "You coming or not?" he asked, and Fielding was surprised. Reuben meant him, not Woodie; he was looking straight at him.

With a surge of gratitude, glad to be doing something at last, Fielding joined him.

Ten minutes later, they were climbing the flight of stairs to Trish Jackson's apartment. Fielding held his revolver awkwardly in front of him. He hadn't held a loaded gun since his days with the Special Forces team.

They were on the third floor now, in front of Apartment 3C.

Reuben nodded to Fielding to release his safety, get ready to shoot.

They listened. Not a sound from inside.

Reuben mouthed: "One, two, three!" and together they barged in through the flimsy wood door, sending paint chips flying.

The apartment seemed unnaturally silent. They stole quietly through the living room, then the kitchen. Slick wasn't here. But in the bedroom, they saw a body under the sheets. Fielding noticed the hair right away. Dirty blond, not copper red. The girl wasn't Kate. And she wasn't hurt. She was Trish Jackson and she was only sleeping.

Fielding felt faint with relief. The moment of relief passed and his fears flooded back. Where was Slick? And where was Kate?

———————

Kate woke to pain and discomfort.

She was sagging limply against a metal pole, her arms tied behind her back, her feet in a mud puddle. It was dark and raining, and she felt frightened. She wanted to shout, but there was a gag in her mouth. The rain had ruined her silk dress, which hung clammily on her. She didn't care so much about the dress, but her mother's gold swordpin was gone. She missed that swordpin. It would have given her courage.

She peered into the darkness. It was pitch black, and yet she could sense she was in some kind of enclosure. A very narrow enclosure, tall and wooden, with four sides but no roof. That was why she felt the rain. And now the rain, which had been a cold penance, was her deliverance. For her opening to the rain was the only thing about these four walls that didn't remind her of a coffin.

Slick had done this to her. Where was he? Watching? Waiting?

Soon he would return. Of course he would.

She tried to think what to do, but the back of her head ached. Her entire body felt stiff and bruised and battered. In the puddle of rainwater, her bare feet felt like ice. But she was most anxious about her hands. Her wrists were bound so excruciatingly tight, her fingers were losing circulation. They were heavy and numb. Grimly determined to save her hands, she began to exercise her fingers, flexing and unflexing them, trying to force warmth back into them. She also tugged experimentally at the rope binding her wrists, but it wouldn't give.

She thought again of Slick. When he came back, God knows what he would do to her.

But, no, he wouldn't find her. She would see to that. She began, with passionate intensity, her struggle to break free. She twisted and tugged and pulled. Time passed, and the rope refused to give. Her battle became a grueling trial. Whenever she yanked, the rope bit deeper into her wrists. Her damp, frazzled hair fell into her eyes. She tossed her head back, kept on twisting and pulling at the unforgiving rope. Finally, she sagged against the metal pole, drenched in sweat, utterly broken, full of despair. She let out a sob, muffled heartbreakingly by the gag in her mouth. She could not go on.

Just then, she let her arms relax, and something unexpected happened. Her arms slid down the pole! Her struggling had loosened the rope, after all. Her wrists were still bound tight, but now she could raise and lower both arms and slide them up and down along the metal pole to create friction. Maybe she could escape, after all.

Charged with frenzied energy, she renewed her efforts to fray the rope and make it snap. Don't let him come, she prayed. Please, God. Don't let him come.

Their visit with Trish Jackson paid off because she told them about Rees. "With Rees in the picture," Reuben said, "anything can happen."

Trish gave them coffee while she had whisky, then they headed back down the worn wooden stairs, outside into the rain. They sat in Reuben's unmarked police car, shivering, because they were wet and it had turned cold. They watched the windshield wipers metronome back and forth. They weren't sure where to try next, when Woodie radioed in: "We located her Volvo. She got in a fender-bender on Fourteenth and Ashton. That's a block from McKeldin Courthouse."

"Only a block, huh?" Reuben said. "Maybe she went in to get out of the rain. Let's check it out."

Reuben drove them to the courthouse. Fielding was silent all the way. He was first up the stairs to the State's Attorneys Office. He knew, even as he entered the room, that Kate had been here, but it was Woodie who found the note.

The white sheet of paper was still rolled in the typewriter. It read: "SHE MUST SUFFER FOR HER SINS. REMEMBER, I LOVED HER TO DEATH. SLICK."

"Jesus." Reuben winced. "He should write greeting cards. Anything else?"

"Yeah," Woodie said, and hesitated. "Her purse."

Fielding turned. "Her purse? Let me see that." He tried to act businesslike, as if he had some purpose for wanting to see her personal effects. The truth was, he only wanted to be close to her. He felt such tenderness toward her as he touched the things that she had touched—her wallet, her lipstick, her comb—and he felt pain, too. It was as though she was already dead and these trivialities were all he had left of her. And yet, there *was* hope, wasn't there? There was still hope.

Suddenly a call for backup came crackling over the walkie-talkie. There was a robbery in progress on Thirteenth and Main, Fort McHenry Liquors. There were two suspects. Caucasian males. One a tall, muscular blond. The other, short with doughy cheeks.

"Sound familiar?" Reuben looked at Fielding. They were both thinking the same thing: Slick and Rees.

Reuben grabbed his jacket. His olive eyes were bright and alive and Fielding began to understand the detective, how he thrived on being a cop and needed his violence-prone job to be at peace with himself. "You coming?" he yelled to Fielding. "We'll get him now. We're even in the neighborhood."

Reuben was already at the door, and Fielding hurried after. He ran with taut, smooth control but his mind was a jumble. Should he be elated? If Slick and Rees were busy holding up a liquor store, how could any harm come to Kate? Unless harm had *already* come to her. . . .

K
ate watched the sunrise, thinking: this is beautiful, thinking:
I may never see this again. She
had worked the ropes through
the long night but she could not
break free. Slick was sure to come back again. And when he did,
she would be helpless to defend herself.

With unbearable sadness, she envisioned the morning going on
around her. Molly would be worried about her, but she would not
tell Ian. Ian would pad barefoot down the hall, rubbing sleep from
his eyes, his biggest question of the day what to have for breakfast,
Cheerios or Pop Tarts? Baby Lily would coo and watch him eat.
She would not sense that Kate was in danger. Her whole world was
the kitchen—Ian's babblings while he ate his cereal, the sound of
the kettle boiling, the pillowy softness of Molly's breast. And Kate's
father? He would be worried about her too, but he would take refuge
in routine. He would drive to the hospital, and perhaps something

in the crisp morning air, after the rain, would remind him of Lily's optimism, and he would miss her. Perhaps he would miss Kate too, when she was gone.

But no, she shouldn't think this way. She shouldn't give up.

Although she was shivering with exhaustion in her damp dress, she hadn't wasted the night. She had made progress. The rope was fraying. And now, as the day heated up and the margarine sun melted across the white plate of sky, light spilled into her enclosure and she could see where she was. Her eyes ran along the angled neck of a giant steel crane. She read the words: JPC Construction.

The Public Safety Building. Slick had trapped her in the construction site. Her enclosure was a wooden form, a temporary part of the foundation. And she was tied to a steel piling that was anchored in concrete.

But why here?

She got her answer soon enough. She heard a deafening clamor, the roar of engines, orders shouted back and forth, and then, the giant yellow crane that towered above her moved mechanically against the sky. The construction crew was starting work.

Excited, Kate forgot about the gag in her mouth and shouted "Help!" only to choke futilely on her own saliva. Still, she did not despair, for surely they must see her. Up on the ridge, there was a workman in a green hard hat. She tried to wave to him, but her hands were held fast. Another workman joined the first. They were talking, laughing. She was directly below them. Why didn't they look down? If they would only look down, they would see her.

The two workmen gestured to the driver of a cement mixer. The cement mixer labored backward and then stopped. What was happening?

Kate shuddered with the sudden realization. They were going to pour concrete. They were going to pour concrete on *her*. No wonder Slick never came back for her. He didn't need to. If the workmen didn't see her, if she didn't escape, she would be buried alive.

She watched, horrified, as the cement truck's rear opened up.

Gray sludge and gravel poured into the wood form only yards away from her. Every second counted now. Breathless, heart racing, she slid the rope up and down along the steel piling. The rope bit deeper into her wrists, but she wouldn't give up.

They began to pour concrete into the form next to hers.

Feverish, she continued to jockey the rope up and down. She felt the first braid give a little and then snap. Cement avalanched into the nearby form. Loose gravel rained down on her shoulders and head, and gray sludge splattered her. Still, she worked the rope. Finally, incredibly, the last braid snapped and she pitched forward onto her knees, into the mud. The rainwater splashed in her face, she was on all fours like a stray animal, her dress torn, her skin grimy, her hair gritty with clumps of mud, but she laughed into her cloth bandanna. She was never so happy in all her life.

She ripped off the gag and scrambled to her feet just as the cement truck backed up directly above her. She didn't hesitate. She threw her shoulder into one wall of the wooden form, felt the plywood crack and give. But the wall remained upright. She lifted her bare foot and gave one last savage kick at the plywood, watched triumphantly as it crashed to the ground. A torrent of gray sludge spewed from the cement mixer, but she was safely away, bounding lightly across the flattened plywood. Suddenly, though, her joyful escape went terribly wrong. When she came to the end of the plywood, the ground vanished beneath her feet and she tumbled into a ditch. She hit hard, on her right leg. She felt the bone snap painfully on impact.

———

Peter Coe strode briskly down the corridor of the Shock Trauma Unit in Baltimore's Community General Hospital. The handsome State's Attorney wore his blue pin-striped suit and an Yves St. Laurent tie. The nurses were staring at him and he liked that. Still, he didn't flirt with any of them. He wasn't interested. Couldn't they tell from the glow on his face, he was practically a married man?

He planned to be engaged by the end of this week; he just needed an evening alone with Kate. He knew Kate better than anybody, and he knew she was ready to be swept off her feet. After her scare at the construction site, she would realize what was valuable in life and what wasn't. She would realize how lucky she was to have *him.* He had money, prestige, and good looks, and he would treat her like gold. This time when he proposed, she would accept.

He regretted that last time, proposing to her in his office. He shouldn't have yelled at her to get out, but he was so angry! He thought he might break something, and he didn't want her to see him do that. At the time, he thought she was rejecting him, and that's why he got mad. But he realized that wasn't it at all. The problem was he didn't propose to her in a romantic setting. That was the only possible explanation because of course she loved him, of course she would marry him, he had simply caught her offguard. This time when he proposed, he would have a limousine drive them to the door of Tio Pepe's, he would seat her at the best table and treat her to the best champagne. He would pay for the violin player to come around and serenade her, and if she didn't like the man's singing, he would pay for him to go away. Nothing was too good for his Kate. Really, he would do anything for her. She was hurting now. He heard they were treating her for hypothermia and a compound fracture of her right leg. That was fine with him, he would take time off from work, nurse her back to health, bring her chicken soup, whatever she wanted. All he asked from her was one simple thing: that she become Mrs. Peter Coe III.

Three people were gathered outside her door. Judith, Woodie, and a tall man with a raggedy mustache. Peter knew him, but for a moment he couldn't place him. He was Kate's expert at the Buckner trial. The shrink. What was his name? Yes, Fielding.

Just now, Fielding was saying to Judith: "Have we met?"

"No," Judith said.

"Not at some party or function?"

Judith frowned. "I don't attend parties."

Fielding fixed his brown eyes on her, nodded. Then he said politely: "I'm Todd Fielding. And you're . . ."

"Judith Moore. Ms. Riley's secretary. Perhaps we met during the trial."

"Yes, I'm sure that's it," Fielding said. He shook Judith's hand warmly.

This guy could run for office, Peter thought. He's got charm, charisma, all the right moves. Instinctively, Peter didn't like this Fielding. He didn't like the fact that Fielding was here, and most of all, he didn't like what Fielding was holding in his hand: a dozen long-stemmed roses.

Roses! Why did they have to be roses? And they were red roses too, just like the ones Peter had brought to the airport to welcome her back from Mexico. Peter scowled. Why did this guy have to *remind* him? And yet, wait a minute. Maybe Fielding knew something he didn't. Maybe Kate was *crazy* about roses, maybe she adored them. And maybe she hated carnations.

He stopped suddenly at this thought. He was far enough away so that no one had seen him. He wouldn't visit Kate just yet; he would slip downstairs to the florist's. So what if Fielding brought her a dozen roses? He would buy her two dozen. No, make that three. He smiled as he hastened down the corridor. On the way, he held the carnations stiffly away from him, and, as soon as he could, he trashed them.

Judith Moore. Fielding knew he had seen her someplace. He couldn't remember where, and it bothered him. But then Judith went off for a cup of coffee and he forgot about her. He stood there in the corridor with Woodie, outside the door, and all he could think of was that he had to see Kate. He turned to Woodie and said: "I know she's sedated, but I'll only stay a minute. Will you let me in?"

"It's against hospital regulations," Woodie grinned, "but I don't see why not."

Woodie accompanied him into the room as he walked over to the bed where she lay sleeping, her red hair splayed on the white pillow. She was dressed in a hospital gown. She looked so small and frail and vulnerable, while the cast on her leg looked so big. His eyes filled with pity. Her leg, which was elevated to prevent swelling, was mummified in a plaster cast that ran all the way from her thigh to her foot. Her bare toes were covered by a cut-off ski sock. The cast was bent in the knee to give her mobility: she would be able to use crutches. Still, it had to be a very messy fracture. Fielding winced to think of the pain she must have suffered, the night she had endured.

He studied her sleeping face. Even when she woke, would he be able to tell her how much he loved her? She was more precious to him than his own life, more precious than sunlight or air.

After one last yearning look at her, he followed Woodie outside into the corridor and handed him the roses: "When she wakes up, tell her . . . well, just tell her I stopped by."

Woodie nodded, then said: "I'm glad she's safe, but I'd sure as hell like to nail Carlson. I can't believe he got away last night."

"I know," Fielding said, remembering. Last night had been a fiasco. Too many police were involved and there'd been a mixup. Roadblocks were set up, but Slick and Rees, fleeing the liquor store, somehow managed to slip through. Now, no one knew where they were. Fielding had slept only two hours last night and he was exhausted. Still, he wished he could help capture Slick. But there was no hostage situation anymore. Reuben no longer needed him. "Well . . ." he said. He was about to leave, but just then Woodie's walkie-talkie beeped and Reuben's voice came through: "We got a lead. Bungalow on Pulaski Highway. A real dump. We think they're hiding out. Listen, Fielding around? Yeah? Ask him if he wants to come along."

Only minutes after Fielding left, Kate stirred toward wakefulness. She felt dazed and confused, but when she finally focused her vision, she realized she had a visitor. Seeing him, she felt like a little girl again. She was, again, the frail six-year-old who suffered from ear-aches, whose father rocked her on his knee to soothe her pain. She had forgotten that, hadn't she? Those nights he had denied himself sleep to comfort her. But she remembered now, perhaps because she was in pain again, and perhaps too, because she let herself remember.

"Dad," she said. "Hi."

"Kate." He nodded. He wore his white lab coat. He must have been on his rounds upstairs. Perhaps he had come to see her only because it was convenient. But was that fair? His eyes behind his spectacles looked sad and worried.

"It's not as bad as all that," she said wryly. She tried to sit up against the pillows, but it hurt too much to move. "Sorry to run out on you and Moll last night. But I learned my lesson." She gestured dramatically at her cast. "I won't be running anywhere for quite some time!"

Her father, to her great delight, laughed. Then they fell silent. They found they had little to say to each other. She watched him glance absently around the room. It was bare and impersonal, white walls, no window, no view you could call your own. She felt sure he would comment on the sad lack of a window or something to that effect and they would end up talking about hospital rooms and then hospitals in general. But he surprised her. In the sterility of that room, he made personal feelings triumph. He turned back toward her and reached across the white bedsheet for her hand.

"Painful, is it?" he said, when he saw her eyes fill with tears.

But she only shook her head, and smiled.

After her father left, Woodie came in.

Kate told him that she was going home, her father was arranging it. She wanted to be in her own bed. Was that all right with him? Sure, Woodie said. Makes no difference. I'll be with you, either way.

Woodie stepped out for a moment, then brought in Fielding's roses. He told her where Fielding had gone. Kate wanted to ask him, would Fielding be safe? But she knew he could not promise her that.

She was thinking about Fielding, when Judith and Peter breezed in. Behind Peter, there were three hospital orderlies, each one's face hidden behind a lavish assortment of roses.

"Wait a minute! Hold on," she told Peter. "Can I take the flowers with me? Because I'm not staying here. I'm going home."

The disappointment on Peter's face made her wish she'd spoken more gently. So she said, purely for his benefit: "Peter, the roses —they're beautiful."

"You like them? You really do?"

She looked at him. His passionate desire to please her was almost ominous in its intensity. Or was it simply that she was groggy from the sedative and reading into things?

I n the tumbledown bungalow off Pulaski Highway, Rees poked Slick in the ribs with the gun.

This took Slick by surprise.

Just minutes ago, they were mingling their sweat in the shafts of morning sunlight on the lumpy mattress on the floor. The mattress was the only thing in the place. The kitchen was bare, unless you counted the roach spray and the mousetrap as company.

"What is it, old buddy?" Slick was hunched over, lacing up his sneakers. He eyed the gun. It was the same gun Rees had waved around in the liquor store last night. "Something I said?"

Rees didn't reply. The gun didn't move either.

Slick quit lacing his sneakers and straightened up to face his old cellmate. Imagine his horror last night when Rees found him. He felt sure Rees was going to kill him, but Rees was as friendly as ever, so he relaxed, he figured he was safe. Now, though, he knew he was in trouble. "Hey, man, what gives?"

After an interminable moment, Rees sighed. His voice was very soft when he said: "You left me behind."

"So what?" Slick said. Sweat trickled down his cheeks. The room was too warm. "You're here now, aren't you? A free man."

Rees shook his head and dug his .44 Magnum Predator deeper into Slick's ribcage. His eyes sparkled oddly. "You promised you'd take me with you."

"Well, I was going to—" Slick began, sweating profusely now.

"Save it," Rees said. And now there was a click. The telltale sound of a gun being cocked.

Slick's heart froze. Just then, the bungalow door crashed open. What's going on? Slick thought wildly. Who are these guys? Slick swallowed raggedly. He recognized Reuben, the cop. The other guy he didn't know. Slick was mesmerized by them and by the two four-inch barrels of the police specials pointing, very definitely, at him and Rees.

Kate was home.

She was sitting up in bed, her cast elevated by two plump pillows. Her crutches stood against the wall, within arm's reach. She felt tired and battered, and her leg was throbbing, yet she considered herself lucky. This morning at the construction site, she might have been hurt far worse. She might have died.

She was also grateful for her friends. Woodie was in the living room. Peter and Judith were with her in the bedroom. Judith sat in the desk chair while Peter busied himself arranging bouquets of roses around the room. Kate felt overwhelmed by all the flowers. She inhaled their sweet fragrance and let herself remember the house on Stoneleigh and Mom in her garden. Mom would tend her roses under a hot sun, intent on her work, yet she was always happy to take a break if Kate skipped over and sat down next to her, in the soft grass, to talk. . . . Yes, the roses were beautiful. Peter had bought too many of them, but that was okay, he meant well. And Fielding? Kate found herself wondering which roses were his. They had gotten mixed in with Peter's. It shouldn't matter, really, which flowers he had held in his hands, but it *did* matter. It mattered to her.

She was thinking this, wondering how Fielding was, was he safe? when her reverie was interrupted by sounds outside her window. Drum rolls, trumpets, and trombones: music from a marching band. And from a farther distance came the sharp percussion of firecrackers.

"That must be the parade," said Judith.

"It doesn't start for another hour," Peter observed from the far end of the room. He placed a towering arrangement of roses on the windowsill and leaned out: "Yeah, looks like they're still getting organized. It's the same every year on Fort McHenry Day. The 10-K race first, then the parade." He made a face. "If you ask me, it's a stupid idea. Only clogs up traffic."

Kate and Judith looked at him.

"I think it's grand," Judith said. "All the high-school bands. The children get the day off from school. They love it."

"I agree," Kate said.

"Okay, so I'm outnumbered." Peter shrugged, suddenly taciturn. Kate guessed what he was thinking. He wanted her all to himself, he didn't like Judith being here. But Kate liked having Judith. And besides, she knew Judith needed to be here where she could feel helpful.

Peter turned from the window and approached her bed. His mood abruptly altered. He asked her, in a thoughtful, caring tone: "Kate, they say after a bad experience it's good to talk about it. You want to talk about last night? What it was like?"

"It was horrible," Kate said, remembering last night despite herself. "The wood form was so tall and narrow, I felt claustrophobic. It was like being in a coffin."

"And you felt trapped?" Judith prompted gently.

"Yes," Kate shuddered. She looked at Judith, then. Their eyes locked. Did something of her pain flicker across her face? Because Judith abruptly stood up. "Peter, perhaps we should go now. Kate needs her rest."

Kate smiled weakly, acquiesced. She *did* need to rest. Her dose of Tylenol and codeine had long since worn off. And the shattering pain in her leg made her tired. She had, the doctors told her, a nasty comminuted fracture of the middle-third tibia. There was lots of bone fragment. She had been told to keep the leg elevated and to watch for swelling.

Peter Coe glanced up from the roses: "Yes, we had better get the show on the road. But we'll be back. We're going grocery shopping for you."

"Oh, thanks, but that's not necessary. You'll miss work," Kate said, thinking she would rather they didn't come back, she would rather sleep.

"No bother," Peter insisted. "No bother at all." He arranged the last of the roses and smiled, seeking her approval. He said teasingly, but she knew he meant it: "Remember, the good-looking ones are mine, the thorny ones are Fielding's."

She sat in bed looking after him, even after he was gone. Peter was so moody, she found him hard to understand. One moment he could be so sweet, buying her all these roses, the next he could say something like that.

Her mind was still on Peter when she noticed Judith lingering by her bed. "Before I go," she said, "any special requests?"

"You're wonderful," Kate said. "But no thanks, I can't think of anything."

"Perhaps I'll get you a small surprise. Your birthday is tomorrow, after all."

"Oh, Judith, you've already done too much!" she protested, remembering the briefcase in Judith's apartment and the perfume. "You're spending too much money."

"But it's my money to spend," Judith said. "And it gives me

great joy to spend it on you." She paused, then added, with tortured honesty: "Kate, you're the closest thing to family I've got."

Alone in her bedroom, Kate reflected on her birthday. She was turning thirty tomorrow, and for once, the prospect did not dismay her. Thirty wasn't so very old.

She gazed upon the roomful of roses, inhaled their perfume. She thought about Fielding and her feelings for him. Her love for him was so pure, a reflection of her finest self, could she regret it? Did it matter even that he could never return her love? Perhaps it only mattered that in a world that could encompass Slick, her love could exist.

She was engrossed in these thoughts when Woodie startled her by appearing at her bedroom door: "Just checking on you."

"I'm fine," she said. "Worried, though."

Woodie was watching her carefully. He strode into the room. "Is it Reuben you're worried most about? Or Fielding?"

She only stared at him.

"All right. Don't answer that. It's none of my business. But when he came to the hospital and he saw you sleeping, well, don't ever say nobody ever loved you because it wouldn't be true. . . ."

Kate could not respond. Her mind was in total confusion. Was what Woodie said possible? Could Fielding really love her too? If he loved her, and he was out there with Slick, in danger . . .

———

"Drop your weapon!" Reuben commanded.

Rees ignored the warning, removed the gun from Slick's ribs, and started blasting. Fielding fired in response, but it was Reuben who safely defended them, who stopped Rees with a bullet to the stomach. In the shocked aftermath, Slick acted first. He snatched up the fallen gun and fled out the back of the bungalow. The screen door banged after him.

"Let's go!" Reuben cried.

Fielding started to run, but his knees wobbled and he sagged forward, light-headed and ill. It was the blood. Blood had never bothered him before, but it did now. Rees on the mattress, and all that blood.

Reuben halted at the door: "You coming?"

"I . . . can't."

"Call Woodie, then, and get some backup." With that, the detective plunged outside, alone.

Fielding felt ashamed. Reuben was counting on him, but he'd let him down. . . . He had no further time for thought but doubled over to vomit. When he finished, he wiped his mouth on his sleeve. He felt fractionally better. He stood upright and his mind began to clear. He immediately hurried to the phone and dialed Woodie at Kate's. While he was dialing, he heard Rees on the mattress still groaning. He was alive.

"Woodie? Listen, we found Slick, but he got away. We need assistance. You know the address. Oh, and send an ambulance."

"I'm on it," Woodie said.

Fielding slammed the phone down, grabbed his gun, and sprinted for the back door. Even as he darted outside, he felt his disappointment keenly. He had failed himself, failed Kate, failed Reuben. He was not the brave man he thought he was. He was a coward.

Behind the bungalow, he looked right and left. To the left were more bungalows. To the right, a sparse woods edging a junkyard. Gun drawn, eyes alert, Fielding went right. He thought only about Slick now. He got into Slick's mind and tried to imagine where Slick would go. He did not realize that he presented an interesting picture. A tall, ruggedly handsome man in white shirt and dark slacks, running under a hazy yellow afternoon sun, dodging pine branches, leaping over old tires. His gun hand was trembling as he ran. For this, he chided himself. He did not realize he had begun to be brave.

36

S lick cast an anxious, backward glance as he stumbled through the junkyard. Were they coming? He stopped to listen. At first he could only hear his heart pounding. But then he heard them. He heard the branches snapping underfoot as they ran. What should he do? All around him, abandoned automobiles rotted in the sun. To his left, shimmering in the heat, was the shell of an old Thunderbird, the kind Elvis Presley used to drive, with shark fins for fenders. When Slick saw the car, his green eyes flashed. He crawled inside behind the ratty upholstered seat and hid.

He listened intently. The footsteps were close now. He peeked out and spotted only one of them: Reuben, the supercop. Reuben was very careful. He held his .44 out in front of him. He was ready. But he didn't see Slick in his hiding place. He walked right past the Thunderbird, just like Slick hoped he would. Slick let out his breath in a whoosh. Reuben was ten paces ahead now and moving forward, his gun in front of him. It was time. Slick piled out of the car, leveled his gun at the cop's back, and ordered: "Stop! Drop your gun or I'll flat blow you away."

It went smoother than he thought. He snatched up the gun, then stepped in behind Reuben and nudged him forward with his own gun: "Move!"

"Where we going?" Reuben asked.

"Just move!" Slick hissed, hustling the cop down the junkyard's gravel driveway. At the end was a dilapidated shack with blistered red paint and shattered windows. He grabbed Reuben in a necklock and backed him up against the outside. "Here's where we wait."

"For what?" Reuben's black midnight eyes showed no fear.

Slick had to give the cop credit. He was cool. He should be sweating bullets, but he wasn't. Just for fun, Slick jabbed him in the ribs, hard, with the gun: "How's it feel, cop? Now *I'm* arresting *you!*"

Reuben didn't flinch. He only said: "You enjoy this, don't you?"

"Yeah," Slick smirked, "I do."

But then Reuben—was he putting him on, or what?—made a sad face. "Kate Riley died this morning. It's over. Give it up, Slick."

"Died? No way, man. I never touched her."

"Slick, in about ten seconds, five million cops'll be crawling all over this place, and we're gonna do more than dump cement on you, I promise."

"Cement?" He snickered. "What's with the cement? You got cement on the brain, or what?"

"The Public Safety Building. You telling me you didn't—"

"Quiet!" Slick heard crashing sounds. Branches snapped in the nearby woods.

"Wait. Just tell me. Did you—"

"Shut up, I said!" Slick clamped his hand over the cop's mouth. He frowned, listened. Footsteps approached the shack. Slick timed it perfectly. He stepped out from the shadows, holding Reuben in front of him like a shield.

Oh, what a kick, seeing the astonishment wash over the tall man's face!

For dramatic effect, he ground the gun muzzle into Reuben's ear. Mirth bubbled up inside him. This was easy, so easy, he could get hysterical laughing about it. But he didn't laugh. He thought of what Kate Riley did to him and how he could never hurt her, she always managed to get away, and he was mean, he was angry, when he ordered: "Toss your gun down or he gets it!"

––––––––

The parade made it impossible for Kate to sleep, but that didn't matter. She was too anxious to sleep anyway. She sat up against the pillows, her leg throbbing painfully. She sighed and tried not to be afraid that, with Woodie gone, with this leg, she was alone and vulnerable. She eyed the crutches against the wall. Without them, she was helpless.

Before Woodie left, she had very nearly called him back. She had puzzled out a few things and she was dismayed by some of the conclusions she had reached.

In her lucid, awake moments this afternoon, when she had felt something less than wretched, she had been thinking. She had been thinking about the note Woodie found in the office. Just now she reached for the note on her bedside table. She held it in her hands and, as she heard the trumpets and trombones outside her window, the sporadic pop of firecrackers, she read: SHE MUST SUFFER FOR HER SINS. REMEMBER, I LOVED HER TO DEATH. SLICK.

Something was off here, but what? First of all, this note was typed and she couldn't picture Slick typing. He had handwritten his other note to her. Second, the bit about suffering for "her" sins sounded too academic, coming from Slick. Too consciously aware. Slick was confused about his mother and about women generally, but Kate doubted he knew it.

235

If Slick hadn't typed the note, who had, and why?

But it was more than the note, wasn't it? It was last night. Had it really been Slick who'd knocked her unconscious, dragged her to the construction site, and left her there? Slick, or somebody else?

She swallowed raggedly.

Any minute now, Peter and Judith would appear with her groceries. She began to dread their return. Lately, Peter frightened her. She thought of him now. His jealousy and possessiveness. She hesitated, then she lifted the phone to call Anthony Reed.

Standing by the shack in the junkyard, with Reuben captive beside him, Slick commanded: "C'mon! Drop the gun. Drop it right now!"

The tall man hesitated and Slick felt sure he would toss down his weapon, but then the man's mustache curled as he smiled slowly and said: "And if I don't?"

"Then I shoot him, stupid. I *told* you that!"

"But I'm like you, Slick, I don't always do what I'm told," the tall man said.

"What?" Slick was puzzled and angry. He couldn't believe this! Why wouldn't the tall man obey him? He was looking at him, studying him, and in that split-second he was distracted enough to lower his gun, just a fraction, from Reuben's skull. The tall man saw this and so did Reuben. In that instant, Reuben twisted free and the tall man fired off a warning shot and said: "Give it up, Slick." But Slick wouldn't give it up. He was too angry. He didn't care so much about Reuben now, he only wanted to get the tall man. Grinning savagely, he turned on him and aimed straight for his heart. But the tall man surprised him again! Slick's shot rang out, but the tall man didn't come crashing down. Incredibly, he remained standing while Slick himself staggered backward, his chest a fiercely burning pain.

His face contorted with fury, Slick raised his gun to fire again.

Reuben, to his left, scrambled to his feet, but Slick ignored him. It was the tall man he was after. The tall man had to die. Snarling, Slick leveled the Predator and began to squeeze the trigger, but Reuben slammed into him and brought him down with a thundering tackle.

Slick's gun exploded, but he knew the shot was wild. The muzzle was pointing to the sky. Reuben rolled off him, but still he couldn't breathe. Slick didn't understand, but then he remembered he'd been shot. Dazed, he gazed down at his bare chest. There was a ragged hole gushing blood. He touched the blood curiously with his fingertips. Red. Bright red. Pretty, like roses.

He blinked. Yeah, he was shot all right. The tall man's bullet had mushroomed in his chest. The scary part was, it didn't hurt that bad. His body was closing down, trying not to feel. The pain was faraway. It was like somebody else was shot, not him.

Lying on his back, Slick looked up at the treetops. He saw the sky was white, not blue. He would have liked a blue sky, with some clouds. His chest heaved. There was a loud roaring in his ears. He felt a sharp, tearing pain and could not breathe.

He coughed painfully, then he smiled a thin, malicious smile. He would find Kate Riley again. He would seize her and take her to bed. Of course she would resist, but that would only double his pleasure. It would be the best struggle ever, just him and her, that body, that red hair. He could hardly wait. . . .

Fielding and Reuben stood over the body.

Fielding looked away toward the pine trees and sighed mournfully. Slick was dead and Kate was safe. He was waiting to feel elated, but he didn't. He felt unspeakably depressed. Slick's dying made him realize his own mortality and the fragility of life in general. Everything seemed questionable and tenuous just now. *Everything,* he thought, *except Kate. I know how I feel about her.* He turned to Reuben: "It's over, then."

"Maybe not," Reuben said.

"What do you mean?"

"Something Slick said. Come with me." Reuben set off briskly, then suddenly slowed and waited for him to catch up: "By the way, thanks."

"What for? I let you down."

"Hardly." Reuben laughed and clapped him warmly on the back. "You saved my life."

The bungalow was alive with activity. Woodie was there and so were a dozen other cops, half in uniform, half in plainclothes. There was a SWAT team and paramedics. A crowd of gaping onlookers stood behind the orange police line. Fielding called for a stretcher for Slick while Reuben marched across the blood-splattered room and stopped the paramedics who were about to wheel Rees out the door to a waiting ambulance: "Hold it! Is he conscious? Good. I need a word alone with him."

Reuben motioned for Fielding to come listen. Fielding hurried over to find Rees glassy-eyed but awake. The big blond country boy, his face white as chalk, lay flat on the gurney. Fresh blood was being fed intravenously into his arm.

"I'll cut you a deal with the State's Attorney," Reuben said, "if you talk to me."

The pale Rees nodded.

"Just answer me one question. Did you and Slick dump a lady in a construction site last night?"

Rees shook his head no.

"C'mon. Sure, you did. Slender? Red hair? Name of Kate Riley."

Again Rees shook his head. He spoke slowly because it hurt him to talk: "See, he was following her . . . but I . . . stopped him."

"Oh, really?" Reuben was skeptical. "Why should I believe you?"

Rees's lips stretched into a tight smile. "I kept my eye on him, see, all night, and don't say I didn't. I . . . was waiting . . . to kill the bastard."

"I see," Reuben said. "Well, you've been a big help, Rees. I appreciate it." Reuben leaned closer. "By the way, our little agreement about the State's Attorney? So happens, me and Peter Coe aren't pals. He can't stand me, matter of fact. Better luck next time, big guy."

Reuben stepped away from the gurney and let the paramedics wheel Rees away, then he walked outside. Fielding followed. Outside, it was muggy and oppressive, but it was an improvement over that sordid room and bloody mattress.

Reuben said: "I don't think it was Slick."

Fielding looked at him: "I've been thinking the same thing. Because of what Rees said. And because it didn't sit right."

"How's that?"

"Slick was obsessed with Kate. He wouldn't just leave her to die. He was after a more personal satisfaction." Fielding shuddered even though he was sweating. It had to be ninety degrees in the shade. He mopped his brow with the back of his hand. "What worries me," he added somberly, "if it wasn't Slick, who was it? Who would want to hurt her?"

A loud marching band was parading past her window so Kate didn't hear when handsome Peter Coe, looking pleased with himself, strode into her bedroom. "Peter!" she said, startled. She glanced at her crutches propped against the wall. The bulky cast on her leg felt heavier than ever.

"Yes, we're back." Peter spread his hands expansively. "We got your groceries."

"Oh, thanks." She tried to sound grateful, but food was the very last thing on her mind right now.

Peter walked toward her, grinning: "So how goes the bed rest? How's my favorite patient?"

"Fine," she said uneasily. "Just fine." And yet her feelings betrayed her. Her eyes shifted to the phone on her bedside table. She was expecting a call back from Anthony Reed. He was taking his medication when she tried before. She spoke with his wife. Anthony was in a good deal of pain, Jesse said, but was it important, what she needed to talk about? Yes, Kate said, it's urgent. So Jesse said, "As soon as he's able, I'll have him call you back."

Peter was watching her skeptically. "What's the matter?" he frowned. "Aren't you glad to see me?"

"Sure. Sure I am." She tried to smile.

"The parade got you down?"

"What?"

He gestured toward the window. "All the noise."

"Yes, that must be it. Listen," she kept her voice neutral, "Judith around?"

"She's putting the groceries away. Why?"

"Nothing. No reason," she said, but Peter frowned again. He knew she was lying.

He turned and walked angrily away. His back was toward her as he looked out the window at the parade.

She tried to soothe his hurt feelings by asking him to describe the parade to her, what everybody looked like, what instruments they were playing. He was warming to the task and becoming friendly again, when Judith walked into the room. She appeared neat and trim in her blue skirt and jacket, her graying hair pulled severely back. Kate would never have guessed she had just battled the humidity and the parade crowds to go shopping.

"How are you?" Judith asked.

"The parade's giving her a headache," Peter said, "or maybe it's me."

"No, no," Kate shook her head. "Peter's doing wonderfully. He's telling me about each band as they pass by."

"Wonderful. I know it must be hard for you," Judith sympathized, "you can't look out the window and enjoy the parade." She paused thoughtfully. "Perhaps now is a good time for your treat."

"My treat?"

"Yes. Think of it as an early birthday present and a token of my esteem." Smiling, she bestowed her gift. It was a small brown paper bag.

Kate accepted the gift wordlessly. She wasn't alone now. She had both Peter and Judith by her bedside, and if she accused one, the other would afford her protection. Was this the time? Should she speak up? She decided, finally, to wait. She still wasn't sure, not until she talked to Anthony Reed. She determined instead to concentrate on the gift. She unfolded the top of the brown paper bag and peered inside. She inhaled the sharp, sweet aroma of fresh coffee beans.

"Colombian," Judith said. "It's the best, and I wanted you to have nothing but the best for your birthday. Turning thirty is so special. Oh, I know it's just a small present, but . . . well, can I fix us some?"

Kate was about to respond but, just then, the phone jangled. She picked it up, then turned to Peter and Judith: "Give me a minute?"

"Perfect," Judith said. "I'll brew the coffee."

But Peter was impatient. "Don't be long," he said, his tone sounding like a warning.

Kate watched them close her bedroom door behind them, then returned to the phone. She took a shallow, shaky breath before she spoke. "Anthony, it's about my mom and that car accident. The article. I seem to remember reading . . . and I hope I'm wrong, but, well, the girl who was hurt? Was her name Sandy?"

"Yes."

"And her last name?"

"Shepherd," Anthony said.

"Oh, no . . ." Kate said, her voice trailing off. She flashed back to that day in the office. She was going through her mail, telling Judith, rather idly, how everyone seemed to be spelling her name wrong these days: "Wiley. Rilly. Ridely," and Judith said: "I know what you mean. You can spell Shepherd so many ways."

"Shepherd?" Kate had said.

And Judith had answered: "Yes. My married name."

———

Back at the bungalow, the police were climbing back into their squad cars. The ambulance carrying Rees was long gone.

Fielding was thinking about that secretary, Judith Moore, and wondering where he'd seen her before. He knew he had. He glanced over at Woodie, who was talking to a sniper from the SWAT team. He frowned and said to Reuben: "Kate's alone in the apartment, do you realize that? And with that cast on her leg, she's practically an invalid. I don't like it."

"Me neither. Let's give her a ring."

But when they called, the line was busy.

———

The line was busy when Molly tried to call.

She hung up reluctantly.

She had been doing some thinking, and now she was afraid for Kate. Who was with her there in the apartment? Kate was bedridden. Her health was frail. If anything should go wrong, she would be powerless to defend herself.

She tried Kate's number again, but again it was busy.

Molly had the feeling she was wasting precious time.

She put the kitchen phone down and stood there, taking stock. Lily was napping. Heather, the baby-sitter, a bright, good-natured teenager, was baking oatmeal cookies with Ian. Molly had been helping them, but now she took off her apron. She looked at the baby-sitter: "Listen, Heather, are you okay for a few minutes? I need to go out."

———

"Shepherd." Kate clutched the receiver. "Are you sure?"

"Yes," Anthony said. "Something wrong?"

243

She was silent, remembering that other time in the office. Peter was teasing her about her thirtieth birthday, but Judith didn't join in. Judith's eyes were sad as she said, very solemnly: "My daughter will never turn thirty." Well, Judith was right. Sandy Shepherd was the same age as Kate, but mentally she would always be a child. Brain damage, from the accident.

"Kate? Are you there?" Anthony's voice was heavy with concern. "Tell me what's wrong."

She considered telling him, but she didn't want to burden him. He sounded so tired. Besides, Peter Coe was just outside. She was safe with him here. "Honestly, everything's fine. I'm just a little woozy from my medicine."

"I know the feeling, having just had the doctor here myself," Anthony chuckled weakly, "but you're still not a very good liar, Kate. Whatever it is you're up to, take care. And call me back if you need help."

"I will," she promised.

"God bless," Anthony said.

There was a pause, and then she said, without meaning to: "Anthony, I love you."

"I love you, too."

She hung up with tears in her eyes, wondering if she would ever see Anthony again, but now wasn't the time for that: Judith was here. She came bustling in with a silver tray.

Kate tensed and sat bolt upright in the bed. It was Judith, wasn't it? who had done those terrible things to her. Judith, who'd tried to undermine her career, who'd smashed the photograph of her mother, had bound and gagged her in the construction site and left her to die. Yes, Judith had very nearly killed her and yet Kate couldn't simply hate her: Judith was a troubled, tormented soul. If Judith would go quietly with Peter and agree to psychiatric treatment, Kate would not press charges. She would not expose Judith to the infamy of a criminal trial. She would let her retain her dignity. If, in the past, Lily had made the wrong choice, speaking to the

Annapolis crowd rather than picking up Sandy at her house (and who knew if Lily was wrong or right to do what she had done), Kate's generosity now would be a small measure of atonement. No one could erase the night of the accident and make Sandy well and whole again, but Kate could do this one small thing.

As Judith fussed over their coffee cups on the silver tray, Kate said to her: "Can you get Peter, please? I need to speak with him. In private, if you don't mind."

"Oh, Peter," Judith said cheerfully, "he's gone. I sent him back to the store for some pastry tarts. We must have some sweets with our coffee, don't you think?"

As they drove toward Kate's, Fielding brooded in the passenger seat. Judith Moore, he said to himself. Judith Moore. He drew a complete blank on her, then, suddenly, he remembered. Community General Hospital, the North wing, the fourth floor. He got lost. He'd barged into the wrong ward, and there she was with her daughter. Madonna and child, they looked like. The daughter temporarily off her Spiroshell respirator, her eyes glassy and faraway. And Judith Moore cuddling her, stroking her sandy hair.

Today, in the corridor outside Kate's hospital room, he had asked her: "Have we met?"

"No," Judith Moore said, but her eyes told him they had.

Curious. Why would she lie to him? It was disconcerting. It made him afraid for Kate. "Come on," he told Reuben. "Can't you drive any faster?"

Molly rang the buzzer twice, but Judith Moore didn't answer. She could be out. But suppose she was in and just wouldn't come to the door? Molly *had* to talk to her.

Molly tried the buzzer again.

Ever since Mexico, she'd had her doubts about Judith. She remembered what Judith had said when Kate was walking toward them on the beach: "She's got everything, that girl." And the look of passionate jealousy that crossed Judith's face.

She tried the buzzer once more, and, feeling frustrated, turned the doorknob. She felt sure the apartment would be locked, but strangely, the door opened. She stepped in gingerly, saying: "Hello, Judith! Hello!" but no one replied. In the living room, a calico cat sprang off the sofa, startling her. The cat came purring over to her and nuzzled against her leg, but she gently pushed him away and continued down the hallway, opening doors. "Judith," she called. "Judith." She flung open the door on the right, then pulled up short, gaping in bewilderment and disbelief. The floor was neatly swept, the furniture dusted, the bed perfectly made: It was like a museum. But that wasn't all. The room, from the bed to the rug to the curtains in the windows, was exactly like Kate's! There was her identical briefcase on the floor, with her initials. Next to the briefcase, Kate's navy high heels, size seven. And on the bed, as if laid out for work, were Kate's executive-style blazer and skirt, an ivory silk blouse, and next to the blouse, nylon stockings and a navy purse. Molly was stunned. How far had Judith been willing to carry the charade? Molly opened the purse and looked inside. There was a bottle of Jontue perfume, a handkerchief with Kate's initials on it, and . . . what was this? Oh my God, the gold sword-pin. Mom's gold swordpin.

Molly shuddered in horror. What did all this mean?

Deeply troubled, wondering what to do, Molly turned to the window. It was there she saw the framed photograph on the desk. It was of a pretty girl, a teenager, with long, sandy-colored hair and a winning smile. Molly picked up the photograph to study it and accidentally knocked a folder off the edge of the desk. Dozens of black-and-white photographs came spilling out. All of the photos were of Kate, and all were candids: Kate by their old house on Stoneleigh Road, Kate playing with Ian in the backyard . . .

Molly's hand holding the pictures began to tremble.

The room, the swordpin, the photographs, it was all too much. Molly feared for her sister more than ever.

Where was Judith? She could be anywhere. But if she had this obsession with Kate . . .

Molly hurried to the phone, tried Kate's again. The line was still busy.

She hesitated only an instant, then she called the police.

The sergeant on duty wasn't helpful, he wasn't even listening: "You want us to check on your sister? All our uniforms are out on the streets. What? You want *me* to go? Lady, I can't even move. Not with this parade going through, you got to be kidding."

———

They were on North Charles Street when the traffic became bumper-to-bumper. The last runners in the 10-K race were coming through, and behind them, the baton twirler leading the parade. There were streamers and floats and bands playing, people on the sidewalks behind the barriers, parents holding their youngsters up so they could see.

Reuben honked his horn in frustration and said: "We can't go anywhere in this."

But Fielding jumped out of the car. He ran up to a male runner and thrust his wallet at him: "You a size ten? I'll give you eighty bucks for your sneakers." The runner, overweight and sweating in the humidity, was only too happy to oblige. And so Fielding jammed on the sneakers and started running in the direction of Federal Hill Park, and Kate.

———

Another band marched by outside her window and people were cheering, but Kate wasn't listening. She looked helplessly at the cast that ran from her thigh to her ankle. She looked at her crutches against the wall. Her heart raced, but she kept her expression calm as she watched Judith set down the silver tray. Judith raised her eyes and smiled at her. Hers was a pleasant smile, entirely well meaning and without guile, and suddenly Kate thought that she must be mistaken. This cheerfully efficient woman could not be dangerous.

On the silver tray were two pairs of cups and saucers, Kate's best flowered china. The cups were filled with steaming brown coffee. Judith brought Kate her cup and placed it on the bedside table. "Here, dear. Black with a dash of cream, just how you like it."

"Thank you." Kate said. She felt faint.

"Come on, drink up. It'll get cold."

"I will," Kate murmured, but made no move toward the coffee.

"It's your birthday present," Judith insisted, her impatience beginning to show. "I bought it specially. Now drink. It will perk you up."

Kate was about to reach for the cup, but then the word "birthday" hit her. Judith didn't want her to reach her thirtieth birthday, did she? At least last night she hadn't. She had left Kate in the construction site to die. And now she had purchased this coffee. "Specially," she said. And wasn't she just a bit too adamant that Kate drink it?

Kate thought quickly. She didn't want to risk a confrontation, not in her weakened condition, not with this cast on her leg. Instead, she said: "No sugar? I'd like some sugar in my coffee."

Judith's facade began to crack, the false smile tightened. "You don't take sugar. I've made you countless cups in the office."

She gave Judith her most disarming smile: "I feel like a treat. And, as you said, it's *my* birthday."

"Oh, all right, then," Judith said. She went to the kitchen to fetch the sugar.

Alone in the bedroom, Kate reached for the cup of coffee, raised it to her nose, and sniffed the hot brown liquid. She noticed a distinctly pungent smell, a smell that was *not* Colombian coffee. With trembling hands, she set the china cup down. She regarded her phone. She should call for help. She couldn't reach Fielding and the others, she would simply call the police at 911. She lifted the receiver and put it to her ear, but before she tapped out even the first digit, the line went, eerily, dead. A voice came on, nasal, from a computer: "If you'd like to make a call, please hang up and dial again. If you'd like help, please hang up and dial the operator. . . ."

She fumbled the receiver back into its cradle. She felt, for the first time, truly alarmed. She was alone in her apartment with a woman who had just taken her phone off the hook, from the kitchen. A woman who was trying to poison her.

38

Judith Moore gazed disbelievingly at the receiver in her hand. Then, with a queer smile, she laid the phone down on the kitchen counter.

She had been waiting so long for this opportunity.

Oh, yes, she was a secretary because she was divorced and needed the money. But why had she interviewed for the job in the State's Attorneys Office, turned down other, higher-paying positions? Because she wanted to be close to Kate Riley.

Kate was everything Sandy was not—beautiful, popular, successful in her career. Many nights in the hospital room, keeping vigil over her daughter, Judith would look at Sandy's pale face, those faraway eyes, and remember Kate, so warm and glowing and alive, and she would think: It's not fair.

Finally, this summer, Judith knew it was time to act. She did not want to hurt Kate. She had grown, despite herself, attached to the girl. And yet, there was Sandy in the hospital, and Judith could not allow the injustice to continue. The girls were the same age, and it was not right that one of them should enjoy everything, the other nothing.

But her attempts to undermine Kate's career had failed. The altered pleadings, the stolen videotape, even the smashed photograph had not quenched Kate's indomitable spirit. In the courtroom the girl was too good, she could do the impossible: She got Buckner convicted. Imagine Judith's surprise when she heard the verdict! And imagine her surprise when she realized that she herself had helped Kate. For it was *The Great Gatsby,* which Judith had substituted for the videotape (a private joke intended to wound Kate), that had inspired Kate to win the case! And yet, when the verdict came in, it would be wrong to say that Judith was unhappy. She was pleased that Buckner was found guilty. Drinking and driving, he was a criminal, like the man who'd injured Sandy: He deserved to be punished.

After the trial, during her stay in Mexico, Judith took time to reflect. If she could not destroy Kate's career, more drastic measures had to be taken. She had to get personal. In the meantime, she took photographs of Kate with her expensive, top-of-the-line Nikon camera. Kate on the beach. Kate cuddling baby Lily. She had hundreds of pictures of Kate, for Judith had followed her everywhere—to work, to her apartment, to Stoneleigh Road, to Molly's house, even to her psychiatrist's. It was in Mexico that Judith took her best picture of all: Kate on the balcony with Ian. She must have found something he said amusing because she tossed back her mane of copper hair and laughed. There. Click. The moment—Kate Riley laughing—was frozen forever. It would be a wonderful picture to remember her by. . . .

The construction site last night? Judith hadn't planned on it, not really. But she was at L'Escargot and saw Slick kidnap Kate, and so she followed, at a safe distance, in her car. She tried to stay with them, but there was that awful thunderstorm, it was dark and raining, and she lost them in the maze of downtown streets. She was about to give up and drive home when she spotted Kate's car near the courthouse. Apparently it had been in some kind of accident with that station wagon. She crept forward in her car and then she saw Kate herself, head down, hastening through the rain. And, goodness, there was Slick chasing her!

Both fascinated and terrified, Judith braked her car and eased over to the curb. She cranked down her window and peered out in time to watch Kate climb the courthouse steps and Slick follow after. Kate entered the building and Slick wasn't far behind when he stopped and turned. A big, blond man stepped out from behind a tall Grecian column. Judith didn't know who the man was but Slick did. They were talking. They turned and came back down the steps. Slick didn't look too happy, but the big man was urging him on. Where were they off to? Judith watched until they disappeared into the rain, then she began to think. Her mind wandered from Sandy to Kate and back to Sandy again. She didn't want to harm Kate, but there would be Sandy to answer to, in the morning.

Suddenly, the thought struck Judith: If something *did* happen to Kate, the police would assume it was Slick. No one would ever suspect her.

Judith's eyes blazed while she herself became icily calm. Should she do it? Yes, yes, yes! Smiling thinly, she switched off the ignition and hastened into the courthouse. She tiptoed into the office, pausing only to grab one of Peter's softball bats by the door. In the near-darkness she crept up behind Kate, who now sensed another human presence, who was warily alert. Feeling strong and righteous, Judith crashed the bat down on Kate's skull. Kate crumpled over. Was she dead? Judith leaned close and could hear her breathing. She raised the bat again, about to strike. Then she noticed, it made her heart skip a beat, how Kate resembled Sandy. So vulnerable, so innocent, like a little child. Judith lowered the softball bat. Now what? She could kill Kate, leave her body here. But they would give her a funeral, they would sing her praises, and Kate would become a heroine. Judith gazed out the rain-streaked window into the dreary night. She saw the blinking orange lights of the construction site across the street. It was like God speaking to her. Judith knew what to do.

She would bury the body in the foundation. No one would ever find it. It would be Judith's little secret. And, what's more, the concrete would preserve Kate just as she was now: She would remain, throughout eternity, God's child.

Judith laughed for joy.

Oh, it was so easy to type up a note and sign it "Slick." Not so easy to transport Kate to the foundation. Judith cast about in vain until she spotted the library book cart. Groaning with effort, she lifted Kate and lowered her into the deep, rectangular cavity, then wheeled her out of the office and into the service elevator.

She exited the building from the basement and hurriedly crossed the slippery street to the construction site. It was hard to push the cart. Kate was a slim girl but tall. The final fifteen feet were the toughest, when Judith had to abandon the cart and drag Kate through the mud to the wooden form. She found rope in her car and an old bandanna and used these to truss her up. The rain was relentless. She got soaked to the bone as she fastened Kate to the steel piling. "Ye shall be as little children," she quoted from the Bible as she proudly surveyed her work. Yes, Kate looked like a little child, but something was wrong. She was wearing Lily's swordpin and that contaminated her. Judith removed the swordpin from her dress. There. Much better. She also removed Kate's shoes. Now Kate would enter the kingdom of heaven barefoot and meek.

Was that everything? No. Judith scouted about for a hammer and nails, then pounded the loose plywood board in place. Now the wooden form was complete, all four sides up. Perfect. Kate was tied up and helpless, trapped, just like Sandy on her respirator. In the morning they would pour concrete, and Kate would be dead. . . .

But Kate was not dead, she had got away, and now she was safely in bed, surrounded by roses and everybody's love. It should be *Sandy* everybody loved, not Kate, so Judith, standing alone in the kitchen, feeling that icy calm again, knew she had to finish what she'd started. Before, she had cared that she would not get caught. This had changed. She wanted Kate to be dead before she turned thirty tonight at midnight. She wanted Kate dead and that was all. Only when Kate was dead could Sandy come home from the hospital. Sandy would step into Kate's shoes, Kate's clothes, Kate's life, and then Sandy would finally have the acclaim she deserved and so would Judith, as her mother.

Judith closed her eyes and gripped the counter to steady herself. A flash of blinding pain, a lightning volt through her temples. Another migraine. She had them a lot lately. The doctor had given her a Valium prescription. The bottle was in her purse now, half-empty. It was full when she'd first entered the apartment, but now, half the capsules were in Kate's coffee.

The pain eased. She let go of the counter, opened her eyes, and immediately spotted two coffee stains on the counter. Two stains and a sprinkling of coffee grounds. She had neglected to tidy up before, when she had fixed their coffees. She scolded herself for this oversight, grabbed a sponge, wetted it, and wiped the counter sparkling clean.

She was about to return to the bedroom when she remembered why she was here. She had come to the kitchen to fetch Kate's sugar. She searched the kitchen cupboard, then reached past the Skippy peanut butter and granola bars for the yellow box. She flipped open the spout and began to pour granulated white sugar into the dainty, flowered sugar bowl. She was staring into space, thinking of Kate's birthday, when she saw sugar overflowing the bowl, sugar bouncing on the counter, sugar everywhere. Suddenly and irresistibly enraged, she seized the yellow box and hurled it at the floor.

The sugar slowed to a trickle, then stopped. This made Judith even more furious. She nudged the box on the floor, then kicked it, sent it spinning across the kitchen tiles. She ran over and pounced on the box, ground her heels in, crushed the air out of it, stomped and stomped and stomped on it until finally she realized she was in Kate's kitchen, standing on a battered yellow box of granulated sugar.

She sighed. Gradually, she regained her equanimity, picked up the box, and tossed it into the trash. She found the broom and dustpan and swept the sugar up from the floor, every last granule. She sponged off the countertop once again. She washed her hands thoroughly with soap and water and dried them with a paper towel. Kate was running low on paper towels, she observed. She was going to jot down "paper towels" and "sugar" on a list for her, but then she realized this would not be necessary.

She surveyed her work. Floor clean. Counter clean.

Good. It paid to be neat. Cleanliness was next to godliness.

She smoothed her graying hair back neatly from her face, pinched her cheeks pink like she used to do in the old days when she wanted a boy to ask her to dance, took the sugar bowl, and, striding smartly in her nylons and heels, looking every bit the trim and efficient secretary she was, started for the bedroom.

39

Kate cast a desperate glance at the door. She must hurry. She tried to ignore the pain, but she grimaced as she swung her broken leg off the pillows and dangled it over the side of the bed. She stretched to reach her crutches against the wall, she almost had them, but she was too late: Judith walked in.

Kate tensed. Her heart fluttered wildly.

"What is it, dear?" Judith asked.

She groped for an excuse: "I was getting up. The parade. I wanted to watch."

"You shouldn't be up. Doctor's orders. Here, I'll help you get comfortable."

She did not protest as Judith settled her back in bed. Outside, the parade grew noisier. There were cheers and shouts as the floats drove past, then the boom of cannon from Federal Hill Park as the school bands gathered to parade their colors.

Judith stuck a dainty spoon into the sugar bowl. "One lump or two?" she asked. Then she noticed Kate's empty cup. "Oh, good girl! You've already drunk it."

"No," Kate said.

"No?"

"The cup is empty because I poured it out. See? Here in the wastebasket by the bed."

"I'm very sorry you did that," Judith said grimly. Her face was ashen, her lips drawn. She turned her back on Kate and walked over to the desk where her purse was. Kate couldn't see what she was doing.

Kate studied her secretary's back. She wanted to understand Judith, and the key to understanding her was to understand her pain. "You want to kill me," Kate said. "Why?"

But Judith didn't answer. She whirled around with a gleaming .22 in her hand.

Kate's eyes fixed on the gun. She had not expected this. Judith pulled out the desk chair and primly sat down. She pointed the gun at Kate, with some familiarity, Kate noticed, as if she knew how to use it. Kate's mouth went dry.

The last of the parade was marching past her window. There were loud trumpets and drums and the clash of cymbals, and Kate suddenly realized, with a despairing heart, that even if she yelled for help, no one would hear.

Her only hope was to hold out until someone came. Peter would soon return from the store. Fielding, Reuben, and Woodie—they were possibilities too.

In the meantime, she would talk to Judith, get Judith to talk to her.

Kate regarded her with compassion: "It's painful for you, isn't it? You see me and I remind you of Sandy, of what she can never be."

"How do you . . ." Judith's voice cracked, ". . . know about that?"

"I know my mom felt terrible."

"Your mother. Ha! Bigshot in A.A. she was. She sent flowers. She kept asking to see Sandy, but I sent her away. She was too late, too late."

"I know," Kate said. "I'm sorry."

"Indeed!" Judith's voice shook with suppressed fury. "How could you know what it's like to visit my daughter in the hospital! To see her strapped to that respirator, to hate it that she's trapped there, dependent on a machine to pump air in and out of her lungs. You said you were trapped in that construction site? That it felt like a coffin? You know nothing!" Judith's face twisted in anguish and her words kept pouring out: "When I visit, they take her off the respirator for five minutes. Five minutes, so I can hold her. My daughter who will turn thirty in one month. My Sandy. Do you know she dribbles saliva down the side of her mouth? She sucks her thumb. She doesn't even recognize me, her own mother! Jesus, God, and you have the audacity to say you're sorry! As if your being sorry makes up for it, all the pain."

"You're right. I don't understand your pain. Tell me about it, Judith, so I *can* understand."

"No, damn you! No! It wasn't supposed to be like this!"

"Like what?"

"You weren't supposed to talk to me. You were supposed to drink the coffee and—"

"Die? But you *want* to talk about it, don't you? It must be lonely for you, keeping all this inside, bottled up."

"No, no! Stop it! I know what you're doing. You're only stalling for time. Peter will be back soon and perhaps others you've contacted. You don't really care!"

"Yes, I—"

"I'm not a fool, Kate!" Judith raised the gun now and seriously aimed it. "I want you to close your eyes. I can't shoot with you staring at me like that."

Kate did not close her eyes. She looked steadily at Judith and said quietly: "Put the gun down. You don't want to shoot me." As she spoke, she eyed her crutches against the wall. She calculated how far away they were and what kind of leap she would have to make. "Please, Judith, put the gun down. Let's talk."

"No."

"Tell me about Sandy. How do you feel? I'd like to—"

"No! Close your eyes. Do as I say!"

She watched Judith's eyes narrow. There was no reasoning with her now, she had to act. In one fluid motion, she lunged for her crutches. They clattered down with her as she tumbled from the bed.

She landed roughly on the hardwood floor, where her fractured, now traumatized leg complained furiously of abuse. Her vision was swimming. When she could focus again, she saw the gun still aimed at her, a deadly threat. She fought down her rising panic and determined what to do. She seized one of her crutches and swung it at Judith, connecting with her arm. The gun, knocked free, went skittering along the floor. Kate dove after it. She almost had it! Her fingers began to close around the handle when Judith, looming above her, stomped on her hand. Kate cried out and released the gun, and Judith bent over and snatched it up.

Panting for breath, Kate watched in dismay as Judith pointed the gun at her again. "Judith, please," she said. She struggled to remain calm. She sat up on the floor and let her back rest against the bed. Her leg throbbed in its plaster cast.

"Peter will be back," Judith said, mechanically, unfeelingly. "I have to do it now."

For a moment, Kate felt complete and unutterable despair. Judith was going to shoot her and there was nothing she could do. Yet there *must* be something, because Kate understood how Judith felt.

She understood because of her own grief. She fixed her eyes on Judith and said, boldly, hoping that this would puncture her rage and reach the real person inside: "Judith, if you kill me, will you feel any less guilty?"

Judith's face contorted to reflect her inner torment: "I don't feel guilty!"

"Oh? Then tell me, what were you doing the night of the accident? Why didn't *you* drive Sandy to the meeting?"

"Because I . . ." Judith was confused. She fractionally lowered the gun.

"Well?" Kate persisted.

"The evening it happened," Judith began haltingly, "I was home. Stephen . . . my husband . . . he was my husband then, we had quarreled and he stormed out. My marriage was in trouble, you see. I suspected Stephen was cheating and indeed, as I later discovered, he was." Judith's eyes clouded with the pain of that memory. "This particular evening, I was feeling blue. I took a bath and crawled into bed with a book. Around eight, Sandy came to my door. I knew that your mother had changed plans at the last minute. But now Sandy told me the person who was supposed to drive her to the meeting hadn't shown up. She asked me if I could take her."

"Yes. And?"

"I said, did she really need me because I was awfully tired."

"Go on," Kate urged. "You're doing fine."

"And Sandy said, she said . . ."

"Yes?"

"She said, Oh, it's all right, Mom, I can drive myself. And I said, Are you sure? She laughed: Oh, hell, I've driven enough places half-crocked, I should be able to get there sober! I said, I'm so proud of you." Judith stopped. "Those were my last words to her . . ."

"You sound like a wonderful mother," Kate said. "I'm sure Sandy would tell you that, if she could."

"But," Judith's lip trembled, "she asked me to drive her and I didn't! If I'd only known—"

"But you couldn't have," Kate said gently.

Judith stared at her a long moment, absorbing what she had said. Tears brimmed in her eyes. She gazed, at first in wonder and then in horror, at the gun in her hand.

There was a commotion at the door, but Judith was oblivious. She blinked, surprised, when Fielding and Reuben burst into the room. For one long moment she looked at the intruders, looked at Kate. Then, abruptly, she raised her arm and pressed the muzzle of the gun to her temple.

"No!" Kate cried.

But Judith did not appear to hear. She did not lower the gun. She was about to squeeze the trigger.

"Judith, no!" Kate repeated, and now Judith heard. Kate had reached her, after all. Judith's eyes filled with gratitude and love for Kate, and Kate began to smile, but this new and fragile peace was instantly destroyed when the gun exploded.

The shot reverberated in the small room. Kate's ears rang. "Oh, please, no!" She scrambled forward on the floor and yanked Judith's motionless body toward her. Judith, who was alive, who wasn't hurt, began laughing and sobbing both at once: "I didn't shoot it. It went off by itself."

"You scared me," Kate said. "But it's okay now. Everything's okay."

A moment later, Reuben stood over them and gave Judith a hand up.

Fielding, meanwhile, had eyes only for Kate. He was gazing fondly down at her.

She squinted up at him through a wayward strand of red hair. She was so glad to see him! "I'm sorry," she said, almost rapturously, "you'll have to come down to my level."

He smiled and knelt beside her. She felt his strong arms enfold her, heard him murmur huskily into her ear: "Are you all right?"

"At this particular moment?" she said. "Yes."

"Happy birthday!" Fielding said. He appeared in her bedroom with a tray, scrambled eggs and toast for the two of them. She smiled.

He put the tray down, sat beside her on the bed, and took her hand.

She gazed deeply into his eyes and hoped she would be able to recall this moment, the feel of her hand in his, the roses in the vase in the window, their red petals on fire in the white sunlight. She gave him a level glance: "I'm sorry about your wife. But maybe you'll both be happier."

"Yes," he said. He gently brushed an auburn tendril from her forehead.

"By the way, thanks for staying here last night."

"I wanted to."

She gestured at her cast. "Maybe next time you won't have to sleep on the couch. As soon as this leg heals . . ."

"We'll celebrate properly," he said, and they both laughed.

He quickly became serious again: "I've been wanting to know. You were very good with Judith yesterday. How did you reach her?"

"I knew she would feel guilty because I did. Remember my dream?"

"Yes."

"I think the dream meant that I was running away from myself. When my mom died, I felt guilty for surviving her. That's why in my dream I was up there on the cliff, thinking I had to jump into the ocean and drown, I had to die, too. Now I realize that's a natural feeling. Part of us does die when someone we love dies. But we're still living, after all, and so that's what we should do."

"And Judith?"

"Well, her daughter didn't die, but the old Sandy is dead. Judith needed to grieve for her, but I don't think she ever let herself. In that way she reminded me of myself. And," Kate looked at him, "she reminded me of someone else too."

Fielding could not meet her gaze. He glanced away.

Kate's face filled with tenderness. She longed to comfort him, yet how could she draw him out? Fielding had never uttered his son's name in front of her and she doubted he ever mentioned him. He had been traveling through life, as she had, wanting to keep his grief private and small, a hard kernel of pain inside him. But the pain, which was not so small after all, had not healed. Look at his sad face. She took a deep breath and said to him, much as he'd said to her once: "Is there anything you'd like to talk about?"

He swallowed and clasped her hand more tightly. "Remember you said I didn't tell you things? Well, it's not just because I was your doctor. I don't talk about him. I pretended to forget him, even though he's with me every day. Kate, my son's name was Keith. Keith Patrick."